The faculty of Union University h
ment to the community of Christian colleges and others
through the essays presented in *Shaping a Christian Worldview,* to stay focused on our core mission: the advancement of Christ-centered learning. These essays manifest a deep commitment to Christian worldview thinking, to theological depth with appropriate ecumenical breadth, and to constructive engagement with secular disciplinary scholarship. This volume will help renew the calling of evangelical Christian teacher-scholars to thoughtful Christian distinctiveness in the academic disciplines, and is a useful introduction to this key characteristic of Christian higher education.

Stanton L. Jones
Provost, Wheaton College

Principled worldview formation is a characteristically Christian species of intellectual work, and no less now than at any other time in history it is work needful to be done. Dockery, Thornbury, and their colleagues at Union University have produced an engaging and pedagogically useful taxonomy for Christian worldview reflection across the disciplines and it should be welcomed by educators and their students alike.

David Lyle Jeffrey
Senior Vice Provost
Distinguished Professor of Literature and Humanities
Baylor University

Exemplary! This fine book by obviously talented and thoughtful members of the faculty and administration of Union University is a model in multiple ways.

In design, this work first lays a solid theological and philosophical foundation upon which a Christian worldview is then effectively applied to a variety of disciplines and educational concerns.

In content, it is informed by clear thinking, penetrating insights, and current scholarship.

In vision, it reflects a deep understanding of the very *raison d'être* of Christian higher education in seeking to form genuinely Christian perspectives on the whole academic enterprise. It successfully shows how a full-bodied biblical piety and scholarship can be united in a most fruitful way.

Union is an innovative Christian university that is setting the right example for the rest of us to follow.

David K. Naugle
Professor of Philosophy, Dallas Baptist University
Author, *Worldview: The History of a Concept*

This lively volume displays the intellectual energy made possible when faith and reason work with, not against one another. The essays are written in a style that makes them accessible to laypersons and scholars alike. A welcome addition to an ongoing cultural debate.

Jean Bethke Elshtain
Laura Spelman Rockefeller Professor of Social and Political Ethics, University of Chicago
Author, *Jane Adams and the Dream of American Democracy*

SHAPING
A CHRISTIAN
WORLDVIEW

SHAPING
A CHRISTIAN
WORLDVIEW

THE FOUNDATIONS OF
CHRISTIAN HIGHER EDUCATION

EDITED BY DAVID S. DOCKERY
& GREGORY ALAN THORNBURY

BROADMAN
& HOLMAN
PUBLISHERS NASHVILLE, TENNESSEE

0–8054–2448–2

Published by Broadman & Holman Publishers
Nashville, Tennessee

Subject Heading: CHRISTIAN EDUCATION

6 7 8 9 10 07 06 05

To
Carl F. H. Henry
and
Charles Colson

With deep appreciation
for their profound influence
on our lives, our thought, and our work

ABRAHAM JANG

November 7, 2007

CONTENTS

FOREWORD

CHARLES COLSON

SINCE THE PUBLICATION three years ago of the book *How Now Shall We Live?* I have been heartened by the burgeoning interest in Christian worldview on the part of Christians from all branches of the church. Nowhere has that interest been more enthusiastic than among the scholars of Union University who have produced the very impressive writings that constitute this book.

The apostle Paul tells us that we can prove the value of our service to the Lord only through the renewing of our minds and the offering of our whole lives as living sacrifices to him (Rom. 12:1–2). Christians all over America are waking up to this challenge and are beginning to take the necessary steps to "prepare [their] minds for action," as the apostle Peter put it (1 Pet. 1:13).

The need for such worldview thinking and living on the part of the Christian community has never been more urgent, because we live in an era which for lack of a better term is called *postmodern*. What this really signifies is not the emergence of a new coherent philosophy but rather a reaction against modernity and its reliance on reason to determine truth. Postmodernists say that reason fails because there is no absolute truth to be found. There are no principles, only preferences, they say. As postmodernity has taken hold, we have witnessed the inevitable consequences: relativism, pragmatism, social fragmentation, ethical and cultural erosion, along with individual disillusion and despair.

Some Christians welcome the postmodern development, arguing that the death of rationalism gives the Christian church a fresh, new opportunity; they say we should take advantage of postmodernity and rely on image over words and feelings over reason to present our case. Admittedly, the argument has a certain superficial appeal. After all, encountering Jesus is the ultimate personal experience, and the vacuum of these times gives us a clear shot at souls set adrift. Happily, the authors of this book are under no such illusion, which is why, in the very first chapters, the authority of Scripture is persuasively asserted.

Even if postmodernity were to offer an opportunity for the church, if an emphasis on image over the word were to result in multitudes being drawn into our churches, our victory would be short-lived. For postmodernity, left unchallenged, would continue our cultural slide into chaos, making the church's task of fulfilling its cultural mandate—to take dominion and bring God's truth to bear on culture and society—ever more difficult. Soon enough the fulfillment of the Great Commission would be hampered as well.

Just look at what postmodernity has done to our culture's most basic suppositions about life and the world. Consider just the three "unalienable rights" grandly set forth in the Declaration of Independence.

The right to life has been diminished beyond recognition. The leading ethicist at Princeton University, for example, openly advocates infanticide (and more recently bestiality. And why not, if the human is no more than one of many morally equivalent species?). Assisted suicide—read that "euthanasia"—has become the law in one state and more or less openly practiced elsewhere. Laws enacted by the people banning the grotesque practice of partial birth abortion have been repeatedly and consistently struck down in the courts. And scientists are gleefully setting about to create life (and dispense with it) in the test tube. The notion of the sanctity of life is hardly recognized in centers of cultural influence.

Or take the second of the Declaration's rights: liberty. Our founders created a careful balance between individual rights and a system of order protecting the common good. They called it an experiment in "ordered liberty." But postmodernity has erased the "ordered" half of the equation. We have so expanded the definition of individual liberty that it is impossible to agree on any binding moral judgment of the common good.

This radical redefinition has been enshrined in the law. In the now infamous and breathtakingly sweeping language of the "mystery clause" in *Casey v. Planned Parenthood* (1992), the Supreme Court defined liberty as the right to make "intimate and personal choices . . . central to personal dignity and autonomy . . . the right to define one's own concept of existence, of meaning, of the universe, and of the mystery of human life." How can any moral truth-claim survive when an individual has the constitutional right to find his or her own meaning in the universe?

The third liberty in the Declaration is the "right to happiness." The founders who used that term in the Aristotelian sense—that is, happiness is the fulfilled, *virtuous* life—would hardly recognize today's debased definition. While classically, happiness might have included the notion of deferred gratification, in the postmodern era it has no higher meaning than instant gratification or sensual pleasure. That is, pure hedonism.

The result is that the Christian church is increasingly unable to communicate to a postmodern culture. The worldviews are worlds apart. We no longer speak a common language; the same word too often has antithetical meanings. If we do not understand what the postmodern mind thinks and how to counter its most outrageous assertions, if we don't have a well-formed and well-grounded biblical worldview, we have no hope of making an appealing case for Christian truth in today's culture.

Almost a century ago, the great preacher J. Gresham Machen warned his Princeton Seminary students that avoiding the great issues of the day would result in "preaching to the air." If we do not engage the great issues of our day, we, too, will be "preaching to the air"—a dereliction of our biblical duty.

Postmodernity must be challenged by a bold and vibrant faith. Nothing less than a clash of worldviews—shaped by the truth of God's Word heroically engaging the postmodern colossus—will suffice to keep American society from free-falling into what Jacques Barzun has called the futility and absurdity of decadence. And nowhere is this engagement more urgent than on the college and university campuses of the land.

I rejoice that the scholars of Union University understand this. As readers will see in this most timely and readable book, they are girding up for the great intellectual contest for the mind of our culture.

Christian colleges once held forth boldly and without compromise for a view of life with Christ at "the bottom" (to paraphrase an early motto of Harvard College) and the Word of God central to all we think, say, and do. Over the past century, that vision has been compromised and largely lost. Today's Christian colleges and universities, for the most part, struggle to find their sea legs amid the flotsam and jetsam of the postmodern storm.

Happily, however, exciting progress is being made. Here and there, Christian colleges and universities are beginning to articulate a clear and compelling vision of life lived in its totality under Christ. Union is a sterling example of a faculty and administration working together to bring full biblical integrity, not only to the curriculum, but also to every aspect of university life. This book is a testimony to their commitment and vision. The chapters that follow mark out the pathway of biblical worldview thinking that Christian colleges and universities all over the nation must begin to walk. Only as we teach the young people of the church to examine every aspect of life from the perspective of God's Word will they be equipped to go and take every thought and every arena of life captive for obedience to Christ (2 Cor. 10:3–5).

That the administration and faculty of Union University have dedicated themselves to this task—and gone on the public record with this book—marks an extremely hopeful development in the history of this institution, and perhaps in the history of Christian higher education in America.

I heartily commend this book to the growing legion within the church that is committed to the renewal of the mind, defense of the biblical worldview, and the fulfillment of the cultural commission.

PREFACE

SHAPING A CHRISTIAN WORLDVIEW is a shared project of representative faculty members from every academic area of Union University. Yet it is not so much an in-house dialogue as a call for worldview thinking by Christians in the academy. Union University is one of thirty-six hundred institutions carrying out the work of higher education. Yet only about 5 percent of those colleges and universities do so with a Christ-centered mission. The essays in this volume call for these institutions to be rigorously academic and unapologetically Christian. We recognize the need for tough-minded Christianity.

The essays in this volume are written at various levels, though all are generally targeted for the beginning college student. We trust, however, that the book will serve as a healthy refresher for faculty members, a guide for trustees and administrators, a stimulus for serious Christian engagement for graduate students, and a helpful and informative work for pastors and others interested in Christian higher education.

The volume is divided into two parts. The first section deals with the biblical and theological foundations of a Christian worldview. The second points to ways that a Christian worldview is important for various disciplines across the curriculum of higher education.

We want to thank all the contributors and the many other colleagues on our campus who encouraged us in this project. We are grateful for Cindy Meredith's coordinating efforts. The trustees of Union University and our friends across the Council for Christian Colleges and Universities have offered much support. Len Goss and David Shepherd at B&H have been patient with us. For their friendship we are most thankful. We owe a special word of thanks to our spouses, Lanese and Kimberly, who have helped us through yet another publishing project. We are grateful for Cindy Meredith's coordinating efforts and also for the indexing work of Sarah Jane Head. To two people in particular we express our profound appreciation for their partnership in the gospel and their mentorship in worldview thinking. We dedicate this work to Carl F. H. Henry and Chuck Colson.

This volume is not intended to be an exhaustive exposition of a Christian worldview. It is, we trust, a capable articulation for beginning college students. Hopefully, it will spur additional thinking and rich conversations in classrooms, hallways, dining halls, dorm rooms, and offices in days ahead. We will rejoice if this takes place. As always, we dedicate our work to the glory of God.

Soli Deo Gloria

David S. Dockery
Gregory A. Thornbury

SHAPING A CHRISTIAN WORLDVIEW

David S. Dockery

ONE OF OUR LOCAL NEWSPAPERS recently ran a series of articles focusing on the rise of crime in our region. Each author addressed the crime issue from the standpoint and perspective of economic deprivation. After reading the articles I thought I must be missing something. One approach was anthropological, another sociological, another economic—each dealing with systemic issues, which I do not doubt for a moment exist. But missing from the articles was any sense of responsibility. Crime was discussed without raising the issue of morality. I could not believe it. Then it dawned on me that there were diverse worldviews at work.

EVERYONE HAS A WORLDVIEW

A Chinese proverb says, "If you want to know what water is, don't ask the fish." Water is the sum and substance of the world in which the fish is immersed. The fish may not reflect on its own environment until suddenly it is thrust onto dry land, where it struggles for life. Then it realizes that water provided its sustenance.

Immersed in our environment, we have failed to take seriously the ramifications of a secular worldview. Sociologist and social watchdog Daniel Yankelovich defines *culture* as an effort to provide a coherent set of answers to the existential situations that confront human beings in the passage of their lives. A genuine cultural shift is one that makes a decisive break with the shared meaning of the past. The break particularly affects those meanings that relate to the deepest questions of the purpose and nature of human life.[1] What is at stake is how we understand the world in which we live. The issues are worldview issues. Christians everywhere recognize there is a great spiritual battle raging for the hearts and minds of men and women around the globe. We now find ourselves in a cosmic struggle between Christian truth and a morally indifferent culture. Thus we need to shape a Christian worldview and lifeview that will help us learn to think Christianly and live out the truth of Christian faith.[2]

The reality is that everyone has a worldview. Some worldviews are incoherent, being merely a smorgasbord of options from natural, supernatural, premodern, modern, and postmodern options. An examined and thoughtful worldview, however, is more than a private personal viewpoint; it is a comprehensive life system that seeks to answer the basic questions of life. A Christian worldview is not just one's personal faith expression, not just a theory. It is an all-consuming way of life, applicable to all spheres of life.

DISTINGUISHING A CHRISTIAN WORLDVIEW

James Orr, in *The Christian View of God and the World*, maintains that there is a definite Christian view of things, which has a character, coherence, and unity of its own, and stands in sharp contrast with counter theories and speculations.[3] A Christian worldview has the stamp of reason and reality and can stand the test of history and experience. Every chapter in this book is predicated on a Christian view of things, a view of the world that cannot be infringed upon, or accepted or rejected piecemeal, but stands or falls on its integrity. Such a holistic approach offers a stability of thought, a unity of comprehensive insight that bears not only on the religious sphere but also on the whole of thought. A Christian worldview is not built on two types of truth (religious and philosophical or scientific) but on a universal principle and all-embracing system that shapes religion, natural and social sciences, law, history, health care, the arts, the humanities, and all disciplines of study with application for all of life.

James Orr in 1891[4] and Abraham Kuyper in 1898[5] brilliantly articulated a Christian worldview at the turn of the nineteenth century. James Sire, C. S. Lewis, Carl F. H. Henry, Francis Schaeffer, Arthur Holmes, and Charles Colson, among others, have articulated well the essence of a Christian worldview in the twentieth century. The purpose of this book is to articulate a Christian worldview for the twenty-first century, with all of its accompanying challenges and changes, and to show how such Christian thinking is applicable across the educational curriculum. At the heart of these challenges and changes we see that truth, morality, and interpretive frameworks are being ignored if not rejected. Such challenges are formidable indeed. Throughout culture the very existence of normative truth is being challenged.

For Christians to respond to these challenges, we must hear afresh the words of Jesus from what is called the Great Commandment (Matt. 22:36–40). Here we are told to love God not only with our hearts and souls but also with our minds. Jesus' words refer to a wholehearted devotion to God with every aspect of our being, from whatever angle we choose to consider it—emotionally, volitionally, or cognitively. This kind of love for God results in taking every thought captive to make it obedient to Christ (2 Cor. 10:5), a wholehearted devotion to distinctively Christian thinking (or as T. S. Eliot put it, "to think in Christian categories").[6] This means being able to see life from a Christian vantage point; it means thinking with the mind of Christ.

The beginning point for building a Christian worldview is a confession that we believe in God the Father, maker of heaven and earth (the Apostles' Creed). We recognize that "in him all things hold together" (Col. 1:15–18), for all true knowledge flows from the One Creator to his one creation.

A worldview must seek to answer questions like:

- Where did we come from?
- Who are we?
- What has gone wrong with the world?
- What solution can be offered to fix it?

In addition, a worldview must seek to answer the key questions of life, whether the general implications or specific applications. It is to these foundational questions and attending issues that we now turn our attention.

WE BELIEVE IN GOD, MAKER OF HEAVEN AND EARTH: A WORLDVIEW STARTING POINT

A worldview must offer a way to live that is consistent with reality by offering a comprehensive understanding of all areas of life and thought, every aspect of creation. As we said earlier the starting point for a Christian worldview brings us into the presence of God without delay. The central affirmation of Scripture is not only that there is a God but that God has acted and spoken in history. God is Lord and King over this world, ruling all things for his own glory, displaying his perfections in all that he does in order that humans and angels may worship and adore him. God is triune; there are within the Godhead three persons: Father, Son, and Holy Spirit.

To think wrongly about God is idolatry (Ps. 50:21). Thinking rightly about God is eternal life (John 17:3) and should be the believer's life objective (Jer. 9:23–24). We can think rightly about God because he is knowable (1 Cor. 2:11), yet we must remain mindful that he is simultaneously incomprehensible (Rom. 11:33–36). God can be known, but he cannot be known completely (Deut. 29:29).

We maintain that God is personal and is differentiated from other beings, from nature, and from the universe. This is in contrast to other worldviews that say God is in a part of the world, creating a continual process, and that the process itself is God—or becoming God. God is self-existent, dependent on nothing external to himself. God is infinite, meaning that God is not only unlimited but that nothing outside of God can limit God. God is infinite in relation to time (eternal), in relation to knowledge (omniscience), and in relation to power (omnipotent). He is sovereign and unchanging. God is infinite and personal, transcendent, and immanent. He is holy, righteous, just, good, true, faithful, loving, gracious, and merciful.

God, without the use of any preexisting material, brought into being everything that is. Both the opening verse of the Bible and the initial sentence of the Apostles' Creed confess God as Creator. Creation is the work of the trinitarian God. Creation reveals God (Ps. 19) and brings glory to him (Isa. 43:7). All of creation was originally good but is now imperfect because of the entrance of sin and its effects on creation (Gen. 3:16–19). This is, however, only a temporary imperfection (Rom. 8:19–22), for it will be redeemed in the final work of God, the new creation.

The Creator God is not different from the God who provides redemption in Jesus Christ through his Holy Spirit. God is the source of all things. This means that God has brought the world into existence out of nothing through a purposeful act of his free will. A Christian worldview affirms that God is the sovereign and almighty Lord of all existence. Such an affirmation rejects any form of dualism, that matter has eternally existed, or that matter must, therefore, be evil since it is in principle opposed to God, the Source of all good.

A Christian worldview also contends that God is set apart from and transcends his creation. It also maintains that God is a purposeful God who creates in freedom. In creation and in God's provision and preservation for creation, he is working out his ultimate purposes for humanity and the world. Human life is thus meaningful, significant, intelligent, and purposeful. This affirms the overall unity and intelligibility of the universe. In this we see God's greatness, goodness, and wisdom.

WHO ARE WE? WHERE DID WE COME FROM?

God has created us in his image and likeness (see Gen. 1:27). At first this might appear to refer to our physical makeup, meaning that we look like God. This, however, is not what the Bible means by the terms *image* and *likeness* of God.

Some have suggested that the "image of God" is what enables humans to relate to one another, while others have suggested that it has more to do with personality, spirituality, or rationality. It is best not to choose only one of these options. Rather, because men and women are created in the image of

God, they possess rationality, morality, spirituality, personality, and the ability to relate to God and other humans, while rightly exercising dominion over the earth and the animals (see Gen. 1:26–28; Ps. 8).

We must be cautious in our thinking so as not to imagine the image of God as only some aspect in men and women but to see that humans are in the image of God. By this we mean that nothing in us is separable, distinct, or discoverable as the divine image. Each person individually and the entire race corporately are the image of God, but no single aspect of human nature or behavior or thought patterns can be isolated as the image of God. Since men and women have been created in the image of God, they are the highest forms of God's earthly creation. All other aspects of creation are for the purposes of serving men and women and are thus anthropocentric, or human centered. Yet humans have been created to serve God and are thus theocentric, or God centered. Thus a Christian worldview helps us fulfill our responsibility for God-centered thinking and living.

WHAT HAS GONE WRONG WITH THE WORLD?

Even though men and women are created in God's image, the entrance of sin into the world has had great and negative influences upon God's creation, especially humans created in God's image. As a result of sin, the image of God, though not lost, is severely tarnished and marred. The role of exercising dominion (see Gen. 1:28) has been drastically limited by the effects of sin on humans and the course of nature. The ability to live in right relationship with God, with others, with nature, and with our very own selves has been corrupted. Ultimately all are spiritually dead and alienated from God (see Eph. 2:1–3). This does not mean that we are all as bad as we can be but rather that not any of us are as good as we should be. We are therefore unable to reflect properly the divine image and likeness (see Rom. 1:18–32).

It is important to see that the fall into sin (see Gen. 3) was not just a moral lapse but a deliberate turning away from God and rejection of him. The day that Adam and Eve disobeyed God they died spiritually, which ultimately brought physical death (see Gen. 2:17). Sin's entrance has brought about a sinful nature in all humanity. Therefore men and women are not simply sinners because they sin, but they sin because they are sinners. People thus think and act in accord with their fallen natures.

This idea is most significant when reflecting on our relationship to God. Because of the entrance of sin into the world and our inheritance of Adam's sinful nature (see Rom. 5:12–19), we are by nature hostile to God and estranged from him (see Rom. 8:7; Eph. 2:1–3). We have wills that do not obey God, eyes that do not see, and ears that do not hear because spiritually we are dead to God.

While we function as free moral agents with a free will, our decisions and actions are always affected by sin. In seeking to understand what has gone wrong with the world, we recognize that human choices are negatively influenced by sin. In regard to our relationship with God, we do not genuinely repent or turn to God without divine enablement, for we are by nature hostile to God.

Any articulation of a Christian worldview must wrestle with the problem of sin. The result of sin (what theologians call depravity) refers to the fact that all aspects of our being, including our thinking and emotions, are negatively influenced. People still do right and good things as viewed by society, but these thoughts and actions, no matter how noble or benevolent, fall short of God's glory (Rom. 3:23). We can affirm that people choose to do good, but a Christian worldview helps us distinguish between the good and the ultimate good, which is the goal of pleasing God.

Answering the question about what has gone wrong in the way we have does not mean all are totally corrupt. Factors such as environment, emotional makeup, heritage, and the continuing effect of our having been created in the image of God influence or limit the degree of our corruption. Yet a Christian worldview recognizes that all types of immoral actions, whether lying, murder, adultery, seeking after power, homosexuality, pride, or our failure to love one another are related to our alienation from God. All in this world are estranged from

God. The good news is that our sin was judged at the cross of Jesus Christ. He has regained what was lost in Adam (Rom. 5:12–21). The grace of God has provided restoration for believers and has brought about a right relationship with God, with one another, with nature, and with ourselves.

WHAT SOLUTION CAN BE OFFERED?

At the core of a Christian worldview is the foundational truth that Jesus Christ's life and death exemplified divine love and exerted an influence for good and sacrifice. More importantly, Christ's death provided for sinners like you and like me a sinless sacrifice that satisfied divine justice. This incomprehensibly valuable sacrifice delivered sinners from their alienation and reconciled and restored sinners from estrangement to full fellowship and inheritance in the household of God.

Christ's work on the cross provided atonement for sin (Rom. 3:25; 1 John 2:2; 4:10; Heb. 2:17). Jesus provided not only atonement but also redemption. Jesus Christ has broken the power of sin, guilt, death, and Satan, bringing about a people who have been bought with a price (see Col. 2:15; 1 Pet. 1:8–19).

Jesus' work on the cross has made it possible for those who have been redeemed by placing their faith in him to be reconciled to God. Believers in Christ no longer stand under God's judgment. Jesus' reconciling work involves bringing humanity out of alienation into a state of peace and harmony with God. Our separation and brokenness created by sin have been restored and healed in Christ. We have been delivered from estrangement to fellowship with God. God now accepts us and treats believers as children rather than as transgressors (see 2 Cor. 5:18–20; Eph. 2:12–16; Col. 1:20–22).

Central to this Christian worldview message is the resurrection of Jesus Christ (see 1 Cor. 15:3–4). The resurrection establishes Jesus' lordship and deity, as well as guaranteeing the salvation of sinners (see Rom. 1:3–4; 4:24–25). The resurrection provides new life for believers, enabling them to see, think, and live anew.

GENERAL IMPLICATIONS
OF A CHRISTIAN WORLDVIEW

A Christian worldview becomes a driving force in life, giving us a sense of God's plan and purpose for this world. Our identity is shaped by this worldview. We no longer see ourselves as alienated sinners. A Christian worldview is not escapism but is an energizing motivation for godly and faithful thinking and living in the here and now. It also gives us confidence and hope for the future. In the midst of life's challenges and struggles, a Christian worldview helps to stabilize life, anchoring us to God's faithfulness and steadfastness.

Thus, a Christian worldview provides a framework for ethical thinking. We recognize that humans, who are made in God's image, are essentially moral beings. We also recognize that the fullest embodiment of good, love, holiness, grace, and truth is in Jesus Christ (see John 1:14–18).

A Christian worldview has implications for understanding history. We see that history is not cyclical or random. Rather, we see history as linear, a meaningful sequence of events leading to the fulfillment of God's purposes for humanity (see Eph. 1). Human history will climax where it began—on the earth. This truth is another distinctive of Christian thinking, for Christianity is historical at its heart. In the sense that according to its essential teaching, God has acted decisively in history, revealing himself in specific acts and events. Moreover, God will act to bring history to its providential destiny and planned conclusion.

God who has acted in history in past events will also act in history to consummate this age. So when we ask, "How will it end?" we do not simply or suddenly pass out of the realm of history into a never-never land. We pass to that which is nevertheless certain of occurring because God is behind it and is himself the One who tells us it will come to pass.

Developing a Christian worldview is an ever-advancing process for us, a process in which Christian convictions more and more shape our participation in culture. This disciplined, vigorous, and unending process will help shape how we assess culture and our place in it. Otherwise, culture will shape us and our thinking. Thus a Christian worldview offers a new way of thinking, seeing, and doing, based on a new way of being.

A Christian worldview is a coherent way of seeing life, of seeing the world distinct from deism, naturalism, and materialism (whether in its Darwinistic, humanistic, or Marxist forms), existentialism, polytheism, pantheism, mysticism, or deconstructionist postmodernism. Such a theistic perspective provides bearings and direction when confronted with New Age spirituality or secularistic and pluralistic approaches to truth and morality. Fear about the future, suffering, disease, and poverty are informed by a Christian worldview grounded in the redemptive work of Christ and the grandeur of God. As opposed to the meaningless and purposeless nihilistic perspectives of F. Nietzsche, E. Hemingway, or J. Cage, a Christian worldview offers meaning and purpose for all aspects of life.

PARTICULAR APPLICATIONS

While many examples could be offered, we will conclude this introductory chapter with six particular applications where a Christian worldview will provide the difference in perspective. Many others will be expanded in the chapters that follow:

1. *Technology*—Technology can become either an instrument through which we fulfill our role as God's stewards or an object of worship that will eventually rule us. A Christian worldview provides balance and insight for understanding this crucial aspect of twenty-first-century life.

2. *Sexuality and marriage*—Sexuality has become a major topic for those entering the third millennium. Much confusion exists among Christians and non-Christians. Sexuality is good in the covenant relationship of mutual self-giving marriage. Sexual intimacy, separated from covenant marriage, in heterosexual or homosexual relations is sinful and has a distorted meaning, a self-serving purpose and negative consequences.

3. *The environment*—Environmental stewardship means we have a responsibility to the nonhuman aspects of God's creation. Since God's plan of redemption includes his earthly creation, as well as human (see Rom. 8:18–27), we should do all we can to live in it carefully and lovingly.

4. *The arts and recreation*—The arts and recreation are understood as legitimate and important parts of human creativity and community. They express what it means to be created in the image of God. We need to develop critical skills of analysis and evaluation so that we are informed, intentional, and reflective about what we create, see, and do.

5. *Science and faith*—For almost two centuries science has been at the forefront of our modern world. We must explore how we see scientific issues from the vantage point of a Christian worldview. An understanding of God includes the knowledge we gain through scientific investigation. With the lens of faith in place, a picture of God's world emerges that complements and harmonizes the findings of science and the teachings of Scripture.

6. *Vocation*—Important for any culture is an understanding of work. Work is a gift from God and is to be pursued with excellence for God's glory. We recognize that all honest professions are honorable, that the gifts and abilities we have for our vocation (*vocatio*/calling) come from God, and that prosperity and promotions come from God.

These are only a few examples that could be cited that will help shape our thinking in other areas.

TOWARD CHRISTIAN THINKING IN HIGHER EDUCATION

As we enter this new century, there are inescapable choices to be made, and these choices have great implication for all aspects of life, and particularly for higher education. Those who teach and study in Christ-centered institutions should take to heart the words of the apostle Paul: "And do not be conformed to this world, but be transformed by the renewing of your mind" (Rom. 12:2 NASB).

What is called for in this volume is intellectually challenging. It is not the easiest option, but it is the option faithful to the calling upon Christ-followers. In what follows there is an amplification of the meaning of the biblical and theological foundations of a Christian worldview. Also there are discipline-specific applications of a Christian worldview. Certainly what will be seen is that there is no room for antiintellectualism in Christian higher education. We are to have the mind of Christ, and this certainly requires us to think and wrestle with the challenging ideas of history and the issues of our day. For to do otherwise will result in another generation of God's people ill equipped for faithful thinking and service in this new century. A Christian worldview is needed to confront an ever-changing culture. Instead of allowing our thoughts to be captive to culture, we must take every thought captive to Jesus Christ.

This call for serious Christian thinking built on the foundational truths outlined in this introductory chapter affirms our love for God and our love for study, the place of devotion and the place of research, the priority of affirming and passing on the great Christian traditions and the significance of honest exploration, reflection, and intellectual wrestling. These matters are in tension but not in contradiction and are framed by a faith-informed commitment.

A Christian worldview is not just piety added to secular thinking, nor is it merely research that takes place in a Christian environment. Being a faithful Christian scholar involves much more than mere piety. As Chuck Colson says, "True Christianity goes beyond John 3:16—beyond private faith and personal salvation." History shows that a commitment to piety alone will not sustain the ideal of a Christian university. The Christian intellectual tradition calls for rigorous thinking, careful research, and thoughtful publication. Christian scholarship is far broader than biblical and theological studies, though these disciplines help provide the framework for serious intellectual wrestling with literary, philosophical, scientific, historical, technological, and social issues.

Such a Christian worldview provides the framework for Christian scholarship in any and every field. This worldview, which grows out of the exhortation to take every thought captive to Christ, begins with the affirmation of God as Creator and Redeemer, for the dominating principle of Christian scholarship is not merely soteriological but cosmological as well. We thus recognize the sovereignty of the triune God over the whole cosmos, in all spheres and kingdoms, visible and invisible.

Such an initial reference point avoids the error of a spiritualized Gnosticism on the one hand and a pure materialistic metaphysic on the other. This premise forms the foundation for our affirmation that all truth is God's truth—truth that is both revealed and discovered. Thus we respond, on the one hand, with grateful wonder at what has been made known to us and, on the other, with exerted effort to discover what has not been clearly manifested. In such exploration we dare not misconstrue our previously stated premise so as to wrongly deduce that all scholarship or all research even if carried out by Christians is necessarily God's truth. No! We want to affirm the Christian intellectual tradition that recognizes that all scholarship, all invention, all discovery, all exploration that is truth—is God's truth.

In the large majority of our institutions, it is teaching that is rightly prized and prioritized, but we also need a complementary place for Christian scholarship. Rightly understood Christian scholarship is not contrary to either faithful teaching or Christian piety. Christian scholarship provides a foundation for new discovery and creative teaching, as well as the framework for passing on the unified truth essential to the advancement of Christianity.

Can we then summarize this serious Christian thinking for which we are calling? I believe we can, and I would like to suggest six overarching characteristics:

1. We call for Christian thinking that is derived from the unifying principle that God is Creator and Redeemer.
2. We call for Christian thinking that seeks answers through curious exploration and serious wrestling with the fundamental questions of human existence.
3. We call for Christian thinking that aspires to be internally consistent and flows from a comprehensive worldview.
4. We call for Christian thinking that recognizes the need to be aware of contemporary cultural, social, and religious trends.

5. We call for Christian thinking that lives in tension, by reflecting an outlook (worldview) while simultaneously having a particular discipline-specific focus—which means it will at times reflect an engagement mind-set and while at other times it needs to take on an antithetical perspective from the avenues of thought pursued by others in the academy. This approach will not entirely please those who see truth as a battle in which it is perfectly clear who stands with the forces of light or darkness. Sometimes the issues with which we wrestle are filled with ambiguities. For at this time, even with the help of Scripture and Christian tradition, we are finite humans who still see as through a glass darkly.

6. Ultimately, Christian thinking grows out of a commitment to "sphere-sovereignty," whether in the arts, science, humanities, education, business, health care, or social areas.

Thus Christian thinking must surely subordinate all other endeavors to the improvement of the mind in pursuit of truth, taking every thought captive to Jesus Christ (2 Cor. 10:5). At three places in the book of 2 Corinthians, Paul reminds us that we cannot presume that our thinking is Christ centered. In 2 Corinthians 3:14 we learn that the minds of the Israelites were hardened. In 4:4 Paul says that the unregenerate mind is blinded by the god of this world. In 11:3 the apostle says that Satan has ensnared the Corinthians' thoughts. So in 10:5 he calls for all of our thinking to be liberated by coming under the lordship of Christ.

So today, as in the days of the Corinthian correspondence, our minds and our thinking are ensnared by the many challenges and opposing worldviews in today's academy. Like Paul and Bernard of Clairveaux several centuries after him, we must combine the intellectual with the moral and spiritual expounded in Bernard's famous statement:

Some seek knowledge for
The sake of knowledge:
That is curiosity;
Others seek knowledge so that
They themselves may be known:
That is vanity;
But there are still others
Who seek knowledge in
Order to serve and edify others;
And that is charity.

And that is the essence of serious Christian worldview think-ing—bringing every thought captive to the lordship of Jesus Christ in order to serve and edify others. That is a high calling indeed as we move forward and faithfully into the twenty-first century.

PART I

BUILDING A FOUNDATION

CHAPTER I

THE AUTHORITY OF SCRIPTURE

George H. Guthrie

AMONG THE ISSUES facing Christians involved in academic life, who seek to integrate faith with learning their academic disciplines, none is more fundamental or vexing than the question of authority. Complex in its formulation and vast in both its scope and its implications, our answer to the authority question, in its broadest sense, molds how we think about data and interpretation, how we think about life's moral framework, even how we think about thinking. Thus it presents the point of departure for how we address *all* questions of truth and reality.

The authority crisis faced by Christians in the academy, moreover, is an extension of (and at times an impetus for) the crisis in the church and draws its force from currents of thinking in the cultures of the world at large. Rather than "our crisis," grappling with the issue of authority has become the elemental struggle of modern, or perhaps more appropriately, postmodern life.[1] Thus, the pressures on Christian thinkers to consider carefully their approaches to authority will not abate anytime soon.

The current volume is an apologetic, primarily through modeling, for "shaping a Christian worldview." The implied "shapers" in the title are those involved in educating others in thinking from the perspective of a Christian worldview as they engage all aspects of life and thought. That the worldview espoused here is "Christian" means that it is grounded in a form of the Christian religion (for us an evangelical form), and this brings us to the question of the specific role of the Christian Scriptures for believers involved in academic life, since, for most

Christians, their general belief system rests in some way on the Bible.[2]

The chief query of this chapter concerns the nature of the Christian Scriptures as authoritative for a Christian scholar or university. That is, how can an academic community, such as the one behind the writing of this volume, work within a confessional context, based in some way on ancient literature of a specific religion, and carry out academic work with rigor and integrity? Can the Christian worldview, in part, form the very axis around which a thoughtful life of research might revolve?

The canons of most academic disciplines, learned by Christians in the secular graduate programs of the world—the "tools of the trade," if you will—normally do not address biblical thought and material. Chemists learn the fundamentals of chemistry, not theology; students of literature study Dickinson and Melville, not Daniel and Matthew; and business students study organizational behavior, not the organization of the early church—and rightly so. Our proposal here is not that the Bible addresses all the necessary technical aspects of modern inquiry. In the Bible we do not find specific research procedures to track chemical reactions, for instance. Yet the Bible does offer a view of reality and principles for interacting with that reality, that is, a general framework for how one thinks about life, thought, inquiry, and the implications of research.

In other words, the Bible has much to say to a Christian immersed in any of the academic disciplines at the level of presuppositions. Thus, we suggest there is a basis for a specifically "Christian" approach to higher education and academic life in general. Such an approach seeks proactively to integrate the Christian worldview with the wide variety of disciplines in the academy.

Of course for the vast majority of our colleagues who do not hold to a Christian worldview, a specifically "Christian" approach to academics is an exercise in "masks and moonshine." For example, in 1988 "a subcommittee of the American Association of University Professors proposed that the AAUP declare colleges and universities that have placed academic freedom within the bounds of religious commitment to have forfeited 'the moral right to proclaim themselves as authentic seats of higher learning.'" In response to the suggestion that Christian perspectives might have some relevance to academic scholarship generally, Bruce Kuklick, a historian, labeled the idea "loony."[3] The presupposition here is obvious: for one to come at the task of academic life from within the framework of a specific, authoritative worldview is to forfeit the necessary freedom to do credible academic work.

FIRST THOUGHTS ON THE NATURE OF SCRIPTURAL AUTHORITY AND THE ACADEMY

Let's begin by being clear that *adherence to what might be called "authority structures" is a universal human phenomenon among those who have the ability for any kind of volitional activity.* Authority structures are the network of dynamics by which one makes decisions of any kind—from what clothes to put on in the morning, to what to eat for lunch, to which chemical to include in an experiment. Why do we make the decisions we do? Why do we think about things the way we do? What drives us? Our authorities do. Thus even a person claiming to eschew all authority has gone with the authority of their own antiauthoritarian perspectives. Of course here we are using the term *authority* very broadly rather than technically.

Thus our emotions at a given moment, our presuppositions learned in a psychology class during freshman year at university, cultural mores, and even the television commercial with an especially catchy jingle that plays in our heads as we choose a cereal at the grocery—all constitute forms of authority.

As we approach academic life and specific academic disciplines, we all come with presuppositions, "authoritative" principles, processes, and propositions that we embrace as appropriate to processes of thinking, researching, interpreting, and communicating the topic under consideration. However, it should be acknowledged that whether a person approaches research as pragmatist, hedonist, naturalist, behaviorist, Marxist, Christian, or one with no readily identifiable worldview, presuppositions are in place and have a profound effect on the way one thinks about research and conclusions. We may think this is not the case for the so-called "hard" sciences, but *every* form of science has its theoretical framework. What Thomas Kuhn pointed out in his *The Structure of Scientific Revolutions* is that there is no completely objective science; all of us are influenced by social and psychological factors in the way we approach our disciplines, in our cultures and eras.[4]

As one scholar has put it, "There is no such thing as an 'immaculate perception.'"[5] Our *Vorverstandnis,* our "preunderstanding," plays an important role in our interpretations of data and our interpretations of others' interpretations of data. Scientific frameworks of all stripes embody views of the world, and these views always color outcomes in interpretation. Of any approach to academic discipline—not just a specifically Christian one—we could ask, "Why do we understand and interact with our disciplines the way we do?" and "How does our worldview affect our interpretation of data?" This book is an attempt to bring a confessed worldview front and center, not that it might proactively "mold" or "guard" the data uncovered in whatever research is at hand, but that the presuppositions at play might be acknowledged as authoritative, in terms of a general view of the world, and engaged in processes of investigation.

Second, *it should not be assumed that a Christian approach to the authority of Scripture necessarily conflicts with many of the general models and fruits of research in the broader academy.*[6] While it is true that forms of fundamentalist Christianity in the past century were and are antiintellectual, other branches of the Christian movement have embraced honest intellectual pursuit as both a worthy vocation and an act of devotion to God. Many insights gained in academia through scientific investigation, historical research, or reflection on the humanities, by both Christians and non-Christians, can be embraced by Christians as aspects of general revelation, that is, God's revelation of truth through the created order, history, or the makeup of human beings. This posture holds that for a Christian there is no real division, in the search for truth, between "secular" (i.e., nonreligious) and "sacred," since "all truth is God's truth."[7]

Thus, a Christian approach has nothing to fear from sound research in any branch of the sciences and, in fact, celebrates excellent work done with rigor and sound tools in any field of inquiry. A truly Christian perspective celebrates excellent work being done in chemistry, literary analysis, or music theory, for example, regardless of whether the research question has to do with a specifically biblical or religious theme, because we celebrate the discovery of truth. As this book demonstrates, in all branches of the academy, Christians are doing good work with tools used generally in their various disciplines. Rather than constituting a conflict of interest, this use of sound tools for historical, philosophical, linguistic, scientific, or literary inquiry fits the Christian commitment to truth in its many expressions—a commitment which itself is based on Scripture's authority.

Although it is true that a Christian might skew the data uncovered in, for instance, a sociology research project or a physics experiment, is this not a danger with any person regardless of the worldview in play?[8] Yet, there is another factor that should be important from the Christian perspective: integrity. In the warp and woof of the Christian worldview, there exists a commitment to an honest approach to life. Thus, Christians are under obligation to allow their perspectives to be molded by genuine insight offered by good research. This does not mean, of course, that those outside the Christian worldview cannot do research with integrity, nor that all Christians do their research with integrity, but rather that integrity is a specific mandate within the Christian worldview rightly understood.

Third, the *process of integrating the Christian view of the world with academic discipline*—that is, working out how the authority of Scripture works with other forms of authority in the academy—*has been neither simple nor simplistic.* For millennia Christian academics have wrestled with how a God-oriented view of the world integrates with nontheological aspects of learning. In the Middle Ages, young men training for ministry were taught the classics, especially Aristotelian logic, and classical languages alongside Paul and Augustine, since the classics were considered important for a well-rounded education. Yet the perennial challenge was how to wed the pagan authorities with the teachings of the church.[9]

The Reformation, with its models of education that evidence, among other influences, the impact of Renaissance humanism, demonstrates a continuance of grappling with integration of faith and learning. It was the Reformation that formed the immediate backdrop to the establishment of the first universities in America. Most of the major universities of North America started as institutions committed both to education in the liberal arts and to a Christian worldview. Yet, with the coming of the Enlightenment and the rise of modernity, these eventually would transition to institutions fostering "a culture of unbelief," as George Marsden has shown.[10] The twentieth century witnessed numerous unsuccessful attempts at maintaining a Christian worldview among church-related institutions.[11] Thus, the endeavor to shape a Christian worldview, on the basis of scriptural authority and within the context of academia, is neither new nor easily sustained.

As this book attests, there exists a vibrant movement built around integrating Christian faith and learning among modern evangelicals, and the movement is beginning to draw some attention from those in the broader academy.[12] We focus our attention on evangelicalism in order to delimit the study and because it is the broader community context of which the writers of this volume are a part. Regardless of the exact expressions of evangelicalism in this movement, all forms in some way confess a specifically biblical worldview as foundational for their institutions. Thus, the Bible is held to be authoritative.

Our goal in the following pages is not to deal exhaustively with various positions on the nature of revelation or the inspiration and infallibility of Scripture. For that the reader may look to the systematic theologies referred to below. Rather, our task is to provide a brief introduction to recent arguments for Scripture as an appropriate authority for shaping one's worldview.

EVANGELICALS AND
THE AUTHORITY OF SCRIPTURE

Historically, evangelicals, as exemplified in such institutions as the Billy Graham Evangelistic Association, *Christianity Today* magazine, and Wheaton College, have held to a high view of Scripture, meaning that they hold Scripture to be inspired by God and, thus, normative for all aspects of life. Mark Noll states, "When examining the evangelical study of Scripture, everything hinges upon a recognition that the evangelical community considers the Bible the very Word of God."[13] Evangelicals insist that sound historical investigation reveals this to have been the position of Jesus and the early church (as reflected, for example, in the manner in which the Hebrew Scriptures are quoted), the church fathers, the Reformers, and orthodox believers to the present day. Thus evangelicals see themselves as holding to a key community value that reaches back to Jesus himself and has been adhered to by the community of faith for millennia.[14] It is on this basis that evangelical Christians have maintained that the biblical worldview is the appropriate worldview and the Bible itself the foundational authority for life.

The Traditional Approach

In arguing for the authority of Scripture, evangelicals traditionally have followed a general logic that moves from revelation, to inspiration, to authority.

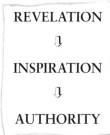

$$\textbf{REVELATION}$$
$$\Downarrow$$
$$\textbf{INSPIRATION}$$
$$\Downarrow$$
$$\textbf{AUTHORITY}$$

This pattern can be seen, for example, in the works of Carl F. H. Henry, Millard Erickson, and David S. Dockery, among many others.[15] Carl F. H. Henry set the evangelical standard for placing the doctrine of revelation at the epistemological center of evangelical theology. Henry located the source for Christian confidence in "God Who Speaks and Shows" and "God Who Stands and Stays." In the expansive fourth volume of *God, Revelation and Authority,* Henry focuses his efforts around the topic of authority from the very beginning. The logic internal to his discussion follows the pattern indicated above and assumes that the authority of Scripture is born of God's revelation and rests on the Bible's inspiration, as well as its inerrancy.[16]

Following Henry, Millard Erickson,[17] in his *Christian Theology,* the systematic theology most used currently in evangelical universities and seminaries, begins his section on "Knowing God" with "God's Universal Revelation," a discussion of what is often referred to as general revelation, or God's revealing himself through nature, history, and the makeup of human beings. From this foundation of general revelation Erickson moves to a discussion of "God's particular revelation," or special revelation, through historic events, divine speech, and, preeminently, in God's incarnation in Christ. This revelation, moreover, has been preserved through God's act of the inspiration of Scripture, which constitutes the Holy Spirit's influence on the writers of Scripture, an influence that rendered their writings both accurate records of God's revelation and works that themselves constituted an act of God's revelatory activity (i.e., the very Word of God).[18]

From his discussion of inspiration, Erickson moves to a discussion of inerrancy, suggesting that the Scripture is fully dependable. Rather than an irrelevant issue, the author sees the question of inerrancy as crucial, calling it "the completion of the doctrine of Scripture." For, "If God has given special revelation of himself and inspired servants of his to record it, we will want assurance that the Bible is indeed a dependable source of that revelation."[19] Having covered the various approaches to inerrancy, Erickson ends the section on knowing God with a discussion of Scripture's authority. Under this topic he deals with definitions of authority, the nature of religious authority, the question of how a reader comes to understand the meaning of Scripture and comes to affirm its divine origin, the role of the Holy Spirit, various views of illumination, and the distinction between historical and normative authoritativeness, among other topics.

In *Christian Scripture*[20] David Dockery follows this general pattern as well. Dockery argues that based on the plenary inspiration of the Bible, the Bible is true and normative. The writings of Scripture proclaim God's saving acts, are historically proximate to his saving acts, and are based on the authority of the prophets and apostles.[21] This revelation proclaims that all people are creatures of God, and relationship with him is the true locus of life's meaning. Thus, God has authority over all his creation and calls for people to respond to that authority. This authority is "communicated in the church and its tradition, in human reason, in conscience and experience, in nature and history, in Christ and the Bible, and is ultimately revealed in the incarnation."

Today the Bible is the primary vehicle for God's authoritative self-disclosure. The Bible witnesses to Jesus' authority as he lived for and acted on behalf of God the Father. This authority is witnessed to by his forgiveness of sins, the casting out of demons, Jesus' teaching, which was with authority, and his raising others from the dead. Indeed, he has been given all authority in heaven and on earth (Matt. 28:18–20). Moreover, Jesus' authority is exercised in his headship over the church, and his authority uniquely rests with the apostles whom he appointed. Their writings, and the writings of those with whom they were closely associated, communicate their authoritative teachings, and, therefore, constitute the standard of authority for the people of God.[22]

The traditional approach holds that knowledge of God can come only by revelation. This, in fact, he has done through a variety of means, but most clearly in his acts of special revelation, as he worked in and through the Jewish people and later the Christian community, and supremely in the person of his Son, Jesus Christ. Having revealed truth about himself, God has therefore acted to preserve that revelation in a dependable form, the written Scriptures. Since the Scriptures have their ultimate source in God's activities, as witnessed by the biblical writers, they carry both a historical and normative authority.[23]

So, in answer to why Scripture should be held as a foundational authority for shaping a Christian worldview, the traditional evangelical approach replies, "Because God is the God of
all truth and has revealed truth generally via the created order
and specifically through historic events, his spoken words, and,
ultimately, in his Son, Jesus Christ. Moreover, God's revelation
is preserved through his inspiration of the Scripture. Thus,
every area of human life and inquiry has at its foundation the
reality reflected by God's revelation in Scripture." Therefore,
Scripture forms the appropriate beginning point for shaping a
worldview.

The Scripture and Community:
The Postmodern Program of Stanley Grenz

In recent years a number of theologians have worked to pave
new paths of thinking about the nature and authority of
Scripture, especially as those paths relate to the Christian
movement as a "community." One of the more influential
thinkers in this regard is Stanley Grenz. In his *Theology for the
Community of God* and elsewhere, Grenz has moved his doctrine of Scripture out of a foundational position for doing theology to a subcategory of pneumatology, the doctrine of the
Holy Spirit. Grenz states:

> The demonstration of the divine authorship of the
> Scripture or its status as revelation need not constitute
> the prolegomenon to our theology. Sufficient for
> launching the systematic-theological enterprise is the
> nature of theology itself as reflection on community
> faith. And sufficient for the employment of the Bible in
> this task is its status as the book of the community, the
> source of the *kerygma*—the gospel proclamation—in
> the early communities and consequently in the contem-
> porary community.[24]

Critical of tendencies evangelicalism has inherited from fun-
damentalism (and thus Protestant scholasticism)—namely orienting itself to biblical authority because of its commitment to
biblical inspiration and its focus on propositions as central to

the faith—Grenz has suggested evangelicalism is off course. Specifically, he understands contemporary evangelicalism to have moved away from being gospel focused, understanding the Bible as a tool of the Spirit's working, to being Bible focused, consumed with the propositions of biblical ortho-doxy.[25] Accordingly, Grenz has rejected the idea, reflected in the traditional approach, that inspiration can serve as the founda-tion for biblical authority.

Rather, inspiration is tied more closely to illumination as an aspect of the Spirit's working in the community.[26] The result is that Scripture, rather than playing the foundational role for the whole program of theology, comes alongside, albeit as the prominent player, of tradition and culture as the norms for doing theology in the community of faith.[27] In answer to our question about why the Bible should be held as authoritative for a Christian university, Grenz, perhaps, would answer, "Because it is the community's book."[28]

Grenz's approach has offered a number of suggestive correc-tives, including a caution against wedding evangelical theology too closely to Enlightenment ideals, the importance of the impact of culture and specific community contexts on individ-ual knowledge, and the danger of excessive individualism.[29] Yet the ultimate weakness in understanding knowledge as relative to a particular community is, in part, the underestimation of the complexity of communities, both internally and vis-à-vis other communities.

Of which so-called Christian communities are we speaking? How many subcommunities are in play and what is their nature? He speaks of the contemporary Christian community as if it were fairly uniform, which is not the case. Consequently there is the problem that this approach diminishes one commu-nity's, or one subcommunity's, ability to speak authoritatively to another. Christianity has at its base, for instance, the mission of communicating its message to those currently outside the community. The New Testament itself also reflects theological dialogue within the first-century Christian movement (e.g., the Jerusalem Council of Acts 15), as the community sought to sort out truth from error. Grenz's program seems to weaken such a dialogue. Millard Erickson comments:

> Grenz contends that knowledge is relative to the group or community of which one is a part. That undoubtedly is the basis for rejecting the more radical conclusions of postmodernism. The question, however, is, Why this community rather than another, a non-Christian community? And within the broadly Christian realm, which of the countless subcommunitites is the one within which our beliefs are to find their validity? Rather different doctrinal formulations are made by liberal Episcopalians and Southern Baptist fundamentalists, for example. Why one community rather than another? Without some answer to such questions, postmodern evangelicalism will sound like Emil Brunner's response to the question about how a Muslim hears "his master's voice" within the Koran, as a Christian does within the Bible: "We are not Muslims."[30]

In his attempt to move evangelicalism from an entrenchment to propositionalism, it seems that Grenz simultaneously has given up important ground on the authority of Scripture as a basis for speaking of theological norms. His program, consequently, seems to offer no firm basis for why we are to hold to traditional Christianity, or a specific evangelical form, rather than some other belief system. Thus, the position would seem to lessen the basis of a Christian in the university, seeking to argue as a discussant in the broader interchange of ideas for a specifically Christian perspective. Erickson is right to raise the question whether a theology oriented to postmodernism does not inherently have a theological inertia that eventually will undo being able to say anything specific about theology at all.

Kevin Vanhoozer: God's Speech Activity

Kevin Vanhoozer is another contemporary evangelical scholar who is sensitive to the dynamics within communities, and specifically to the role of language and communication both within and without communities. Rather than offering a full-blown systematic theology, his endeavor, detailed in his book *Is There a Meaning in This Text?* addresses the task of biblical interpretation, and, therefore, the roles of the author, text, and reader in interpretation—the central issue in modern, hermeneutical discussions. Vanhoozer's book offers a nuanced critique of modern philosophical hermeneutics, addressing first the problems with current trends and then offering solutions, seeking ultimately to offer a metaphysics and ethics of meaning. Like those of the traditional approach who argue for biblical authority, he suggests that right interpretation begins with right theology, specifically what the trinitarian God has revealed about himself.

Addressing the issue of biblical authority, he suggests that postmodernity's approach to literary criticism, which renders the author's voice "undecidable and indecipherable," has undermined biblical authority.

How does such authorial laryngitis affect biblical authority? The answer is brief but massive in its implications: *biblical authority is undone.* The Undoers effectively strip the Bible of any stable meaning so that it cannot state a fact, issue a command, or make a promise. Furthermore, without the author to serve as touchstone of the distinction between meaning and significance, every interpretation becomes just as authorized a version as another. A text that cannot be set over against its commentary is no authority at all. Finally, biblical authority is undermined by the instability of meaning because, if nothing specific is said, the text cannot call for any specific response. Interpreters can give neither obedience nor belief to texts that lack specificity. If there is no meaning in the text, then there is nothing to which the reader can be held accountable.[31]

Vanhoozer seeks to answer the removal of the author from the task of interpretation (and the consequent hyper-focus on the autonomy of modern communities), as well as the supposed instability of a text's meaning, via speech-act theory. This approach was originated by John Austin and has been extended by John Searle and, in biblical studies, by Anthony Thiselton.[32] Simply put, speech-act theory suggests that utterances cannot be reduced simply to declarations of what is true and false but rather have a significant role as performatives in community. An author of a text, therefore, is an initiator of a speech act and, therefore, must be considered in the process of interpretation. A text, moreover, is an act of communication performed by that agent and fixed by writing. The concept of genre, along with communication conventions in place when an author produces a text, provides a means of stability in the meaning of texts. This flies in the face of modern literary approaches, such as the reader-response criticism of Stanley Fish. Moreover, an author must be respected as "an other" if a text is to be received with ethical integrity, as an act of communication.

Thus the interpretive community, rather than the place where meaning is born, is where interpretive virtues are cultivated. The reader, as part of an interpretive community, enters into a covenant of communication with the author. To read responsibly is to respect the otherness of the author and to receive an act of communication humbly. In this way individuals or their communities can be changed, or kept from inappropriate change, by authoritative texts. A text can challenge the preconceptions of a reader or a whole community, and readers can be freed from the tyranny of their own perspectives or the perspectives of their communities.

When dealing with the authority of Scripture, Vanhoozer's speech act approach simultaneously carries Grenz's sensitivity to the importance of community contexts for interpretation but at the same time is able to stand the text of Scripture over against a community as an authoritative speech act. In answer to why the Bible is authoritative for us, Vanhoozer responds, "Because the Bible communicates the gospel of Jesus Christ— the account of what God has said and done as sovereign Lord and as suffering servant for our salvation."[33] Ultimately, therefore, the Scripture, in essence, is communicative action initiated by God, and this gives Scripture its ultimate authority.[34] His answer, therefore, to our question on why Scripture should be held as authoritative in the Christian university might sound similar to those of the traditional approach: God has performed a speech act via Scripture that serves as the authority for the Christian community and speaks an authoritative word to all people.

Kevin Vanhoozer's engagement of modern philosophical hermeneutics exemplifies the agenda of *Shaping a Christian Worldview*. He has critically and constructively interacted with prominent, highly influential currents of thought, learned from them, but then brought the Christian worldview to bear on those currents. In his hermeneutical sophistication, he has offered a way to draw on important contributions of traditional evangelical arguments for Scripture's authority. At the same time, he has expressed the nature of Scripture in a way conversant with modern understandings of the nature of language.

Further Thoughts

Let me add three clarifying points concerning the authority of Scripture in line with Vanhoozer's orientation to speech-act theory.

First, the vehicle God has used to communicate his authoritative word via Scripture is human language and not something else. As Calvin noted, God has accommodated his revelation through Scripture to human language.[35] Thus the Bible is a divine-human book. God has initiated the revelation, but he has used human beings with their capacities and within their historical contexts to communicate truth. That God has inspired the writers of Scripture does not mean that he dictated the words to them, nor that he incapacitated their normal abilities (e.g. as in a trance).[36] Inspiration means that God exerted supernatural influence upon the writers of Scripture that rendered their writings "an accurate record of the revelation or which resulted in what they wrote actually being the Word of God."[37] Yet the vehicle used was human language in historical contexts.

Second, this vehicle of human language in and of itself is limited because language uses symbols to communicate rather than somehow transferring a comprehensive knowledge of the complete reality of any given referent. For example, when we say, "God is love," the assertion communicates neither all that God is nor all that love is. At the same time, we suggest human language can communicate, specifically and accurately, in a way that corresponds to reality (i.e., what is true proposition-ally) and that is adequate to accomplish intended, relational results. Thus, it can both be true and adequate for accomplish-ing the designs God had for his revelation in establishing and maintaining his covenant communities. J. I. Packer comments:

> It is asked whether biblical language is adequate to communicate knowledge about God. . . . The key fact . . . is the theomorphism of created man, whom God made a language user, able to receive God's linguistic communication and to respond in kind. But it is impor-tant, in saying this, not to appear to claim too much. If we ask what knowledge about God biblical language communicates, the answer is, not exhaustive knowledge of Himself and of all things in relation to Him—the knowledge that is distinctly His—but only knowledge of those matters that He sees to be adequate (i.e., suffi-cient) for our life of faith and obedience.[38]

Third, and closely related to the second point, human lan-guage, even when used by God to communicate his authorita-tive word, is not impervious to misunderstanding. As Vanhoozer notes:

> Access to the reality of Jesus or to anything else of which Scripture speaks is textually mediated. The process of mediation, however, is not guaranteed. For though the communicative act may be successfully per-formed, and though meaning may really be "there," there is no guarantee that the interpreter will behave in a rational, or indeed moral, way. The covenant of dis-course may be broken. Communicative action calls not only for hermeneutic rationality but also for commu-nicative ethics. Literary knowledge requires not only the right interpretive methods but also the right

interpretive virtues. For the reader too is a covenantal agent, and the communicative act remains in suspended animation until the reader responds.[39]

Interpretation skills and virtues are demanded of those who hear; thus, misunderstanding, while not inevitable, is possible.

So the fact that God has accommodated his revelation to human language does not mean that the communication revealed constitutes exhaustive knowledge; or that the revelation is impervious to misunderstanding. Neither does it mean that the communication is, because it is given in human language, of necessity errant or unintelligible. By way of analogy, when I say to my wife, "I love you," that statement is true and, since she can understand it, adequate to accomplish the encouragement I intend towards my wife; this in spite of the fact that the statement does not communicate all that the word *love* means. Moreover, Pat could misunderstand the phrase given a certain context. If I were an insensitive husband who used sarcasm consistently, she might misunderstand the assertion "I love you" as meaning, "I am frustrated with you and do not like you right now." Nevertheless, none of this changes the fact that the assertion is true and, given sensitivity to the author's intended meaning, adequate to accomplished its intended effect in community. Yet the intended meaning is crucial.

This understanding of language explains several phenomena related to the reception of authoritative Scripture in a Christian community. The fact that the human language in which the biblical materials were originally communicated is neither exhaustive nor impervious to misinterpretation explains why, for instance, there are significant variations in modern translations. The act of translation is, inherently, an act of interpretation. Translators must make decisions concerning which possible meaning of a term from the biblical era (words have ranges of meaning in any language) is the appropriate meaning given the context.

Furthermore, some suggest that Christianity cannot be true since there are so many contemporary expressions of the Christian community, or denominations, which conflict in their understandings of basic Christian teachings, regardless of the fact that they, at least to some degree, claim the Bible as a primary authority. However, since the human languages in which the Bible was written are not perfect vehicles and must, therefore, be interpreted, variations in how the Bible is read and understood should be expected.

If somehow God had directly transferred truth to the human soul, without the mediation of human language (and it is hard even to imagine such an experience), then the difficulties involved in communication, perhaps, would have been alleviated. However, this is not how God chose to communicate and preserve his specific revelation. Thus humans in general, and the church specifically, will always have to wrestle with interpretation when dealing with the Scriptures. These facts, however, diminish none of Scripture's truthfulness or authority.

Back to the Question of Scripture in the Academy

The Christian community specifically has been established as an act of God's initiative. God has spoken and acted on our behalf, and he has invited response to his speech acts. Preeminently his communication is focused in the person of his Son, Jesus Christ. Hebrews 1:1–2a reads, "Long ago God spoke many times and in many ways to our ancestors through the prophets. But now in those final days he has spoken to us through His Son" (NLT). Thus, the Son is the authoritative Word to whom all written revelation points and bears witness.

> At the heart of the Christian faith lies not so much a set of abstract ideas or beliefs but a person. We must resist the temptation to speak about Christianity as if it were some form of "ism," like Marxism, Darwinism, or Hegelianism. These are essentially abstract systems which have become detached from the person of their founder, and reduced simply to sets of doctrines. Although the ideas which we call "Marxism" were originally developed by Marx, the ideas are now quite

independent of him. All that Marx did was to introduce them. The relationship between Jesus and Christianity is, however, quite different.[40]

Specifically, Christ, who was sent from God the Father, founded a covenant community based on a Christological hermeneutic; that is, he taught his followers to interpret Scripture in light of his person and work. That community both followed and produced authoritative texts, inspired by and illumined by the Spirit. As Christians today, we form an extension of that interpretive community: we hold to the same texts and teachings, and we are children of the same Spirit. As God spoke to the first Christians through the Scriptures, as illumined by the Spirit with whom they were in interpretive community, they received the speech act of God as authoritative and responded accordingly. As Christians in the academic community, we too hear the Scriptures as authoritative for building our view of the world. This worldview, rather than being antithetical to academic life, offers certain community values that can contribute to the academic enterprise. For as Christians, our authoritative worldview carries with it a love for and commitment to truth, a confidence in the ultimate unity of reality, and the community virtues of integrity and respect for others.

Applications

How then might this position on the authority of Scripture work itself out in an individual or institution seeking to live both under that authority and within the broader academic community? Let me offer several principles of operation and concluding suggestions.

1. *We must work out a clear understanding concerning how the authority of Scripture relates to our tasks of doing our academic disciplines.* In other words, we must reject the fragmentation of life that suggests a clear demarcation in life between the sacred and secular. If God is the originator of all there is, he can be followed into the task of thinking well about any area of study. We may well ask, What ways are our

presuppositions concerning our approaches to research and reflection shaped by the Christian worldview?

2. *We must make a distinction between the authority of Scripture and our own interpretations of Scripture.* By highlighting this need, no evasion of confidence in the great doctrines of the Christian faith is implied. Because Scripture is clear, so are the great axioms of the Christian worldview. Nonetheless, all Christians must feel the burden of becoming more faithful interpreters of Scripture. This means, first of all, that those engaged in the integration of faith and learning will have to work hard at the task of learning theology, in order to discern the distinctions between the primary components of the Christian worldview (e.g. the holy Trinity, God as Creator of the universe, Christ as Son of God and Savior, etc.) and what have been seen as secondary or tertiary issues in the history of the church (e.g., how long God's creation of the world took in terms of duration).

Being more faithful interpreters will mean, furthermore, that hermeneutics, the art/science of interpretation, will also have to be studied. As the Christian scholar brings the Christian worldview to bear on discussions of various fields, he or she must learn to avoid positions that would be rejected among evangelical biblical scholars, for example, as based on poor hermeneutics. This will help Christians avoid putting forth a perspective in the broader academy as *the* Christian positions on a topic, when in reality they only constitute a weak biblical interpretation by an individual. This operating principle speaks to the need for more collaboration between theologians and those doing work in other fields.

3. *We must embrace the presuppositions of the guild critically, analyzing them in light of biblical authority.* Christians need to seek to understand not only their own worldview, but also the worldview held by mentors in their various disciplines, and to assess critically what aspects of the mentor's worldview are based on research and what aspects are part of the professor's personal, philosophical system of thought. The wide-eyed graduate student enters a prestigious program of study with a renowned scholar, and the scholar offers his views with

confidence and expertise. The Christian scholar should be able to think critically in this context, and it will serve as a training ground for interacting well in the broader arena of scholarly meetings and publications. This operating principle witnesses to the need for undergraduate Christian institutions to teach their students the skills of critical thinking as well as the various major worldview systems.

4. *We must work with integrity and excellence, and bear witness gracefully.* Poor work, or work skewed to fit one's own prejudices, bears false witness to the Christian worldview and the authority of Scripture. Christian scholars should live under the authority of the propositional truth of the Scriptures as well as the relational virtues mandated by the Scriptures. This will mean that work will be approached "as unto the Lord, rather than human beings," and, thus, work done with excellence and work done honestly. It also will mean that engagement with others in the guild, those who have worldviews contrary to our own, will be carried out with grace and humility. Arrogant, angry Christians who are easily provoked and made defensive do little for the advancement of the Christian worldview as a credible authority structure.

C. S. Lewis once suggested that Christian intellectuals have an important ministry of engaging the broader world of ideas on behalf of our brothers and sisters in the church, to stand in the gap for them, offering well-conceived reflections on reality from the Christian point of view. If in our generation we are to carry out this weighty task and, thus, play a role in "shaping a Christian worldview" in those under our voices or pens, then we will have to do so in all the disciplines of the academy, working at integrating faith and learning beginning at the level of presuppositions, and, ultimately, with an orientation to the authority of Scripture.

CHAPTER 2

THE LESSONS OF HISTORY

Gregory Alan Thornbury

By all accounts, Christian higher education faces the twenty-first century with newfound strength and respectability. Across the denominational divide, Christian colleges and universities report record enrollment, boast impressive faculties, and look toward a very bright future.[1] In a recent conference sponsored by the John F. Kennedy School of Government at Harvard University, participants from "a broad range of Christian denominations . . . portrayed the cultural climate as increasingly welcoming of religious scholars and hospitable to religious institutions."[2] Such news heartens Christians on many fronts in the church as well as the academy.

AN "OPEN" INSTITUTIONAL FUTURE?

Although evangelicals will not likely feel as though they are winning the culture war, new opportunities present themselves to institutions of theological conviction and ecclesiastical heritage. Such signs offer hope to evangelical Christian liberal arts colleges and universities. University of Notre Dame historian George M. Marsden, author of the path-breaking book *The Soul of the American University: From Protestant Establishment to Established Nonbelief,* sounded a positive note as a participant at the Kennedy School conference. Marsden, whose *Soul of the American University* chronicled American higher education's long march toward secularism, expressed confidence that Christian colleges and universities need not repeat the trajectory of the past.

"The general consensus," Marsden commented, "is that there's no reason to have to continue along the slippery slope toward secularism. . . . This is a moment of opportunity for religious colleges."[3] Evangelicals among these religious colleges, whose strides in higher education are finally being noticed across the academy, cannot afford the luxury of savoring the moment for long. Rather, evangelicals in Christian higher education must refuse to afford the "reason" for another "slippery slope" to which Marsden referred.

Recently, evangelicals received an additional boost from an unlikely source: *The Atlantic Monthly* in a provocative article entitled, "The Opening of the Evangelical Mind." In a positive, if measured, approbation of certain developments in Christian higher education, Alan Wolfe of Boston College praised institutions such as Wheaton College and Calvin College, as well as Baylor and Pepperdine universities, for producing academic communities in which vigorous discussion and passion about ideas characterize the classroom.[4]

For those of us in the evangelical guild, Wolfe discovered something we have known all along: Christian colleges and universities need not take a back seat with respect to rigorous academic preparation and engagement of the mind. But even as Wolfe welcomed evangelicals back from what he deemed a self-imposed obscurity, he nonetheless cautioned his academically separated brethren against a return to the doctrines that consigned them to exile in the first place.

Those encouraged by Wolfe's openness—indeed, a hopeful development—must also read between the lines of Wolfe's argument. What struck Wolfe so positively about students studying at evangelical institutions of higher learning was that they, unlike their faculty mentors, were genuine pluralists. Reflecting on an interview with a Wheaton College student, Wolfe contrasted the student's worldview with that of her own institution and evangelicals at large. Referring to the recent flap at Tufts University in which the student government association sought to defund a Christian organization for barring a lesbian student from its leadership, Wolfe observed of this Christian college student that "unlike those Tufts students—and, indeed, like

Wheaton's own president—she and other students like her are genuine pluralists; in their view, evangelicals ought to be able to stand the competition of coexisting with other faiths." To which Wolfe adds, "Evangelical faculty members could learn from their students."[5]

In other words, evangelicals are respectable only insofar as they are good pluralists. According to Wolfe, evangelicals have to give up their doctrine of salvation, welcome Roman Catholics as fellow evangelicals, "put their defensiveness to one side," and learn the art of non-interventionist religious conversation.[6]

Wolfe's prescription poses serious questions for evangelical Christian colleges and universities. What must we do to receive greater standing and acclaim among our peers in the academy? What, if any, theological distinctives are at stake in order to achieve such an end? If historically evangelical convictions are forfeited or even downplayed, will we thus provide the very reason for a downgrade to which Marsden referred? How might Christian college students, faculty, administrations, and trustees prevent the drift toward secularism that haunts the biographies of so many formerly Christian institutions? First, we must learn from the mistakes of the past, those slow and often imperceptible choices that serve to loosen us from our theological moorings. Second, we must put accountability structures in place that remind and demand of us faithfulness to the Lord we confess and to the churches we serve.

BUCKNELL UNIVERSITY
A CASE STUDY

For those unfamiliar with why a chapter with a title such as this one is needed, the place to start is with George M. Marsden's *The Soul of the American University*, cited earlier, and James Tunstead Burtchaell's *The Dying of the Light: The Disengagement of Colleges and Universities from Their Christian Churches*.[7] Both volumes masterfully chronicle the demise of the Christian worldview within some of the most noted colleges and universities in American higher education. The books complement each other.

Where Marsden provides the sweeping historical narrative of universities that increasingly severed ties from their distinctive religious tenets, Burtchaell offers specific case studies of the phenomenon organized denominationally. Burtchaell remarks that the failing of the churches that sponsored these now-famous schools lay not in an attempt to hold their colleges accountable but rather in holding on to them as long as the churches did. Burtchaell summed up his conclusions:

> Until the later nineteenth century it was conventional for colleges in the United States to be identified by association with a Christian church. Their founding faculty, students, funding, piety, morality, and religious study (but not much other study) were braided together into a cord that tethered college to church. Yet we have seen that this church-college relation could be feeble on the brightest of days, and in the longer judgment of history the churches may be more harshly judged for continuing to claim colleges than for nagging them.[8]

Simply put, Burtchaell contends, blame rests not only on those colleges and universities that repudiated the faith of those who founded their schools. Burtchaell also finds fault with those denominations and churches who persisted in identifying themselves with institutions that no longer concurred with their own confession. In other words, a composition of church with school is not possible when differing worldviews cannot be composed.

For his part, Marsden lamented the exclusion of belief as a corollary of scholarship in the once-religious schools he surveyed. For Marsden, scholars of deep religious conviction now hope merely for a place at the table of discussion in the academy because "while the procedural rules of academia may preclude some religious attitudes and viewpoints, there is no reason why it should be a rule of academia that *no* religious viewpoint shall receive serious consideration."[9] Marsden's follow-up work, *The Outrageous Idea of Christian Scholarship*, brought the irony of the disestablishment of religion in American university full circle.[10]

Arguing persuasively for his cause, Marsden appreciated the position in which Christian intellectuals find themselves in the current academic economy: that the disciplines may be pursued from a thoroughly Christian worldview is indeed an "outrageous" proposition to the modern mind. As a result, Marsden's analysis caused his colleagues in the academy to regard their Christian counterparts via a simple appeal to pluralism, if nothing else.

Both Marsden and Burtchaell's splendid volumes provide an explanatory mechanism through which we can explain the hard times upon which the Christian worldview has fallen in the secular academic community. More pointedly, they chronicle the loosening of the ties between colleges and universities and the churches that founded them. But what Marsden and Burtchaell do not provide is a prescription for how current Christian institutions might stay faithful to their own confession and the churches that support them. Clearly this is not a shortcoming of Marsden and Burtchaell's work, for theirs is primarily a work of description.

The best inductive way to start analyzing the demise of the Christian worldview in higher education in the United States is simply to choose any college initially founded by Christians for the purpose of Christian education. In order to demonstrate the widespread nature of the slippery slope toward secularization in American higher education, I chose Bucknell University in Lewisburg, Pennsylvania, as an example. Although Bucknell certainly developed an impressive reputation as one of a handful of elite independent universities in the Northeast, the institution is not as immediately recognizable as the schools that Burtchaell and Marsden review. The fortunes of the Christian worldview at Bucknell University remind us that the presuppositions of modernity do not discriminate on the basis of geography, ecclesiastical roots, or institutional size. In other words, "the dying of the light" is not limited to institutions with immediate name recognition.

Bucknell University began classes in the basement of the First Baptist Church in Lewisburg, Pennsylvania, in the fall of 1846. After a review of the need for an institution of higher learning among Baptists in Pennsylvania, the Northumberland Baptist Association founded the school for the express purpose of furthering the cause of Christ and the Christian ministry. In a "corresponding letter" sent to its sister associations throughout the state, Northumberland Baptists expressed their earnest desire and intention for the university. They purposed "to see that the cause of God, the honour and glory of the Redeemer's Kingdom [is] promoted in all our bounds, and spreading far and wide until the Kingdoms of this world shall become the Kingdoms of our Lord and his Christ."[11]

Although the founders of Bucknell University never narrowly conceived of their mission as the preparation of ministers for their Baptist churches, they nonetheless saw Bucknell as an organ for the spread of Baptist theological convictions and polity. Indeed, the Rev. Howard Malcom, an early president of Bucknell, acted to establish a department of theology, whose "main purpose should be the spread of Baptist doctrine."[12]

Perhaps most importantly, Bucknell University clearly emerged as a *denominational* school, accountable to the churches that supported it. Initially, the charter of the university required that the overwhelming preponderance of the trustees (four-fifths) be members of regular Baptist churches.[13] Clearly, the founders of Bucknell wished for the school to reflect both the theological convictions and ecclesial fidelity of its Baptist patrons.

Like many denominational schools, Bucknell prescribed in the "general regulations" of the institution that students would be in attendance "upon public worship in some church in town on Sunday." Another aspect confirming the Christian character of Bucknell was the initiation of a daily chapel service that consisted of Scripture reading, prayer, and the Gloria Patri, a practice that continued until 1960, when the practice was made voluntary and then subsequently abandoned.

Bucknell found its initial sustenance, encouragement, and resources from the benevolence of local churches, and such contribution to the institution was recognized in the makeup of the school's students, faculty, and administration. In an appeal to Pennsylvania Baptists to support the new institution, Stephen

William Taylor, formerly of the Hamilton Theological Institution in New York and general agent for the then still "University at Lewisburg," implored his fellow Baptists:

> Unite; and in the wisdom and strength which God has given you, rise and build. One noble effort will bring into existence a University which will remain to supply the subordinate schools with well qualified educator's [sic]; the missionary field with able laborers, and Bible Societies with correct translators—to minister the benefits of sound learning to all the learned professions, and to all the great departments of honest industry, and to every benevolent institution, during all coming time.[14]

Such language sounds strikingly familiar (albeit anachronistically) to a well-crafted mission statement of any Christian liberal arts college. Consider the elements involved: the advance of the Christian gospel, the honoring of the Word of God, and the application of divinely given resources throughout the disciplines of human inquiry. Taylor's appeal represents the heart of every truly Christian institution: to bring all fields of knowledge under the sovereignty of the Lord Jesus Christ.

Sadly, in time, the spherical nature of Bucknell's Christian identity and ecclesial commitments unraveled. As the university prospered both in terms of student population and resources, its earlier commitments quickly dissipated. From the start, Bucknell did not put into place any confessional requirements for the faculty or trustees. Participation in Baptist life stood as the only requirement for the board of trustees, and, predictably, such a standard was one of the first markers of the Christian character of the institution to go. In order to strengthen the financial stability of the university (i.e., to place more patrons of financial means on the board), President John Howard Harris eased the requirement that four-fifths of the board of trustees be members of regular Baptist churches and changed the standard to a simple majority in 1929.[15] The move accomplished its intended effect, as Bucknell successfully survived the Great Depression and prospered in institutional resources.

As Bucknell grew in size, importance, and financial freedom, a concomitant decrease occurred in the Christian identity of the institution. By 1945, an internal study of the university recommended the removal of the requirement that a majority of the board of trustees be Baptist and suggested instead that members of the board be selected "because of their ability 'to make a valuable contribution to the conduct of the university.'"[16] Gone was any sense of gratitude and deference to the churches that gave Bucknell its initial and long-standing support. By 1953, President Merle Odgers brushed aside any responsibility to the American Baptist Convention (formerly Northern Baptist). In a remarkable attempt at revisionist history, Odgers averred that the "liberal Baptist tradition has been Bucknell's Christian tradition."[17] Ogders's remarks signalled an evolving shift in Bucknell's institutional identity from Baptist controlled and Baptist operated to Baptist affiliated, to broadly Christian, and then broadly religious.

Today, Bucknell claims no religious heritage as a distinctive of the university. A visit to Bucknell's Web site reveals no information that the school was initially denominational in origin or that a Christian impulse once marked its educational philosophy. In effect, present-day Bucknell commits a sort of modern ecclesiocide, a wiping away of the memory of classes in the basement of the First Baptist Church of Lewisburg, mission statements that acknowledge the glory of God, and the desire "to see that the cause of God, the honour and glory of the Redeemer's Kingdom [is] promoted in all our bounds, and spreading far and wide until the Kingdoms of this world shall become the Kingdoms of our Lord and his Christ." In fact, citizens of Lewisburg, Pennsylvania, are far more likely to open their local newspaper and read an article subversive of the Christian faith by a faculty member at Bucknell than read one supportive of historic Christianity.[18]

To be certain, Bucknell's move away from ecclesial accountability and Christian distinctives meant greater financial stability and freedom. Additionally, and to be fair, no confession of faith or governing documents anchored Bucknell to the faith that its early supporting churches confessed. In other words, no obstacles prevented or at least impeded Bucknell's secular drift. Consequently, some of the blame for the ever-dimming Christian witness of a school such as Bucknell lies at the feet of the churches themselves who failed, whether from lack of foresight or courage, to preserve their university from wholesale abandonment of its initial mission and scope.

LEARNING FROM HISTORY IN CHRISTIAN HIGHER EDUCATION

The preceding account should sober any student, faculty member, administrator, or trustee in Christian higher education. The leading moral of the demise of Christianity at schools such as Harvard, Yale, Bucknell, and others, is this: the same thing can and will happen to Christian colleges if they are not alert and do not learn from the lessons of history. Simply put, the status of many Christian colleges and universities as distinctly evangelical is only tenuous at best unless certain safeguards keep them accountable to their own theological convictions. Evangelical institutions that intend to remain evangelical must put into motion action plans that concretize their intellectual commitments.

Unfortunately, evangelicals often seem to be the last persons who recognize that their own emerging beliefs do not square with their established beliefs. Evangelicals, caught up in the epistemological trends of the moment, often congratulate themselves on the ideological currency of their newly revised theologies. Outside observers, however, remain singularly unimpressed and wonder what, in fact, makes one an evangelical if one's presuppositional boundaries appear so fluid and accommodating to the winds of secular philosophical thinking. Bemused observers of recent evangelical intellectual projects may wonder if the five *solas* of the Protestant Reformation have given way to a message to the secular academy which says, "Anything you can do, we can do thirty years later. We can do anything later than you."

Consequently, evangelicals abdicate the task of self-criticism to non-Christian journalists and academics. Writing in a recent article on the evangelical fascination with all things postmodern, *Lingua Franca* author Charlotte Allen was left to ask the question, "If Derrida is in the classroom, can the devil be far behind?"[19]

Evangelical Christian colleges and universities must develop internal criteria by which they can measure their fidelity to the missions that marked them from the start. Such criteria need not mean a stultification of academic progress, intellectual growth, and institutional achievement. To the contrary, by rooting themselves to their fundamental beliefs and practices, Christian institutions ensure that their progress will be forward in nature, an advancement of the kingdom of God and his Christ. In this configuration, such colleges and universities have, as the apostle Paul instructed the Corinthians, "divine power to demolish strongholds. We demolish arguments and every pretension that sets itself up against the knowledge of God, and we take captive every thought to make it obedient to Christ" (2 Cor. 10:4–5).

"Every thought captive" must be the refrain of every evangelical educator who realizes that each presupposition either honors or dishonors, reflects or deflects, the truth as revealed by the triune, holy, and personal God. By living this way, as Reformed theologian Douglas Wilson observes:

> This will result in knowledge of the *antithesis*—the same antithesis Christian colleges have lost. Because the Bible tells us that sin is real, everything is either in submission to God or in rebellion against Him. Every person is either in submission or rebellion. Every action is either in submission or rebellion. Every thought is either in submission or in rebellion (Col. 2:6–10). *No neutrality exists anywhere.*
>
> The modern opium dream that education can be religiously neutral should, in our minds, be equivalent to the question of whether or not, to use Dabney's phrase, "schoolrooms should be located under water or in dark caverns." Neutrality about the ultimate questions can be *pretended* in education, but it cannot be accomplished.[20]

What criteria, then, might Christian colleges and universities develop to increase the likelihood of ongoing institutional fidelity? I propose that such criteria be distilled from the lessons of mistakes past. Think again about our present case study—Bucknell University. What choices did the presidents and trustees make that proved later to be the undoing of the Christian character of the institution? Three primary issues spring to mind: first, the slow but steady severing of the university from the body of Christ in the local church; second, the lack of any clear theological standard to which the institution was accountable; and, finally, the loss of the missiological impulse of the school. The placement of some combination of these elements into the guiding documents of a school acts as a kind of antidote to the secular drift. They provide obstacles that in order to remove must be overturned or ignored. In either case, the institution by necessity leaves a clear marker behind when its delinquent custodians alter course.

The three issues listed above—ecclesiastical accountability, theological fidelity, and missiological focus—if placed at the heart of the university's mission, act as a preservative of the Christian character of a school over time. Further, if an institution does stray from its guiding purposes such as those aforementioned, there exists a method and discourse for retrieval. Such principles provide some assurance, if not a guarantee, that a Christian institution will not depend so heavily on whatever combination of evangelical presidents, deans, and department chairs currently hold office. Let us then take in turn aspects which, if instantiated, help keep an evangelical institution evangelical.

Ecclesiastical Accountability

The church, made manifest in the local congregation of Christian believers, gives, through the Holy Spirit, encouragement, nourishment, and sustaining power through the preached Word of God. Since this is true, then it is right for us to reclaim the Protestant precedent for referring to and thinking of the church as our mother. John Calvin, the great Reformer, argued that we must esteem highly the church

into whose bosom God is pleased to gather his sons,
not only that they may be nourished by her help and
ministry as long as they are infants and children but
also that they may be guided by her motherly care until
they mature and at last reach the goal of faith . . . so
that, for those to whom he is Father the Church may
also be Mother.[21]

If the church is indeed our mother, then many evangelicals
find themselves guilty of breaking at least an ecclesial interpretation of the fifth commandment. While not all evangelicals
agree, for example, on the way we receive the grace of God
through the church (Baptists, for instance, do not hold that the
ordinances of the church actually confer grace upon the recipient), we do stand together on the centrality of the church as the
mouthpiece for God in the world through the preaching and
teaching of the Word of God. Through the divine monologue—
the preaching ministry of the church—Christians come under
conviction of sin and into an awareness of their many duties
before their Lord and God.

Regrettably, evangelicals have done a singularly poor job of
promoting the notion of *our* responsibility to the church, both
local and universal. Instead, evangelicals have placed increasing emphasis on how the church must change to appeal to an
ever-evolving culture. Eager to produce results in their
churches, evangelicals alter their worship services, programs,
and ministries to restore interest in church attendance, commitment, and participation. Unfortunately, and despite our
best efforts, a declining trend persists. For example, a 1991
Barna Research Group study showed that less than half of
Americans polled (43 percent) had considerable confidence in
the Christian churches they knew.[22] The church, to be sure,
must always be reformed according to the Word of God. But
perhaps it is time we as evangelicals remind ourselves that it is
the culture and individual persons within that culture who are
to be changed by the preaching of the Word of God.
Throughout Scripture, we find that God always creates his

people by his Word, and by God's own design, the church assumes primary responsibility for the preaching of the Word.

As Baptist theologian and pastor of Capitol Hill Baptist Church in Washington, D. C., Mark Dever writes, "Simply put, we need churches that are self-consciously distinct from the culture. We need churches in which the key indicator of success is not evident results but persevering biblical faithfulness. We need churches that help us to recover those aspects of Christianity that are distinct from the world, and that unite us."[23] Throughout history, churches that place emphasis on the Word of God remain viable churches and retain their voice in contemporary culture.

A unified and healthy people of God, particularly as expressed in local churches, reconfirm the role of church as nourishing mother. And increasingly healthy churches mean a healthier Christian college or university. A healthy church continues to have something to say to the formation of the minds and hearts of young persons, even when those young people have geographically left their charge. A vibrant church continues to offer significant resources to the Christian college and university through both a steady stream of incoming students and other resources, including ever-important financial assistance.

From history, we learn that vibrancy and interest of the local church in the institutions of higher education they support determines the level of the college or university's interest in them. As we saw in the history of Bucknell University, Bucknell's trustees, eager to enhance the financial stability of the school, made arrangements to loosen their relationship with the churches. By remaining a viable presence in the life of the university through student population and financial support, the local church ameliorates the temptation of all schools to value money over denominational commitments. This fact is unfortunate but nonetheless true.

The Christian college or university must never presume, however, that the church need always be reasserting her worthiness before the academy. On the contrary, to presume such a point is to get the whole relationship backwards. Rather, an institution of Christian higher education rightly thanks the church for her many gifts and demonstrates the ways in which that institution serves as an extension of the local church and a promoter of the cause of God and truth in the world. The university owes the greatest debt of gratitude to the godly men and women, the saints of Christ's church, who sacrificed their resources and entrusted their own children to the care of the Christian university. New Testament scholar and biblical theologian D. A. Carson states the issue with characteristic forthrightness:

> *Because of its God-centeredness, the Christian university will recognize that it is beholden to the church, to the world, and to the God who inhabits eternity.*
>
> That means, among other things, that Christians working in a Christian university will put a muzzle on their pride, one of the terrible sins of the universities. In the secular arena, university professors may think of themselves as the elite of society; in the Christian arena, university professors may think of themselves as the elite of the elect. But Christians who attempt to order their lives in light of Scripture will recognize that the societal institution to which they owe primary allegiance is neither the state nor the university, but the church. Moreover, just as the apostle Paul thinks of himself as a debtor to all (Rom. 1:14), so Christians will reflect the same sense of indebtedness.[24]

History teaches us that as the relationship between Christian college or university and the churches go, so goes the Christian character of the institution. By reconfirming its commitment to the churches that support it, the Christian college or university signals its gratitude and responsibility to the many pastors and laypersons who have given so generously to the cause of Christ in helping young men and women develop a Christian worldview.

Theological Fidelity

Our next lesson from history strikes at the great temptation of the university and indeed all human hearts: to rebel against the Word of God and to disbelieve the faith once for all delivered to the saints (Jude 3). The theological convictions of an institution forecast the fortunes of ongoing faithfulness of that school as a distinctly Christian place of learning. Throughout the history of Christian higher education, founders of Christian colleges across the denominational divide placed confessions of faith at the center of the institution's identity to declare to everyone the fundamental convictions prior to educational engagement. Like the people of Israel in the fourth chapter of Joshua who, at the command of God, set up twelve stones at Gilgal to remind them of the Lord's faithfulness to them and their need of ongoing faithfulness to the sovereign Lord who brought them out of Egypt, so too Christian institutions put in place the stones of theological conviction to remind all who come thereafter the convictions upon which the school was founded.

For example, from its inception, Eastern College required that each trustee and faculty member sign a clearly evangelical doctrinal statement, thereby clarifying their allegiance to the intellectual and worldview commitments of the school. In his institutional biography of Eastern College, John Baird recounts a speaking visit from the great evangelical philosopher D. Elton Trueblood on the occasion of the opening convocation for Eastern's academic year. Trueblood watched as trustee and faculty alike mounted the platform to sign, with great solemnity, Eastern's doctrinal statement. When Trueblood rose to speak, he affirmed the importance of this act, stating, "I've been to some of the great colleges and universities of this country and Europe, and not seen an occasion as impressive and meaningful as this. I'm glad you have this statement and the dignified method of observing its importance. It shows you mean business."[25]

By adopting some theological standard, a Christian institution confesses that it "means business," in the words of Trueblood. A confession of faith anchors a Christian organization to the faith of its past and provides a declaration to all who enter of the commitments that distinguish that institution from the dizzying array of secular colleges and universities, both public and private, who by matter of course keep their mission statements vague and their true presuppositions hidden. Christian colleges and universities remand the trend of their secular counterparts by placing in open view their intellectual commitments. Such standards will disclose belief in the triune, personal, self-revealing God who, in the words of the great evangelical theologian Carl F. H. Henry, "speaks and shows, stands and stays."[26] As Henry elsewhere avers:

> The Christian movement has founded and funded great institutions in the past only to lose many of them to others. We are better founders than preservers of our schools. To break out of that spiral of defecting enterprises, evangelical institutions need a discerning, informed, strongly assertive and courageous leadership. Those who would lead educational institutions must stand unwaveringly for the basic Christian doctrines. They must be devoted to the centrality of Christ incarnate, crucified, risen, and returning. They must not falter in their commitment to the governing role of Scripture.
>
> However great their world prestige and financial ability may be, trustees must first and foremost be theologically literate. If the founding vision of a school is to be preserved, the institution's trustees must faithfully share that vision. They must know the objectively given truths or doctrines that revealed religion espouses.
>
> Faculty must impart to students an awareness of the Christian revelation's doctrinal interrelatedness, systematic coherence, and rational consistency.[27]

Christian colleges unwilling to state where they stand with respect to the faith of their forebears run the risk of following the trajectory of schools that in the past refused to do the same. A school such as Bucknell never located a doctrinal statement at the heart of its institutional identity. Universities like Bucknell often were remiss to do so because they assumed their convictions would obtain in the following generation. It was not until the early twentieth century and the advent of the fundamentalist-modernist controversy in the late nineteenth and early twentieth centuries that Christian educators became skittish about committing themselves to a set of theological affirmations in print.

What accounts then for the loss of theological focus among denominational schools? As a discipline, theology fell on hard times in the nineteenth century when rationalist and empiricist criteria increasingly precluded the right of theologians to speak to the most pressing questions faced by both society and the university. Instead of launching a full-scale orthodox critique of modernity, theologians accepted the philosophical terms of the debate and sought to show that Christianity could keep current with new intellectual trends. Ironically, a reverse trend occurred. Even as conservative theologians jockeyed for academic respectability, they continued to lose credibility among their peers. As the theologians conceded epistemological and theological ground, they hemorrhaged older expressions of doctrine for newer ones more amenable to modernity. As the academy grew more alienated from traditional forms of metaphysical speculation, theologians continued to lose face, in part, it seems, because they gave up their beliefs so easily.

Consequently, as British theologian Colin Gunton maintains, there emerged a "self-conscious thought in the public realm . . . that theology has abandoned the right to a place [in the academy] because theologians spend more time undermining than defending the faith that they are believed to hold."[28] If the theologians could not hold their ground, then the fact fails to surprise us that Christian colleges and universities without theological standards for their boards and faculty members appeared less Christian with each succeeding generation.

A recovery and utility of confessional standards in Christian higher education prevents the same kind of downgrade that occurred in previous generations. While not perfect (after all, our God as revealed in Scripture is our only "bulwark never failing"), confessions of faith preserve institutional memory and remind administrators, students, and faculty alike that giants in the faith once walked the corridors of their buildings, and not without price. A statement of faith can be ignored, but it can also be recovered. For Christian educators and alumni who want to avoid lamenting a Christian *alma mater* that once was, an agreed-upon series of theological commitments will help assuage such a possibility from becoming an inevitability. A confessing church must mark God's people while simultaneously being the one thing the world cannot understand. In Alan Wolfe's otherwise friendly *Atlantic Monthly* article on evangelical Christian higher education, Wolfe stumbled over the exclusivity of Wheaton College's doctrinal statement. After noting Wheaton President Duane Litfin's response that a Wheaton professor who became a Roman Catholic "would be asked if he would not be more comfortable working elsewhere," Wolfe immediately followed with the comment, "Of all of America's religious traditions, evangelical Protestantism, at least in its twentieth century conservative forms, ranks dead last in intellectual stature."[29]

For many moderns, theological confessionalism in higher education is a scandal. The idea that certain presuppositions or beliefs are axiomatic and required purportedly comprise the unthinkable thought to free inquiry and academic freedom. But Christians know that confessionalism of a secular variety persists unassailed in the modern university. The cults of political correctness, tolerance of all perspectives except for the idea of absolute truth, and pragmatism are well-known to careful observers of contemporary culture and familiar to students of public and private colleges and universities everywhere. If the secular academy is allowed its nonnegotiable worldview presuppositions and conclusions, then surely evangelical Christians find warrant for theirs.

A return to confessional subscription of some kind does not imply any admission of the inerrancy of such documents but only that we take the individual theological propositions to reflect faithfully the teaching of Scripture. Even as the early church attested, "I believe in God the Father Almighty, Maker of heaven and earth" as an accurate statement of the true orthodox faith found in Scripture, so too we may construct such statements to state our beliefs before the watching world. The tired, hackneyed charges that confessions of faith impinge unduly upon freedom of conscience miss the mark. A Christian college or university possesses the right to know whether its faculty gladly and without reservation identify with the faith of the churches that support it. From the witness of Justin Martyr to present-day doctrinal statements, Christians across denominational lines happily affirm the faith that they profess.

Some Christians might get the idea that any kind of confessionalism obligates the Christian college to profess the Christian faith in precisely the same fashion as did the Reformers, the Puritans, or other stalwarts. Nothing of the sort is intended. Confessional statements look as different as the denominations they represent. The statements of faith of evangelical colleges and universities may be long or short, basic or detailed, as tradition and historic precedence dictate. But in our affirmations, we do well to treat our forebears in the faith with the consideration requisite to their contribution to Christ's church. "In matters spiritual we owe a debt to the past," writes church historian Gerald Bray, "which cannot be ignored or derided in one-sided polemic. We cannot debate with Athanasius or Augustine, with Calvin or Luther, as if our opinions were on par with theirs. The reputation of these giants is assured, and it behoves us to respect that fact, even if we wish to disagree with them or modify their points of view."[30]

A recovery of at least some theological touchstones aids the ongoing spiritual health of the Christian college and university. Confessions alone, however, do not suffice to preserve the Christian character of the university if not utilized and remembered. To those institutions unwilling either to place or use theological confessions in the governing documents of the school, a warning: your identity as a Christian organization is as close to theological amnesia as a new president, dean, department chair, or influential faculty member (see Exod. 1:8).

Missiological Focus

Certain sectors in Christian higher education express uneasiness at the thought that the Christian college or university holds an evangelistic mandate as a part of the educational enterprise. Christian higher education, or so the argument goes, finds its identity in the Great Commandment (Matt. 22:34–39) but not the Great Commission (Matt. 28:18–20). Such thinking, although understandable, falls short of the scope and outreach potential of an evangelical organization. The attempt to wed mind and heart by deconstructing any sort of pietistic dualism surely comprises the central mission of any institution that seeks to develop a Christian worldview. Nonetheless, we deceive ourselves if we think that our teaching, writing, and sending of students is not profoundly missiological in nature. We do, in a very real way, proclaim the gospel that Jesus is Lord over all of life and make disciples who will, upon graduation, commence in earnest kingdom-building enterprise.

Colleges that began the race but eventually flagged in their Christian commitments quickly lost the centrality of this missiological impulse. During the nineteenth century, as the German model of the university arose and specific educational methods enjoyed prominence, universities with Christian foundations moved away from the idea that the university's task is largely to produce ministers of the gospel. In the place of this ideal, universities advanced the millenial optimism of the nineteenth century that new advances in natural philosophy would usher in the kingdom of God on earth. As George Marsden asserted, "The evangelicals who dominated American higher education at mid-century confidently awaited the arrival of the millenial days . . . that in the last days almost everyone would be converted to Christianity."[31]

Subsequent to this belief came a tacit understanding that knowledge itself was a kind of gospel. In effect, such schools pursued a Great Commandment agenda apart from a concomitant emphasis on the Great Commission. Such sentiment caused the traditional conception of missions to fade in the consciousness of university administrators. Although the student missions movement later revived the idea, it would do so without the official sanction or support of the university.

Evangelicals in Christian higher education must never operate under the illusion that their task is not, at least in a broad sense, evangelistic. The Great Commission presents a twofold mandate to Christian higher education.

First, the Christian faculty member or administrator will undoubtedly encounter students who, by their own admission, express doubts or explicit rejection of the fundamental truths of the gospel. In this case, Christian institutions have the opportunity to bear witness to the risen Lord. This fits Jesus' first directive in the Great Commission: proclamation.

Second, these same schools also receive students who, through lack of serious Christian education at the primary or secondary level, lack the intellectual tools necessary to form their beliefs into a comprehensive world and life view. This task falls under Jesus' instruction for us to make disciples as well as to "love the Lord our God with all our heart and soul and mind." Despite the most conscientious admissions criteria, every Christian college admits students whose hearts have not discovered the intellectual coherence of the faith they profess or students whose minds have not yet yielded to the triune personal God and the completed work of Jesus Christ.

History teaches us that higher educational institutions of formerly evangelical conviction sacrificed their commitment to the Great Commission before they abandoned attempts to fulfill the Great Commandment. By keeping both commandment and commission in view, evangelical institutions increase the likelihood that they will continue a strong, growing commitment to Christ, his church, and his Word.

CONCLUSION

If evangelicals intend to keep their colleges and universities evangelical, they must deal soberly with the realities of the past. This means that we cannot fool ourselves into thinking that as long as we have a good president and make the right faculty hires, we have met our obligation to future generations in preserving our cherished Christian institutions. While we rejoice when our scholars gain a wider hearing in the academy, we dare not think that such developments indicate a growing acceptance of the fundamental axioms of the Christian worldview that have scandalized the secular mind for nearly two millennia. If we believe, teach, and practice as the church has in times past, we invite the same credulity and criticism as the saints before us have.

The only other option is to change the message that we teach to ameliorate our differences with the culture. Christians tried this approach in the past in order to achieve, in the words of former British Prime Minister Neville Chamberlain, "peace in our time." In his scathing *Attack upon "Christendom,"* Søren Kierkegaard upbraided both priests and parents for accommodating the message of Christianity to the culture. By offering a vision that all is right between God and the world, such Christian educators believed the ethos of anti-Christian thought and convinced themselves of falsehoods for the sake of comfort. As a result, Christian children were taught a sweet, easy going, but ultimately ruinous version of the Christian worldview.

"Under the name of the Christian education of children," Kierkegaard charged, "they jabber foolishly out of the stock of paganism along the lines suggested: 'It is an extraordinary benefice that thou didst come into existence, this is a fine world into which thou hast come, and God is a fine man, only hold fast to Him, He will to be sure not fulfill all thy wishes, but He's a help all the same.'" To which Kierkegaard added, "Sheer lies."[32]

Kierkegaard offered a warning to Christian educators not to decrease their view of God and increase their estimation of the world. Instead, Kierkegaard exhorted, we must "think Christianly."[33] His invective still applies to those of us who, in the twenty-first century, find ourselves beset by the same temptations as before. The Christian college needs to be unapologetically Christian in its confession, accountability, and mission.

CHAPTER 3

THEOLOGICAL AND PHILOSOPHICAL FOUNDATIONS

Brad Green

THE ISSUE OF EDUCATION is not one that may be treated in a vacuum. The question of education leads quickly to a discussion of ultimate truths and convictions, as it should. When one broaches the subject of education, one inextricably asks a host of other questions having to do with God, man, the past, the future, and the destiny and purpose of our lives. T. S. Eliot has written, "Education is a subject which cannot be discussed in a void: our questions raise other questions, social, economic, financial, political. And the bearings are on more ultimate problems than even these: to know what we want in education we must know what we want in general, we must derive our theory of education from our philosophy of life. The problem turns out to be a religious problem."[1]

Thus, an essay on education raises many other issues, and this essay reflects that reality. While the assigned topic of this essay is "theological and philosophical foundations," no attempt to drive a wedge between theological foundations and philosophical foundations is intended. This essay thus follows a twofold organizational scheme. The first section deals with the schema of what is sometimes called "the history of redemption" (creation, fall, redemption, and the lordship of Christ), and the second section deals with particular themes (truth, faith seeking understanding, knowledge, communication, the past, and the future).

CHRISTIAN HIGHER EDUCATION
AND THE HISTORY OF REDEMPTION

Creation

At the heart of historic Christian orthodoxy is the affirmation that we live in a created world. In identifying the Christian God, the Nicene and Apostles' Creeds speak of "God, the Father Almighty, maker of heaven and earth." Scripture is clear that God has created all things, and that he created all things out of nothing (Gen. 1–2; Ps. 33; John 1:3; Heb. 1:3; Col. 1:16; Acts 17:24–25). This good world is created freely by a good God, and he creates without being under any compulsion or necessity. The historic Christian doctrine of *creatio ex nihilo* is central to an understanding of education for several important reasons.

First, there is a "givenness" to things with which the Christian must come to terms. There is indeed a reality outside of the human person, and the human being finds himself in a world that is not of his own making.[2] Thus, while man is certainly given dominion over the world in Genesis 1:26–30, he is given dominion over something that already *is*. He is not called to manipulate things into any shape he wishes. Rather, he is called to work with and shape and rule over something that is already structured in a certain way, is already constituted in *this* way, not *that* way. Thus, from the very beginning of their existence, human beings find themselves in relation to the rest of the created order, and this relation already has a structure we must recognize and respect.

A doctrine of creation also implies that there is indeed *something* that can be known. There is indeed a real world, and what we see around us is not simply a fantasy or an illusion (as some Eastern religions profess). Rather, this world is truly *there* (or "here"), and it can be encountered and known. But this creation is not simply a chaos or a random association of stuff. Rather, this world is an *ordered* reality, and when Christians further affirm that God is a *speaking* God who has created man as *knowing* creatures, there is powerful theological grounding for education. Literary scholar Richard Weaver suggested that the idea that there is a world of truth that is "worth knowing and even worth reverencing" ultimately *requires* a doctrine of creation: "Clearly this [i.e., that there is a body of data worth knowing] presumes a certain respect for the world as creation, a belief in it and a trust in its providence, rather than a view (as if out of ancient Gnosticism) positing its essential incompleteness and badness. The world is there *a priori*; the learner has the duty of familiarizing himself with its nature and its set of relations."[3]

The psalmist makes this point vividly clear when he writes, "When I consider Your heavens, the work of Your fingers, The moon and the stars, which You have ordained" (Ps. 8:3 NASB). Consider Psalm 19:1–2: "The heavens are telling of the glory of God; and their expanse is declaring the work of His hands. Day to day pours forth speech, and night to night reveals knowledge" (NASB).

As Marion Montgomery (borrowing from Aquinas) suggests in his recent book, education is concerned with coming into contact with "the truth of things." Historic Christianity roots the "truth of things" in the fact that we live in a good, created, and orderly world.[4] A Christian view of education is therefore concerned not simply with the world of speculation but with the world *as it is*. Richard Weaver suggests that much of modern educational theory is ultimately Gnostic. Weaver means two things by his use of "Gnosticism": (1) creation is inherently evil, the work of a demiurge that is limited in power; (2) man does not require salvation from outside himself but is already in a state of "Messianic blessedness."[5] Gnosticism, according to Weaver, "is a kind of irresponsibility—an irresponsibility to the past and to the structure of reality in the present."[6] Gnosticism fails because its advocates, on Weaver's understanding, "are out of line with what is."[7]

Gnosticism fails on several fronts. First, whereas Gnosticism predicates evil of the world itself, Christianity sees a good world that has been now caught up in the sin of human beings. Second, whereas Gnosticism sees evil and chaos in the world from the beginning, Christianity sees a good, ordered world which has not lost all traces of goodness and order (sin notwithstanding). Third, whereas in Gnosticism, the world is to be manipulated and transformed by sinless man, in Christianity the world is to be ruled by sinful man (Gen. 1:26–30), but this rule is under, and in accord with, the ultimate rulership of the triune God. Fourth, whereas Gnosticism affirms that man is sinless and can do what he wants, Christianity affirms that man is sinful and must act in accord with standards *not* of his own making.

The doctrine of creation also affirms that there is a thoroughgoing distinction between Creator and creature. We are simply *not* God. We receive our being from someone else—God. As creatures, our interpretation of all of reality must accord with the God who has made us and has given us life. Since the Creator God has spoken to us about the world he has created, it is *his* interpretation of reality that must pervade all of our educational endeavors. As Graeme Goldsworthy has written, "God made every fact in the universe and he alone can interpret all things and events."[8] That is, as created beings, we are not autonomous.[9] Our freedom must always be seen as a created freedom, not a radical, autonomous freedom. Our learning, therefore, must always seek to understand God's interpretation of reality that has been revealed in Scripture, and we are always seeking to understand all of reality in light of the triune God, and in light of what the triune God has spoken.[10]

Fall

We do live in a good world, but we live in a good world gone bad. We live amid the ruins of a glorious past. Any Christian understanding of higher education must wrestle with the reality of sin and how sin affects the endeavor of education. G. K. Chesterton somewhere quipped that if you took all the devils and put them into school, you would not end up with angels, but simply with educated devils. Any vision of education that does not take sin seriously will miss the mark and in the end will be sub-Christian.

Scripture teaches that all of us are somehow caught up in the error and rebellion of our first parents, Adam and Eve. Adam represented us, and when he sinned, we sinned (Rom. 5:12–14;

1 Cor. 15:20–24).[11] We have all sinned in our own time and place as well. Indeed, it is not the case that we simply "sin." We *are* sinners. That is, we are not simply good folks who occasionally sin. We are sinners, and even as believers this old sin nature continues to plague and haunt us. Before conversion we were dead in our sins (Eph. 2:1–3; Col. 2:13); we were enemies of God (Rom. 5:10); we were alienated from God and hostile in our minds to God (Rom. 8:5–8; Col. 1:21); we were unable to submit to God's law (Rom. 8:7).

It is important to point to such texts, whose language may strike the twenty-first century reader as harsh or overbearing. But such texts must be engaged and believed and must help inform a truly Christian view of man. For without a good understanding of who we *are,* we will not forge a truly Christian vision of who we should *be.* Now, with conversion we truly are new persons in Christ: "Therefore if anyone is in Christ, he is a new creature; the old things passed away; behold, new things have come" (2 Cor. 5:17 NASB; see also Gal. 6:15; Eph. 2:10). We have been born again (John 3:3); like Christ, we have been raised from the dead (Rom. 6:4). However, we are still sinners, and we still struggle with sin. We are new persons (2 Cor. 5:17), but Paul can still command Christians to "put on the new self" (Eph. 4:24 NASB). We see here what New Testament scholars generally call the "already-not-yet" tension in the New Testament. The kingdom of God has *already* come with Christ (Matt. 12), but it is *not yet* here in the fullest sense (1 Cor. 15:24–28). The Christian is *already* a new person (2 Cor. 5:17), but we are *not yet* all that we will be (Eph. 4:24). The Christian is *already* sanctified (1 Cor. 6:11), but we are *not yet* completely sanctified (Heb. 4:10; 12:14; 2 Cor. 3:18).[12] In short, sin is still a reality in our lives, and education, at least for the Christian, takes place in this time between conversion and the consummation of our salvation in glory.

But why does this matter? Keeping the reality of sin at the forefront of our minds when thinking on education is crucial for at least the following reasons.

First, genuine Christian education is always aware that education can have *adverse* effects on students. Students can become puffed up, arrogant, and conceited (1 Cor. 8:1). Like the Athenians in Acts 17, students can become those who "spend their time in nothing other than telling or hearing something new" (Acts 17:21 NASB). Students can become lost in the maze of thinkers, ideas, and intellectual movements, with little ability to make sense of what they are learning. When the accumulation of knowledge, facts, ideas, and thinkers are not brought into relationship to higher ends (such as wisdom), and made "captive to the obedience of Christ" (2 Cor. 10:5 NASB), then genuine Christian education has not taken place, and the teachers and administrators should begin asking serious questions about their efforts.

The second reason we should be attentive to the reality of sin is that sin truly affects our noetic (knowing) faculties and abilities. Scripture can speak of sin as a hostility in the *mind* (Col. 1:20). John Calvin taught that the mind is a factory of idols, and he had good scriptural warrant for such a claim.[13] Not only is our knowing ability *limited* (which is already the case simply by being *created*), but our knowing ability is also *injured* or *corrupted* by sin. According to Paul in Romans 1:18–23, the bent of sinful man is to worship the creation instead of the Creator. Man *will* worship, and if man does not worship the triune God, he will create idols to worship. Since a Christian vision of education ultimately affirms a Christian way of knowing, it is important that Christians recognize that our knowing is not somehow "neutral." Even our knowing is caught up in sin, and this must be recognized in forging a Christian view of education. But how would this insight affect Christian higher education day to day?

Ultimately, genuine Christian education must recognize sin's impact on the noetic faculties and provide a context in which the student is encouraged to be conformed to the image of Christ (Rom. 8:29). Teachers model Christian character by living exemplary lives of genuine Christian piety and faithfulness. Christian teachers model humility rather than arrogance about their advanced knowledge in their fields (1 Cor. 8:1). Christian teachers are constantly showing their students how *all knowledge* coheres in Christ (Col. 1:17). Abraham Kuyper could write of how God looks out at every square inch of his creation and says, "Mine." Christian teachers likewise are always about the business of helping students to understand how there is not a single fact, idea, or concept that escapes the lordship of Christ, or that is autonomous from the reality of Christ. Any Christian education that does not move students toward "taking every thought captive to the obedience of Christ" is at risk of forging an institution that facilitates students' becoming idolaters (Rom. 1:18–23).

Redemption

At the heart of the Christian faith stands the gospel of Jesus Christ—the death, burial, and resurrection of Jesus Christ for sinners. The second person of the Trinity took on human flesh, suffered on the cross for our sins, and was raised for our justification. This past event of redemption is applied to the sinner when he or she believes. Redemption *accomplished* in the past is *applied* to the believer in the present.[14] But how does redemption relate to the task of higher education? I want to suggest two key interrelated areas where the reality of redemption shapes how a Christian thinks about education: (1) the renewing of the mind and (2) the *telos* of human life.[15]

First, at the heart of God's redemptive purposes is the renewing of the human mind. We have mentioned that Scripture speaks repeatedly of the non-Christian mind as hostile to God (Col. 1:21; Rom. 8:7), how the non-Christian mind is death (Rom. 5:6), and how the non-Christian can be spoken of as actually an enemy of God (Rom. 5:10). For the redeemed sinner, there is a radical change in one's orientation, and this radical change includes the life of the mind. For the Christian, part of the Christian life is the continual renewing of the mind. Just as the Christian is a new person at conversion (2 Cor. 5:17) but continues to grow in grace (Phil. 2:12–13), so the Christian has a new mind at conversion but continues to be transformed in mind throughout his or her life (Rom. 2:1–2).

Thus, "redemption" in its fullest sense is both something applied to us at a certain point (i.e., it is punctiliar) and process. Thus, central to a Christian vision of education is the affirmation that God is constantly renewing the mind of his children: "And do not be conformed to this world, but be transformed by the renewing of your mind, so that you may prove what the will of God is, that which is good and acceptable and perfect" (Rom. 12:2 NASB). But note in this text that the Romans are commanded to "*be* transformed." While certainly this transformation is God's act, it is simultaneously the act of the Christian. That is, we are commanded to *be* transformed, which means that somehow *we* must do *this* instead of *that* or that we must make *this* decision instead of *that* decision.

A similar phenomenon is seen in such passages as Philippians 2:12–13. The Philippians are commanded to "work out your salvation with fear and trembling" (NASB). Is Paul teaching salvation by works? Not at all, for in the next verse he continues: "For it is God who is at work in you, both to will and to work for His good pleasure." Paul can teach, therefore, that *we* must work out our salvation, but *in the very same act* it is *God* who is at work in us.

The renewing of the mind is a common theme in Paul's writings. He can contrast futile minds with redeemed minds. For example, in Ephesians Paul can speak of Gentiles who walk "in the futility of their mind," who are "being darkened in their understanding." The redeemed, on the other hand, have been taught Christ and should thus "lay aside the old self" and "be renewed in the spirit of your mind, and put on the new self." (Eph. 4:17–24 NASB). Again, note that while Christians are *already* new creatures in Christ (2 Cor. 5:17), Paul can command his readers here in Ephesus to "*be* renewed in the spirit of your mind," and to "*put on* the new self." There is both an *already* and a *not-yet* reality to the life of the Christian—including the renewing of the mind.

It is important for professing evangelicals to probe the relation between the gospel and education a bit further. If evangelicals proclaim the centrality of the *gospel*, it is proper to ask how the gospel is central to education. We have noted above that unregenerate persons are dead in sin and that this state is often portrayed in terms of the *mind* and *thoughts*. Colossians 1:20 speaks of being enemies in our *minds*, and Ephesians 2:3

speaks of the *thoughts* of the sinful nature. We have shown that redemption includes the transformation of the mind. Romans 12:2 (NASB) reads, "Be transformed by the renewing of your *mind*." First Corinthians 2:16 (NASB) says, "But we have the *mind* of Christ." Ephesians 4:23 (NASB) speaks of being made new "in the spirit of your *mind*."

Evangelicals should note that the redemption of the human person includes the redemption and transformation of the mind, and that ultimately this redemption of the mind springs from the gospel. That is, the reconciliation and transformation of the mind is something that ultimately flows from the cross. What this means is that our intellectual development as Christians, which should always be seen against the backdrop of being conformed to the image of Christ (Rom. 8:29), is something that is rooted in, and that proceeds from, the cross.

For example, in the Colossians passage noted above, our hostility as unregenerate persons is a hostility of the *mind* (Col. 1:21). But note the very next verse: "*But* now he has reconciled you by Christ's physical body through death to present you holy in his sight" (Col. 1:22). Thus, it is Christ's death on the cross that reconciles us—including our minds—to God.

Augustine was compelled to make a similar argument in battling with the Neoplatonists. The Neoplatonists held that the goal of man is to ascend to the One (God), and that this was achieved by the will and action of man. Augustine countered that the only way one can *ascend* to God is if he has *descended* to us. Christ descends for us, dies for us, and if we are in him, we ascend with him to the presence of God. Augustine writes, "Christ is the Principle by whose incarnation we are purified. . . . [B]ut the incarnation of the unchangeable Son of God, whereby we are saved, [enables us] to reach the things we believe, or in part understand."[16] Not only the incarnation, but the cross is necessary. If we are truly to *see* God (1 Cor. 13:12), then we (our minds) must be purified: "The only thing to cleanse the wicked and the proud is the blood of the just man and the humility of God; to contemplate God, which by nature we are not, we would have to be cleansed by him who became what by nature we are and what by sin we are not."[17]

As one commentator has put it, summarizing Augustine: *"There can be no intellectus* [understanding] *apart from the concrete sacrificial act of Christ."*[18] Indeed, it is the gospel that is at the heart of true understanding and the true *intellectual* life.

The second key point to recognize in relating redemption to education is that this emphasis on the constant renewing of the mind shows us that there is a true *telos* or *goal* to the Christian life. If a Christian view of education had nothing else to offer the secular world (and indeed it has *much* to offer the secular world), a Christian world and life view affirms that there is indeed a true *telos* to the created order. Creation is *going* somewhere. There is a purpose and plan to history, and our lives in the twenty-first century are ultimately a part of God's plan and purposes. The notion of ultimate or first and final causes is foreign to much of the modern world—at least in the sense that there really *are* such things. Richard Weaver has written, "Questions of first and final cause are regarded as not within the scope of education, which means that education is confined to intermediate causes."[19]

In a Christian approach to education, both intermediate causes as well as first and final causes are fair game, and ultimate causes are not rejected out of hand, as if the empirical method is the only way of knowing. It is hard to overemphasize the importance of a *telos* that gives meaning to all of our endeavors. Such language as "goal" or "telos" used to be commonplace. In Augustine's *De Trinitate*, one of the most commonly quoted Scripture texts is 1 Corinthians 13:12 (NASB): "For now we see in a mirror dimly, but then face-to-face; now I know in part, but then I will know fully just as I also have been fully known."

This text from Paul forms what we might call the theological substructure of Augustine's treatise on the Trinity. For Augustine, the Christian life is one long quest for the vision of God. Augustine is not simply expounding the doctrine of the Trinity. Rather, he is exploring the reality of the triune God against a certain backdrop: Christians look forward to, indeed yearn for, this future vision where they will see God face-to-face.

Thus, his exploration of the triune God is not a dry listing of abstract propositions or theses. Rather, Augustine wants to explore the question, Who is this God whom I and all other believers will one day see face-to-face? Thus, there was a *telos* that informed and provided a backdrop against which Augustine wrote and thought.

And note, the backdrop is one that could truly energize Augustine's intellectual efforts, for the vision of God is not simply a game played by academics; it is an existential and beautiful reality of the deepest sort that provides Augustine's writings with a passion and attractiveness rarely matched in contemporary theological tomes.

The Lordship of Christ

At the heart of all things Christian is the lordship of Christ. As sinful creatures we are always seeking to dethrone Christ from his rightful place as Lord of his universe. It is the role of Christians in every endeavor of life to be constantly working not to dethrone Christ from his proper place of lordship.[20] Ultimately a true "liberal" education—one that prepares men and women to live truly free lives—can only be a *Christian* education. For only when all of our learning is devoted to and submitted to the lordship of Christ is freedom possible.

Christopher Derrick makes this point eloquently. Although Derrick is a Roman Catholic writing for Roman Catholics, it takes little adjustment to apply his proposition to evangelicals: "If Christ is indeed the great and only Liberator, if the world without Him is indeed a prison and a slavery, it follows that any real liberal education must be ordered at *every point* towards Him and governed *at every point* by the Faith of His Church." He continues, "A genuinely liberal education will be one based upon the objective and final truth of the Catholic Faith, and upon an uncompromising application of that Faith to every question that arises with the educational process."[21]

The apostle Paul says something similar in his correspondence to the Corinthians: "We are destroying speculations and every lofty thing raised up against the knowledge of God, and we are taking every thought captive to the obedience of Christ"

(2 Cor. 10:5 NASB). *Every thought captive.* That should be the motto of the Christian student and scholar. The lordship of Christ is exhaustive and brooks no compromise. As Lord of his universe, all things—every thought—are to be placed under his lordship. This "taking every thought captive" is generally not something that will take place completely naturally. Due to our sin, the Evil One, and the radical influence of secular culture, this task is ultimately part of any truly Christian discipleship. If Jesus meant what he said when he said the greatest commandment is to love God with our *minds* (Matt. 22:37), then, like the rest of the life of discipleship, it is a task that will take work— although in the end it is God "who is at work in you, both to will and to work for His good pleasure" (Phil. 2:13 NASB).

The reality of the lordship of Christ is something that cannot be emphasized enough. This question, and the extent to which the members of a university or college truly recognize and confess the lordship of Christ in every area, will determine whether an institution can truly claim the name *Christian.* As Richard John Neuhaus has written, "If Christian truth does not illumine and undergird every quest for truth, it is questionable that Christianity is true." Indeed, "the question that those who lead a Christian university must answer, and answer again every day, is whether the confession that Jesus is Lord limits or illumines the university's obligation to seek and serve *Veritas*—to seek and serve the truth."[22]

CENTRAL THEMES

Revelation, Scripture, and the Possibility of Knowledge

At the heart of Christian higher education is the affirmation that God has spoken. The God of Scripture is a God who has revealed himself. This is a crucial affirmation, not a peripheral one, and a biblical doctrine of revelation has profound implications for a Christian understanding of education. It is common to speak of "general" revelation and "special" revelation. General revelation is "God's self-disclosure of Himself in a general way to all people at all times in all places" (e.g., in nature, human experience, and God's providential ordering of history), while special·revelation is "available to specific people at specific times in specific places" (e.g., God's historical acts, the incarnation of Jesus, and Holy Scripture).[23]

Scripture should play a prominent place in any truly Christian understanding of higher education.[24] The lives of the entire college or university community should be saturated in Scripture, and Scripture should shape and determine the course of the institution. Scripture, as *norm normans non normata* ("the norm that norms that is not normed"), is the ultimate standard and guide for all of the Christian life, including the task of education. Since Christians affirm that *God* really has spoken in Holy Scripture, Scripture must be at the center of the educational task.[25]

In speaking of "special" and "general" revelation, it is particularly important to note that "general" revelation is still *revelation*. The intellect does not "discover" and learn certain truths about God through a "reason" that is autonomous or separate from revelation, a reason that is then complemented by special revelation. Quite the contrary. We can know something of God by looking at nature because God *reveals Himself* through nature. Romans 1:18–25, perhaps the *locus classicus* for general revelation, states, "For the wrath of God is revealed from heaven against all ungodliness and unrighteousness of men who suppress the truth in unrighteousness" (NASB). What truth is suppressed? The following verse tells us: "Because that which is known about God is evident within them; *for God made it evident to them.*" That is, God *revealed* it to them. When verse 20 says, "For since the creation of the world His invisible attributes, His eternal power and divine nature, have been clearly seen, being understood through what has been made, so that they are without excuse" (NASB), we must remember that certain of God's attributes are "clearly seen" because he has revealed these attributes.

There are several implications for education that flow from a thoroughgoing doctrine of revelation. First, since God is the source and content of *all* revelation, there is a coherence and complementary relationship between "general" and "special" revelation. That is, there is a unity to all of God's revelation. As

Richard John Neuhaus has written, "A Christian university has as its premise the knowledge that all truth is one and all ways to truth are one because the Author and the End of truth is One."[26]

Second, it is mistaken to think that somehow we are "active" in relation to "general" revelation but simply "passive" in relation to "special" revelation. The whole man (intellect, heart, will) is both active and passive with all of revelation, although we should tilt the scales in favor of our *passive* position before a just and holy God. Thus, when we study a beautiful constellation, *God* is communicating to us—hence we are in a sense "passive"—but we are also engaged in the task of studying, reflecting, thinking—we are in a sense "active." Similarly, when we study Scripture, it is *God's* Word to *us* we are studying—thus we are in a sense "passive"—but it is *we* who must open the text, attempt to clear the fog from our minds, and apply ourselves to the task—we are in a sense "active."

Following Augustine, Ronald Nash writes, "Human knowledge is made possible by two lights, the uncreated light of God and the created, mutable light which is human intellect. Just as the moon derives the light it reflects from the sun, so the rational human mind derives a created ability to know from its origin, God."[27] Nash continues, "Because humankind was created in the image of God, the human mind is a secondary and derivative source of light that reflects in a creaturely way the rationality of the Creator. A harmony or correlation exists therefore between the mind of God, the human mind, and the rational structure of the universe."[28]

Third, since the whole created order reveals the triune God, we are forced to say that ultimately, *all* objects of our knowledge are pervaded with the self-revelation of God. That is, wherever we look in the created order, there are traces of the self-revealing God.

Fourth, we must also say that knowledge is always and thoroughly moral and ethical at its core. In particular, the knowledge of God that surrounds us makes us accountable to God. To suppress such knowledge, and to refuse to honor God and give him thanks in light of such knowledge (Rom. 1:21) is to store up wrath for one's self. But even in a more general sense, since the whole created order gives evidence of God, we are accountable to take all our knowledge and subject it to and relate it to the lordship of Christ, to tease out the relationship between what we are learning and reality of the triune God. Indeed, we are to make all of our knowledge captive to the obedience of Christ (2 Cor. 10:5).

But we must also make a bolder claim if we are to approach a thoroughly Christian understanding of knowledge. Ultimately, all knowledge—whether of the empirical, or rational, or intuitive sort—is predicated on the existence of God, the reality of a world created and sustained by God, the noetic (or "knowing") structure of the human mind, and the coherence of all things in Christ (Col. 2:8), the *Logos* (John 1:1–5). That is, *all knowledge,* not just knowledge of God, is predicated on the reality of the Christian worldview. While knowledge of God is particularly important, I wish to claim that *all* knowledge is rooted in the reality of Christ. As Ronald Nash has written, "Jesus Christ, the eternal Logos of God, mediates all divine revelation and grounds the correspondence between the divine and human minds. This eternal Logos is a necessary condition for the communication of revealed truth; indeed, it is a necessary condition for human knowledge about anything."[29]

What is being said here? The central thesis can be outlined as follows: (1) Christ, the second member of the Trinity, is the divine *Logos* (Word); (2) the Logos is the agent, or medium, of creation—both of the human and nonhuman world (John 1:3; 1 Cor. 8:6; Col. 1:16; Heb. 1:3); (3) the Logos is the means by which God sustains the world (Col. 1:18); (4) the Logos was active in creation, the nonhuman created order bears marks of this Logos (Ps. 19; Rom. 1:18–20), and man himself is an image-bearer (Gen. 1:26), whose mind is marked by the Logos; (5) since man's mind is shaped and structured in accord with the divine Logos, and since the nonhuman created order is ordered according to the Logos, man is capable of knowledge, both of God and of the rest of the created order.

John 1:9 (NASB) is important here. Speaking of Christ, the Logos, John writes, "There was the true Light which, coming into the world, enlightens every man."[30] What this text suggests is that somehow Christ illumines every human mind. Augustine picks up on this idea, and it helps constitute his own understanding of how we know. In his work *The Teacher* (*De Magistro*) Augustine is engaged in a discussion with Adeodatus (the actual name of his son). The majority of the book is an extended dialogue on the nature of words, signs, and reality. Augustine argues that the purpose of speech is to teach and that words are an instrument by which we are brought into contact with reality.[31] But Augustine eventually asks how we know that *this* word refers to *that* reality. He argues that the only reason we know that *this* word refers to *that* particular thing is because we *already* know the thing.[32] Indeed, we simply do *not* learn because of words themselves: "We do not learn anything by means of the signs called words."[33] But if this is the case, if we learn *nothing* from signs called words, how *do* we learn?

Augustine concludes that we learn because we each have a Teacher within—Christ. Christ is the Teacher who illumines the human mind to comprehend and understand reality. Augustine writes: "Regarding, however, all those things which we understand, it is not a speaker who utters sounds exteriorly whom we consult, but it is truth that presides within, over the mind itself. . . . And He who is consulted, He who is said to 'dwell in the inner man,' He it is who teaches—Christ—that is, 'the unchangeable Power of God and everlasting Wisdom.'"[34]

Indeed, the human person "is taught not by my words, but by the realities themselves made manifest to him by God revealing them to his inner self."[35]

While there is disagreement over exactly how to interpret Augustine's doctrine of illumination, we can certainly affirm with him that, while words have been given by God to assist with communication, it is Christ who illumines every human mind, and that *every* act of knowing is made possible because Christ is the Teacher who, by his grace, teaches us.[36]

Perhaps it goes without saying that any Christian view of education must affirm the possibility of knowledge. But in the contemporary milieu it is indeed necessary to make this affirmation clear. Dallas Willard has written, "The heart of the university crisis is, in my view, the simple fact that its institutional structures and processes are no longer organized around knowledge. The life of knowledge is no longer their *telos* and substance."[37] Willard continues: "But the idea of knowledge that guided the universities for almost a millenium—the same idea which inspired both classical thought and the rise and development of modern science—is one according to which to know is to be able to think of things as they are, as distinct from how they only seem or are taken to be, and to be able to do so on an appropriate basis of experience or thought."[38] On Willard's view, knowledge has been displaced as the proper *telos* of the American university due to three main reasons: (1) egalitarianism, (2) empiricism, and (3) the absolutizing of freedom.[39]

John Henry Newman could argue that knowledge was its own end. That is, knowledge is not obtained *primarily* to serve some other end, whether to make us better persons, to help with the division of labor, etc.[40] Newman writes, "Knowledge is capable of being its own end. Such is the constitution of the human mind, that any kind of knowledge, if it really be such, is its own reward."[41] Whether one agrees completely with Newman, it is clear that Newman and virtually the entire Christian tradition affirm the possibility of genuine knowledge.

The Truth of Things

If what I have argued above about revelation and knowledge is indeed true, then it follows that genuine education must affirm that the student is on a quest for an encounter with the "truth of things."[42] There is indeed a reality apart from the student, and through study and reading and the whole endeavor of education, the student wishes to come into contact with this reality. But the Christian should not assume that all persons (particularly in the academy) would indeed affirm such a reality. Education is an *intellectual* task. But if "intellectual" comes from the Latin *intellectus*, which means understanding, true education must posit that there truly is something *there* to be understood. And moving one step further, the Christian must affirm that the thing there *can* be understood.

In the twentieth century some education reformers argued that what was needed was a return to the "Great Books." Mortimer Adler and Robert Maynard Hutchins implemented such a program at the University of Chicago, and similar models have sprung up elsewhere, perhaps most noticeably at St. John's College (Annapolis, Maryland, and Santa Fe, New Mexico). The recovery of great books is certainly important, but it must be remembered that in the end, the question is still one of truth. That is, the goal is not simply to know the history of thought. Knowing the history of thought *is* a part of what it means to be educated. But true education is about seeking *wisdom* and about seeking the *truth*. As Christopher Derrick has written, "The object of a liberal education is reality or truth, not the different things that men have thought and said about reality and truth, useful though these will be as aids to thought."[43]

The exciting advantage of a genuinely Christian institution of higher learning is that it has the opportunity to introduce students to the central and classic texts of their tradition, while doing so against the backdrop of a Christian world and life view that serves as an interpretive grid for such a task. Thus, the "Great Books" are read and studied as a part of a thoroughgoing quest for truth and wisdom and as part of an educational endeavor that sees the reading of such books as a central means to the end of being a truly wise and Christian person who has learned to submit all things to the lordship of Christ.[44]

Lastly, we should note that for the Christian there is a unity to all of truth. This unity is predicated on the fact that this world is created by God. Since this world bears the mark of its Creator, and since God is ultimately *one*, there is a unity to all knowledge. Indeed, there is a unity of all truth. John Henry Newman made this point in his seminal work *The Idea of a University*: "I have said that all branches of knowledge are connected together, because the subject-matter of knowledge is intimately united in itself, as being the acts and the work of the Creator."[45]

Faith Seeking Understanding:
A Christian Understanding of Reason

In a paper such as this I can only begin to discuss the classical Christian understanding of *fides quaerens intellectum* ("faith seeking understanding"). But the issue must be broached. A Christian vision of higher education must take a stand on the reality of reason and its relation to Christian faith. This issue is of particular importance because here we come to grips with one point at which an evangelical understanding of Christian higher education differs from a Roman Catholic understanding of Christian higher education.[46] A Christian understanding of reason (and indeed, of the whole life of the mind), must wrestle with how the lordship of Christ is central to the whole of the Christian life.

Perhaps the key biblical text to inform such an effort is Colossians 2:8. Paul writes: "See to it that no one takes you captive through philosophy and empty deception, according to the tradition of men, according to the elementary principles of the world, rather than according to Christ" (NASB). This text has often been used to cast a dark shadow over the enterprise of philosophy in general, to argue that philosophy is a non-Christian enterprise. The text need not be taken that way. However, there *is* a contrast that Paul is making. The contrast is not between "Christianity" and "philosophy," but rather between Christian thinking and non-Christian thinking. Paul speaks of "philosophy and empty deception," "the tradition of men," and "the elementary principles of the world," and all these are contrasted with Christ. Thus, Paul's point appears to be that Christ is the foundation of all thought, and the Christian is not to be taken captive to any other alternative. In short, Paul is making a plea for the radical lordship of Christ.

Another key biblical text that helps inform a Christian understanding of the centrality of faith to understanding is Proverbs 1:7: "The fear of the LORD is the beginning of knowledge" (NASB). Texts such as this have formed the backdrop for the position of "faith seeking understanding." There is a priority of faith in the intellectual task. Augustine could write, "I believe, in order to understand; and I understand, the better I to believe."[47] Similarly, Anselm could say basically the same thing, "Believe, that you might understand."

This Augustinian (and ultimately biblical) inheritance is central to any Christian understanding of education, and I believe that until it is properly understood, there will simply *be* no Christian college or university worthy of the name. Part of the difficulty of appropriating this insight from Augustine is that we live in such a different age. Augustine breathed different air than we breathe. Human nature remains the same throughout the ages, and indeed, there is nothing new under the sun, but there are genuine differences between Augustine's age and ours.

Perhaps the key difference is that when Augustine speaks of "faith seeking understanding," there is no dichotomy between the two, and indeed, *the two can never be separated.* For modern Christians, "faith" and "understanding" are two things that must be brought together, or integrated. But we are off to a bad start if we begin this way. The truth is, "faith" and "understanding" are *never separated to begin with.*[48] Faith ultimately is a type of understanding, or knowledge (i.e., it is not simply a subjective feeling). At the same time, on a Christian understanding, faith is an essential part of *all* knowing. That is, knowledge or understanding *never* occurs without faith.

This has been articulated particularly forcefully in our own century by Cornelius Van Til. Van Til argues that the Christian worldview is the necessary precondition of any predication whatsoever. That is, any person who utters a sentence either knowingly or unknowingly uses the Christian understanding of the world.[49] This does not mean that the person is a Christian but simply that the only worldview that comports with the presuppositions necessary for any speaker's utterance is the Christian worldview. As Van Til has written, "On the presupposition of human autonomy human predication cannot even get under way."[50] Indeed, "The only 'proof' of the Christian position is that unless its truth is presupposed there is no possibility of 'proving' anything at all."

One of Van Til's chief interpreters, Greg Bahnsen, paraphrases this same contention as follows: "God's revelation is more than the best foundation for Christian reasoning: it is the only philosophically sound foundation for any reasoning whatsoever."[51] Indeed, "only the truth of Christianity can rescue the meaningfulness and cogency of logic, science, and morality," for "only the Christian worldview provides the philosophical preconditions necessary for man's reasoning and knowledge in any field whatever."[52] Bahnsen continues, "From beginning to end, man's reasoning about anything whatsoever (even reasoning about reasoning itself) is unintelligible or incoherent unless the truth of the Christian Scripture is presupposed."[53] Finally, Van Til can write, "I understand no fact aright unless I see it in its proper relation to Christ as Creator-Redeemer of me and my world."[54]

Even if someone balks at Van Til's way of stating the issue, it is essential that a Christian understanding of higher education come to terms with the fact that every act of understanding is ultimately a *faith*ful act, in that every act of understanding presupposes any number of things that are often not consciously "proven" and indeed could never be proven by the scientific method. Take science for example. If a non-Christian student goes into the lab on Monday afternoon, he is assuming (by faith) any number of things that are not provable by the scientific method. He is trusting that the floor will support his weight, that room 25 is the same yesterday as today, that the test tube in his hands is really a test tube and not a hamburger, that his eyes are really seeing real letters and numbers on the textbook, and that his mind is really interpreting such letters and numbers, etc. All of these things are believed by faith, and they cannot be proven by the scientific or empirical method. If this is true, then *all* learning is, on one level, *faith*ful learning, and there is no *need* of "integrating" faith and learning.

But we must push our case further and affirm that *all* learning by *all* persons (Christian and non-Christian alike) takes place against the backdrop of a belief in the triune God of Scripture. That is, we trust that our eyes see things, our minds can grasp reality, etc., because God has made and sustains such a world and because it is impossible to live in this world and *not* see the handiwork and see certain attributes of God. Indeed, according to Romans 1:18–20, *every* person knows God, but the unbeliever suppresses such knowledge. There are no atheists, according to Paul. Thus, *all persons* think, reason, and learn against the backdrop of a belief in God. But some are nonetheless engaged in their intellectual tasks against the backdrop of a willful rejection of the knowledge of God who made them—the willful rejection of what they know to be true. The Christian, however, has been redeemed from such suppression of the knowledge of God because God has shone in his heart to give him "the Light of the knowledge of the glory of God in the face of Christ" (2 Cor. 4:6 NASB).

The puzzling thing is this: if Christians have been redeemed, and if they have come to such a "knowledge of the glory of God in the face of Christ," why do so many Christian students and academics see little relation between faith in Christ and academic and intellectual tasks? The simplest answer is that they have not grasped the radical nature of the lordship of Christ. They *function* as rebels who refuse to recognize the sovereignty of God over every area of their lives—including their disciplines. *Functionally,* such persons live as autonomous rebels, who would rule themselves and who suppress the knowledge of God in certain areas of their lives. When this is the case, and it is the case for every Christian to some degree, there *is* the need for the "integration of faith and learning."

But ultimately, what is needed is for genuine Christian faith to be at the heart of the intellectual task, and for students and scholars to constantly seek to allow their faith commitments to inform and drive their intellectual endeavors. What is really needed is "taking every thought captive to the obedience of Christ" (2 Cor. 10:5 NASB). All of our intellectual work flows from *some* faith; what is central is to constantly be asking if our scholarly endeavors, whether as students or as professors, are truly flowing from Christian faith, or is our scholarly work rooted in alien faith presuppositions that must be rooted out? The integration that must take place is the task of making sure that we are not subtly severing our academic work from the lordship of Christ. Our work *will* be rooted in a whole world of presupposition and faith commitments. The key task is to ensure that such work is truly consistent with our faith in Christ and our commitment to the historic Christian faith.

Hence, the work of the Christian student and scholar is the *constant* work of making *every* thought captive to the obedience of Christ. If for evangelicals the Christian church is *semper reformanda* (always to be reformed), then the Christian mind is *semper capiens* (always taking captive).[55]

The Possibility of Communication

While most people take it for granted, it is necessary to affirm the real possibility of communication. The biblical God is a God who speaks. As creatures we have the capacity to understand this self-communication and the self-revealing God. Likewise, as communicating creatures, we have the capacity to communicate with one another. It is no accident that one of the central Christological texts centers on the centrality of the Word. John writes (John 1:1, 14): "In the beginning was the Word, and the Word was with God, and the Word was God. . . . And the Word became flesh, and dwelt among us, and we saw His glory, glory as of the only begotten from the Father, full of grace and truth" (NASB). Here the Word is preexistent and eternal, but it becomes flesh in time. Indeed, the Word is not simply an impersonal "thing" but Christ himself, as verse 14 so clearly teaches. Christ himself is the Word, and we can believe that our words can be meaningful because they are ultimately rooted in the reality of Christ himself, the eternal and divine Word.

A Christian worldview provides a meaningful backdrop for the possibility of communication. Augustine outlines such a beautiful theology of communication, largely predicated on the incarnation. He writes, "Thus in a certain fashion our word becomes bodily sound by assuming that in which it is manifested to the senses of men, just as the Word of God became flesh by assuming that in which it too could be manifested to the senses of men. And just as our word becomes sound without being changed into sound, so the Word of God became flesh, but it is unthinkable that it should have been changed into flesh. It is by assuming it, not by being consumed into it, that both our word becomes sound and that Word became flesh."[56] Thus, in Augustine's thinking our words have meaning, because at the heart of the universe there is the second person of the Trinity, the *Word*, who himself became flesh in order to redeem us and to communicate to us—and our words have meaning because they are analogical to *the* Word.

Augustine also outlined, in brief, a Christian understanding of words in his *On Christian Doctrine*. Augustine contends that there are "signs" and "things." A word is primarily a sign, although a word is also a thing, "because if it is not a thing at all then it is simply nothing."[57] Things are either to be *used* or *enjoyed*.[58] In short we *use* things, and these things lead us to those things that are to be *enjoyed*. Ultimately, the only "thing" that is to be enjoyed is the triune God, who is *the* "Thing" (*res*).[59] Augustine's teaching, then, is that our words ultimately have a *telos*—the triune God. There is a *telos* to all communication, and that *telos* is the vision and presence of the triune God. All words are types of signs, or pointers, that find their culmination and goal in the triune God of Scripture.

It is no accident that movements that are skeptical of the possibility of genuine communication subtly or not so subtly reject the *Logos*. Jacques Derrida is honest enough to reject the existence of a Logos-centered universe ("logocentrism"), and his denial of objective truth and meaningful communication flows quite naturally from this rejection.[60] As George Steiner has remarked, "The archetypal paradigm of all affirmations of sense and of significant plenitude—the fullness of meaning in the word—is a *Logos*-model."[61] It is exactly this "plenitude" of meaning that Derrida has rejected. But Derrida's honesty *is* admirable and should force Christians to the realization that the reality of the triune God really is the necessary precondition for meaningful communication.[62]

The Importance of the Past

The Christian faith takes the past seriously. At the heart of the Christian faith is the gospel—the death, burial, and resurrection of Jesus—a *past* event that radically shapes reality *now*.[63] Thus, while the Christian faith has a radically *future* orientation, in that it is looking forward to the completion of salvation and to the ultimate and complete establishment of the kingdom of God, the Christian faith also has a *past* orientation, in that certain first-century events—i.e., the gospel—form the axis of history and determine the trajectory of current and future events.[64] In one sense, the whole Book of Deuteronomy is a lesson to the Israelites before they enter the Promised Land: Do not forget the past! Do not forget what the Lord has done for you. Even at the very end of the Old Testament, in Malachi, the last of the prophets, Scripture admonishes the Israelites to look *back*: "Remember the law of Moses My servant, even the statutes which I commanded him in Horeb for all Israel" (Mal. 4:4 NASB). Indeed, the very last verse of Malachi does not speak of something primarily *new* but of a *restoration*: "He will restore the hearts of the fathers to their children" (Mal. 4:6 NASB).

This emphasis on the past should shape a Christian vision of education. Christians are people who *remember*. History often repeats itself, and the lessons of the past must always be remembered—often they have been hard earned! God is not simply the God of the modern age but the God of all of history, and if he truly has been sovereign over all of history, history is worth studying. Since Christians view the idea of "progress" with some skepticism, they know that there is little reason to believe that all goodness and light dwells in the last one hundred years. Since this is God's world, and he is sovereign, Christians recognize that the history of the world is in a sense *one* big story—the drama of creation, fall, redemption.

To be educated is to know where you have come from, and this means understanding what has come before you. For Christians in the Western world, this means knowing, at least in broad terms, the flow of history, from the cradle of civilization in Mesopotamia, through the Greeks and Romans, on through the ancient, medieval, renaissance, reformation, and modern worlds. Thus, any truly Christian and liberal education will be one in which students are immersed in the central texts of the past, the literature, history, philosophy, and theology of millenia.

The central texts are not approached as magic talisman or as equal purveyors of wisdom. Rather, the student recognizes that the past must be approached critically (e.g., 2 Cor. 10:5) but also humbly, knowing that through study of such classic texts our provincial blinders are removed, captivating stories of beauty, courage, and tragedy become a part of our intellectual makeup, and we discover how our forebears dealt with numerous problems and concerns, most of which we are still wrestling with today.

Perhaps the most insidious aspect of modern education is its arrogance and chronological snobbery and its attempt to cut students off from the past. This is seen in a myriad of examples, whether in simple historical ignorance, in the disdain for (or ignorance of) the contribution the elderly can make to the family, church and cultural life, in the loss of the humanities at both the college level and below, and in the often-adamant insistence that certain (often Southern) symbols be removed from public places. This war on the past is fundamentally anti-Christian in that it seeks to cut people off from their past. It is essentially a Gnostic obsession with the immediate. Richard Weaver has written that such Gnostics are "attackers and saboteurs of education." Indeed, "in the way they have cut the young people off from knowledge of the excellencies achieved in the past, and in the way they have turned attention toward transient externals and away from the central problem of man, they have no equal as an agency of subversion."[65] Perhaps the chief way to avoid being victim to such "attackers and saboteurs of education" is by a deep immersion in the writings of the past. Only by being saturated by the events, figures, and texts of the past can contemporary students keep from being cheated out of a good education by idealogues and educational Gnostics.[66]

The Centrality of a *Telos*

The conviction that there is a *telos* or goal to all of human life helps form the warp and woof of a Christian vision of education. In exploring what might be meant by a Christian culture, T. S. Eliot was clear that constitutes a Christian culture is not this or that political party, or these or those particular laws. Rather, a Christian culture was a culture with a certain type of *telos* or goal. For Eliot, the key question was, "To what *end* it is arranged?" As cited earlier, Eliot wrote, "We must derive our theory of education from our philosophy of life. The problem turns out to be a religious problem."[67] The Christian affirms that ultimately the world created by God is a world that is moving in a certain direction, under the sovereign hand of a loving and just God, and that there is larger story and purpose to life, and all of our reading, learning, and studying are to be related to, and ultimately should serve, these sovereign purposes.

So the task for any Christian view of education is to articulate the *goal* or *telos* of education. What exactly is education for? What is the goal? The ultimate goal of education, for the Christian, should be the glory of God (1 Cor. 10:31). *All* things are to be done for God's glory, and this includes education. At the same time, it is worthwhile inquiring about subordinate goals, those goals that are good in and of themselves, but that should ultimately always be construed as serving the ultimate goal of the glory of God.[68] Regarding the goal of education, the Christian must be particularly astute and bold in rejecting and confronting the unchristian and idolatrous philosophies of the non-Christian mind.

In the United States, the pragmatism of John Dewey has been particularly influential, and it is hard to measure the harm Dewey's thought has had on the course of education in the United States.[69] Dewey was explicit in his rejection of transcendent goals for education: "In our search for aims in education," Dewey stated, "we are not concerned, therefore, with finding an end outside of the educative process to which education is subordinate."[70]

Contra Dewey, the role of education is not "equality," "democracy," or the like. Dewey saw education (especially and centrally the public school system) as the best tool for creating a radically "equal" society that would serve the purposes of "democracy." At all levels of education, from pre-school to graduate study, such a vision must be jettisoned by the Christian. The Christian parents' goal in educating their young child is simply not the furtherance of "equality" or "democracy," nor is the graduate student's pouring over lengthy volumes done so that he or she might take his or her dutiful place in the furtherance of "equality" or "democracy."[71] The goal of education is along a different line. Russell Kirk suggests the following: "The immediate object of education is the mind and heart of the person. Formal education perpetuates culture through developing the private understanding and imparting to the individual the heritage of civilization."[72] One does not have to affirm a thoroughgoing Enlightenment individualism to agree with Kirk that education is concerned with the mind and heart of *this* person. That is, the goal is not some abstract notion of "democracy" or "equality."

Rather, the immediate goal of education is to develop *this* person's mind and heart, and *that* person's mind and heart. There is a proper biblical individualism that looks at every student as an image-bearer and sees the development of *this* person's mind and heart as the goal of education. Kirk, speaking of the *telos* or *goal* of education, has written elsewhere, "I hold that the higher learning is an intellectual means to an ethical end; that the college is meant to join knowledge with virtue, so helping to develop persons who enjoy some wisdom because they subordinate private rationality to the claims of what T. S. Eliot called 'the permanent things.'"[73]

On a Christian view, education *does* prepare students for life in *this* world but also prepares students for their ultimate *telos,* the vision and presence of God. A fascinating example of the conviction that education helps prepare students for their ultimate destiny is found in the script from the case, *Wisconsin v. Yoder* (1972). In the following exchange, the prosecuting attorney ("Q") is trying to bully the Amish witness, John A. Hostetler ("A"), into admitting that the purpose of education should be ultimately secular. The exchange is priceless:

Q. The principal purpose to attend high school is to get education, is it not? Isn't that the primary purpose?

A. Yes, but I think there is a great deal of difference what education means—education for what?

Q. To put it bluntly, education so the child can make his or her place in the world.

A. It depends which world.[74]

Hostetler's testimony is a powerful witness to the fact that education, in its ultimate sense, prepares Christians for their ultimate destiny, the presence of God. However, a Christian view of education must also reckon with the reality that, short of the Lord's return, there is a proper Christian concern for our lives in the here and now, in this time and place, and in this culture. That is, a Christian view of education must prepare students for life in this world: how to live and love, how to raise a family, how to shape and transform culture along biblical lines, such that the whole earth "will be filled with the knowledge of the glory of the LORD, as the waters cover the sea" (Hab. 2:14 NASB).

Genuinely Christian education passes on to the next generation true wisdom, from both Christian and non-Christian sources, that can inspire and motivate the future generations in their task of cultural stewardship and dominion (Gen. 1:26–27). This cultural task includes the realms of the individual, the family, the church, civil government, and other institutions. However, we will surely fall into the wrong track if we allow our ultimate goal of the glory of God to be overshadowed or marginalized. We cannot allow an "eclipse of heaven."[75] As James V. Schall has noted, when we forget the reality of ultimate ends, we end up with tyranny in the here and now. Thus Schall can refer to Machiavelli as "an Augustinian realist without the City of God."[76]

This point has been made quite eloquently by C. S. Lewis in a sermon he gave at Church of St. Mary the Virgin, Oxford, in the fall of 1939.[77] Lewis asked why students should devote themselves to studies such as literature, philosophy, science, and history when war was raging and they might not even finish their studies. Lewis makes essentially an Augustinian point: all knowledge and learning are to be related, ultimately, to God. He posited, "I mean the pursuit of knowledge and beauty, in a sense, for their own sake, but in a sense which does not exclude their being for God's sake."[78] This sentence is wonderful. Note that the pursuit of knowledge and beauty can be for "their own sake," but only in a sense. For ultimately, the pursuit of knowledge and beauty (i.e., an education) is for God's sake.

Lewis's key (Augustinian) insight is that the pursuit of knowledge and beauty is both (1) something pursued for its own sake and (2) something pursued for God's sake *at the very same time and in the very same instant*. That is, the Christian scholar and student recognizes that at the very instant he or she is seeking to understand Plato's story of the cave in *The Republic*, that quest for knowledge is being pursued for God's sake. Samuel Johnson articulates this same truth, when he writes of "the obligation we were under of making the concerns of eternity the governing principles of our lives."[79] Indeed, these eternal concerns are the only things that ultimately give our temporal concerns their proper place in our lives.

CONCLUSION

The mission of Christian higher education (at least in the U.S.) has not always been particularly successful. Over time, most schools compromise their confessional commitments, become secularized, and at times have become thoroughly hostile to historic Christianity.[80] I have attempted to argue that genuinely Christian higher education must be shaped by certain things: a commitment to the core Christian realities of creation, fall, redemption, and the lordship of Christ, as well as such central themes as revelation, Scripture, and the possibility of knowledge, the truth of things, faith seeking understanding, the possibility of communication, the importance of the past, and the centrality of a *telos*, or goal. There are certainly other themes and indeed nuances that could be added. But certainly any vision of a truly Christian higher education will contain no *less* than these commitments. The odds are against any large renaissance of genuine Christian higher education, but we can pray that God may be pleased to bring just such a renaissance about.[81]

CHAPTER 4

THE INFLUENCE OF C. S. LEWIS

HARRY L. POE

PERHAPS NO ONE in the twentieth century has had a more far-reaching influence on the intellectual dimension of the Christian faith in the English-speaking world than C. S. Lewis. *Time* magazine featured Lewis on the cover of its September 8, 1947, issue with the caption, "His heresy: Christianity." While most writers can hope to do no more than speak effectively to their own generation, Lewis has continued to speak to new generations almost forty years after his death. His books continue to come out in new editions, and collections of his essays that were unavailable during his lifetime have been published in edited volumes. As was said of the Puritans a generation ago, the study of Lewis has become a minor industry.

Lewis also breaks all the rules in terms of his appeal. One would expect Reformed Christians to read Edwards, Arminian Christians to read Wesley, and Catholic Christians to read Newman—but everyone reads Lewis. He has that rare appeal that one also finds in Francis of Assisi, whom everyone wants to claim as their own. Perhaps it is the inner recognition that if I were to be the kind of Christian I ought to be, he is what I would be. Perhaps it was simply his ability to put matters of intellectual complexity and eternal significance into plain English. It is one thing to understand difficult matters and quite another to make difficult matters understandable.

Many people have written about the influence of C. S. Lewis on their lives. Sheldon Vanauken in *A Severe Mercy* and Charles Colson in *Born Again* have described the part Lewis's writings played in their conversions. Lewis presented

Christianity as intellectually reasonable. Many more people have written about how Lewis helped them to develop as a Christian. In *C. S. Lewis at the Breakfast Table,* edited by James Como, many of Lewis's former students and friends contribute specific accounts of how Lewis influenced them. One continues to run across brief essays written by former students of Lewis who found that Lewis had helped to shape their career.

W. Brown Patterson, former dean and professor of history at the University of the South at Sewanee, contributed a brief essay to *Sewanee,* the alumni magazine of the University of the South in 1999. Patterson studied with Lewis as a Rhodes scholar during the period 1953–1955. In his essay, Patterson describes the tutorial method of Oxford University that sets it and Cambridge apart from any other universities in the world. Lewis could have such a formative impact on his students because he spent an intense hour with each student individually every week of their time at Oxford. These tutorials were times devoted to the study of English literature rather than to the exploration of Christian faith.

Patterson notes that he went to Oxford in hopes of discussing with Lewis the great religious and moral questions raised in his books, which Lewis was happy to do "as long as the questions related to the subject of the week."[1] In other words, Lewis did not use his teaching in an artificial way to raise issues of faith. Issues of faith either pertain to the material at hand or they do not. Lewis focused on developing the minds of his students in such a way that they could recognize what pertained and what did not.

With these ground rules in mind, however, Lewis believed that certain ideas and values, that any literature of any culture would reflect, could only be understood with reference to some standard which all civilizations recognize. In *The Abolition of Man* Lewis refers to this standard as the *Tao.*[2] Patterson remarks that he came to understand Lewis's approach as a "'natural law' point of view."[3] We might substitute the term *worldview* for what Patterson refers to as Lewis's point of view. At least, we should understand that natural law comprised a part of Lewis's worldview.

This essay will not attempt to repeat yet again the significance of Lewis's popular writings. Instead, it focuses on Lewis as a model for how to take one's Christian worldview seriously in one's scholarship and teaching. We would do well to recall that the popular writings for which Lewis is so well known were not his principal work as teacher and scholar. Yet they represent the by-product of his work. If he had not been involved in serious scholarship of English literature, he could not have produced the popular volumes that he did. Lewis serves as a model for how to do good scholarship, regardless of one's field, and yet to do so informed by a Christian worldview. All scholarship proceeds from some worldview. Lewis refused to be bullied into believing that the Christian perspective of reality stood in an inferior position to naturalism.

To illustrate how Lewis's faith informed his scholarship and how his scholarship informed his popular writing, we may examine his scholarship during the war years from 1939 to 1945. When war broke out, the London office of Oxford University Press moved its operations to Oxford. One of the editors who came to Oxford was Charles Williams, a man who wrote a series of novels fantastic in their imagery of Christian and occult themes. Although he lacked the university education of Lewis and his literary circle who called themselves The Inklings, Williams possessed a remarkable mind and profound knowledge of literature and poetry in particular. After hearing Williams's lecture on *Paradise Lost,* Lewis began a serious study of that neglected poem.[4]

The study of *Paradise Lost,* which Williams inspired, resulted in one of Lewis's most successful series of lectures. Lewis delivered the eleven lectures that became *A Preface to Paradise Lost* at Oxford during Michaelmas term (fall semester) 1939. He revised these lectures for the Ballard Memorial Lectures at University College, North Wales, in 1941. Oxford University Press published the final revision of the lectures in 1943.[5]

While focusing his literary scholarship on *Paradise Lost,* Lewis also produced in the same period his most important work on the Christian faith. As will become apparent, his work on *Paradise Lost* provided the reflective and rigorous thought necessary to produce his popular work. During this period he wrote *Perelandra, The Screwtape Letters, The Abolition of Man,* and *The Great Divorce,* and he broadcast the radio talks that would be edited as *Mere Christianity.*

A Preface to Paradise Lost

Lewis approached *Paradise Lost* in a straightforward fashion. He began his *Preface* by providing the critical guidance a person of the twentieth century would need to understand a form of literature that had disappeared from living experience. Lewis wrote to help a modern reader understand and appreciate an ancient form of poetry. He wrote with passion and insight so that the reader who has never cared for poetry is left wondering how he could have wasted his life so long without poetry. Lewis's *A Preface to Paradise Lost* begins with his simple yet firm conviction about how to understand a text:

> The first qualification for judging any piece of workmanship from a corkscrew to a cathedral is to know *what* it is—what it was intended to do and how it is meant to be used. . . . The first thing the reader needs to know about *Paradise Lost* is what Milton meant it to be.[6]

Milton meant to write an epic poem, and epic poetry has conventions and techniques that Lewis explained. It does no good to evaluate epic poetry on the same basis one uses to evaluate lyric poetry. Since most people have greater familiarity with lyric poetry, Lewis devoted some attention to comparing the two forms, including why a person might have no difficulty reading a brief lyric poem yet stumble on an epic poem.

Lewis joined Milton in believing that the lyric poetry of the Hebrew psalms was superior aesthetically to Greek lyric verse quite apart from any religious or moral consideration and proposed, "[I]f any man will read aloud on alternate mornings for a single month a page of Pindar and a page of the Psalms in any translation he chooses, I think I can guess which he will first grow tired of."[7] In so simple (or difficult) a matter as writing a poem, the poet must decide the form in which the idea and experience for the poem should be expressed. An epic poem will be quite different from a lyric poem.

Lewis's *Preface* represents his scholarship, but it also demonstrates that his scholarship was not an end in itself. Scholarship is a teacher's tool. The teacher in Lewis would not allow that people who did not understand poetry could not learn to love it. People can understand the differences between literary forms. Once they recognize the patterns, they can see the patterns in any piece of literature. Lewis rejected T. S. Eliot's view that only poets can properly judge poetry. Eliot's view represents the kind of specialization and fragmentation of life that Lewis found objectionable.[8] The whole issue of critical judgment is at stake, and it goes far beyond the matter of evaluating poetry. If a person cannot evaluate poetry, then he cannot evaluate much in life at all.

Lewis argued that it is not necessary to be skilled in a field to recognize those who have skill. He admitted that specialization limits the extent to which people may make judgments, but reason provides access at a basic level to some basis for evaluation. This view represents a foundational matter for Lewis as a literary critic, and it comes from his understanding of the kind of universe God created. He recognized a certain orderliness to creation that people may comprehend through the mind. This fundamental view arises from faith in a Creator God who created an orderly universe that may be known. It assumes that people are made in the image of God and share the quality of mind that allows for knowledge of the ordered patterns of the universe. It assumes a degree of reliability between the universe one perceives and the universe that is actually there.

Without the basic faith assumptions with which Lewis approached his work as a scholar, the concepts of knowledge, reason, and reality are at risk. In the process of writing *A Preface to Paradise Lost,* Lewis raised a number of questions related to literary criticism or the themes of *Paradise Lost* that have social, moral, political, and theological significance for his generation. While he wrote as a literary critic from a faith perspective, he did not artificially use his *Preface* as a theological tract. Nonetheless, the discussion of *Paradise Lost* provides the backdrop for the popular writing Lewis undertook during the war years. While the examination of *Paradise Lost* raises the issues, Lewis would have to discover his own creative way to move the discussion from literary criticism to personal faith. As he suggested in his discussion of understanding what Milton or any author meant to do in a piece of literature, every literary form has its conventions. Authors use different literary forms to accomplish different objectives. Although he wrote from a faith perspective, Lewis did not use literary criticism as an apologetic or evangelistic device. For those purposes he would turn to more creative forms.

The Danger of Subjectivism

In assessing the role of repetition of stock words, phrases, and lines in epic poetry, Lewis insisted that the critical question concerns what the repetition does for the person hearing the epic, not the person composing or reciting the epic. Instead of the subjectivism and self-absorbed expressionism of the twentieth century that focuses on the experience of the artist, Lewis emphasized the success of the artistic piece in communicating to the audience. Thus, "Music means not the noise it is nice to make, but the noises it is nice to hear. Good poetry means not the poetry men like composing, but the poetry men like to listen to or to read."[9]

When Lewis makes statements such as "the common ground of all oral poetry," he gives an indication of his worldview.[10] The very notion of "common ground" provides a basis for rationality, judgment, and communication. This common ground provides the background that enables people to make judgments between things that share the common ground—in this case, epic poetry. The issue of subjectivism appeared in other pieces of work Lewis produced at this same time. One can see how Lewis recognized the implications of literary criticism for how one approached life. The underlying philosophical assumptions one brings to literary criticism or life will determine how one approaches either. At stake was the matter of whether any objective values exist. In his discussion of this issue, Lewis anticipated the deconstruction movement in literary criticism by twenty-five years.

The Abolition of Man

When invited to deliver three lectures at Durham University in 1943, Lewis took the opportunity to address the question of the meaning of language and the idea of moral absolutes. These lectures would be published as *The Abolition of Man*. In *The Abolition of Man* Lewis used a new elementary English textbook to illustrate a dangerous trend in culture that was influencing the thought processes of schoolchildren during World War II. Lewis learned of the book from his own students who had used it in school. In *The Control of Language* by Alec King and Martin Ketley, Lewis discovered a subjectivist view of language and morality set forth.[11]

The textbook made the simple claim that when a person makes a remark, such as "the waterfall is sublime," they really mean "I have sublime feelings."[12] This approach to the elementary study of literature crept into the educational system from A. J. Ayer's theory of emotivism: "The contention that when one says 'X is good' he is saying only 'I like X.'"[13] Lewis argued that children who read this text would believe two things: "Firstly, that all sentences containing a predicate of value are statements about the emotional state of the speaker, and, secondly, that all such statements are unimportant."[14]

The danger arises, Lewis believed, not because the authors intended to undermine society or even that they understood the implications of what they had said. The danger arises because the text will be read by "a boy who thinks he is 'doing' his 'English prep' and has no notion that ethics, theology, and politics are all at stake. It is not a theory they put into his mind, but an assumption, which ten years hence, its origin forgotten and its presence unconscious, will condition him to take one side in a controversy which he has never recognized as a controversy at all."[15]

While failing to distinguish good literature from bad, the authors focused their attention on debunking human feelings with the possible intention of making a clean sweep of traditional values. Lewis insisted that the authors of this English textbook had staked out "a philosophical and not a literary position."[16]

In a remarkable critique of Lewis in *The Inklings* in which he takes Lewis to task for his prejudices, Humphrey Carpenter dismissed *The Abolition of Man* as an overreaction to "a handful of remarks about subjectivity made by the authors of a school textbook for the teaching of English."[17] Carpenter does not appear to take the problem seriously and faults Lewis: "Even supposing these remarks to be truly representative of modern thought, Lewis does not give them a chance."[18] Furthermore, Carpenter criticized Lewis's failure "to examine those elements in his opponents' case which have a potential for good."[19] Carpenter did not have the vision to see the direction of culture that Lewis saw so clearly from the road map of a textbook and the influence it had already begun to have by 1942. Humphrey published *The Inklings* in 1978 but failed to recognize the growing influence of postmodernity and the challenge to objective truth.

In the struggle between intellect and emotion, Lewis argued that "the head rules the belly through the chest." The chest represents magnanimity, emotions that have been organized "by trained habit into stable sentiments."[20] Lewis argued that the assumptions of the English grammar text produced "Men without Chests."[21] One might substitute the idea of character.

While he anticipated an approach to literary criticism that would not have a major impact in the scholarly world until after his death, Lewis also responded to an approach to criticism that had great influence during his life. Some scholars approached the treatment of epic poetry by first supposing an earlier form of the epic and then imagining what that earlier form might be like. This clever approach could justify virtually any conclusion or predisposition of mind that a scholar might have. Lewis distrusted the critical method that would "suppose" an earlier version of an epic (or of the Gospels) in order to develop a theory of the meaning and purpose of the text. Though it may be possible to imagine a previously unknown version, the text creates no necessity to do so.[22] In terms of the value of interdisciplinary conversation for biblical studies and theology, Lewis's views on the interpretation of a text have important implications for biblical criticism.

Mere Christianity

Lewis understood history to have a pattern or design, and he argued that people who do not perceive the design have no basis for attaching more significance to one event than to another. From this perspective he explained that primary epic poetry such as *Beowulf* or the *Iliad* was not concerned so much to express a great national subject as to reflect on individual heroism. The heroic age had no great world-changing event to which it could point, such as the founding of Rome or the fall of man. Without the pattern or design against which the great event can be understood, people have nothing to fall back on but futility and despair.[23] Secondary epic, on the other hand, reflects a sense of meaning to history. Actions matter. Virgil's *Aeneid* may deal with the same siege of Troy with which Homer's *Iliad* dealt. Yet Virgil painted a picture that spans centuries as he explained how a sequence of actions led to the founding of Rome:

> Poetry certainly aims at making the reader's mind what it was not before. The idea of a poetry which exists only for the poet—a poetry which the public rather overhears than hears—is a foolish novelty in criticism. There is nothing specially admirable in talking to oneself. Indeed, it is arguable that Himself is the very audience before whom a man postures most and on whom he practices the most elaborate deceptions.[24]

This whole line of thought proceeds from a fundamental view of the universe. Lewis believed that patterns could be recognized because the patterns were actually there. Pattern implies purpose and meaning. Purpose implies one who intends purpose. The recognition of order and purpose and the universal understanding of good and evil received a considerable amount of Lewis's attention at the outset of the war. He explored these issues for the public in a series of talks on BBC radio.

During August 1941, Lewis broadcast a fifteen-minute talk every Wednesday evening for the BBC on the subject "Right and Wrong: A Clue to the Meaning of the Universe?" This four-part series was followed by a second series on the subject "What Christians Believe." These first two series were published in July 1942 as *Broadcast Talks*. They were later published in the United States as *The Case for Christianity*. A third broadcast series on "Christian Behavior" began in September 1942. In late 1943 Lewis prerecorded a series that would be broadcast in February, March, and April of 1944 as "Beyond Personality: The Christian View of God." This last series was published later in 1944. After the war, these talks were edited as a single volume under the title *Mere Christianity* (1952).[25]

Because *Mere Christianity* represents several different series of radio broadcasts, it has several major themes not normally found in one book. The opening section represents a modern restatement of the moral argument for the existence of God. Lewis considered the existence of a universal concept of good and evil to be beyond question. It was too easily demonstrated to question seriously. From this observable phenomenon present in all cultures at all times, Lewis proceeded to account for its presence. He argued that the ultimate basis for all judgment "is farther back and higher up" than any alternatives, such as dualism or even personal preference.[26]

Mere Christianity provides an apologetic for the kind of God in whom Christians have faith, but it also presents an apologetic for the major doctrines of the Christian faith and the norms of Christian behavior. *Mere Christianity* does not provide a biblical teaching about the Christian faith, although its approach is based on the biblical teaching of the apostles. Instead, it provides a philosophical examination of what Christians believe in order to demonstrate the reasonableness of the Christian faith. In this sense, Lewis's approach to Milton has informed how he approaches the Christian faith. In his *Preface* he strives to help his reader understand exactly what Milton meant. He brushes aside prejudices against the epic form of poetry as well as modern ideas that prejudice the reader. He takes the same approach to the Christian faith for the modern reader in *Mere Christianity*. The result is a book that does not come across as a dogmatic diatribe but as a reasonable conversation between reasonable people.

Part of his approach includes the demonstration of universally held ideas and values. In his discussion of the cardinal virtues of prudence, temperance, justice, and fortitude, he observes that these Christian virtues "are those which all civilized people recognize."[27] He goes so far as to say that Christianity does not introduce any new morality so much as it reminds us of the natural law of which all people are aware.

The Virtue of Stock Responses

Milton's *Paradise Lost* has been criticized for the presence of "stock responses," by which "I. A. Richards means a deliberately organized attitude which is substituted for 'the direct free play of experience.'"[28] In this discussion of "stock responses," Lewis explored what we might call "universal values" today. Lewis took the opposite view, arguing that just such deliberate organization of attitude constitutes a necessity of human life. People enjoy entirely too much free play of experience that calls for more "stock responses." Because human response to the whole range of life circumstances has grown increasingly uncertain, "stock responses" to pride, treachery, pleasure, death, and pain provide "a delicate balance of trained habits, laboriously acquired and easily lost, on the maintenance of which depend both our virtues and our pleasures and even, perhaps, the survival of our species."[29]

Lewis finally returns to the idea of "stock responses" when he treats the Fall at the end of his *Preface*. In describing how Eve's decision to offer the fruit to Adam represents the moment of decision to commit murder, Lewis points out the subtle progression of the mind:

> No man, perhaps, ever at first described to himself
> the act he was about to do as Murder, or Adultery, or
> Fraud, or Treachery, or Perversion; and when he hears
> it so described by other men he is (in a way) sincerely

shocked and surprised. Those others "don't understand." If they knew what it had really been like for
him, they would not use those crude "stock" names.[30]

Adam has placed conjugal love above any other claim. This
decision creates the false impression of noble sacrifice if one
forgets that there were higher values in Milton's and Adam's
world.[31]

The Screwtape Letters

On the question of Satan as the "hero" of *Paradise Lost* as
Dryden suggested, Lewis insisted that such a view could not be
entertained until recent times. Milton would have had no such
intention, for Lewis insisted that "we know from his prose
works that he believed everything detestable to be, in the long
run, also ridiculous; and mere Christianity commits every
Christian to believing that 'the Devil is (in the long run) an
ass.'"[32] During the same period in which Lewis developed his
lectures on *Paradise Lost* from which his *Preface* comes, he also
wrote *The Screwtape Letters* (1940). Between July 1940 and
February 1941, Lewis wrote *The Screwtape Letters,* which
chronicle the misadventures of a young devil working on his
first "patient" through a series of thirty-one letters from a
senior devil, his uncle Screwtape.[33]

In exploring why Satan would be the best drawn of Milton's
characters, or for that matter of any poet's or novelist's characters, Lewis explained that one need only release imaginatively
those worst passions that constantly strain at a person. All people have a bit of Satan within, on which they can rely in painting a picture of him. Drawing a picture of those real, high
virtues that a person does not possess, however, does not come
quite so easily. Lewis's understanding of humanity after the Fall
informs this literary insight as he observes, "We do not really
know what it feels like to be a man much better than
ourselves."[34] This fact prevents Satan's predicament from being
truly comic: it lies too close to home.

"Evil and God"

Lewis wrote an article for *The Spectator* in February 1941 that dealt with the relationship of evil and God. Lewis rejected the notion of a dualism that allowed for "two equal, uncreated, antagonistic Powers, one good and the other bad."[35] In dualism, good and evil exist mutually, but they do not explain each other. The condition of their mutual existence would have greater ultimacy than their existence would have. The condition of two equal powers existing, or the cause of their existence, would be more ultimate.

The moral problem for dualism lies in the way that it gives evil a "positive, substantive, self-consistent nature, like that of good."[36] In such a situation, with both values having equal weight, no superior value exists to make the judgment that one is good and one is evil. Neither can be judged right or wrong. The only basis for judgment would be human preference. Since some people prefer evil, then it would be good and right for them on the basis of preference.

Lewis insisted that "a sound theory of value demands . . . that good should be original and evil a mere perversion; that good should be the tree and evil the ivy; that good should be able to see all round evil (as when sane men understand lunacy) while evil cannot retaliate in kind; that good should be able to exist on its own while evil requires the good on which it is parasitic in order to continue its parasitic existence."[37]

Lewis recognized that a Christian shares a number of assumptions with the Zoroastrian, but important distinctions exist. The Christian goes one step further than the dualist in their views of spiritual forces and ultimate reality. If Michael is right and Satan is wrong, then "they stand in two different relations to somebody or something for further back, to the ultimate ground of reality itself."[38]

Christians often mistakenly assume that a strong sense of good and evil in a creative work like the *Star Wars* movies or J. R. R. Tolkien's *The Lord of the Rings* represents a Christian view. The presence of such strong statements on good and evil stands in contrast to the broad moral relativism of the twentieth century, but other belief systems have strong values. The dualism of *Star Wars* with its impersonal Force in no way approximates the God of Abraham, Isaac, and Jacob. Good may triumph over evil, but only as luck would have it.

The theological perspective of Tolkien's *Ring* has more to do with the dualism of Norse mythology than with the sovereign God of Scripture. One could argue that his tale is full of Christ figures, but Hemingway's fiction has an ample stock of Christ figures. Lewis's *Chronicles of Narnia*, on the other hand, makes quite clear throughout that Aslan will always win the battle because his is the greater, deeper magic. Even when the contest between good and evil rages, Aslan's unseen father remains in the background as the ultimate authority.

The Great Divorce

While Lewis appears to dread the possibility that he may "seem to be merely moralizing," he nonetheless brings his worldview as one of the "tools" at his disposal as an educated man called to literary criticism. Successful understanding of the meaning of the text requires a consideration of matters that modern people prefer to ignore: "But the truth is that the aesthetic value of every speech in this debate partly depends on its moral significance, and that this moral significance cannot easily be exhibited without indicating those situations in human life which resemble the situation of the devils in Pandemonium. They resemble it not because Milton is writing an allegory, but because he is describing the very root from which these human situations grow."[39]

Lewis raised the possibility of escape from hell through "humiliation, repentance, and (where possible) restitution."[40] But Milton does not explore this option for his devils, who raise it themselves, only to conclude that they will never repent. The door of hell is locked on the inside. Lewis returned to this idea when he wrote *The Great Divorce*. Lewis first conceived the idea for *The Great Divorce* in 1933, but he did not finally write it until the war, when it was published in fourteen weekly installments in *The Guardian* from November 1944 to April 1945.[41]

Perelandra

In his discussion of Milton's treatment of Adam and Eve, Lewis exposed those attitudes and expectations within himself that had prevented him from grasping the significance of the Fall. He had wanted the newly created parents of humanity to be naïve and simple because they lacked experience. Milton made clear, however, that they were innocent but not childish. They were "created full-grown and perfect."[42] While he devoted only a few pages to this subject in his *Preface*, Lewis drew upon his scholarly observations related to *Paradise Lost* to provide him with a full outline for a novel. In the second volume of his science fiction trilogy, Lewis imagined what kind of struggle took place in the Fall and what it would have meant had the Fall never taken place. George Sayer remarked that *Perelandra* as a story "is very much that of Genesis or *Paradise Lost*."[43] In fact, Lewis would have been working on *Perelandra* at the same time he was preparing *A Preface to Paradise Lost* for publication.

The Problem of Pain

One cannot read *Paradise Lost* without being aware that it explores the question of why pain and suffering exist in a world made perfect by God. The role of Satan, the failure of Adam and Eve, and the ultimate plan of God for redemption play through it all. During the same period in which he delivered his lectures on *Paradise Lost* in Oxford, Lewis wrote a little book on perhaps the greatest question of faith, *The Problem of Pain*. Written during fall of 1939 and winter of 1940, the book went into publication during the fierce Battle of Britain, when so many civilians lost their lives during the blitz.

Lewis explored many of the same themes that he explored in the *Preface*, but he went beyond what Milton thought to how a person of the modern world might think about the same issues. He combines his training as a philosopher with his faith as a Christian. His primary contribution to the question comes in chapter 2 of the ten-chapter book in which he seeks to clarify the meaning of the omnipotence of God. In his discussion, he primarily clarifies how people think about the options available to God in creating a universe in which people have freedom of action. Lewis approaches the subject with remarkable humility as he acknowledges the difficulty of his subject, but he succeeds in presenting an argument that the presence of suffering in the world does not preclude the existence of a loving God.[44]

CONCLUSION

One misses the point from this survey if one concludes that Christian scholarship means the study of angels and devils. The discussion of Milton's understanding of the Fall and all of the theological foundations for that understanding emerge from the primary concern Lewis had for how to understand a text. Understanding arises because of the communication that can occur between two minds in an objective universe characterized by order. The scholarly problem Lewis faced in writing *A Preface to Paradise Lost* might just as easily have been addressed if he had written a preface to Spenser's *The Faerie Queene*. In fact, we almost have a preface from Lewis to *The Faerie Queene*.

When Lewis went to Cambridge as professor of medieval and renaissance English, he delivered a series of lectures on *The Faerie Queene* just as he had done at Oxford on *Paradise Lost*. Lewis died before he could write a book based on the lectures, but one of his students published a manuscript based on his notes of the lectures. In *Spenser's Images of Life* edited by Alastair Fowler, we find the approach to understanding a text that Lewis demonstrated in *A Preface to Paradise Lost*. To read *The Faerie Queene* with understanding, a person must enter into the way of thinking of the Elizabethans. It does no good to read it from the perspective of a modern worldview. Neither does it help to approach it as a journey into Spenser's inner psyche. Just as it was important to understand the role and function of epic to read Milton with any understanding or pleasure, it is necessary to understand the role of pageant and the function of allegory to understand Spenser. The book represents Lewis as a Christian scholar but not as a writer of theology.

It is not difficult to find traces of Plato in Lewis's thought. His emphasis on mind and order might easily be called Platonic thought rather than Christian thought. Many Christians before Lewis have appropriated Plato's system and have taken it for the correct Christian worldview. While Lewis believed that "mind" lay at the heart of reality, that belief answered only part of the question. The more important question that he addressed over and over in his writings was, "What sort of mind?" The sort of mind behind the universe provides the explanation for the presence of universal values and the ability to make distinctions between things. Value judgment and all critical judgment depend upon this mind whom Lewis came to know as the God of Abraham, Isaac, and Jacob—the Father of our Lord Jesus Christ.

The way Lewis approached the text of *Paradise Lost* is also reflected in his other scholarly writings, including *English Literature in the Sixteenth Century, excluding Drama* (1954), *An Experiment in Criticism* (1961), *The Discarded Image: An Introduction to Medieval and Renaissance Literature* (1964), and his earliest major scholarly work as a young Christian, *The Allegory of Love: A Study in Medieval Tradition* (1936). During a time of growing crisis within the academic discipline of literary criticism, Lewis held out for an objective, knowable world. In the face of positivism, naturalistic materialism, subjectivism, linguistic analysis, and the grab bag of literary critical experiments that marked the cultural crisis of the twentieth century, Lewis held out for a coherent world that could be known and spoken about.

The influence of C. S. Lewis extends far beyond his field of medieval and renaissance English literature. Yet he continues to serve as a model for how to go about excellence within one's academic field while informed by faith. Rather than interfere with or jeopardize the quality of his scholarship, faith gave Lewis an extra tool in his scholarly tool kit by which he could understand his discipline.

CHAPTER 5

CHRISTIAN WORLDVIEW, ETHICS, AND CULTURE

DAVID P. GUSHEE

ONE OF THE GREAT FLAWS of the moral instruction that young Christians typically receive is the failure of teachers, preachers, and parents to ground moral norms in a broader Christian worldview. High schoolers may know that they are not supposed to have sex before marriage but not why they should not do so. They may have learned to oppose abortion-on-demand but not why abortion is wrong or the complex issues involved in considering exceptions. The outcome of this failure is that when young Christians get exposed to the wider world and encounter people of strongly held, diametrically opposed moral convictions, often they have not been well prepared to give good reasons for the moral convictions they hold.

Even those who are able to ground their moral beliefs in particular biblical passages find that appeal to Scripture is unpersuasive to those who do not share a submission to biblical authority. To argue against the legitimization of homosexuality, for example, on the basis of the half-dozen or so passages that address the issue directly leaves dialogue partners unconvinced. Such frustrating attempts at dialogue can leave the young Christian in despair about the prospects of civil conversation about the day's hot-button issues, and perhaps even with some quiet doubts about the cogency of his or her own Christian views.

Dialogue about controversial moral issues with those committed to alternative perspectives poses a great challenge for any Christian, young or old. But the key to making progress in such dialogue, or at least in representing Christian positions well, is to reflect more deeply on the connection between Christian moral convictions and the Christian worldview. In this chapter, we will do just that, seeking to answer three basic questions:

- In what ways are moral norms grounded in worldviews?
- What are the central elements of the Christian worldview as it relates to Christian morality?
- How can Christians best communicate and advance their moral convictions in a contemporary pluralistic western culture such as our own?

GOING ON TOUR: WORLDVIEWS AS THE FOUNDATION FOR MORAL NORMS

The religious convictions of ancient Sumerian society, which flourished over five thousand years ago, are found in a text called the *Epic of Gilgamesh*. Among other things, this colorful and fascinating ancient writing tells the story of aggressive warrior lords like the part-human, part-divine Gilgamesh himself, his struggles with men and gods, the gods' struggles with one another, and the sexual couplings between the gods that result in the fertility of the earth. This universe of thought, not coincidentally, was inhabited by a society in which contentiousness and aggression characterized the entire social order, warrior virtues such as violence and courage were lifted up and prized, and religious rites included orgiastic temple prostitution.[1]

Epicurus (341–270 B.C.) was an unhappy refugee whose life was caught up in the chaos of a contracting Greek Empire just after the early death of Alexander the Great. Forced to flee the island of Samos, where he had spent his childhood, Epicurus settled in Athens to ruminate on questions philosophical. Epicurus was a convinced materialist who denied the existence of transcendent gods or any divine involvement in human life. In ethics, not coincidentally, Epicurus counseled, as Stanley Grenz puts it, an "austere hedonism": the rational human being will seek to avoid pain and enjoy the pleasures of this life while he can.[2] The goal of human life is to attain peace of mind regardless of external circumstances—such as, perhaps, the chaotic circumstances of his own life.

Karl Marx (1818–1883) was one of the most significant shapers of twentieth-century history, although he did not live long enough to see it himself. Marx rejected both the Jewish and the Christian strands of his religious/family background and instead became, with Friedrich Engels, the founder of the Communist movement. Marx viewed the entirety of human history as the struggle between economic classes, and especially as the fight of oppressed groups to throw off the chains of their oppression and enjoy the fruits of their own labor. Marx saw religion as the "opiate of the people," consisting of the anesthetizing lies that oppressors told the oppressed in order to keep them happily occupying their place in the social order.

The movement that Marx set in motion established as its highest and nonnegotiable good "the categorical imperative to overthrow all circumstances in which man is humiliated [and] enslaved."[3] This, in its way, laudable moral goal ultimately developed into an unrestrained revolutionary ideology in which the moral obligation of the Communist was to advance the cause by any means necessary and with absolutely no "extra-class" moral scruples, as Lenin put it. Current estimates of the twentieth-century death toll under what became a global ideology now run as high as one hundred million.[4]

Adolf Hitler (1889–1945) grew up Catholic in lower Austria and rose to become dictator of Nazi Germany. Hitler's worldview was a crazy quilt of anti-Semitism and pseudoscientific racism, social Darwinism, extreme authoritarianism, strident militarism, and ardent German nationalism. In one of the great tragedies of all human history, the Austrian corporal managed to get his hands on power in troubled Depression-era Germany and then led that nation into the abyss of evil. His worldview caused Hitler to lift up martial virtues, to honor inhuman hatred and cruelty to (supposed) racial subhumans and other national enemies, and to celebrate the triumph of the strong over the weak. The result was a demonic regime pursuing ruthless policies of genocide and global war, with twelve million civilian victims and a total wartime death count of at least fifty-five million.

What do all these stories have in common? Simply this: they show that worldviews are the ultimate foundation of moral norms. *Human beings live their lives on the basis of the stories that they tell and the convictions that they hold about ultimate reality.* It is easy to miss this if we are limited in our experience to the one particular culture in which we are born and raised. One of the best ways to know the morality-shaping power of worldviews is to step outside of our own cultural context, whether in imagination or in reality. Then the conclusion simply becomes undeniable.

In a forthcoming work about Christian ethics called *Kingdom Ethics* (InterVarsity Press), Glen Stassen and I offer a model for the nature and structure of moral norms that reflects the claim I am making here. In brief, the model argues that there are four essential levels of moral norms.

The first level is the *particular judgment*. Two things characterize a particular judgment as we define it: the moral judgment applies to one specific situation, and we do not necessarily give reasons for the judgment that we make. Imagine a conversation in the hall at school in which you say, "It's wrong for Sally to lie to Sam about her true feelings for him and pretend she cares about him more than she does." This is a particular judgment, and we make such judgments quite frequently in everyday life.

Of course, if asked about why we make the particular judgments that we do, we sometimes are able to offer reasons for our views. Thus, you may say that Sally's behavior is wrong because it violates the moral rule that we should tell the truth. A *moral rule* applies not just to one immediate case but to all similar cases, and a rule tells us concretely and directly what to do or not to do. So it turns out that your particular judgment about Sally's behavior is actually grounded in the moral rule that people should tell the truth to one another.

Now consider what your answer would be if your conversation partner asks why this rule is important to be followed or why the truth-telling rule exists at all. If you dig underneath rules to this next level, you discover *moral principles*. Principles are more general than rules. They do not tell us directly what to do or not to do, but they do provide the ground upon which moral rules sit (or ought to sit). If pressed for the principle that supports the rule demanding truth-telling, one might say that the principle is respect for persons, especially those with whom we are in intimate relationships. So you might say that it is simply disrespectful, a diminution of Sam's personhood, for Sally to be deceiving Sam about her true feelings for him.

Here is where it really gets interesting. Let's say your hallway friend is simply unwilling to let the issue go and thus asks you why respect for persons is such an important principle. If you think deeply about the issue for just a minute, you might say—if you're a Christian—something like, "It says so in the Bible," or, "God made us in his image, and this governs how people should be treated!" Stassen and I call this the *ground-of-meaning* or *foundational conviction* level of moral reasoning. Foundational convictions, by this definition, are the core beliefs about reality, God, human nature, and so on that actually serve as the bedrock support for our moral norms. You cannot dig any deeper than such convictions. In the language of this chapter, in foundational convictions we encounter a person's worldview. Whether in ancient Sumer or Athens, twentieth-century Moscow or Berlin, or twenty-first-century America, worldviews lie at the foundation of how people live and what they believe to be morally right and wrong.

If worldview shapes ethics, then it becomes incumbent on the thoughtful Christian to do at least three things. First, she must understand as well as possible the worldview/s that shape the ethics of secular and pluralistic American society. Then, she must dig deeply into the Christian worldview for comprehension of its foundational convictions and the moral principles and rules that flow from it. Finally, she must learn how to bring the two worlds together in dialogue and advocacy for Christian beliefs. A complete treatment of the first question would carry us outside of our purview in this chapter. It will be considered along the way in the next section as we undertake the second of these tasks. We will conclude by addressing the third.

TRUTH, STORY, AND PROPOSITION: FOUNDATIONAL CONVICTIONS FOR CHRISTIAN ETHICS

Christian ethics stands against the tide of modernity and postmodernity in its continued commitment to a belief not only in such a thing as truth but also divinely grounded and divinely revealed truth.

It turns out that prior to any particular claims about what is morally right and morally wrong is the issue of how one could possibly find out such a thing or upon what foundation moral truth-claims stand. We have already tipped our hand in the prior section by arguing that moral judgments, rules, and principles ultimately rest upon basic theological convictions. Another way to say it is that Christians continue to believe that God is the source and the revealer of moral truth. This belief distinguishes us sharply both from those who believe moral truth is discovered in other ways and from those who—more radically—believe there is no such thing as moral truth at all.

At the very heart of our faith is belief in a God who is moral in his very nature and who as a reflection of his character has created a morally structured world. All moral truth is ultimately traceable to its divine source. This does not mean that every moral conviction held by every Christian (or anyone else, for that matter) carries divine authority. It does mean that genuine moral truth is God's creation rather than human invention, that it is *discovered* rather than *created* by us, and that whenever we make our way to moral truth we are drawing closer to an aspect of God's character and creation.

As to exactly how humans discover divinely grounded moral truth, the classic theological distinction between *special revelation* and *general revelation* continues to be helpful. Special revelation is truth that God communicates to particular people in particular contexts through his words or deeds. The Bible clearly stands out as the high point of special revelation, with instances of divine communication to groups or individuals in encounter with God (Moses and the burning bush, for example, or insights gained in prayer) pointed toward the telos of inscripturated revelation. General revelation is truth that God embeds in creation, history, and conscience and thus makes available in principle to all persons willing to receive it (see Rom. 1:18–20). The faculty of reason, rightly employed and illumined by God's Spirit, is the primary way in which we receive general revelation. Underlying the concepts of both special revelation and general revelation is the bold and marvelous claim that God wants human beings to know the truth and thus reveals it to us.

The Christian life, then, ought to involve the serious effort to discern God's revealed moral will. The Christian, and Christian community, ought to be characterized by consistent Bible study, prayer, corporate dialogue for purposes of discernment, the disciplined use of reason to reflect on creation, history, experience, and tradition, and any other legitimate means to arrive at knowledge of the truth God is revealing to us in the area of morality. There is such a thing as moral truth; God is its source; God desires us to know that truth and thus reveals it to us. It is hard to think of more foundational convictions than these or convictions more out of step with the (post)modern temper.

It is important to strike a note of caution and humility and offer a bit more nuancing before continuing. The (divinely revealed and empirically confirmed!) doctrine of sin reminds us that the human capacity to apprehend—not to mention live out—God's moral will is deeply marred by the effects of sin. While God's will is fairly described as objective and absolute truth, Christian comprehension of that will is limited and incomplete. "We see through a glass, darkly," as Paul wrote (1 Cor. 13:12 KJV). This helps to account for such problems as the differences of opinion among Christians over what stance to take on major moral issues, differences in emphasis concerning which moral issues are most important, and the obvious variations in the shape of Christian moral convictions across time and culture.

This is why the work of Christian ethics is never quite done; we are involved in an ongoing "moral quest," as Stanley Grenz puts it,[5] and we must remain open always to correction and revision of our moral norms and practices—in submission to the divine will, of course, not to passing fads in culture.

Turning to the actual content of the moral truth God has revealed to us, we will follow customary evangelical Protestant practice by emphasizing the cardinal truths communicated in Scripture. However, we first want to introduce a distinction concerning the forms in which moral truth can be found in the Bible. The basic distinction here is between proposition and narrative.[6]

Moral truths are sometimes found in (or can be derived from) Scripture in terms of direct declarative statements of God's will. Large sections of Scripture take this shape, such as Old Testament law (beginning with the pivotal Ten Commandments in Exod. 20), the declarations of the prophets, the teachings of Jesus, or the instructions of Paul and Peter to their communities. It is also possible to derive moral propositions from central theological doctrines that coalesce in Scripture, such as the doctrines of sin, salvation, Christ, or eschatology. Of course, it is important to state here that sound interpretation of these texts, and sound understanding of these doctrines, is no mean feat.

Many Christians assume that it is precisely and only in moral commands or propositions that God's moral will is communicated in Scripture. However, closer examination of the Bible reveals that much of it takes the form of stories, and that these stories are embedded in a "master narrative" running from Genesis to Revelation. God communicates moral truths to his people in such classic stories as the account of Naboth's vineyard, David and Bathsheba, or Jesus' restoration of Peter. The master narrative of Scripture begins with God's creation of the world, offers the sad tale of human sin, details God's redemptive covenantal relationships with first Israel and then, in Christ, the church, and promises a final consummation of human history when Jesus returns.[7] Details of interpretation related to aspects of this "Story" will always be debated, but all good Christian theology and ethics is conceived within the framework this story provides.

Indeed, it is fair to say that any sound Christian worldview will be rooted and grounded in a thorough understanding of the Christian master narrative and its implications.

Traversing the length and breadth of Scripture in this way, are there particular moral principles and rules that emerge as most central for Christian ethics?

Love

Jesus was asked a question just like this, and his response is the best place to begin: "'Teacher, which is the greatest commandment in the Law?' Jesus replied, 'Love the Lord your God with all your heart and with all your soul and with all your mind.' This is the first and greatest commandment. And the second is like it: 'Love your neighbor as yourself.' All the Law and the Prophets hang on these two commandments" (Matt. 22:36–40).

The summit of biblical revelation is found here—love. At the heart of the Christian faith is the good news that the deity is most characterized by love and that the proper response to God is therefore love (cf. 1 John 4:7–11). Rooted in the love of God for us and the response of love for God, the believer's fundamental moral obligation is to love his neighbor, whom Jesus defines expansively as anyone, especially anyone in need (cf. Luke 10:25–37). Love is the driving moral principle of the Christian life, and love thus serves as the foundation for every legitimate moral rule; at least, no moral rule can be described as legitimate if it fundamentally contradicts the principle of neighbor-love.

Justice

God is one who sets things right. "The LORD longs to be gracious to you; he rises to show you compassion. For the LORD is a God of justice. Blessed are all who wait for him!" (Isa. 30:18). Human sin creates endless conditions of wrong. Far from being impassive and uninvolved with us as we continue to ruin each other's lives and our own, the God revealed in Scripture intervenes constantly to correct the results of our wrongdoing. At least as often, though, God calls his people—all people—to live according to justice and to redress the wrongs done by injustice.

Justice is often defined rather dryly as "giving each what is due." But justice is described passionately in Scripture as a state of affairs in human life that God actually "loves" (Isa. 61:8). What God loves is when he sees the vulnerable protected and the victimized healed and restored to life in community. Justice is not cold impartiality but food for the hungry, shelter for the homeless, a fair trial for the poor, a family for the orphan, and liberation for the oppressed. Justice redresses wrong and opens up the possibility of that wholeness and peace (*shalom*, in Hebrew) that is God's intent for every member of the human family. "Let justice roll on like a river, righteousness like a never-failing stream!" (Amos 5:24).

The Sacredness of Human Life

Perhaps the most significant narrative in the entire Old Testament, the creation account, tells us of God's intimate and loving effort to make the human species. The account in Genesis 1 climaxes in these stirring words: "So God created man in his own image, in the image of God he created him; male and female he created them" (Gen. 1:27). Theologians for centuries have pondered what it means to say that we are made in the image of God. In essence, *imago dei* means that human beings share certain *attributes* of the divine that no other species on the face of the earth shares. We wretched and frail human beings were made to resemble God, astonishingly enough, and God even declares us as "a little lower than the heavenly beings, and crowned . . . with glory and honor" (Ps. 8:5). This extra-ordinary status confers dignity upon each and every human life and establishes a central moral principle at the center of the moral life—a respect for persons so deep that some, myself included, have called it "the sacredness of human life."

Another aspect of the *imago dei* concept has to do with the significant *responsibilities* that the Creator has laid upon humanity. "You made him ruler over the works of your hands; you put everything under his feet" (Ps. 8:6). God has essentially deputized human beings as his representatives to the rest of the creation, and we are thus accountable for our treatment of the created order and nonhuman species of all types. More broadly, the concept of moral responsibility is embedded in the moral structure of the world. Human beings have far greater powers than other species and have correspondingly greater responsibility, whether in individual life or in societies. Thus the concept of the sacredness of human life entails both respect for persons and a profound sense of moral responsibility.

Participation in Community

Recent work in theology and ethics reveals yet another central moral motif—participation in community. This idea is rooted most foundationally in an appropriately relational understanding both of God and of the image of God. If God is triune in his very person, then the deity himself is always in rich and abundant relationship. Relationality is constitutive of what it means to be God, and the same is true of we who are God's image-bearers. Modernity, with its market-driven individualism, managed to obscure the fundamental significance of human relationality until the modern world itself began showing its own signs of strain. But now we see what the ancients knew all along—that solitary human existence is inconceivable. We exist in community. We now understand that a key aspect of human moral responsibility as God has revealed it is to do all we can to enhance the experience of human community for all persons.

God is relational. God called a *people* (not just scattered individuals) into covenant relationships—first Israel and then the church. God rescued the people Israel from slavery and then constituted them as a community in the desert. God's moral commands constantly call Israel to include the marginal and the vulnerable (the widow, orphan, alien, and sojourner) in community and prescribe all manner of moral norms for the life of the entire community.

When Jesus walked among us, one of his characteristic activities was restoring/including into community people who had been excluded (the crippled, the ill, tax collectors, prostitutes, Gentiles, women, and children). Much of the New Testament prescribes norms for life in Christian community and how to deal with violations of such community norms. The New Testament vision of the consummation of all things ends not in the mystical ecstasies of the individual believer but in the perfect community of the heavenly city, the new Jerusalem (Rev. 21). A right understanding of Christian ethics will involve, then, concern for the well-being of communities at every level, beginning with the faith community, but including families, localities, nations, and the entire human family.

Love, justice, the sacredness of human life, and participation in community do not exhaust the normative content of Christian ethics, to be sure. We have already indicated under these rubrics other key moral themes such as liberation, peace, and responsibility. One could also mention such central moral norms as truthfulness, holiness, and integrity. And of course, these broad moral principles serve to anchor hundreds of particular moral rules also revealed in Scripture. As has long been noticed by ethicists, the moral life is like a kaleidoscope that can be viewed in different ways, depending on "the way the light strikes" and your angle of vision. But one could do worse than to approach particular judgments in everyday life with a perspective rooted in love, justice, sacredness, and community—themselves all rooted in the character of a God worthy of all praise.

INTO THE FRAY: ENGAGING CULTURE WITH CHRISTIAN MORALITY

Suitably equipped with an understanding both of the relationship between ethics and worldviews and of the central moral norms emerging from the Christian worldview, the issue that remains before us is how Christians might best communicate and advance our moral convictions in contemporary culture.

The significance of this issue can hardly be overemphasized. It is at least arguable to claim that it is the single most discussed concern in contemporary evangelical Christian circles in North America. We are deeply frustrated over what seems to us to be the continuing erosion of our moral influence in American society, and we want to do something about it. But what?

I want to propose that only a multifaceted response will do in facing a problem that is multifaceted in its nature. American culture must be engaged vigorously for Christian moral truth, but a variety of arenas of engagement will be required. The good news is that the engagement is already occurring. Let's consider four arenas for the engagement that is needed.

Worldview Formation: Academia and the Intellectuals

If it is in fact true that worldviews shape ethics, that we actually live our lives based on the stories we tell ourselves about reality, as I argued above, then the single most important arena of cultural engagement is likely that of worldview formation. The primary institution involved in worldview formation at its deepest level is academia, and thus academia is one arena that we must engage.

Our nation is not one that always takes its intellectuals very seriously. We do not generally exalt academics to the position of cultural influence they have in some other nations. Yet it remains true, as someone said long ago, that the ideas articulated in the universities in one generation will be taken for granted on the street in the next. Ideas do matter.

An interesting example of this can be found on the issue of divorce. The legitimization of mass divorce as the American way of life began to occur in the mid-1960s. Before and while divorce rates began to rise, certain strands of American academia began to offer increasingly sophisticated intellectual rationales for the dethroning of the older religio-cultural norm of lifetime marriage. Popular opinion did not immediately reflect the attitudes of the avant-garde. But now, even a week spent watching *Oprah* or reading the advice columns reveals a titanic shift in the basic cultural understanding of both marriage and divorce.[8] The street in 2001 reflects the ivy towers in 1969.

Thus it may be that some of the most important work happening "in" Christian ethics today is the increasingly sophisticated Christian engagement with, say, scientific naturalism—an encounter that is not being undertaken by ethicists at all. To get at the roots of the modern, and now the postmodern, worldview, is a worthy task indeed and one that is at least conceptually prior to an engagement with moral issues.

Values Formation: Popular Culture

Popular culture is another critical arena of engagement for Christians today. It is increasingly impossible to deny that the movies, video games, music, and television shows produced by the entertainment industry exert a profound influence on every one of us. And it is also hard to deny that much of what is produced by popular culture is morally noxious in the extreme. All one has to do is test the offerings at the local cineplex this weekend against the moral norms of love, justice, and the sacredness of human life.

I had opportunity not long ago to go to Hollywood and engage in dialogue with writers, directors, and others in the industry. The majority of those present at the event were Christians who are attempting to infiltrate and change the entertainment industry as professionals. They are gifted by God to do the work that Hollywood does, but they also have the sense of calling to bring a Christian presence and Christian values into their workplaces and creative projects.

My time with these Christians in Hollywood reminded me that there are many different ways to engage an area of concern, not all of them either helpful or in keeping with Christian norms. Christians sometimes attempt to engage Hollywood through attacks on those in the industry, boycott threats, and other approaches that reflect a strategy of confrontation. While there are times when confrontation is called for, it should not be seen as the primary or only Christian strategy for cultural moral engagement. This is true both on grounds of effectiveness and on the Christian norms of love and respect for persons.

Still, it remains critical for Christians to engage the entertainment industry because of its profound influence as a shaper of values in American culture and around the world. Whether through exposure of the marketing of inappropriate materials to children or through permeating the industry from within, Christians have important work to do on this particular front of cultural engagement.

Character Formation: Evangelism and Discipleship

A close look at the New Testament reveals no power lunches with high Roman entertainment officials. Jesus commissioned his church to "go and make disciples of all nations . . . teaching them to obey everything I have commanded you" (Matt. 28:19–20). This was the primary strategy undertaken by the early church. The original eleven apostles, Paul, and those who followed after them spread the good news of the gospel of Jesus Christ with relentless zeal and energy, taking it across the Roman world within a generation. Meanwhile, those who were won to faith in Christ were assimilated into vibrant communities of faith and character formation—schools for training in love, justice, and the sacredness of human life. Within three centuries after the death and resurrection of Jesus, the cruel and pagan Roman Empire had officially given its allegiance to Jesus Christ, a remarkable occurrence indeed.

It is possible to overdraw the lessons one might glean from the church's world-transforming strategy as depicted in the New Testament. The church did begin as a tiny religious minority, a splinter group within Judaism, and thus had no access to political or cultural power. It used the only strategy it really had available to it—winning the culture, one soul at a time, and establishing vibrant countercultural communities of faith as laboratories of the Christian moral vision.

But it is hard to see how the strategy can be improved on. Evangelism is the beginning point of Christian efforts to change society, because—as we have seen—moral norms are rooted in worldviews and the primary allegiances of the human person. The soul truly won to Christ and initiated into the Christian worldview is the beginning of social change.

The church, understood as an assembly of changed people gathered in Christian community, is critical at every level one can imagine. In the church, the ongoing work of character formation can occur in a context of moral modeling, mentoring, instruction, and accountability. Likewise, as the church makes moral progress in its own life in such areas as marital permanence and racial reconciliation, for example, it offers an embodiment of the kind of existence toward which it is inviting the society to strive. The church is a beachhead of God's kingdom. It is (or should be) a community of such remarkable moral change that all but the morally obtuse will want a part of what the church enjoys.

The church rightly undertakes its social mission in the world if it offers constant demonstration projects for government and civil society of efforts that can advance and serve public justice. Finally, the church also functions as a support base for individual Christians called to their variety of particular missions in the world. The church, then, for all these reasons, is *in itself* a social change strategy as it embodies the Christian moral vision.[9]

Policy Formation: Christian Political Engagement

I have argued that the church must engage the culture with its moral vision by addressing arenas of worldview, values, and character formation. It would be a mistake to conclude this essay, however, without considering the place of policy formation as a form of Christian moral engagement in the culture. Here we are thinking of the Christian witness to the state, especially through public policy activism.

A veritable cottage industry of Christian political activism currently exists. As I wrote in a recent work on this subject: "Christian[s] are more involved in political action and engagement as of 2000 than at any time in living memory."[10] Every major denomination and most minor ones operate Washington offices, from which they churn out policy declarations and lobby political leaders. A host of parachurch organizations does the same thing both in Washington and around the nation. Numerous Christian publications chronicle the ups and downs of political campaigns and policy debates. While it is not at all clear that the typical person in the pew is paying much attention, it is definitely true that some Christians are exerting considerable effort to influence the outcome of the American political process.

The fallout of the Clinton scandals, however, hit conservative evangelicals particularly hard. Many evangelicals were outraged that our now-former president managed to survive the Lewinsky scandal, and other scandals, and remain in office. Conservative Christian disillusionment with the political process became profound. Taken in historical perspective, this pattern of intense activism (accompanied by high hopes) followed by bitter disillusionment (accompanied by a temptation to withdraw from politics) is characteristic of evangelical engagement with politics.

Rather than this political boom-or-bust cycle, what we need instead is the same kind of long-term investment in the policy formation process that we have in other kinds of social change strategies. Christians have known for centuries that evangelism does not always win converts, that disciple-making programs do not always produce saints, that intellectual engagement does not always change minds, and that efforts to reform popular culture do not always transform what goes on in town on Friday nights (or on TV every night). But there is no sign that evangelical Christians as a whole are therefore tempted to withdraw from these other forms of cultural engagement. So why are we inclined to treat political activism differently or to expect more from it than from other kinds of social change efforts?

A strategy for Christian political activism that is worthy of God's people will dig in its heels for consistent and dogged efforts to accomplish incremental change in the direction of God's moral will as we understand it and will not give up when that change seems very hard to come by.

CONCLUSION

The conclusion just reached fits quite nicely with the overall Christian worldview and illustrates, by way of closing, our perennial need to remain rooted and grounded in the master narrative that Scripture unveils.

Our story speaks of God's creation of a good world populated by, among others, human beings made in the divine image. It accounts for all that is horribly wrong here by recounting the way in which the primeval man and woman strayed from God's will and brought disaster on themselves, all who followed, and the creation itself. It portrays a God who resisted the perfectly justifiable inclination to give up on us and instead has spent the whole of human history entering into redemptive covenant relationships with human beings. It tells of how God himself entered the human story in the flesh in the God-man Jesus of Nazareth, the inaugurator of God's kingdom. Here creation and all who dwell therein were reclaimed for God. And yet the final consummation of the mystery of redemption still awaits Christ's return and the end of history.

In the time between the first and second comings of Christ, we catch glimpses of what N. T. Wright calls "the victory of God," but we are not privileged to see that victory in all of its fullness. The church remains a pilgrim people, on the way to the heavenly city but not yet there, meanwhile called to reclaim the earthly city for Christ and experiencing both victory and defeat in so doing. This is who we are, where we are, what we are doing, why we are doing it, and what we can expect. It is our worldview, the story of our life and the life of the world.

PART II

APPLYING
A CHRISTIAN WORLDVIEW

CHAPTER 6

FAITH AND LEARNING

Jimmy H. Davis

MANY INTERESTING TRENDS are present at the beginning of the twenty-first century. Two of these trends are the information explosion and the vibrancy of religious faith. One of the world's leading forecasters, John Naisbitt, touched on some aspects of the information explosion when he wrote:

- Between 6,000 and 7,000 scientific articles are written each day.
- Scientific and technical information now increases 13 percent each year, which means it doubles every 5.5 years.
- But the rate will soon jump to perhaps 40 percent per year because of new, more powerful information systems and an increasing population of scientists. That means data will double every twenty months.[1]

Since John Naisbitt wrote *Megatrends*, the information explosion has continued. From 1990 to 1996 in the United States, the number of periodicals published increased by 3 percent while the number of books published increased by 46 percent.[2] The Internet has compounded the information explosion; from 1997 to 1998, the number of registered domains increased by 118 percent.[3] In the United States, 760 households join the Internet per hour.[4] It seems that we are bombarded almost daily with information about Martian meteorites and microfossils, solutions to the human genetic code, atrocities worldwide, new ways to make us healthy and wealthy, cloning and Dolly the sheep, global warning, and so on. How does one deal with all this information? As Naisbitt wrote, "We are drowning in information but starved for knowledge."[5]

Although information and knowledge are sometimes used interchangeably in conversation, they are not the same. Information implies a random collection of material. Knowledge implies understanding and wisdom that come from an orderly synthesis of the collection of material.

In the past many forecasters predicted that religious faith would disappear as knowledge increased. Governments of the past and present have attempted to squash all religious faith. Yet, at the beginning of the twenty-first century, religious faith flourishes around the world. Worldwide, 71 percent of people say that they are adherents of a religious tradition; the followers of monotheism made up about 53 percent of the world's population; and about 34 percent of the world's population profess to be Christian.[6] In the United States the expression of religious faith is even stronger. About 87 percent of the adults consider themselves members of a Christian denomination with only about 5 percent indicating no religious preference.[7]

In this chapter, we will first examine different ways of knowing. Then we will examine how a person of faith, especially one with a Christian worldview, relates his or her faith to knowledge.

WAYS OF KNOWING

One way that we know is by observation. I know that the day begins with a sunrise because I observe the sun appearing in the east each morning. I know that the day ends with sunset because I observe the sun disappearing in the west. Because I have observed these sunrises and sunsets countless numbers of times, I know that the day begins with sunrise even on a very cloudy day when I do not directly see the sun. Yet I also know that the sun is not moving around the earth but rather the earth is rotating on its axis while revolving around the sun. I also know that the earth's rotation on its axis causes the appearance of sunrise and sunset. Yet I have never been at an observation point where I could see the earth rotate on its axis. All my observations are of a "moving" sun and a "stationary" earth.

Where do I get the idea of a moving earth? I obtain it from scientific texts. Why do I accept the scientific text over my direct observations? In philosophy, one would say my epistemology reflects the ontology. Epistemology refers to theories of knowledge, while ontology refers to characteristics of reality. In my mind why do I believe that my observations about the earth and sun do not reflect the reality as well as the scientific statement of a moving earth and a stationary sun? For one thing, we live in a society transformed by science and technology. Within the last two hundred years science and technology have greatly changed how we view our world: the plagues of old are now diseases moderated by science; our community has moved from our birth village to the world; travel has moved from draft animals to cars and planes; our work and play have drastically changed; wars have become much more destructive; many view themselves as one animal among many.

We have been taught that the scientific way of knowing is the best way to gain knowledge about the physical universe. This idea that science is the dominant way of knowing has been present for over a century. Charles William Eliot, president of Harvard University, proclaimed in 1877 at the opening of a new wing of the American Museum of Natural History, "In every field of study, in history, philosophy, and theology, as well as in natural history and physics, it is now the scientific spirit, the scientific method which prevails."[8] To Eliot, science would provide the knowledge needed to solve pressing social problems. As Eliot said, "[To] guide wisely the charitable action of the community; give a rational basis for penal legislation."[9]

If science is the modern way to knowledge, let us review how science works. Science begins with the assumption that the universe is knowable, regular, predictable, and uniform. This is an assumption that cannot be confirmed by the scientific method. If the universe were capricious, the scientific way of knowing would not work. A traditional view of science is that scientists go about their business in an objective, empirical, and rational manner.[10] The view was proposed by Francis Bacon (1561–1626) in *Novum Organum* (1620).

Bacon said science must be objective by removing speculation, preconceptions, and emotion; empirical by employing neutral, objective, reproducible observations; and rational by being rigorously logical. The traditional view saw scientists objectively collecting a set of observations (data) and then organizing and classifying this data to discover basic principles about nature. After discovering these basic relationships, most scientists want to know what is happening to cause these relationships.

But asking what is happening to cause these relationships moves from the arena of Baconian empiricism to the arena of creative imagination. Now the scientists must formulate a hypothesis, model, and theory. A hypothesis is a provisional guess about how nature behaves; a model is a mental picture of things too small (atoms), too far away (planets), or too slow (oil formation) to be observed; a theory is an overarching concept to explain observations. Since there are no logical rules to guide in formulating a hypothesis, model, or theory, the scientists must speculate or guess. Thus, the scientist goes beyond Bacon's objective, empirical, rational method.

In formulating a hypothesis, model, or theory, the scientist relies on his or her training and experiences. These guide the scientist in determining what questions to ask, what observations to make, and what conclusions to draw. The worldview (paradigm) of the scientist is a window that allows the scientist to see some things but not others. An example of this effect of a worldview is provided by scholars discovering the nature of combustion. When a wooden match burns, the match appears to lose weight by losing something to the air and leaving only an ash. In 1702, the German scientists Johann Becher and Georg Stah proposed the phlogiston theory to explain combustion. They proposed that when a substance burns the chemical phlogiston escapes into the air. Plants absorb phlogiston from the air, which explains why dried plant material is so combustible. The phlogiston window directed chemistry for the next eighty years. The phlogiston theory directed chemists to isolate and study gases. During this period hydrogen, nitrogen, nitrous oxide, nitric oxide, carbon dioxide, sulfur dioxide, hydrogen chloride, ammonia, and oxygen gases were isolated and studied. Also, during this period, the phlogiston window caused chemists to ignore certain questions dealing with mass changes.

The Frenchman Antoine Lavoisier (1743–1794) was a businessman who was also a chemist. He approached the combustion problem through the window of the balance sheet. By asking questions about the relationship of the masses in the combustion reaction, Lavoisier discovered that there is no phlogiston and that combustion is the reaction of oxygen with a material. He also discovered that the mass of the products equals the mass of the reactants (the Law of Conservation of Mass). For his work, Lavoisier is considered one of the founders of modern chemistry; for his business work (tax collecting), he was guillotined during the French Revolution.

Lavoisier's experiments and interpretations led to a worldview or paradigm shift: combustion is the reaction with oxygen and the mass is conserved in chemical reactions. Some contemporaries of Lavoisier could not make the paradigm shift; Joseph Priestley (1733–1804) could not. Priestley spent the rest of his life fighting for the phlogiston theory against the oxygen theory. Priestley was a good experimentalist; he identified seven gases, including oxygen. Both Priestley and Lavoisier performed the same reactions. Yet, how they collected and interpreted their observations depended on the assumptions flowing from their worldview. Priestley's worldview was so strong that he could not see the data any other way. Bacon's hope for an objective and rational science is an impossible dream. As the example of Priestley shows, going from information to knowledge is much more than just the facts. One's worldview will color how information is processed into knowledge.

In this chapter, we will argue that faith can be a valid factor in directing the collection and interpretation of observations. Faith is a window through which understanding comes. Faith is a valid factor in processing information into knowledge. Before examining how faith can guide understanding, let us examine different ways faith and knowledge have related to each other.

WAYS OF RELATING FAITH AND KNOWLEDGE

Since the earliest days of Christianity, the question has been asked, "How should a person of faith relate to knowledge?" Tertullian (ca. 155—ca. 230) expressed the question elegantly when he asked, "What indeed has Athens to do with Jerusalem? What concord is there between the Academy and the Church? What between heretics and Christians?"[11]

Recently, Ian Barbour, retired Bean professor of science, technology, and society at Carleton College, presented four ways that science and faith have related to each other: conflict, independence, dialogue, and integration.[12] Although any taxonomy system places complex concepts into simple categories and although some people have moved from one category to another,[13] Barbour's categories are a convenient way to discuss faith and knowledge interactions.

Conflict

When I recently began writing a book[14] on the relationship between science and religion, a common comment was that I would have to write a short book because the two are in conflict. Amazingly, I experienced this reaction both within and without the academy; within and without the church. Some within the church see the knowledge of the academy as a challenge to faith.[15] Growing up in a country church, I heard a few sermons warning that too much knowledge could ruin one's faith. Those outside the church see the conflict category in terms of religion trying to restrict science. Two works that popularized this view were J. W. Darper's *History of the Conflict between Religion and Science* (1874) and A. D. White's *A History of the Warfare of Science with Theology in Christendom* (1896). Although there have been conflicts between faith and science over certain issues, I do not believe that faith and knowledge have to be in conflict.

Independence

Those holding the independence view see no connection between faith and science. This view states that each has its own sphere and each should keep out of the other's way. In this view, faith is a private matter dealing with *why* while science is a public matter dealing with *how*. The neoorthodoxy theological renaissance held the independence view. As Paul Tillich said, "Science is the cognitive approach to the whole of finite objects, their interrelations and their processes. Religion is the total approach to that which gives meaning to our life. . . . All statements about facts, structures, processes and events in nature, man and history, are objects of scientific research and cannot be made in the name of religion."[16]

Another example of the independence view is that expressed by the scientist Stephen Jay Gould in *Rocks of Ages: Science and Religion in the Fullness of Life* (1999). He calls this independence nonoverlapping magisteria (NOMA). Gould says, "I do not see how science and religion could be unified . . . but I also do not understand why the two enterprises should experience any conflict. Science tries to document the factual character of the natural world. . . . Religion, on the other hand, operates in the equally important, but utterly different realm of human purposes, meaning, and values."[17]

The independence view does create a split in the human mind. As John Dewey wrote, "If the physical terms by which modern science deals with the world are supposed to constitute that world, it follows as a matter of course that qualities we experience and which are the distinctive things in human life, fall outside nature."[18] Thus, according to the independence view, love, beauty, and faith would fall outside of reality. Independence is not a satisfactory viewpoint for one who believes that there is one reality; such a viewpoint leads one to the categories of dialogue and integration.

Dialogue and Integration

Since there is a wholeness to truth, and all truth is God's truth,[19] faith has much to say in the conversion of information into knowledge. As Pope John Paul II said, "Science can purify religion from error and superstition; religion can purify science from idolatry and false absolutes. Each can draw the other into a wider world, a world in which both can flourish."[20] As Harold Heie, mathematician and director of the Center for

Christian Studies at Gordon College, wrote, "I believe that every discipline is informed by ontological assumptions. . . . But ontological assumptions are also part of my biblical and theological understanding. . . . And I also believe that every discipline is informed by axiological assumptions about what is of value. . . . But value commitments are also part of my biblical and theological understanding."[21] Faith and knowledge have much to share with each other. Faith is another window through which understanding comes.

FAITH AS A WINDOW ON KNOWLEDGE

Many say that injecting faith into the information-gathering, knowledge-formation process results in a dead end. They say once God is invoked, further exploration is ruled out. An example of this thought process is represented by Robert Pennock in *Tower of Babel* when he discussed Michael Behe's book *Darwin's Black Box*. Behe proposed that certain biochemical processes are so complex that they could have arisen only by intelligent design. Pennock writes:

> The most that Behe has done there is to point to a number of interesting research problems. One wonders why he, as a biochemist, does not begin the research himself. . . . Of course, Behe has no motivation to pursue the research himself, since he thinks he already knows the answer—biochemical complexity was produced by the intentional action of an intelligent designer. With intelligent-design theory, Behe has found a way to save himself a lot of work.[22]

Pennock confuses how to carry out an experiment with how to interpret an experiment. The worldview of the experimenter will influence what questions are asked and how the experimental results are interpreted.[23] As we saw in the case of Priestley and Lavoisier, the same experiments and the same experimental results can lead to vastly different conclusions due to the worldview of the investigator. Another example of the power of presuppositions is Albert Einstein's belief in the static model for the universe. Einstein's theory of relativity predicted that the universe should be expanding. Because Einstein believed that the universe is static, he modified his equations to predict a static universe. Einstein let his worldview dominate his prediction. Einstein later said that this was the greatest mistake of his life.

My reading of history reveals that faith has made many positive contributions to the accumulation of knowledge. In many cases, faith did not stifle the acquisition of knowledge but provided the insight needed to advance understanding at many key points. Let us examine several examples of key insights provided by faith in the history of science. Such examples include development of science in the West along with the work of Johannes Kepler, Carolus Linnaeus, Louis Pasteur, George Washington Carver, Georges Lemaître, and the Intelligent Design movement.

Key Insights

When one considers the history of modern science and its contributions to knowledge, one sees that there were many areas of the ancient world that could have been home to our modern way of knowing. The ancient Greeks provided many concepts that are important to our modern way of knowing: observation (Aristotle), theory (Plato), mathematics (Pythagoras), astronomy (Ptolemy), and technology (Archimedes). The ancient Chinese made great discoveries: gunpowder, the compass, papermaking, the rocket, silk production, and accurate astronomy records. Yet neither culture was where modern science developed. Why? Science begins with the assumption that the universe is knowable, regular, predictable, and uniform. To the ancient Greeks, the capricious behavior of gods and goddesses made nature unpredictable. The ancient Chinese were never convinced that humans could understand the divine code that rules nature. Modern science developed in a culture that had a window that saw the universe as knowable, regular, predictable, and uniform. The Christian faith provided such a window.[24]

The Christian belief in a Creator provided the basis for the assumption that the universe was really there and had value. Such an idea would be antithetical to a worldview such as

Buddhism. The Christian faith provided the basis for the assumption that nature could be studied since it was a creation of God, not a god itself who might retaliate against too much probing or curiosity. The Christian view of God as a moral lawgiver also encouraged them to look for natural laws. The Christian faith in an eternal and omnipresent God led to the assumption that any natural laws would be uniform throughout the universe. Thus, the Christian faith had provided a window that saw the universe as knowable, regular, predictable, and uniform.

Experimental science was encouraged by the belief in creation *ex nihilo*. The concept of creation *ex nihilo* meant that God was not constrained by preexisting matter since he created the universe out of nothing. Thus, rational deduction will not provide the details of the universe; one must actually do the observations. Christian belief in the Fall of mankind in the garden of Eden encouraged Christian scientists to develop technology to help alleviate the destructive effects of the Fall. To the Christian, the faith in a Creator God presented nature as another avenue for discovering information about God. As Francis Bacon stated in 1605:

> Our saviour saith, "You err, not knowing the scriptures, nor the power of God"; laying before us two books or volumes to study, if we will be secured from error; first the scriptures, revealing the will of God, and then the creatures expressing the power; whereof the latter is a key unto the former: not only opening our understanding to conceive the true sense of the scriptures, by the general notions of reason and rules of speech; but chiefly opening our belief, in drawing us into a due meditation of the omnipotency of God, which is chiefly signed and engraven upon his works.[25]

Thus, faith encouraged the study of nature.

Johannes Kepler (1571–1630) was the German astronomer who formulated the three laws of planetary motion. Kepler was born near present-day Stuttgart, Germany, on December 27, 1571. He studied theology and classics at the University of

Tübingen. At Tübingen, he accepted the Copernican theory for a sun-centered planetary system. He had planned on becoming a Lutheran minister but instead accepted a chair in mathematics and astronomy at Graz. Kepler had accepted the Copernican theory because of its simplicity. He believed that God created *ex nihilo* and that his creation would be simple and God's plan of creation would be observable. In 1596, at the age of twenty-four, Kepler published *Mysterium Cosmographicum (Cosmographic Mystery)* in which he defended Copernican theory and described a structure of the universe based on the five Pythagorean regular solids.

Kepler's book so impressed Tycho Brahe, the greatest astronomical observer before the telescope, that he invited Kepler to be his assistant in Prague. Kepler gladly accepted, because Catholic persecution of the Protestant minority in Graz was intense. Within a year of Kepler's appointment, Brahe died in 1601. Kepler was appointed his successor as mathematician at the court of Emperor Rudolph II. Importantly, Kepler inherited Brahe's observations and now had the information he needed to determine God's plan of creation. Kepler tried and rejected many models over a six-year period. Although many of his models were more accurate in their predictions than previous models, Kepler was not satisfied because they were not as accurate as Brahe's data. His faith that God created accurately and simply kept Kepler going until he found "God's plan."

Kepler's findings are today called Kepler's laws of planetary motion. The heart of these laws is that the planets travel in elliptical orbits rather than in circular paths. He published his findings in *Astronomia Nova (New Astronomy,* 1609) and *Harmonice Mundi (Harmony of the World,* 1619). Kepler's faith did not discourage his quest for knowledge but rather kept him going at a time when his previous findings were "great" by the standards of his day. On a personal note, although Kepler found "the Harmony of the World," his personal life was anything but harmonious. He faced religious persecution all his life; five of his nine children died before he did; his first wife also died; his mother was tried as a witch. Yet through all this,

Kepler kept searching for the harmony God put in his creation so that Kepler might worship God by finding it.

Carolus Linnaeus (1707–1778) was a Swedish naturalist who developed the binomial system for classifying and organizing plants and animals. Linnaeus was born Carl von Linne in a small town in rural Sweden. His father, a minister, wanted him to study for the ministry. Once he realized Linnaeus's talent with plants, he instead sent him, in 1727, to medical school because it included training in botany.

By 1730, Linnaeus recognized that the current botany classification system was flawed, and he began developing his own method. With a fifty-dollar grant from the Royal Society of Science, he spent five months in 1732 collecting plants in Lapland. During this collection trip, he walked nearly one thousand miles. In 1735, he left Sweden to complete his medical training in Holland. That year he published *Systema Naturae,* which presented his new taxonomic system. (He became known as Carolus Linnaeus because he wrote in Latin.) His system is called binomial nomenclature because it assigned a unique two-word Latin name to each organism. The first word refers to the genus to which the organism belongs while the second word refers to the species. For example, the dog has the scientific name, *Canis familiaris,* where *Canis* is its genus and *familiaris* is its species name.

In 1738 Linnaeus returned to Sweden and was instrumental in establishing the Swedish Academy of Science. In 1742, he became professor of botany at the University of Uppsala. The tenth edition of *Systema Naturae* (1758) extended his system from plants to animals. In this book Linnaeus first classified humans as *Homo sapiens.* His inspiration for a classification system was his belief in God's original creation of fixed "kinds." His faith in God the Creator convinced him that there would be common characteristics within similar types of organisms that would allow him to classify them. Using his faith as a window to knowledge allowed him to classify nearly six thousand plants with names still used today.

Linnaeus's faith in "fixed kinds" might be viewed by someone like Robert Pennock as a research stopper. Rather than limiting Linnaeus's research, this belief spurred Linnaeus to search to see how the concept of "fixed kinds" fit into his classification scheme. At first, based on his observation of a limited number of species in Scandinavia, he thought that species referred to the Genesis kinds. As he was exposed to more organisms from other areas, he became convinced that species can change and that the genus level corresponded to the "fixed kinds." Finally, he revised his thinking to propose that the order level corresponded to the "fixed kinds." The life of Linnaeus is another example of faith providing a window that led to a very productive scientific career.

Louis Pasteur (1822–1895) was the famous French chemist and biologist noted for founding microbiology, proposing the germ theory of disease, inventing pasteurization, and developing vaccines for diseases. Pasteur, the son of a tanner, was raised in a small town in eastern France. In 1847, he earned his doctorate in physics and chemistry from the École Normale in Paris. An important question in Pasteur's day was whether spontaneous generation could occur. Spontaneous generation or abiogenesis is the theory that living organisms can be spontaneously formed from lifeless matter. People thought that toads, snakes, and mice could arise from moist soil, that maggots could emerge from decaying matter, and that flies could arise from manure, and that microorganisms could appear in boiled nutrient fluids.

Pasteur approached this problem through his window of faith in God as Creator of life. He believed that life was more than a set of chemical reactions. Again, Pasteur's faith in God as Creator of life might be viewed as a research stopper. Pasteur could have said that God created life and thus there was no need to investigate spontaneous generation further. Rather, Pasteur used this faith plus his skill as a chemist and microbiologist to devise ingenious experiments to test whether spontaneous generation was occurring. Pasteur's work showed that life does not arise from nonlife. Any microorganisms that "spontaneously" appear come as a contamination from the air or the fluids. (Some of Pasteur's experiments are on display at the Pasteur Institute in Paris and still have no sign of life after over one hundred years.)

These discoveries of Pasteur form the basis of aseptic techniques currently used in laboratories and medical facilities to prevent contamination by microorganisms. Pasteur's faith provided a window that led to new insights in microbiology, fermentation, germ theory, and so forth.

George Washington Carver (1864–1943) was an African-American scientist who won international fame as an outstanding innovator in agricultural sciences. Carver was born into slavery in Diamond, Missouri. He received a bachelor of science degree (1894) and master's degree in agriculture and bacterial botany (1896) from what is today Iowa State University. In 1896, he accepted Booker T. Washington's invitation to become director of the department of agricultural research at Tuskegee Institute (now Tuskegee University) in Alabama. Arriving in the South, Carver found the farmland depleted from intensive cultivation of cotton. Carver immediately began applying his agricultural knowledge to the problems around him: replenish the soil with crop rotation, use legumes as natural fertilizer, improve a diet consisting of the three M's (meat, meal, molasses) with vegetables and fruits.

The legumes Carver chose to promote were plants familiar to the farmers but plants that they considered useless: cowpeas (good only for cows to eat) and peanuts (called by the African name *goober* and considered a weed). As the boll weevil destroyed the cotton crops, farmers began to try Carver's peanuts. Now Carver really had a problem: what to do with all the peanuts. Today, peanut production is a worldwide agricultural activity; then, there were no markets for peanuts. What was the creator of this problem going to do? Carver remembered a verse from Genesis, "And God said, Behold, I have given you every herb bearing seed, which is upon the face of all the earth, and every tree, in the which is the fruit of a tree yielding seed; to you it shall be for meat" (Gen. 1:29 KJV).

Using this faith as a window, Carver began taking the peanut apart. When he was through, he had discovered over three hundred products that could be made from the peanut: cheese, milk, coffee, flour, ink, dyes, plastics, wood stains, soap, linoleum, mineral oils, cosmetics, and of course peanut butter. With the insight from his faith, he created a whole new industry and helped revitalize agriculture in the South.

Georges Lemaître (1894–1966) was a Belgian priest and astronomer who proposed an expanding model of the universe. After being trained as a civil engineer, Lemaître served as an artillery officer in the Belgian army during World War I. After the war he entered the seminary and was ordained as a priest in 1923. Then Lemaître studied astronomy at the University of Cambridge (1923–24) and MIT (1925–27). During his studies, he was exposed to the continuing debate about the nature of the universe: static (as we saw, Einstein modified his relativity equations to maintain a static universe) or dynamic (Edwin Hubble and Harlow Shapley had experimental evidence that implied the galaxies were moving apart). In 1927, he was appointed professor of astrophysics at the University of Louvain, Belgium. After reviewing Einstein's relativistic equations and the work of Hubble and Shapley (galactic red shift data), Lemaître, in 1931, proposed the first scientific creation cosmology or cosmogony. He proposed that the universe began as "primeval atom," which exploded to cause an expanding universe. His faith in a Creator God allowed Lemaître to be comfortable with the concept of a dynamic universe with a beginning, a concept that clashed with the thousand-year-old view of a static universe without a beginning.

The Russian-American physicist George Gamow (1904–1968) further refined Lemaître's proposal into the currently accepted Big Bang model of the origin and structure of the universe. There is consonance between the Big Bang model and theological claims of God creating the universe. Some have carried the relationship beyond consonance to apologetics.

For example, Pope Pius XII in 1951 said that the beginning of the Big Bang provided grounds for belief in God. Lemaître was more cautious; he did not want to tie his window of understanding to apologetics. Lemaître opposed basing one's religious proofs on science because scientific theories are never complete and are subject to refinements. Thus, a faith based on scientific theories appears to crumble when the scientific theory changes. As the case of Lemaître and Pope Pius XII shows, one has to be careful to separate faith's window of understanding from apologetics.

Intelligent Design Movement

The concept of design in nature has been used throughout the history of theism. From the authors of the books of the Bible (for example, Ps. 19:1–4 and Rom. 1:20), to medieval scholars (Thomas Aquinas in the thirteenth century) to William Paley in the seventeenth century, theists have presented arguments about the design in nature pointing toward a Creator God. The modern Intelligent Design movement goes beyond this early work by proposing precise rules for distinguishing an intelligently caused event or object from an unintelligently caused event or object. The modern design movement draws on the work of archeology, artificial intelligence, cryptography, forensic science, and the search extraterrestrial intelligence; in each of these areas, scientists must distinguish an intelligently caused event or object from an unintelligently caused event or object.

A leader in this modern movement is William Dembski, former director of the Michael Polanyi Center at Baylor University. Dembski has developed a flowchart, which he calls the Explanatory Filter, to distinguish between law, change, or design causations. Dembski says that the Explanatory Filter will allow a person to select designed events, which he calls specified complex events, from events caused by chance.

Another leader in the modern design movement is Michael Behe, associate professor of biochemistry at Lehigh University. Behe has investigated the behavior of the biochemicals located in the cell. He has found what he calls irreducibly complex systems, such as vision and blood clotting. Behe says that irreducibly complex systems are so dependent on all their parts that removing one component renders the irreducibly complex system nonfunctional. Thus, he proposes that irreducibly complex systems must have been designed that way by an intelligence.

The faith of those in the design movement allows them to propose new explanations (other than chance) for certain complex events in nature. Does this faith stop research as Pennock has speculated? No. The Intelligent Design scientists, now that they have a framework within which to work, are designing and carrying out experiments to test the limits of their proposals.[26]

FAITH AS A WINDOW, NOT A BLINDER

Anyone who has watched a team of horses work will notice that one or more of the horses will be wearing blinders. The blinders are flaps on the outside of the horse's eyes that keep the horse from seeing anything on the periphery. If one is not careful, any worldview or paradigm can blind one to information that does not fit the worldview. The worldview can make one see only the information that supports a particular point and blind one to information on the periphery that may question the worldview interpretation. One must be careful and make sure that the worldview of faith is not used as a blinder.

There are many cases in the history of science where a worldview has blinded the investigators to peripheral information that challenges the worldview interpretation of the data. The work of Priestley that was previously discussed is an example of worldview blinding the scholar to peripheral information. Let us briefly examine three other cases of where the worldview of the scientists acted as a blinder rather than a window: Piltdown man, Paluxy River human/dinosaur tracks,[27] and Chinese bird-dinosaur.

Piltdown Man

In 1912, the amateur naturalist, Charles Dawson, announced the discovery of fossil bones and tools in gravel at Piltdown in southern England. The fossil find consisted of the cranium of a man and the teeth and jaw of an ape. Since scientists at the time were looking for the missing link between man and ape to support Darwin's theory of evolution, the Piltdown discovery was hailed as this missing link. With time, scientists began looking at the periphery and noticed that no other fossils were in the gravel bed at Piltdown, that the Piltdown fossil did not fit into fossil patterns that were being found at other sites around the world, and the Piltdown fossil looked just like a modern human skull combined with an ape jaw. Finally in 1953, scholars were able to show that Piltdown was a forgery. They reported that the jaw of a modern orangutan stained to look old and a six-hundred-year-old human skull had been used in the Piltdown hoax. Initially, the worldview of the scholars blinded them to the peripheral information that should have raised question about their interpretation of "missing link."

Paluxy River Human/Dinosaur Tracks

Near Glen Rose, Texas, along the Paluxy River are limestone beds that contain many three-toed dinosaur tracks. Mixed in with these dinosaur tracks are elongated tracks between fifteen and twenty-four inches long. In 1939, Roland Bird, paleontologist from the American Museum of Natural History, reported these facts in *Natural History*. Those with a young-earth worldview hailed these discoveries as proof that humans and dinosaurs ("giants in the earth" Gen. 6:4 KJV) had lived at the same time and that this was a startling proof that the earth was young rather than billions of years old.

As in the case of Piltdown man, scholars here let their worldview blind them to the peripheral facts. Careful observation revealed that the so-called human prints actually had faint three-toe imprints similar to other dinosaur tracks; these dinosaurs had been walking by placing weight on their soles and heels. This case is not a direct hoax like Piltdown man. But how people use this information can verge on a hoax. During the Great Depression, it has been reported, some people carved human prints into the rocks to sell to "scholars." Also in the young-earth movement, one can still hear reference to these tracks as proof that humans and dinosaurs existed together.

Chinese Bird-Dinosaur

This third example is included to show that the worldview blinders are still functioning today. In early 1999, an amazing fossil was found at a gem and mineral show in Utah. The fossil was said to be from the Liaoning area of China, a fossil-rich area that has yielded many new species related to birds and dinosaurs. The description of the fossil appeared in the November 1999 issue of *National Geographic*. The article states, "I've seen feather dinosaur specimens before, but [this specimen] takes my breath away. Its long arms and small body scream 'Bird!' Its long, stiff tail . . . screams 'Dinosaur!'"[28] The specimen, named *Archaeoraptor liaoningensis* is declared to be the "missing link" between dinosaurs and birds. The article also discussed two other dinosaur specimens that have fibrous structures that could be feathers.

By January 2000, scientific concerns abut the authenticity of *Archaeoraptor* had been raised.[29] *National Geographic* promised to print a retraction about *Archaeoraptor* in its March issue. However, in the March issue all that was published was a short letter to the editor by Xu Xing, one of the Chinese scientists who originally examined *Archaeoraptor*. His conclusion was, "Though I do not want to admit it, *Archaeoraptor* appears to be composed of a [dinosaur] tail and a bird body."[30]

What went wrong? The scholars let their worldview of the connection between birds and dinosaurs blind them to peripheral data. The peripheral information concluded that the history of the fossil was unknown; it was thought to be a Chinese fossil illegally smuggled into the United States and purchased from a fossil dealer in Utah. The rocks containing the fossil are split, with the bones connecting the dinosaur tail to the bird body missing. *National Geographic* compounded the problem by rushing the "findings" to print before there was peer review. In this case, the good news is that the scientific community quickly raised questions about the validity of this fossil. The bad news is the reputation of *National Geographic* is damaged and the validity of the other "feathered" dinosaurs discussed in the November 1999 article is questioned.

In all these cases, the worldview blinded the scholars to peripheral data that raised questions about the central hypothesis. In all cases, the scientific community ultimately discovered the "facts." With more practicing scientists and faster communication, the time for corrections gets faster and faster. In the case of Piltdown man years, and months in the case of the Chinese bird/dinosaur. There is no grand conspiracy to fool the public; there are a few scholars who have let their worldview make them do sloppy work. Combine sloppy work with the rush to print, and one has a perfect combination for embarrassment. Scholars of faith must be diligent to ensure that they keep the blinders off. If it is just too good to be true, it should be looked at even harder with the full force of all the light coming through the window of understanding.

SUMMARY

In our modern society, the scientific method has become the preferred way of knowing not only in the natural sciences but also in the social sciences. Although some see conflict or independence as the preferred relationship between faith and science, faith has much to contribute to the conversion of information into knowledge. Faith provides a window through which understanding comes. One has to be careful not to let one's worldview blind one to see only what supports that worldview. Faith has provided the window of understanding that allowed modern science to develop in the West and provided key insight to scholars such as Kepler and Pasteur.

CHAPTER 7

CHRISTIAN WORLDVIEW AND LITERATURE

Barbara McMillin

IN THE AFTERWORD to *Contemporary Literary Theory: A Christian Appraisal,* Leland Ryken concludes that Christian criticism "based on the broad foundation of Christian doctrine will intersect at virtually every turn with critical traditions from Aristotle through the latest critical fashion. Some of the intersections will produce collisions, while others will result in smooth mergers."[1] Aware that to embark on studies of deconstruction, Marxism, feminism, and psychoanalytical criticism is to embark on clearly labeled collision courses, what are Christian literature professors to do? Avoid all dangerous intersections, opting instead to travel only the routes characterized by Ryken's smooth mergers? Choosing this option will of course produce students who are not well traveled, students who are ill equipped to navigate the challenging intersections—intersections that will not be optional for the Christian student who later pursues a graduate school itinerary.

On the contrary, literature professors in Christian higher education can and should proceed toward the inevitable collisions that deconstruction and other approaches afford, confident in the truth that the faith of their students will emerge unscathed if not strengthened.

Aware that the road ahead will be hazardous, how then can a literature professor prepare herself and her students for the journey? What device or strategy will best absorb the shock when one's Christianity crashes head-on with a given critical theory? I recommend the following plan of action:

1. *Anticipate the collisions.* Students who are braced for the impact are less likely to sustain ideological injuries when they are confronted with, for instance, the tenets of Marxism. Such forewarning occurs when the professor openly addresses the sectors at which the approach and Christianity collide while introducing a new approach.

2. *Encourage dialogue.* While practicing a specific approach, students should be encouraged to articulate their misgivings, their discomfort, or even their resentment. If these thoughts and feelings are suppressed, students may harbor so much ill will toward the approach that they simply cannot force themselves to experiment effectively with its practical application. Furthermore, some students need to be reminded that being a member of a "movement," such as feminism, is not a prerequisite for practicing feminist critical theory. Allowing students to acknowledge openly their dislike of a given approach tends to make applying it less threatening, less branding. Professors as well should express their concerns—not only to foster a healthy discussion but to remind students that what one must teach and what one professes personally are often diametrically opposed!

3. *Recognize the advantages.* Frequently the literature professor will discover that most critical approaches, even those considered at greatest odds with Christianity, can be applied from a Christian worldview and can yield compelling and insightful Christian analysis of a given text. Allow me to illustrate by casting in a Christian light some basic questions asked by selected critical camps.

Reader-Response Criticism

Granting biblical exegetes the right to scorn the apparent relativism of Stanley Fish's "interpretive communities," the literature professor, working not with divinely inspired texts but with the texts of mere mortals, can assume the role of reader-response critic—at least for the purpose of initiating student interest in a given work. To develop Louise Rosenblatt's "aesthetic readers" (readers whose relationship to a work extends beyond data collection to appreciation and identification),[2] a

Christian professor can and should encourage students to ask the standard question: How does the work make me feel?

For instance, after reading Faulkner's "Barn Burning," students might be asked how they feel about Sarty's having betrayed his father by alerting Major DeSpain of Abner's plan to burn yet another barn. From a Christian perspective, does Sarty do the right thing in choosing to tattle on his father, the pyromaniac? Students at a Christian college will likely recognize in Faulkner's plot a conflict between righteousness and blood loyalty, perhaps even viewing Sarty as one who forsakes all to pursue a higher call.

Furthermore, a student who initially condemns Sarty as a traitor to his family may refine his view as the Christian interpretive community composed of his classmates engages in conversation about the text and thus makes "meaning," for, in reader-response circles, meaning is the product of shared reactions. Thus, a discussion about how a given text makes one feel may not only enhance a reader's involvement with and appreciation for the work, but, when the interpretive community is Christian, the process of sharing one's feelings may also serve to refine or strengthen one's Christian worldview.

Biographical Criticism

The biographical critic approaches a work of literature determined to reveal connections between an author's life and the text that he or she has produced. For the Christian professor, this approach provides an opportunity not only to practice the integration of faith and discipline but also to witness such integration as it happens on the printed page. Responding to "Is the writer a Christian, and, if so, how is his or her Christianity revealed in the text?" a student soon discovers that a writer's faith may either be overtly heralded or more subtly suggested. For instance, a student performing a biographical analysis of Katherine Anne Porter's short story "Noon Wine" will find that the writer's spirituality is scarcely perceptible to an uninformed reader. However, as the student learns of Porter's Catholicism and of her tendency to compose "spiritual allegories in which characters and objects are emblems of universal moral issues,"[3] the spiritual message of "Noon Wine" becomes clear.

As a case in point, students in my most recent short story class were intrigued when I referred to Porter's story as a spiritual allegory, for they clearly had not recognized the work's spiritual dimensions on first reading. Once enlightened regarding Porter's background and style, they enthusiastically set about the task of unravelling the allegory, concluding that "Noon Wine" is, in fact, a modern "Judas" story. (A word of caution is necessary here: at a Christian university students seldom need much prompting to examine the spiritual aspect of a given text. While such cooperation may appear to be ideal, professors must be prepared to corral zealous students who sometimes force a Christian reading of a work when, in fact, there is no substantive biographical or textual evidence for such a rendering.)

Unlike Porter, other writers of faith are far less covert stylistically. Certainly there is little doubt concerning the Christian commitment of the likes of Milton, Bunyan, Donne, Herbert, Taylor, and Bradstreet. With such as these, Christian professor and student alike can have a field day. Conversely, does the knowledge that an author is unapologetically non-Christian preempt any possibility of a learning experience that combines faith and discipline? The answer is a resounding no! British Romantic poet Percy Bysshe Shelley was expelled from Oxford and disowned by his family following his coauthorship of *The Necessity of Atheism*; but his blatant denial of God does not negate the beauty of his poetry—nor does it prohibit professors in a Christian environment from conducting a worthwhile and stimulating analysis of Shelley's works. To illustrate, let's take a closer look at the last stanza of Shelley's "Ode to the West Wind":

> Make me thy lyre, even as the forest is:
> What if my leaves are falling like its own!
> The tumult of thy mighty harmonies
>
> Will take from both a deep, autumnal tone,
> Sweet though in sadness. Be thou, Spirit fierce,
> My spirit! Be thou me, impetuous one!

Drive my dead thoughts over the universe
Like withered leaves to quicken a new birth!
And, by the incantation of this verse,

Scatter, as from an unextinguished hearth
Ashes and sparks, my words among mankind!
Be through my lips to unawakened Earth

The trumpet of a prophecy! O Wind,
If Winter comes, can Spring be far behind?[4]

Tempered by knowledge of Shelley's atheism, students will detect in this apostrophe the author's yearning for vitality, for immortality, and for hope—yearnings that Christians will contend are satisfied not by a mystical bond with nature but only by trusting one's life to Jesus Christ. Recalling their own failed attempts to fill a God-sized void with something or someone other than God, Christian students are likely to recognize and identify, in hindsight, with Shelley's desperation. In short, despite disagreeing with Shelley's solution, students can still confirm the truth of his emotions. For, as Susan V. Gallagher and Roger Lundin remind us in *Literature Through the Eyes of Faith*, "Works of literature that do not articulate specific Christian ideas can express ideas that are congruent with our Christianity."[5]

New Criticism

Reacting to the "affective fallacy" committed by the reader-response critic and to the "intentional fallacy" made by the biographical critic, practitioners of the New Criticism contend that meaning resides in the text and the text alone. Sometimes called formalism or the "Brooks and Warren" approach (in tribute to its "founders" Cleanth Brooks and Robert Penn Warren), New Criticism reigned supreme in literature classrooms during the middle decades of this century, causing Wilcox and Jones to note that, for at least one generation, it was "as powerful in literary criticism as the triumphant capitalist economy has been in the United States for the past ten years."[6]

In the process of *explication de texte* new critics examine only what the text itself offers, asking such questions as these:

1. How are the elements of a short story developed? What is the turning point? How is the main character developed? Is the setting significant? What is the point of view? What is distinctive about the writer's style? Is the story allegorical? How do all of these elements contribute to the story's theme?

2. What poetic conventions are evident in the poem? (In other words, identify any allusions, symbols, paradoxes, sound devices, and figurative language within the work. Describe the poem's tone, its use of irony, and its structure.) How do these conventions contribute to the unity of the text?

3. How is the drama developed? Identify the protagonist and antagonist. Does the play conform to a pyramidal pattern? Examine the dialogue for imagery and foreshadowing. What is the unifying theme?

Given the constraints of such a text-focused approach, if Christianity is to enter into a new critical analysis, then it is clear that it must somehow be inherent to the text. It must reside in the allusions, the symbols, the imagery, or the dialogue, thus directly or indirectly shaping the text's theme. Fortunately, English literature can boast of no shortage of biblical references, a fact confirmed by David Lyle Jeffrey's *A Dictionary of Biblical Tradition in English Literature*. This massive reference work was "designed to help the modern reader understand how biblical motifs, concepts, names, quotations, and allusions have been transmitted through exegetical tradition and used by authors of English literature from the Middle Ages to the present."[7] This text, together with Roland Bartel's *Biblical Images in Literature*, testifies of the ample opportunities available to the new critics who espouse a Christian worldview.[8]

Marxist Criticism

In contrast to the New Criticism, Marxist theory did not begin as a school of literary analysis. Grounded in the teachings of Karl Marx and Friedrich Engels, Marxism began as an "opportunity and a plan for changing the world from a place of bigotry, hatred, and conflict resulting from class struggle to a classless society where wealth, opportunity, and education are actually accessible for all people."⁹ A materialist philosophy, Marxism stands in sharp contrast to Christianity. As Clarence Walhout explains,

> Christianity holds that human beings belong to a created order which is sustained by and always stands in relation to the Creator God, whose existence is metaphysically autonomous. Therefore, all understanding and value are to be defined in terms of the relationship of human beings to the divine Creator as he is revealed in the Christian scriptures.
>
> In contrast, Marxism holds that our historical identity as human beings is formed entirely by and within the material (i.e., historical) order of existence. Spiritual values arise as human beings exercise their powers of consciousness in a continuing struggle to master the forces of the material world. Spiritual life is defined not in relation to a transcendent God but in relation to the conditions of the concrete material world. These conditions are thought to be at the primary level economic or economic/political; that is, social organization for the purpose of survival and mastery is regarded as the most basic of human activities.¹⁰

Although seemingly an attempt to mix oil and water, a dialectical approach that brings both the theists and the atheists to the table can yield a more in-depth analysis of the text in question. As a case in point, let's examine what might happen if students were invited to debate the duke's motive for murdering his wife in Robert Browning's dramatic monologue "My Last Duchess."¹¹

Determined to expose the dominant class and its ideology, the designated Marxist half of the class will no doubt quickly label the duke a member of the bourgeoisie bent on shaping the values of his humble wife, who, because she does not recognize "his hundred-year-old name" and because she is willing to "stoop" to those beneath her station, is put to death, living on only in the painting that Fra Pandolph has produced. These would-be Marxists will also waste no time in pinpointing the duke's materialism, evident in his desire to obtain a new bride with an ample dowry and in his impressive art collection, featuring among other rarities a sea horse cast in bronze by Clause of Innsbruck and the aforementioned portrait of his last bride.

The "Christians," on the other hand, are likely to argue for pride—not class consciousness—as the motive that drives the duke to murder. From the Christian perspective, sin is an individual, not a group, responsibility. In other words, oppression, abuse, and murder are wrong primarily because they are contrary to the commandments of God, not just because they are the results of one economic group attempting to suppress another. Having debated these concepts, students will walk away from the experience with a better understanding of Marxist theory and, ideally, with a better understanding of individual responsibility.

Feminist Criticism

Like Marxist criticism, feminist criticism has its roots not in an academic setting but in a cultural movement to reveal and lament the marginalization of women in society. Feminist critics view the study of literature as yet another opportunity to decry sexism and to promote the accomplishments of female authors. In "Feminist Literary Criticism: A Chorus of Ethical Voices," Susan Van Zanten Gallagher also credits feminist criticism with "incorporating ethical commitment into the critical act."[12] This ethical commitment is the sector at which feminist criticism and Christianity merge. In addition to asking the standard questions raised by the gynocritics, the image-of-women critics, and the deconstructive feminists, a Christian professor should ask students to identify ways in which Christians and feminists share a common goal.

For a practical application, let's consider how a class in a Christian college might approach a feminist study of Henrik Ibsen's play *Hedda Gabler*. Having discussed such issues as how Hedda is shaped (or stifled) by her nineteenth-century Norwegian environment and if Hedda is in any way stereotypical, students can be encouraged to examine the ethics of Hedda's situation. Are any of Hedda's actions unethical? For starters, she tempts Loevborg to abandon abstinence and enjoy the bacchanalian pleasures available at Tesman's bachelor party. Later, out of jealousy she burns the manuscript representing the life's work of Loevborg and Mrs. Elvstead. She admonishes Loevborg to use her own pistol to take his life and thus die "beautifully." Rendered powerless by Judge Brack's knowledge that she has been indirectly involved with Loevborg's death, Hedda opts to take her own life rather than live oppressed by the judge's blackmail.

While it may be impossible for feminists and Christians to reconcile the causes of Hedda's various unethical actions, it is very possible for all involved to agree on what is right and wrong about Hedda's behavior. Such agreement signals the point at which Christianity and feminism intersect: both lament oppression, and both lament the reactions of what one calls a sinner and the other calls a victim. Thus, a student wearing the guise of a feminist may discover that answering the feminist questions unearths issues that are paramount for Christian and feminist alike.

Psychological Criticism

In "Psychological Criticism: From the Imagination to Freud and Beyond," Alan Jacobs admits, following a careful examination of the Romantic concept of the imagination in contrast with Freud's theories of the unconscious, that "right now . . . psychological criticism from a Christian perspective is virtually non-existent."[13] Such a state of affairs is hardly encouraging for the Christian professor faced with the tasks of defining the Oedipus complex and describing the antics of the id. I must contend, however, that hope resides in the analysis of Freudian lingo. While students in a Christian setting may be at worst shocked and at best amused by some of Freud's explanations, these same students will in all likelihood respond favorably if asked to match Freud's terminology with a corresponding biblical phrase or concept.

For instance, a Freudian critic might interpret the monomaniacal behavior of Captain Ahab, of Melville's *Moby Dick,* as a neurotic expression of a repressed childhood emotion; a Christian, on the other hand, might see Ahab's actions as the manifestation of unconfessed sin. Hawthorne's Young Goodman Brown may be dubbed a classic illustration of the struggles between the id, ego, and superego from the Freudian perspective. The Christian critic, however, may just as quickly detect Satan's forces in conflict with the Holy Spirit over the soul of Hawthorne's title character. Admittedly, this substituting of names could be hastily dismissed as an exercise in semantics; its significance materializes when students realize the teleological void inherent in Freud's language. In other words, there is clearly no eternal significance to the labels affixed by the psychoanalytical critic.

Deconstruction

To attempt a definition of deconstruction is to defy the very principles on which the movement rests; however, a few words of explanation are necessary. Having surfaced in the 1960s as a reaction to the structuralism of Ferdinand de Saussure, deconstruction is considered the brainchild of French philosopher Jacques Derrida. Sometimes called the "father of modern linguistics," Saussure had posited that there is no inherent relationship between a "signifier" (a word) and its "signified" (the object that it names).[14] In short, "cat" is simply an arbitrary label for a feline, there being nothing about the feline that conjures up the term *cat.* Furthermore, meaning resides not in a given signifier but in the contrast that occurs between signifiers. In other words, I know the difference between a "cat" and a "hat" because I hear the different initial consonant sounds; meaning occurs when I process different sounds.

Derrida takes Saussure's theories a step further by noting that signifieds are just as relative as signifiers. For instance, an object, let's say a poem, has meaning only in relation to other poems. Simply put, my only means of critiquing "Stopping by Woods on a Snowy Evening" is by contrasting it with another poem. Only then does its value become obvious.

Based on this view of the signifier and the signified, Derrida recognized within Western philosophy a supposed fundamental error: the existence of a transcendental signified—a signified that is absolute, needing no other signified to give it meaning. (For the Christian community, the transcendental signifier is God.) Furthermore, according to Derrida, Western philosophy is also erroneously based on a system of binary opposites. If there is good, there is also bad; if there is truth, there are also lies. If one believes in the existence of a transcendental signified, then one half of each pair of opposites assumes a privileged status. However, if one denies the existence of a transcendental signified, then such privileging cannot occur. In other words, good ceases to be better than bad if there is no absolute standard (i.e., God) that serves to promote goodness. If no absolute standard exists, the result is a meltdown, a deconstruction.

How does this way of thinking impact the reading of a given work of literature? In Alan Jacobs's words, deconstruction "transforms an experience as potentially joyful and exhilarating as reading into an especially bitter form of warfare."[15] He adds that deconstruction

is particularly regrettable in that it does not allow the reader to see the textual encounter as a potentially enriching, even ennobling thing; it makes no provision for the possibility that what a text may exercise over us is not necessarily sheer power but rather a legitimate *authority,* like that which Kent recognized in Lear, or which distinguished Jesus from the (far more powerful) scribes. It further denies us the ability to distinguish between those texts that enrich and those that demean or insult. If every text always deconstructs itself before our very eyes, then we can never learn anything from it; we can only use it for our pleasure, diminish it into a plaything, force it into our already-fixed world of understanding and discourse. Deconstruction makes a prison-house not only of language but also of personhood.[16]

Given such negative effects, shouldn't Christian scholars avoid any approach that even remotely resembles deconstruction? The answer is yes if Jacobs is correct in stating that we can never learn anything from a text that seemingly deconstructs itself. I must contend, however, that the "process" of deconstruction can contribute to an enriched reading of the text—even when the reader is firmly committed to the existence of a transcendental signified.

For instance, students given the task of determining how Flannery O'Connor's short story "A Good Man Is Hard to Find" deconstructs will first attempt to identify the text's binary opposites. The result will include such pairs as good versus evil, truth versus falsehood, past versus present, and age versus youth This step alone can enrich one's understanding of the story, for it is unlikely on a first reading for a student to process a work as a series of contrasts. Next, a class can examine the binary opposites to determine which item within each pair has privileged status. Aware of O'Connor's Catholicism, one would expect goodness and truth to occupy positions of privilege, until the reader admits that telling the truth about the Misfit's identity is what ultimately takes the life of the grandmother and that it is the evil Misfit who walks away the winner at story's end.

Does this apparent "de-privileging" of goodness and truth damage a Christian reader's worldview? Does deconstruction foster cynicism? Certainly it can in this instance if the discussion proceeds no further. However, the Christian professor may discover that engaging students in a deconstructive reading may provide a perfect opportunity to demonstrate how a writer such as O'Connor uses irony to define goodness and reveal truth. After all, the Misfit, murderer that he is, serves as a foil who exposes the grandmother's superficial goodness while he exhibits a greater respect for truth.

Thus, the *tools* of deconstruction, if used only at the most rudimentary levels, can yield discussions within Christian settings that actually enhance the values established by the transcendental signified. The denial of absolute truth and the confirmation of relativism, however, render a full deconstructive reading of a text incompatible with a Christian worldview.

CONCLUDING REMARKS

So what does happen when Christianity and criticism collide? Do Christian travellers on this collision course inevitably sustain serious spiritual injuries? The answer is no—provided the driver (i.e., the professor) has braced all passengers by equipping them for the impact. In fact, these student travelers may discover that having survived the collisions they are now better prepared for what they have yet to encounter on both their spiritual and their scholarly journeys.

CHAPTER 8

CHRISTIAN WORLDVIEW AND NATURAL SCIENCE

GLENN A. MARSCH

Dateline 2001

LIQUID WATER is necessary but not sufficient for life. Whether or not life exists on Mars or any other planet depends first on whether liquid water exists there. Since the early days of Martian space exploration, the Viking and Global Surveyor probes indicated that liquid water had at one time existed on the Martian surface. Sinuous erosional patterns suggested ancient riverbeds. Yet the thin Martian atmosphere is too rarefied to support surface water in its liquid state. Scientists had speculated at the end of the twentieth century that under the surface of Mars, where the pressure was greater, there might still be liquid water.

In the year 2001 the gimlet eye of Global Surveyor's Mars orbiter camera spied the effects of localized torrents of liquid water exploding out the sides of craters, the channels of water etching the sides of the crater walls.[1] Subterranean liquid water exists on Mars, and it is fairly abundant. Scientists searching for extraterrestrial life began lobbying Congress for a manned mission to Mars to learn more.

Dateline 2014

Finally launched in 2012, Europa Orbiter arced through the inner solar system in a languorous, looping trajectory, then outward to Jupiter. In 2014, it entered the Jovian system, and using the massive gas giant's gravity as a braking mechanism, the spacecraft assumed orbit around Europa, the Galilean moon second closest to Jupiter. Did life exist there?

On signal, Europa Orbiter released a probe that fell to the icy jumble of icebergs fused together by geologic processes incompletely understood. The probe fired retrorockets well before impact and settled onto a flat area of the Europan surface. A cylindrical robot was jettisoned from the belly of the probe into the ice. The "cryobot's" inner shell of low-grade plutonium kept the outer surface of the robot hot, and its heated drill bit burrowed the cryobot into the Europan crust. About two kilometers under the surface, the cryobot reached the vast subsurface ocean of the moon, and a smaller submersible robot, utilizing the latest in nanotechnology, engaged its navigation system, propulsion, and sensor arrays to test for the existence of life on Europa.[2]

* * * * * *

The search for extraterrestrial life is just one scientific enterprise that does not at first appear to have a biblical basis or theological framework. Can a Christian legitimately support such research? More importantly, how can these investigations be understood scripturally? Even if the results of modern science appear mysterious to us, and we wonder how scientific discovery fits into God's eternal purposes, I hope to demonstrate that pioneering and revolutionary research is possible only because society was long ago perfused by biblical worldviews.

New information about the universe is overturning the foundations of our society. To many Christians, science seems to exist mainly to challenge the old verities of our faith. Even society at large is becoming wary of the juggernaut of scientific advance, wondering if there isn't more to life than scientific explanation. The search for extraterrestrial life is one such culture-shaking endeavor, but there are others, such as the astounding completion of the sequence of the human genome.

It is my heartfelt conviction that Christians must understand what science is and why our faith was paramount in the development of science. For science was not a pagan interloper in a comfortable Christian society but a perfectly inevitable (and good) outworking of Christian theology. It is high time for evangelicals to interpret science's advance in the light of good theology. If I am convinced that neither life nor death, nor principalities, nor anything else can separate us from the love of God in Christ Jesus, then I am convinced that neither can a paper in a scientific journal. We must be salt and light in the postmodern world without resorting to ancient heresies to accommodate "modern science."

WHAT IS SCIENCE?

To live successfully in a technological age requires a reasonable understanding of the methods and goals of science. Though our society teaches us to elevate scientific truth above other verities of existence, especially religion, only a few can explain what science is. Practitioners of science have not been taught to appreciate a theological framework for their discipline; most of us have been taught the superiority of the scientific enterprise.

Contrary to the usual Spartan precision of dictionary definitions, the *Oxford English Dictionary*'s fourth definition of *science* waxes eloquent. Science is "a branch of study which is concerned either with a connected body of demonstrated truths or with observed facts systematically classified and more or less colligated (joined together) by being brought under general laws, and which includes trustworthy methods for the discovery of new truth within its own domain."

Scientific Truth Does Not Exhaust the Essence of Reality

Every part of this definition is pregnant with assumed worldviews that must be understood before a scientific program can be initiated. Although there is clearly overlap, scientific truth is not historical truth and can't be equated with the narrative of Scripture, but it *is* theological truth in the sense that a Christian worldview is necessary to conduct the scientific program. The real people and events of history are accessible to the human intellect by a unique paper trail of corroborating evidence. Christianity is a religion rooted in historical reality and historical documentation. It is also anchored to the work of the Holy Spirit, who breathed his infallible truth into the Scripture writers and, in a lesser way, illuminates the souls of believers as we grapple with the truths of the Bible.

We must reject scientific triumphalism, the idea that scientific truth reigns supreme over all knowledge, or is in fact identical to all knowledge. Science cannot reduce the essence of a Monet painting to a prescribed orientation of paint blotches, each of which is defined by a specific absorption spectrum, and science cannot better introduce us to George Washington with a clone from his DNA than history can with his letters and the records of witnesses.

Scientific truth is contingent on the quality and quantity of the data and the wisdom and talent of the people interpreting the data. Increasingly discerning experiments enable scientists to deepen their understanding of the world by building better models to describe it. But this sort of inductive reasoning cannot be perfect, simply because God transcends our finite creatureliness. Scientists will rarely tell you that they arrive at an unshakable, inviolate truth about the physical world. Unfortunately, unbelieving scientists will also neglect to tell you that the *presence* of absolute truth allows science to progress. They may not in a superficial sense, but they do in a deeper sense believe in absolute truth themselves.

The Relationship between Absolute Truth and Scientific Truth

How closely can we approach absolute truth in our scientific research?

Science's weakness is perhaps its greatest strength. Scientists should recognize that they may ask only limited questions about reality. But Christians should recognize that scientists answer these limited questions very well.[3] The scientific program is successful because the scientific method probes the physical world effectively. I sometimes hear Christians wield a weak argument against science that goes something like this: "So-and-so is just a theory. It is not fact. Therefore, my interpretation of Scripture invalidates the conclusions reached by scientists. After all, science is proven wrong all the time."[4]

That is only partly true. While cutting edge science requires much more data before uniform acceptance, there is much about the physical world that we won't have to unlearn. We learn real truth. Our scientific theories are models that we construct to define certain phenomena. Some theories are simply untenable after more probing experimentation, and they are flatly rejected. But sometimes better experiments lead to better, more accurate models. A good model may not be perfect, but to use the technical jargon, it is "verisimilitudinous." That is, the model truly reflects reality, and it may later have to be refined but not necessarily overturned.

A good example of model refinement comes from the field of nucleic acids research (DNA and RNA). The standard model for DNA structure was developed by Watson and Crick on the basis of Rosalind Franklin's X-ray diffraction data. (Franklin should get much more credit than she does for the elucidation of DNA structure, but, tragically, she died of cancer shortly afterwards and never received the acclaim she deserved.) The two strands of the familiar double-helix of DNA attract each other (partly) by what we call Watson-Crick base-pairing. We nucleic acids researchers call this structure canonical B-form DNA.

Rank-and-file DNA looks like this double-helical B-form DNA. But not surprisingly, we have refined this model since its development in 1953. We now know that "A-form" helices (usually found in RNAs) and weirder "Z-form" helices form under the correct conditions. There are triple-stranded helices and even, in the case of certain sequences, tetrameric helices, where four strands wind around each other. The base-pairing mechanism that helps hold the strands together is not always "Watson-Crick," either. The bases (letters) of each DNA strand can recognize the letters of the other strand by "Reverse Watson-Crick" base-pairing, "Hoogsteen" Base-Pairing, etc. These structures and types of base-pairing are variations on the theme first discovered by Watson and Crick. We do not have to unlearn what they did. We have learned *more* than they did, which is not in the least bit surprising if you believe that God is perfect in his infinities.

The amount and quality of data we have available to construct theories in the natural sciences are crucial and have analogies in Scripture exegesis. The very spare (but perfect) account of Genesis 1–10 leaves much that can be filled in by archaeology, history, or science without disrupting or perverting the biblical narrative. On the other hand, we have an extremely detailed account of our Lord's passion, and we have no excuse for not understanding the work of Jesus on behalf of sinners. In fact, soteriology in general (the doctrines of salvation) is laid out in such detail because God desires that we know exactly what it means to be redeemed.

Likewise, suppose a historian learns about an ancient Akkadian city from one cuneiform tablet, and she draws a picture of what life was like in that city from this tablet. Another historian is studying the effects of the Civil War on the culture of New York City. This historian has an incredible array of resources at his disposal: libraries, museums, newspaper repositories—and thus his picture of New York City during the Civil War will be much more complete and accurate. The accuracy of the model is a function of the amount of data present.

Science has thus far not caved in to the postmodernism that infects other branches of knowledge. Most of us believe there is a real universe to study, and it has some concrete things to say about itself, if we only study it correctly. In defending critical realism and true knowledge, John Polkinghorne, both a theoretical physicist and a theologian, supplies an excellent example of model revision: the electron.

> J. J. Thompson, the discoverer of the electron, thought about these tiny, electrically charged particles in one way, Niels Bohr in another, and Feynman, Schwinger, and Tomonaga (the discoverers of modern quantum electrodynamics) in yet another. Yet it is perfectly natural to say that they were all describing the same entity and that the difference in their discourse relates to a deepening of our understanding of the nature of electrons. There are continuities in what is being said (all are talking about a particle with a mass

of 10^{-27} g and with a certain electrical charge, a constituent of atoms) and one can see how the classical account of things is a crude approximation to the increasingly more subtle quantum mechanical descriptions of his successors. What is happening is not a discontinuous change, but better understanding.[5]

Thus our understanding of the physical world is becoming more profound, but we must apply a worldview, a philosophical or theological framework, to any data we collect. As John Polkinghorne organized his work *Faith of a Physicist* around the Nicene Creed,[6] I have found it helpful to work within a framework of systematic theology to explicate my worldview.

Our worldview is the filter through which we perceive reality, and mine is unashamedly Christian. But what does it mean to have a Christian worldview informing one's scientific endeavors? It is sometimes stated that science is the West's most exportable commodity. Science is something we are conditioned to admire, or at least respect, but it is not something that all societies develop. Indeed, Loren Eiseley has said that science is "an invented cultural institution, an institution not present in all societies, and not one that may be counted upon to arise from human instinct."[7] Why did the West develop modern science?

THE NATURE OF GOD
MAKES SCIENCE POSSIBLE

I strongly believe, with Abraham Kuyper, that not one iota, not the tiniest volume of space, is unclaimed by Jesus Christ: he is Lord of it all, and he actively rules his universe. And I believe that a society's theological underpinnings either allow science to flourish or inhibit its development. To examine the role of Christian faith in science, we must first examine the role of the Christian God in the universe.

To my mind, the resonance of Hebrews 1:1–4 serves to exalt Jesus Christ in all His manifest excellencies. It is loaded with theological import, and it bears on the issue of God's creation:

> Long ago God spoke many times and in many
> ways to our ancestors through the prophets. But now
> in these final days, he has spoken to us through his
> Son. God promised everything to the Son as an inheri-
> tance, and through the Son he made the universe and
> everything in it. The Son reflects God's own glory,
> and everything about him represents God exactly. He
> sustains the universe by the mighty power of his com-
> mand. After he died to cleanse us from the stain of
> sin, he sat down in the place of honor at the right
> hand of the majestic God of heaven. This shows that
> God's Son is far greater than the angels, just as the
> name God gave him is far greater than their names
> (NLT).

Observe that Jesus Christ himself is said to be the creative power of the Trinity, as we see verified in Colossians 1:15–17: "He is the image of the invisible God, the firstborn over all creation. For by Him all things were created: Things in heaven and on earth, visible and invisible, whether thrones or rulers or authorities; all things were created through Him and for Him. He is before all things, and in Him all things hold together."

These texts also describe something very foundational and, if you will, primordial. The universe came into being because God in his eternal purpose willed it, and God cannot create anything at variance with his eternal purpose and at odds with his beautiful attributes. The universe—its being, construct, mechanism, and meaning—has everything to do with the Lord's nature.

Christians should live and have our being in a God-centered universe, but culture in general lives in a context of multicul-turalism and postmodern thought, and within the halls of acad-eme devoted to science, scientific triumphalism reigns. In this mind-set, everything can be reduced to laws of science, and there is no need to posit God to describe anything.[8] The notion that the attributes and nature of God allow us to do science would be roundly rejected by most practicing scientists. But that's their problem, not mine or God's. And understanding their mind-set can help Christians know how to think Christianly about science.

I do not believe we can predict an experimental result based on a confession of faith, or even on the Bible. I believe God desires his children to go and find out about his universe, and the scientific method is an effective means of doing that. In the Bible I find nothing of electromagnetic theory, of quantum mechanics, or of recombinant DNA technology, beyond notes on the breeding of Jacob's and Laban's sheep! Regarding the natural order, the Scriptures are largely phenomenological: the inspired writers describe what they see, and they do so correctly. A scientific explanation is not given nor required.

But viewing God through the lens of Scripture allows us to focus on the universe correctly; when we are imbued with the knowledge of who God is, when an entire culture is suffused with godly learning, then we begin perceiving the universe in a way that makes science tenable. A scientist (even a Christian one) cannot open the pages of her Bible or consult a creed to help her interpret the latest hot experiment. Nor will logic alone enable full understanding of the physical world: beyond logic we must rely on experimental proof. However, a scientist performs the experiment in the first place because he has, even if subconsciously, imbibed a biblical worldview that allows science to be possible. A scientific society cannot blossom in the absence of a biblical worldview, nor, in my estimation, can it continue for long if it jettisons that worldview. Thus, many precepts and doctrines of Christianity are vital to the health of the scientific enterprise.

J. I. Packer in *A Quest for Godliness* gives his approbation to the earthy worldviews espoused by the Puritans.[9] They loved to talk about the attributes of God, and they had a consuming goal: that "through the preaching and teaching of the gospel, and *the sanctifying of all arts, sciences, and skills* (emphasis mine), England was to become a land of saints, a model and paragon of corporate godliness and as such a means of blessing the world." The Puritan William Ames called theology the science of living to God, and his contemporary William Perkins defined theology as the science of living blessedly forever.[10] In *Knowing God,*

Packer asserts that this emphasis, coupled with their insistence on the primacy of the mind, and the impossibility of obeying biblical truth one has not understood, renders a potent and energetic fuel for the pursuit of the scientific program.

So if science is based on a theological understanding of the world, where do we get that understanding? The *Westminster Confession of Faith,* penned by a committee of theologians and clerics from the mid-1640s, tells us, as do many of the classic creeds of Christendom. After describing the attributes of God's character, the confession begins to describe his relation to man:

> God hath all life, glory, goodness, blessedness, in and of himself; and is alone in and unto himself all-sufficient, not standing in need of any creatures which he hath made, not deriving any glory from them, but only manifesting his own glory, in, by, unto, and upon them: he is the alone fountain of all being, of whom, through whom, and to whom, are all things; and hath most sovereign dominion over them, to do by them, for them, or upon them, whatsoever himself pleaseth. In his sight all things are open and manifest; his knowledge is infinite, infallible, and independent upon the creature, so as nothing is to him contingent or uncertain. He is most holy in all his counsels, in all his works, and in all his commands. To him is due from angels and men, and every other creature, whatsoever worship, service, or obedience, he is pleased to require of them.[11]

Why be so heavy-handed about the theological basis of science? Modern science tells us much about the world, and I believe we are foolish to disregard its findings as being irrelevant to matters of faith. But more problematic is that many theologians pray that maybe (just maybe) trendy science will validate their theology. While we can learn from science, theologians and all Christians must cherish their patrimony delivered once for all the saints. Stanley Jaki, in a preface to his book *Miracles and Physics,* correctly says, "Too many theologians look for dubious handouts from what they think to be science, although they merely receive thereby a doubtful interpretation of it. They should show more appreciation for the treasure they are supposed to hold in their professional hands and hang on to it for dear life. For the treasure is God's word and miracles are the seal on its revealed character."[12] Let us enumerate the theological principles that undergird science, principles that have been adduced by theologians for many centuries.

THE ATTRIBUTES OF GOD

The Scriptures tell us in Romans 1 that God's attributes are so clearly arrayed before us in nature that we are without excuse if we consign him to any role other than complete primacy in our lives, because creation shouts that he is Lord. Paul writes, "Since the creation of the world His invisible attributes, His eternal power and divine nature, have clearly been seen, being understood through what has been made, so that they are without excuse." We do not see the gospel arrayed in nature, but the law, says Protestant Reformer Theodore Beza;[13] we cannot learn of the life and ministry of the Lord Jesus Christ by peering at the stars or standing amazed at the mathematical regularity of the flower of an Echinacea (purple coneflower: look at one some time). The law is branded upon the hearts of all men, and it tells us of God and his goodness, but it also condemns because it shows us we fall short of the glory of God. As Beza says, it lays bare to us the majesty and justice of God.

The attributes of God as revealed in nature reveal God's eternal power, and these generally fall under the rubric of his incommunicable attributes. As Louis Berkhof has written, "While the incommunicable attributes emphasize the absolute Being of God, the communicable attributes stress the fact that He enters into various relations with His creatures."[14] We first turn to the incommunicable attributes as a theological basis of science and then to the communicable attributes. Both are important to the development of science, but their discussion in this forum must be truncated.

The Incommunicable Attributes

God's incommunicable attributes are his self-existence, unchanging nature, and infinities, or those attributes present in infinite measure. Taken together, these cement the notion of *uniformity,* so central to the scientific enterprise.[15] That is, scientists assume that the universe is everywhere governed by the same underlying principles, rendering it capable of being studied.

God's *self-existence* contributes to the concept of uniformity because God requires nothing to add to his glory, and he wrought a universe that reflects his steadfastness and order. His universe, in its very essence, does not depend on us to be what it is. The scientist who knows that God is *unchanging* in his essential being recognizes that he is not capricious, and his creation's fundamental laws will not change in the time that elapses from one experiment to the next. Nor does God's essence change anywhere else in the universe. He is thus immutable temporally and spatially. God's *infinities* are those divine qualities present in infinite measure, and they are reckoned by Louis Berkhof, late president of Calvin Theological Seminary, to be his perfection, eternity, immensity (omnipresence), and unity.[16] To these I would add his sovereignty, which is his effective rule over all the universe.

Taken together, all the incommunicable attributes render uniformity a necessary consequence and enable science to arise. Western civilization long ago learned to look at the world through the eyes of God's incommunicable attributes, consciously or not, and these attitudes about God and the universe persist in the most post-Christian of cultures. No scientist would deny uniformity, even if he were an Eastern religionist and an ardent New Age devotee.

The Communicable Attributes

The communicable attributes emphasize the relationship that God has with his people and are defined by Berkhof to be his *personality, veracity, knowledge, holiness, goodness,* and *love,*[17] to which I have one addendum: His *creative power.* For now, I will devote more space to the latter two.

God has a *personality,* in the sense that he engages with his creation and can be said to have an intelligence that interacts with his creation in accord with his holiness and other qualities. As creatures in his image, we have personality too, and ours helps shape our perception of the universe. As God is a God of *truth,* we have confidence that we are in pursuit of the truth when we explore creation and that we can know truth about it. God's *holiness* displays God's splendor and loveliness through the book of nature, and it is also the grounding for scientific ethics. The *goodness* of God tells us that his creation is good and worthy of study, even though affected by original sin.

Human love embodies multiple concepts, and the highest form of it in Christian thought, *agape,* refers to a life of active service and well-being toward those who are undeserving. The main exemplar of this love is modeled on God's actions to redeem a humanity that had spurned him and enslaved itself to serve evil. Berkhof defines God's *love* in a manner that is not only consistent with this definition but germane to the practice of science. Love is "that perfection of God by which He is moved to self-communication eternally."[18] Naturally, one's attention must turn to the clearest expression of God's revelation, the Holy Scriptures.

THE AUTHORITY OF SCRIPTURE IN THE LIFE OF THE SCIENTIST

If God's love is his revelation to us, then Scripture defines the highest form of love possible. Although it is customary to view the authority of the Bible being at loggerheads with the authority of science, this is not true, and it is helpful to review an evangelical doctrine of the authority of Scripture. An excellent source for understanding the role of Scripture in the life of faith is given in Benjamin B. Warfield's *The Inspiration and Authority of Scripture.*

To what degree is truth in science equivalent to truth in theology? Many seek a consilience of the two disciplines, and many scholars, some evangelical, have written on the topic. By using the Nicene Creed as a skeleton in his elegant *Faith of a Physicist,* John Polkinghorne fleshed out that creed with his understanding of it as a scientist. Many diverge more from an evangelical understanding of theology, some less. I wish to compare science and Scripture in light of an evangelical theology of the Bible, God's special revelation.

As God has created all that is, we cannot limit our definition of his creative impulse to the Holy Scriptures alone but must expand it to include the rest of the created order. It is common for evangelicals to distinguish the book of the law from the book of nature, both of which God has written. The former is often known as special or soteriological revelation[19] and contains those doctrines necessary to understand how to be saved and how to live as a disciple of Jesus Christ. The latter is called general revelation, because it is everywhere and cannot save anyone, although God's revelation of himself is known to everyone (Rom. 1:18–21,25,28,32; 2:14–16). But are the general and special revelation equally accurate? And does the Holy Spirit assist in the understanding of both types of revelation the same way and to the same degree?

First, I would like to make clear my commitment to the Scriptures. Following Benjamin B. Warfield, I believe that the Scriptures are plenarily inspired, meaning that not only general concepts but also the words of Scripture are inspired.[20] Thus all of it, and each word of it, is from God and completely trustworthy; the Holy Spirit said precisely what he wanted to say, and that includes Genesis chapters 1–11. The Scripture is his very exhalation (*theopneustos*, 2 Tim. 3:16), and it possesses his lifeforce in full measure, though the writers are not marionettes in the hands of a cosmic tyrant, as many wish to mischaracterize God. This doctrine has been held by orthodox Christians of every stripe until the modernists decided to tip the apple cart of biblical inerrancy. Orthodox Christians have always said that if you desire to understand your existence, you should go to the Scriptures, for it is there you will find eternal life and the reason for being.[21] This is as true for scientists as it is for anyone else.

Thus Scripture has these perfections: its author is perfect; its content is without error and completely reliable; it perfectly describes God's work in the world; and it has been preserved to this present day. Yet to this I can add another superlative, one that is germane to the scientist's work. The Holy Spirit guides the believer to a proper understanding of Scripture in a way he does not guide the scientist to understand creation. Theologians contrast the terms *illumination* and *inspiration*. The Holy Spirit *illuminates* the Scriptures for the believer, knitting our souls and wills to his truth as revealed in Scripture, but not in an infallible way: we say that our understanding of Scripture is by illumination, not inspiration, the latter term reserved for the writers of the Scripture.

Almost every doctrine has been contested by some faction in the church: some of this is due to "false professors" and heretics, but some errors are due to the fact that the Holy Spirit will not give perfection to our understanding until glorification, when we will see the Lord Jesus face-to-face. Thus Bible believers differ not only on baptism and church government but also on the age of the earth and the proper use of medical technology. A Christian should be assured, however, that he will be granted enough understanding by the Holy Scripture to understand how to be redeemed by the blood of Christ.

By contrast, we must assert some differences in our capacity to understand general revelation. Nowhere in Scripture are we promised we will understand creation in the same way we do the Scriptures, although Paul affirms that God speaks to us through general revelation (Rom. 1 and 2). The creation tells us of God's eternal attributes, but it does not tell us in depth how general revelation works. The specifics of general revelation are not illuminated by the Holy Spirit in the same way he illuminates God in the Scriptures to the redeemed. God is sovereign over all scientific advancement, and he is not surprised by any new scientific finding, as if his fallen creatures were too clever for him. He knew it, and he ordained it. Thus, in a way, the Holy Spirit is operative at some level in the progress of scientific discovery. Even the hearts of kings are in God's hands. But we must not call this providential guiding of the Holy Spirit inspiration or even illumination.

Because of the qualitative differences in the Holy Spirit's work, I believe that a saint in modern times has no general spiritual advantage over a saint who lived a millennium ago,[22] especially if the modern saint has not been trained to take Scripture seriously. On the other hand, scientific truth must be pursued according to the scientific method, with new knowledge added to a corpus of already discovered truth. In a sense the "canon" of general revelation is still being written, unlike the completed canon of Scripture. And there is another repercussion of these differences in the Holy Spirit's work. Provided both unbeliever and believer have the same worldview (approximately) about general revelation, or apply the scientific method equally well, God does not necessarily grant the Christian better scientific knowledge than the unbeliever.

But here's the crux of the matter. The two hypothetical scientists must hold the same worldview about creation. And only a biblically based one will do. There are many unbelieving scientists, but every one of them has to use God's tools to study God's creation, and they are that much more clearly in rebellion if they have the temerity to proclaim either that God does not exist or, if he does, that he is not the God of the Bible. The thought of Cornelius Van Til, late professor of apologetics at Westminster Theological Seminary, is appropriate here: "I contend that you cannot argue against belief in Him unless you first take Him for granted. Arguing about God's existence, I hold, is like arguing about air. You may affirm that air exists, and I that it does not. But as we debate the point, we are both breathing air the whole time."[23]

GOD'S CREATIVE POWER: IN THE IMAGE OF GOD

I believe that humans can perform science because we are made in the image of God. If there are truly communicable attributes that we have because God possesses them, then it follows that the doctrine of man being made in the image of God fits well under a discussion of God's communicable attributes. Man creates because God does; this is one aspect of our image-bearing capacity. I am aware that we cannot create *ex nihilo*, out of nothing, as God does, but when we create out of the pre-existing forms already present in the universe, scientists truly engage in an intensely creative discipline.

But what does it mean to be in the image of God? There are many historical views. The Socinians thought the image was embodied only in man's *dominium* over the earth, an explanation with merit given the context but almost certainly a definition not extensive enough. Karl Barth viewed the image as our maleness and femaleness together, but this too seems inadequate, though with an element of truth. Most of the Protestant Reformers saw the image as consisting in humanity's original holiness and God-reflecting spiritual attributes, which were of course greatly effaced by the Fall. More radically, Luther thought that the *imago Dei* was essentially destroyed by sin. Since the image could be partially restored by redemption, the image was understood mainly as that we could possess God's moral attributes. In other words, our bodies, our corporeality, were not considered by seventeenth-century saints to be a large part of the image. But modern theologians, including very orthodox ones like Louis Berkhof, and G. C. Berkouwer of the Free University of Amsterdam, usually include the whole man, meaning body and soul, as the image.[24]

How does the presence of the image of God affect science, beyond the notion that we create because God does? First, we cannot have dominion over creation unless we understand creation (see below), and understanding the physical world is fulfilled by scientific progress. Second, the idea that our maleness and femaleness reflect the image is manifested by our relationship to the created order. Indeed, Barth's idea is one of relationship. Colin Gunton says that "to be God, according to the doctrine of the Trinity, is to be persons in relation."[25] Thus, the Fall resulted in enormous damage to human relationships, especially those between the sexes, and this damage has spread to the world around us, i.e., the environment. We have a relationship with the created order that has been damaged and ruptured, leading to widespread, deleterious effects on ourselves and on the created order.

So then, to be a Christian in the sciences is to conduct research in such a way that we reflect God's image in its original purity, unsullied by sin. The question arises how this must be done. The answer, in ringing clarity, is supplied in Scripture. It is by redemption through the work of Christ.

In the Old Testament, the image of God was worked out in purely human terms, as we have seen. In the New Testament, the perfect instantiation of the image of God is seen in Jesus Christ, who is also identified as Creator. "With one or two exceptions, the old doctrine in its purely anthropological form has disappeared in favour of the teaching that Christ is the image of God. He is not only the true image of God, but also the source of human renewal in it. 'He is the image of the invisible God' (Col. 1:15); 'predestined to be conformed to the likeness of his Son'" (Rom. 8:29).[26]

In this Berkouwer agrees with Colin Gunton, who furthermore makes the connection that since Jesus is prophet, priest, and king, and we are in the image of God, we have a priestly role to fulfill in our relation to creation. We are not merely kings over creation by our dominion over it, but we are priests and mediators who are responsible for its protection. And because our relationship with God has been healed by his grace, our relationships with others and with creation around us should reflect that same restoration.

CREATION ORDINANCES: GOD GIVES US OUR MARCHING ORDERS

A special emphasis of systematic theologians is the scheme of God's "creation ordinances," those instructions he gave to Adam and Eve before the Fall. Because of their special connection to man in even his sinless state, they apply today and enable us to live successful lives *coram Deo*, before the face of God. The creation ordinances include God's call to man to work, to take dominion over the creation, and to marry and have children.

The Work Ethic

The work ethic is a patrimony of the Reformation, even if a somewhat debased one: Reinhold Niebuhr in *The Irony of American History* chronicled the devolution of the American Puritan work ethic to a shallow Yankeeism, devoid of spirituality and independent from God.[27] Yet the importance of the work ethic cannot be overemphasized, though it is left out of discussions of faith and science. The pagan world (and its modern apologists) knows little of the Christian work ethic. Peter Green wistfully looks towards the insouciant, eat-drink-and-be-merry culture of the ancient Minoans, wishing we still possessed their attitudes.[28] A highly developed and sophisticated doctrine of one's calling, found in its fullest expression in Christianity, is beneficial to science in several ways, some of which may be surprising.

First, an elevated sense of calling renders all work worthy, enabling all to glorify God equally, regardless of vocation, so long as that vocation is licit. The hard work that inevitably follows powers an economy that frees up wealth and leisure for scientific research. We take for granted the importance of science in modern economies and fund it accordingly from the public till as well as from the corporate and even from personal wealth. But science was often in history an activity reserved for the moneyed classes.

Thus, in a sense, the rise of mercantilism before the Reformation and its development after it contributed to the development of science, not because Protestantism demands capitalism or a free-market system or because there is any such calculus like capitalism = science. Rather, like Bainton, I believe that Christians devote themselves to their work as unto the Lord, and they prosper, whatever the prevailing economic system, within reason.[29]

There is another reason, more germane to the essence of science, that the development of a godly work ethic helped propel science to a mature discipline. I find that most people do not appreciate what a practical, hands-on discipline science is. True, theoretical physicists and mathematicians comprise an indispensable part of modern science, and it is axiomatic that modern mathematicians like to ply their trade devoid of any reference to or dependence on natural phenomena. Yet modern scientists, as a whole, recognize the paramountcy of the experiment as the voice of nature and the arbiter of the truth of a theory. And performing experiments is a practical art.

This may not mean much until you see the cultural context. The Greeks came closer to developing science than any other ancient society. There were three classes of investigators in the ancient Greek world that we would today subsume under the rubric of "scientists": mathematicians, natural philosophers, and astronomers.[30] These men had, for their day, international renown in the classical world. But there were very few of these thinkers over many centuries. And they had an aversion to the manual labor necessary to prove their hypotheses, even Archimedes, usually adduced as a true scientist and the exemplar of the finest of Greek thought. This aversion to physical work was the cause of their vitiated work ethic, at least as it pertained to science. The rigid mind-body dualism of the ancient Greeks scuttled any true scientific program because it prevented an appreciation for a material world as it idealized the spiritual, mental world.

This is not to denigrate the Greeks, but I must point out shortcomings rooted in their religious and cultural perspectives. The debate between Jerusalem and Athens is a long one: what culture influenced our own the most, the Greco-Roman or a biblical one, the latter exemplified by the Decalogue? The answer, I believe, is rooted in Paul's exhortation not to be conformed to the world but to be transformed by the renewing of our minds. Thus, ancient codes and institutions of the Greco-Roman world were not just transposed to a more modern usage, but they were transformed—clothed in godliness—by a Christian culture steeped in Greco-Roman tradition but concerned that these institutions undergo a metamorphosis into something pleasing to God.

It is not a problem that our forefathers sometimes made this transformation imperfectly. They made the attempt, and it was, overall, successful. Justinian used the old Roman legal codes as the basis for Byzantine jurisprudence, but they were transformed, not used whole cloth, so that there are some substantial differences between Byzantine and classical Roman law. Greek sexual ethics would be absolutely shocking to a modern America, even to many proponents of the "sexual revolution" and the "gay rights movement." The ancient Greek worldview is simply not our own.[31]

The Greeks were famous throughout antiquity for possessing minds of singular power and subtlety. The archetype of the Greek intellect was Odysseus, king of Ithaka and hero of the Trojan war, who hatched the devilish idea of the Trojan horse. But the Greeks' theological limitations limited an understanding of uniformity. At best, a Platonist might have believed in an amorphous creator, while other Greeks maintained belief in a menagerie of factious, inconsistent tribal deities.[32]

Archimedes of Syracuse is the exception who precisely proves the rule. Every modern physics student rightly studies Archimedes's principle, which describes the physical laws underlying buoyancy. In addition he designed many ingenious implements of war, which gave the Romans fits when they tried to besiege Syracuse. Yet he assumed the rigid mind-body dualism typical of Greek intellectual society, in which mentality is exalted, but the physical universe is inferior.

> Archimedes . . . would not deign to leave behind him any writings on his mechanical discoveries. He regarded the business of engineering, and indeed of every art which ministers to the material needs of life, as an ignoble and sordid activity, and he concentrated his ambition exclusively upon those speculations whose beauty and subtlety are untainted by the claims of necessity. These studies, he believed, are incomparably superior to any others, since the grandeur and beauty of the subject matter vie for our admiration with the cogency and precision of the methods of proof.[33]

Now let us consider two giants who established much of the modern scientific enterprise, Galileo Galilei and Francis Bacon, the former Roman Catholic and the latter Protestant. These men were contemporaries, producing much of their work in the last part of the sixteenth century and the early part of the seventeenth. Galileo jettisoned much of the Aristotelian framework of natural philosophy, a particularly unhelpful philosophy of physics but one of more use in the biological sciences.[34] His dependence on experimental evidence over raw logic enabled him to conceptualize the effect of friction on the motion of objects. Galileo recognized the importance of friction, and he rolled objects down inclined planes of various smoothnesses to test his hypothesis. He recognized that the more polished the slope, the less friction present, and so the object would roll very far. This was a tedious process and not one that a Greek would have wanted to undertake. Yet Galileo's experimentation enabled him to understand that if friction were not present, then all objects, regardless of size and mass, would fall at the same rate.

Francis Bacon was more of a philosopher than what we would today call a practitioner of natural science, yet he laid a theological foundation for empiricism that is necessary to the practice of science. Deeply critical of medieval Scholasticism's excessive rhetorical ornamentation as well as of Renaissance humanism, he sought to overturn the status quo of English education in Elizabethan and early Stuart times. As a Reformed Protestant, he felt that Scholasticism largely ignored what he called the word of God and the works of God, or what we might today call special (or soteriological) revelation and general (or natural) revelation. He believed that scholastic logic helps rhetoric but does not explain nature by itself: metaphysics must at some point give way to probing nature for its truth. He had in one sense a utilitarian view of science, reasoning that science's main goal is to further humanity's dominion over the earth. Indeed, the well-known aphorism "knowledge is power" is a Baconian one. Yet the end of this research—scientific knowledge and its resulting technology—has a religious end, dominion. Prayers were sprinkled throughout his writings, and he was orthodox doctrinally.[35] In Bacon's understanding, God makes science possible.

Though many scientists believe that the search for scientific truth is an end in itself, regardless of utility, it cannot be doubted that the aim to improve man's lot is one of the driving aims of science, and this aim has its origin in the empiricist beliefs of Francis Bacon. I am a biophysicist who applies physics to the study of chemical carcinogenesis, how chemicals damage DNA and cause cancer. The cadre of scientists who study cancer probably number in the tens of thousands worldwide, and funding for cancer research in the U.S is approximately one billion dollars a year. The fact is, if cancer were not a vicious and cruel disease, far fewer people would be studying it; cancer research is a classic example of alleviating the results of the Fall by scientific progress. This is clearly Baconian and leads to a topic related to the work ethic: dominion.

John Milton spoke of the end of learning being to repair the ruins of our first parents, done by empirical study. Bacon writes in *Novum Organum*: "For man, by the Fall, lost at once his state of innocence, and his empire over creation, both of which can be partially recovered even in this life, the first by religion and faith, the second by the arts and sciences."[36]

The Dominion Mandate

Thus we can segue comfortably into what is commonly called (or sometimes vilified) as the dominion mandate, also a creation ordinance. For some reason, this lovely truth is often hated, and usually misunderstood, even in the Christian community. One writer clucks disapprovingly that dominion is "an environmentally insensitive biblical command."[37] This opinion is fairly typical of the breed of environmentalist who has neither the sophistication to exegete Scripture nor the spiritual desire to do so. What does the Bible really say about dominion, and what does the dominion mandate have to do with science?

At the culmination of creation, the end of the majestic cadence of God's work in Genesis 1, the following is said of God's creation of humankind: "Then God said, 'Let Us make man in Our image, according to Our likeness; and let them rule over the fish of the sea and over the birds of the sky and over the cattle and over all the earth, and over every creeping thing that creeps on the earth.' And God created man in His own image, in the image of God He created him; male and female He created them. And God blessed them; and God said to them, 'Be fruitful and multiply, and fill the earth, and subdue it; and rule over the fish of the sea and over the birds of the sky, and over every living thing that moves on the earth'" (Gen. 1:26–28 NASB).

In Genesis 9 the dominion mandate is repeated, but with a malignant twist: the world is fallen, and sin perfuses everything, and now the animals fear man. Finally, the dominion mandate is repeated in Psalm 8.

Bacon's philosophy provides a key to understanding the link. If we are to implement dominion over the earth, then we need technology and therefore science. Perhaps the first step in the scientific enterprise is observation and categorization; if so, then God's command to name all the beasts of the field is in a sense a scientific one.

The Rain Forest Problem

It is hard to deny that science works, and it works well. One could adduce numerous advances that have lengthened life spans, given us wealth and prosperity, and made us less susceptible to the inclement weather and natural catastrophes that have always marked human experience. In fact, the back-to-nature movement has largely been fueled by our mastery over our planet; at one time nature was viewed as frightening, because it had so much power over us for destruction. In an earlier work, I noted that "the wetland is appreciated because it is an incubator to many organisms, and provides efficient filtering of water, but we forget it was once a source of pestilence, much of which has been conquered in this century in developed countries. Likewise, the sublimity of mountain crags inspires us, but we forget these were once insurmountable to human beings and a source of rockfalls, avalanches, and changeable, inclement weather, which inhibit human habitation."[38]

The tropical rain forest provides a case in point. The jungle heat enervates, and parasites too ghoulish for Hollywood to duplicate invade your body. The rain forest is inhospitable, as close to hell as you get on the earth. But the tropical rain forest is one of the most beautiful of all ecosystems, and its importance in the global scheme of things cannot be overestimated. Rain forests are romanticized as fragile, delicate biomes, and environmentalists are rightly concerned for their preservation.

All earth systems are open systems, and thus linked to each other, and we cannot pretend that in our own cozy North American cities we really won't be affected by the destruction of the rain forest.

Now we are cutting down the rain forest. Maybe not as quickly as one cadre of impassioned environmentalists would have you believe, but sooner or later we have to be careful. Destruction is not real dominion either.

The Tyrant Problem

Earthly kings are to have dominion, and we should look to what the Scriptures say about how godly kings should rule.

In Deuteronomy 17:14–20, Moses says that the king should not try to multiply for himself chariots, wives, and wealth, which means that he was not to plunder his people for his own aggrandizement. That is, he was to be a shepherd king who cares only to benefit his people. The Book of Proverbs is replete with pithy sayings about the blessings of wise rule, and we see this personified by Solomon, whose prayer to God as a young man, upon accession to the throne, models humble kingship. Rather than craving the lives of his enemies or great wealth, he desired to rule his people graciously and fairly, so that they could obey God to the very fullest and yet have some measure of protection in order to do this. God's verdict on Solomon's intent was unequivocal—he gave his complete imprimatur to Solomon's reign, precisely because Solomon desired to gently shepherd his subjects. It was when Solomon reneged on his promises late in life that his reign unraveled, as did his whole nation after his death. Many of the Israelites, especially in the Northern Kingdom, became unfairly burdened with supporting a bloated and threatening bureaucracy, and they rebelled.[39]

Dominion demands science, for we cannot exercise dominion over things we do not understand. Our increasing power over nature necessitates some very careful decisions about how to use that power. We are already grappling with the fallout from genetic engineering, which takes many forms, from designer babies to super-tomatoes. And what will be the role of computers in future societies? It sounds far-fetched, but I have heard perfectly mainstream computer scientists give vent to nightmares reminiscent of the movie *The Matrix,* in which computers enslave humanity. Even though that scenario is likely impossible, we must be sure we use any technology wisely.

The Pollution Problem

And these are just the new issues. We are still wrestling with the hydra heads of pollution in all its manifest forms, and nuclear energy is still a controversial topic. I study the toxicity of methyl halides (specifically methylene chloride), important and helpful chemicals ubiquitous in modern society. They are also hazardous when they are sloppily stored in leaky barrels and "sequestered" underground, only to feed a plume of miasma into our groundwater.

J. R. R. Tolkien in *The Two Towers* describes the filth as some of the Fellowship of the Ring approach Isengard and the stronghold of Orthanc, now defiled by the evil Saruman:[40] "No trees grew there, but among the rank grasses could still be seen the burned and axe-hewn stumps of ancient groves. It was a sad country, silent now but for the stony noise of quick waters. Smokes and steams drifted in sullen clouds and lurked in the hollows. The riders did not speak."

Tolkien ascribes the spoliation of the environment to evildoers, who pervert God's order and do not understand how they should cultivate the earth: "A strong place and wonderful was Isengard, and long it had been beautiful . . . . But Saruman had slowly shaped it to his shifting purposes, and made it better, as he thought, being deceived—for all those arts and subtle devices, for which he forsook his former wisdom, and which fondly he imagined were his own, came but from Mordor."

There are real problems with the science we do and the technologies spawned from this knowledge. Thus, many Christians rightly espouse the concept of "stewardship." En route to achieving partial mastery over the created order, we have defiled the earth's systems, and it is apparent that God's creation ordinance of dominion is no less prone to sin than are marriage and work, two other creation mandates.[41] But even as human wickedness cannot obviate the institution of marriage and the duty of work, neither can it blunt the imperative of dominion which God gave us. All of us seek to carve out our niche in this world, a deep imperative no less true for those societies purported to live in harmony with creation. God told us to rule over the earth, but nowhere does this imply rapine and decimation. Instead, dominion strictly implies stewardship, and stewardship, dominion, since one cannot be a steward if he has neither understanding nor control (ability to rule) over what he desires to husband.

It is necessary for Christians to implement a more biblical concept of dominion, entailing a peaceful and beneficial co-existence with creation while extending our mastery over it, and a fulfillment of the mandate will come when this world-view comes to be society's.

Peter Warshall speaks eloquently about that most lowly of all things—the soil of the earth—and believes that the Old Testament's environmental ethic is more profound than mere stewardship. "The Old Testament spends many verses not, as commonly reported, declaring dominion over the soil, nor encouraging land stewardship, but more radically stating that humans should be servants of the soil."[42] I echo this environ-mental ethic, but he is incorrect about the *dominion* ethic: he simply hasn't defined dominion biblically.

Jesus himself said that if you wish to be great in the kingdom of heaven, then you must be servant, and likewise the apostles always called themselves not only bond servants of Jesus Christ but also servants of those people to whom they ministered. Those who hold positions of authority in the church hold true positions of leadership. But they are also shepherds and there-fore servants of those people. Both things—rule and servant-hood—must be perceived correctly by Christians, especially by those in the sciences whose discoveries have repercussions on society at large and on the environment.

MARRIAGE AND THE FAMILY

Marriage and the family are creation ordinances critical to the success of science (and everything else worthwhile, for that matter). Historians of the Reformation are often in sharp disagreement about the true effects of the Reformation. For example, some ascribe the rise of the free market and economic prosperity to the Protestant work ethic. There is much more of a consensus about marriage and the family, with most historians agreeing that the institution was revamped after Luther's reforms. Roland Bainton and many others believe that this was perhaps the Reformation's most lasting achievement.[43]

The training in and mind-set of God-glorifying work toward dominion starts in the home, the primary of God's three great institutions: the family, the church, and the state. Any nation with profligate and dissipated youth need not be surprised that few choose science as a career. Children are often out of control, and almost every public schoolteacher I have spoken with decries the lack of discipline in the classroom, so that the teacher's job devolves into mob control, not education. Christian parents need to educate their children covenantally, so that they understand that all of life orbits around the radiant and lovely person of our Lord Jesus Christ, who reigns supreme over his creation. And children need to be disciplined. Godliness with contentment is great gain, and this godliness is often forged in the fires of discipline, both God's directly and also through his vice-regents, the parents (especially the father). For only the true children of God undergo his discipline: the rest are illegitimate (Heb. 12:4–11). God tells us to become disciples, not just saved.

These spiritual disciplines not only feed the soul but also nurture the skills one acquires in obeying one's calling. Science is great fun; I cannot imagine wanting to do anything else. But it can be hard. As a scientist who knows the discipline and effort required in obtaining an advanced degree in science, I can tell you that slackers need not sign up.

Obtaining the discipline necessary for scientific or other high-level enterprise presupposes that, for the most part, families are functioning biblically. It is not my intention to comment on the fate of the American family and roles, except to say that evangelical families look uncomfortably similar to pagan families. This observation might seem irrelevant to the topic of the foundations of science. It is not. I have heard it said about the

Puritans that they believed and worked toward the end that their children would be better at the family's trade than the parents.[44] I remember hearing a highly competent Christian scientist say that his son, who had just received his Ph.D. in physics, would be a better physicist than he. This happens because godliness can accrue over generations. It is a vision we have jettisoned, or, worse, don't know ever existed. Today we evangelicals just hope our kids manage to scrape by without becoming hellions. But we must be God's instruments to lovingly and compassionately disciple them so they can do more.

We spend millions to send missionaries overseas, and this is very good. But God has given us children who are immortal beings. As C. S. Lewis pointed out, there are no such things as mere mortals.[45] Parents should be biblical and bold in the rearing of their children. Pastors should assist them in this endeavor by having them understand not only the joy of their salvation but also the joy of their callings as they obey God. Ministers need to teach the Word of God faithfully and convince their congregations that it is worthwhile (and critical) to wield doctrine effectively. A robust theology isn't dry; it is the study of our precious and magnificent God, and those who wish to love him with all their hearts and minds will find that they can grapple with deep, intricate issues, including those of a scientific nature. The Puritan soldiers of the New Model Army would sit around their campfires debating sophisticated issues of theology with a thoroughness that few moderns could match. It is no wonder they were also unbeatable on the battlefield.[46]

CONCLUSION

Christian astronomer Hugh Ross has called for a "Jerusalem Council" of leading theologians and scientists to deliberate on whether old-earth creationism is biblical.[47] The same should be done for the issues of genomics, or extraterrestrial life, or any other groundbreaking advancement, in light of biblical, evangelical theology and the ancient creeds of the church. It is my prayer that God would use this essay to stimulate interest in science and better enable the reader to glorify God, who makes it possible to understand the world he has created. If anyone who reads this is spurred thereby to undertake a scientific career, or even just to appreciate science as a part of a godly liberal-arts education, I will be grateful.

EPILOGUE

Dateline 2014

The technology to reach the stars is far off, but the technology to see planets around nearby stars is not. In the mid-1990s, large Jupiter-sized planets were indirectly detected around many of our stellar neighbors by observing the Doppler shift of radiation emitted from stars that had big planets. By the end of 2000, about 50 extrasolar planets had been catalogued. All of them were gas giants incapable of supporting life, but some of them orbited in the "habitable zone." Any large moons orbiting those planets might have the proper temperatures to allow liquid water to form.[48]

In 2011 the Terrestrial Planet Finder telescope was borne aloft into space by NASA's new Venture Star orbiter. The telescope's resolution was enhanced by a technique that physicists call interferometry, but it also had filters and optical blocking devices necessary to shut down the host star's glare so that orbiting planets, some five orders of magnitude dimmer than the star, could be optically detected. The light reflected off the planets was scanned for the telltale signatures of ozone and methane gas; the first substance is associated with an oxidizing atmosphere, the second with the metabolism of life.[49]

CHAPTER 9

CHRISTIAN WORLDVIEW
AND THE ARTS

KAREN L. MULDER

LIVING STONES THAT CAUSE A FEW STUMBLES:
EDUCATING INTENTIONAL CHRISTIANS
IN THE ARTS

ONE CAN HARDLY BLAME Christians outside the discipline for breaking into hives when it comes to a discussion of the arts. The problems with understanding contemporary art fall into a plethora of seemingly irresolvable categories that become even more troublesome under the magnifying glass of Christian propriety.

Some leaders in our camp have suggested that perhaps we, as Christians, need to separate ourselves completely from contemporary art or risk the possible loss of our own purity or integrity. This viewpoint implies that the arts, in what has become an increasingly godless world, have become so pernicious, so pornographic, and so self-centered that we, as carriers of the gospel, should have nothing to do with them.

But if we are truly carrying the gospel into the darkest corners of the world, we must be engaged to some degree in its concerns. Aesthetician Calvin Seerveld, one of the most sincere and learned Christians serving the artistic members of Christ's body, put a fine point on our need to interact with contemporary culture during the 1991 C. S. Lewis Foundation Summer Institute at Oxford University: Any arena from which Christians withdraw goes to hell.[1]

We simply cannot afford the luxury of pulling away from contemporary culture, or cutting off dialogue with it, if we truly love the world as Jesus Christ taught us, by example, to love it.

Love Letters from the Educational Front

If it is true that any arena from which Christians withdraw "goes to hell," where should the Christian artist learn to engage in the arena? It is sound logic to conclude that before we leap into the colosseum, face off with the lions, and dodge the swinging maces and nets of cultural gladiators, we need to practice. We need the discipline and safety of the gymnasium for strength training, stretching, limbering up, and becoming intellectually buff. That gym is the studio classroom of Christian higher education.

A casual survey of fourteen art departments on Christian campuses reveals several interesting patterns.[2] Primarily, regardless of the number of art majors in a given department, an average of one to two graduates go on to master's-level studies in studio art; the number of majors from this modest sampling of fourteen institutions varies widely between thirty-five at Wheaton College, Illinois, to 150 or more at Indiana Wesleyan or Biola University, California. Yet out of an average department of four to six professors who will instruct the art major at a Christian campus, at least four will have the master of fine arts, the terminal degree now required by many Christian universities to secure accreditation status as well as faculty promotion or tenure possibilities.

Another point of interest can be extrapolated by a purely numerical exercise from these "soft" statistics: if this handful of diverse departments reaches a total of approximately nine hundred students and sees thirteen to twenty-six students go on to higher art education each year, then it is possible that every four years, roughly fifty to one hundred students are released from a Christian subculture into the secular academic culture of fine art education. From a modest beginning, this could mean that as many as 130 to 260 potential instructors of art or well-practiced studio artists are released into the culture each decade. At this juncture, we might do well to remember what twelve disciples were able to instigate.

This "release" from the Christian environment to the secular scene is a necessity, since there are no Christian-sponsored M.F.A. programs known to any of the departments surveyed. Many of the studio professors and art historians from the departments surveyed received their graduate degrees at secular art schools. Among several dozen regionally strong universities reported in the informal survey, some Christian professors attained their education at prestigious institutions—even those with a pronounced anti-Christian bias—such as the Claremont Graduate School (Calif.), Boston University's School of Fine Arts (Mass.), the San Francisco Art Institute (Calif.), the Rochester Institute of Technology (N.Y.), and the School of Visual Art (N.Y.).

Also, at this moment in time, Christians in the Visual Arts (CIVA) lists among its membership several students attending elite master's-level studio programs at Yale University, the Rhode Island School of Design, the School of the Art Institute of Chicago, the Massachusetts Institute of Technology, the Graduate Center at New York University, and the Pasadena Art and Design Center. This can only bode well for Christian representation in the future of the arts.

Such findings also indicate a radical change for the young Christian seeking an arts education in the twenty-first century, when compared to the experience of the more isolated Christian art student of the 1970s.

The Ripple Effect in Recent History

What amounted to a "Christian arts movement" in the 1970s was not primarily academic, although its roots were nurtured by an academic. Roughly thirty or forty years ago, a handful of Protestant artists were exposed to the freeing ideas of Hans Rookmaaker, a Dutch art historian from Amsterdam's Free University, and his acquaintance, evangelist Francis Schaeffer, founder of L'Abri Fellowship in Switzerland. Two slim booklets incited euphoric responses from the as yet unconnected community of Protestant artists: Rookmaaker's *Art*

Needs No Justification, and Schaeffer's *Art and the Bible,* along with a more substantial Rookmaaker book, *Modern Art and the Death of a Culture.*[3] These works represented conversations and lectures that Rookmaaker and Schaeffer delivered to small groups of art students in the 1960s and 1970s.

The holy grail of the Christian arts discussion in the 1970s was a question that no one needs to ask today: "Can I be a Christian and an artist?" Faced with the onslaught of modernism and conceptualism—the styles inspired by self-expression, cathartic release, and open-ended explorations of meaning—the question was an ethical one. To answer it, arts fellowships sprung up in various major cities, starting with gatherings like the Arts Centre Group of London and progressing to the New York Arts Group and other city-based gatherings throughout the Western world. The "question" now is answered by scores of practicing artists from the Christian community, inclusive of Fulbright Scholars, Yaddo Fellows, NEA grant winners, and artists with works in some of the finest collections, such as UCLA's Armand Hammer Museum, the Cooper Hewitt and Metropolitan museums of New York, and the Vatican. By this roster alone, it is clear that significant advances are being made. Much of this progress can be traced back to three instigators.

Although it is another "soft" statistic, my phone interviews with thirty-six arts groups leaders in 1986 indicated that approximately 75 percent were inspired by Rookmaaker and Schaeffer, or their ideas transmitted through British arts networker Nigel Goodwin.[4]

In 1983—before every adult, child, and dog had access to a desktop computer, the Web, and E-mail (or even a fax machine!)—I felt called to initiate Christians in the Arts Networking, Inc., an international information network that attempted to keep artists from disparate groups, disciplines, countries, and denominations connected to one another. In support of CAN's aims, and with barely any capital to fund our calling, my partner Phillip Griffith and I traveled to Europe, Australia, New Zealand, and China to make "real" connections with Christian artists. We spanned North America trying to find out why certain programs were successful and why others floundered. Artists, after all, are not stereotypically able administrators, fund raisers, or even "joiners."

During these journeys we heard many anguished and unforgettable confessions by artists who felt mistrusted by their churches because their vocation was artistic, or marginalized by the gallery world for their Christian beliefs and themes. While North Americans never suffered physically—like the Christian artists of Eastern Europe, the former Soviet Union, or Mao Tse Tung's China during the cultural revolution—they still labored under a hindering sense of isolation and dispossession.

Even though few of the 1970s groups survived into the year 2000, these volunteer efforts contributed in untold ways to advance Christian participation in the arts. Groups that have survived, like CIVA, Christians in the Theatre Arts, or the International Christian Dance Fellowship, tended to have at their core a small subset of people committed to one another, as well as to the group's vision. The questions have risen to a much higher level of discourse. One of the most troubling areas for Christians, however, is still the dilemma of Scriptures: what does the Bible say about artistic praxis?

The Biblical Problem

As astounding as it may seem, there is nothing directly and particularly addressed to artists in Scripture about the exact form or approach art should take; God does not dictate a sheet of style points to artists anywhere in the Bible. Artists who profess Christ must heed the injunctions and cautionary inferences that all observing Christians must obey to be in God's camp. In the arena of professional choices and matters of ethics, these often relate as much to who we *are* as to what we *do* or *make*.

Apart from the stern specificity of the second commandment in Exodus 20, which warns us not to direct our worship of God toward idols made by human hands, the only direct mention of God's view of the artist's role and behavior comes out of Exodus 3:30–36:5. Here we receive a laundry list of characteristics about the tabernacle designer, Bezalel. Even a superficial reading of these passages compels us, for we would all do well to emulate such guidelines, regardless of our vocations. Briefly put, Bezalel was chosen by God; filled with the Spirit of God; filled with skill, ability, and knowledge to work in "all kinds" of artistic craftsmanship; and was adept at organizing teams of artists. He worked in partnership with Oholiab—meaning he could operate as a team player and not just a creative maverick. At heart, he was also willing to do the work that the Lord commanded, suggesting he was "in sync" with the designs of the ultimate maker. But most importantly for the educational forum, Bezalel and Oholiab had the ability to teach. If fine craftsmanship, and the aesthetic theories governing it, are not passed down by example, such knowledge can often be irretrievably lost.

In my view, the lack of scriptural specificity about artmaking may be God's way of leaving the door wide open for artistic creativity. Perhaps it is a covenant of infinite possibilities for individuals who are free to exercise their imaginations, provided they remain aware of their essential identity as believers of Christ. The heart of the issue is really about what artists can do with such unlimited freedom and whether they will be helped or hindered, trusted or condemned by the perceptions of their Christian community.

The Problem of Perception, or, as It Were, Misperception

Engaging in the arena of the fine arts is a complicated task. There is the powerful obstacle of misperception to overcome within the camp. Plainly stated, most Christians are unschooled about how to "see" contemporary art; most feel entitled to dismiss it because their gut reaction directs them to do so.

The greatest tragedy about art is that it makes for such an easy target. Art is so accessible that without knowing a thing about it, we are all able to have an immediate opinion about it regardless of the level of education we bring to the viewing transaction. Using our visceral reaction as a guide, any one of us can judge a work of art within a second's time and either savor it or condemn it, none the worse for the wear. But gut reaction is merely one tool of judgment available to everyone on earth; it is not the most responsible one.

The challenge of being redeemers in a world of fallenness is to throw over the natural pattern of reaction with the more considered and powerful option of response. A perfect example of response-motivated behavior is encapsulated by Jesus Christ's reaction to being hung, exposed, and mocked on the cross. Never once did the Lord spit condemnation upon those tormentors who taunted him and dared him to use his self-stated powers to come down from the cross. Jesus Christ did not angrily dismiss them by pointing up his own rightful role as the eventual judge of their eternal plight. Instead, he responded compassionately to the ignorance and limitations of his mockers. Luke alone records this response in 23:34, where Christ says through his pain and humiliation, "Father, forgive them, for they do not know what they are doing."

If Christ gave us this example of response in such an extreme situation, how can we emulate him during the challenges of our far more mundane existences in suburbia, or the workplace, or on the campus?

In my opinion, instilling the "response" instinct rather than allowing the "reaction" response to overrule ought to comprise a key principle of Christian education. It ultimately distinguishes truly educated Christians from milk-fed Puritans trained up with platitudes and superficial attitudes from the safe subculture of American Christianity. True response can bring surprise into the jaded and cynical arena of this confusingly pluralistic postmodern culture. The fact that an element of surprise—unexpected responses to challenges—is not incompatible with Jesus Christ's example ought to be used to the Christian's advantage in all disciplines. What hinders our creativity?

The Problem of Learning How to "See"

When we say, "I *see* what you mean," we infer that seeing is a process with intellectual qualities. In many instances, misperception is enhanced by faulty "seeing"; faulty seeing obscures the process of attaining knowledge.

In medieval Augustinian terms, the mechanics of seeing were integrally tied up with the heart and soul as well as the belly and the mind. A ray of fire from the eye would illuminate the object being seen and send its image directly through the eye, into the soul of the seer. Therefore, if one saw evil, that evil entered directly into the soul and festered there, obscuring the inner light of the seer. Thus it was entirely feasible that an evil soul could throw the evil eye onto another soul, compromising the recipient's spiritual health.

Those of us living in today's highly technological culture suffer not from the evil eye, a medieval superstition, but rather from the bedeviled eye. Nanosecond television editing, MTV-style sequencing, highway billboards, neon competitions at strip malls, and *cyberpaginalia* may force us to edit much of what we see for the sake of personal sanity. Theologian Margaret Miles makes a good case for this shifting perceptual ability in *Image as Insight* (Boston: Beacon Press, 1985). In the sense that Miles suggests—that we involuntarily censor what we see to prevent visual overload—what remains of the act of seeing has been reduced to a voyeuristic and passive activity, best represented by the act of watching television or videos. Miles writes that such rapid imaging cannot "stimulate the mind to greater precision of thought and expression." Unfortunately, the act of "seeing" art—particularly when it is religious in nature—requires far more connection between the brain and the belly of the soul.

"On the contrary," Miles concludes, "the contemplation of a religious image is more likely to rest the mind and to correct its busy craving for articulate verbalization." She infers that this kind of "meditative" seeing, so familiar to the illiterate medieval churchgoer, has all but been erased from the programming of the young twenty-first-century mind.[5]

C. S. Lewis understood this transaction between seeing and deep knowledge as well, writing in "Meditations in a Toolshed": "One could spend one's life looking *at* things, but taking the effort to look *alongside* is a different, richer, deeper matter."[6] This involves a discerning insight. Perhaps the effort of looking "alongside" can be best described by the trick one must use at night to see a star. It just so happens that the actual center of sight in the eye surrenders its best night vision rods and cones to the optical cortex, which connects the circuitry of the eyeball to the brain. This is why seeing a thing at night requires us to look slightly to one side of it; looking directly at a star will actually blot it out of view. During daylight, our eyes work in tandem to alleviate this blind spot, sending two images to the brain that are then combined.

Although Lewis rarely commented on the visual arts, he revealed a few cogent premises in "How the Few and the Many Use Pictures and Music," published in *An Experiment in Criticism*. "Nearly all those pictures which, in reproduction, are widely popular are of things which in one way or another would in reality please or amuse or excite or move those who admire them," Lewis writes. Whether or not Jack's own rubric, the "widely popular," included the museum reproductions of Constable's *Haywain* or Van Gogh's *Sunflowers* that hung in his own home at The Kilns, near Oxford, Lewis does not say.[7] He does, however, bracket the "widely popular" as

> hunting scenes and battles; death beds and dinner parties; children, dogs, cats and kittens; pensive young women (draped) to arouse sentiment, and cheerful young women (less draped) to arouse appetite. The approving comments which those who buy such pictures make on them are all of one sort: "That's the loveliest face I ever saw!"—"Notice the old man's Bible on the table."—"You can see they're all listening."— "What a beautiful old house!" The emphasis is on what may be called the narrative qualities of the picture. Line or color as such, or composition are hardly mentioned. The skill of the artist sometimes is. But what is admired is the realism and the difficulty, real or supposed, of producing it.
>
> This attitude, which was once my own, might almost be defined as "using" pictures. While you retain this attitude you treat the picture—or rather, a hasty and unconscious selection of elements in the picture— as a self-starter for certain imaginative and emotional activities of your own. In other words, you "do things with it." You don't lay yourself open to what it, by

being in its totality precisely the thing it is, can do to you. To be moved by the thought of a solitary old shepherd's death and the fidelity of his dog is, in itself, not in the least a sign of inferiority. The real objection to that way of enjoying pictures is that you never get beyond yourself. The picture, so used, can call out of you only what is already there. You do not cross the frontier into that new region which the pictorial art as such has added to the world.[8]

What might Lewis mean about this idea of getting beyond "yourself" or crossing the frontier into a new region of art appreciation? I'm not sure Lewis knew the answer himself, in visual terms, and I am certain that his taste would not have embraced most contemporary art, had he been alive today. But his insistence that an "extra"-ordinary effort is required to really "see" art is a valid one, and it is also most often what we as amateur viewers protest against. "The first demand any work of art makes upon us is surrender," Lewis writes in *Experiment in Criticism*. "Look. Listen. Receive. Get yourself out of the way. (There is no good asking first whether the work before you deserves such a surrender, for until you have surrendered you cannot possibly find out.)"[9]

The Problem of Terminology

Part of our discomfort with comprehending—or, surrendering to—contemporary art forms can be explained by a simple exploration of the dictionary term for "art." Try to define art without dictionaries or references. Such a simple exercise can take hours, since art is a body of widely disparate productions and objects, appearing in a variety of forms. The traditional definition, in this case paraphrased from the *American Heritage Dictionary*, takes the following line: Art is a conscious arrangement or production of elements that appeal to one's sense of beauty.

Examples of the elements are broadly represented by paint, stone, textiles, wood, videos, film, and various materials in the visual arts; sounds in music; movement in dance; gesture in drama; words in literature, and so on. It is the deep desire of many conservatively aesthetic Christians that this classical terminology should be reinstated as the *alpha* definition for art and that all other art outside of this spectrum should be ruled as invalid. Such a sentiment is tantamount to cultural terrorism but often voiced in conservative Christian circles.

The problem with such a myopic perspective is that most art being made today intentionally travels far beyond the limitations of this traditional definition. Ever since the impressionist "revolution" against the rules of so-called academic painting in the 1890s, artists have undertaken a conscious revolt against this traditional definition. Educationally, it has been decades since the most preeminent American art schools mandated excellence in craft or the concept of ideal beauty as main goals for the burgeoning artist. In fact, the process that influences most contemporary Western art is rigorously *unconscious,* meant to avoid the biases that the artist might build into the work by being too intentional or manipulative. More problematically, beauty has either become merely incidental in current works of art or has entirely evaporated as an artistic guideline. Beauty is no longer the inherent goal of the artistic endeavor from the Western world's point of view. It remains in place, however, because the public craves it.

My own approach to the difficult task of judging contemporary art is to fall upon the root meaning of the word *beauty.* Etymologically, *beauty* is defined as a quality that pleases or satisfies the senses. Unfortunately, this root meaning makes it difficult to avoid the problem of subjective judgment in the critique of art from a professional or a layperson's perspective. A substantial work of art offers continual satisfaction to its viewer, who will return repeatedly to appraise it. Such a sense of satisfaction can move collectors to purchase certain works of contemporary art that might not, at first glance, be described as "beautiful." But here is the rub: these days, beauty is somewhat beholden—better said, chained inescapably—to the eye of its beholder. In any case, most of what the Christian world instinctively describes as "beauty" is limited to the reiterations of classical works innovated in ancient Greece and reiterated during the Renaissance or to realistic reproductions of what we can actually see already. Nothing could be further from most of the art that Christians and nonbelievers are producing today.

This said, nothing is wrong with either approach—realism, or ideal beauty—except the fact that neither one suffices as the exclusive way in which Christians choose to participate in today's art. The high road of ideal beauty in art is influenced by the works of Plato and his followers and cannot be accepted unthinkingly as a purely Christ-driven aesthetic, since the ancient Greeks were pagan by Christian standards. As Yale theologian Jaroslav Pelikan explains in his marvelous journey through the artistic and theological depiction of Christ, *The Illustrated Jesus Through the Centuries,* "the Platonic triad of the Beautiful, the True, and the Good" is somewhat replaced by Jesus Christ's metaphors for himself as the Way, the Truth and the Life in John 14:6.[10] Frankly, such metaphors are often too abstract to concretize in visual terms.

Too frequently, Christian reviewers erroneously assume that the evils of contemporary art would be solved by a return to Plato's ideals as presented during the Italian Renaissance. Renaissance art is broadly perceived as religious, and palatable on the eyes because of its adherence to Neoplatonic ideals concerning beauty. With this, there is an assumption that Renaissance artists were yoked to the church, when in fact they were often simply astute professionals who knew how to please their customers, regardless of whether the clientele was the Vatican or a filthy rich merchant. Fra Filippo Lippi, a Carmelite monk, provides an excellent example of this accommodating duplicity at London's National Gallery, where the viewer can see the same composition applied to *Moses Bringing Forth Water from the Rock,* or *Egyptians Worshipping the Bull God Apis.* (The Egyptians, of course, have racier outfits and look far more gleeful—probably because they can dance.)

As for the low road of realism, it never fails to please the eye when satisfactorily rendered, but it adds nothing to the current discussion about the validity of art practice. In effect, it can inspire a neutralizing or even trite art that will not usually give Christians an entrée to the cultural mainstream. For instance, Thomas Kinkade's impressionistic landscapes are known and loved throughout the nation, and his savvy sense of commercialism has made him the wealthiest artist of the twentieth century, according to some.[11] Despite this financial success, Kinkade's mass-produced canvases are seen as laughable and superficial works in the professional arts world. Even if we grumpily condemn most contemporary artworks to the "laughable and superficial" heap, the ethics of the situation remain. We must ask, Who will enter *that* arena, and speak for Christ on *that* level?

Classicism and realism conform to the more traditional definition of art, but to include contemporary art, one has to come up with a broader description. Joseph Beuys, the influential German conceptualist who dominated art of the 1970s, described art simply as "being and doing."[12] If one chose to stand in a spot because he was waiting for a bus, that was life; if one chose to stand in a spot waiting for a bus because she had decided to produce a performance piece, that was art. Of course, "being and doing" does not suffice as an operative definition for art, although the concept of art as merely "being and doing" does emphasize the current obsession with expressing the "self." My concession to the need to be inclusive about defining art comes to the following premise: Art is a form of deliberate, intentioned human expression. Make no mistake about it: this is a bridge-building definition. It allows artists of any belief to speak to one another about the potential of art, and Christians to enter into the arena of high art. Do not expect you will be "heard" if you bring a traditional definition of art into the arena of contemporary art practices.

The Problem of Art as a Lie

Then there is the problem with the illusionary nature of art, as a concept. Consider the savvy comment of Gustave Flaubert, the nineteenth-century French critic and controversial author of *Madame Bovary*: "Of all lies, art is the least untrue." Or, consider Picasso's paraphrase, "Art is the lie that helps us see the truth."[13] Art can really be the truest of lies, or better said, the truest of illusions. Why should I, as an arts advocate, accept such a statement so willingly?

Simply because art really *is* an illusion. Art is not equal to the substance that it appears to be, as Rene Magritte's rendering of a pipe labeled *Ceci n'est pas une pipe* ("This is not a pipe") confirms in his 1928 painting, *The Treason of Images*. The logical test of reality would be to attempt to smoke the pipe in the canvas, and this would end in failure, of course. It is a logical assertion that three-dimensional reality cannot truly be portrayed in all its fullness by a two-dimensional, or flat, illustration. The line drawn to separate an object from the space it rests within does not truly exist. The mixture of colored pigments that constitute a color is never a true match to the actual seen color, which in turn, is actually a reflection of light waves. The shadow that is painted is never truly solid, in reality. The scene from life that captures a moment of reality is never truly as stationary as it seems to be on a canvas or in a sculpture.

Along a more subtle but empowered line of reasoning, the way an artist interprets reality is going to be several times removed from that actual reality and changed as well as by the artist's personal perception of the scene or idea. Yet there can be no contesting the fact that well-made art delights the viewer when it reconfigures reality and fools the eye and the soul into accepting the illusion.

With religious imagery, the illusionary quality of art challenges us even more. After all, which artist ever recorded the actual face of Christ during his earthly visit? A review of imagery will show that Jesus Christ has been beardless or hirsute, young or lined with wrinkles, blow-dried or sunbaked, placid or wrathful, blue-eyed or brown-eyed, slight or extremely muscled, masculine or feminine or androgynous, and of varying racial types. Contemporary painters striking a banner for inclusivity have even gone further, applying the icon tradition to depict Christ as a Mayan god, a Buddhist monk, a Navajo chief, or an African soothsayer. Ostensibly, this is meant to bring home the point that Jesus Christ is made in all our images, whether or not we are made in his (hers?). In his excellent summation of the historical problem of Christ's appearance, *The Clash of Gods: A Reinterpretation of Early Christian Art,* art historian Thomas Mathews writes:

The imagery that was formed for the new God drew upon a variety of potent sources—the gods, the philosophers, the magicians of antiquity. Its dependence on the Gospel, however, was curiously oblique. Scripture had left no account of the physical appearance of Christ, and in any event its claims for Christ far exceeded all visual symbols. How was the artist to deal with Christ's own self portrait: "before Abraham was, I am"?[14]

In fact, the bloodiest battle of Christendom was sparked by arguments about the artistic countenance of Jesus Christ. The so-called Iconoclastic Controversy came to a boil in the 750s, featuring acrimonious debates that lasted 150 years, and resulting in the final schism between Eastern Orthodoxy and Roman Catholicism.[15] On occasion, orthodox iconographers had their eyes gouged out, and untold masterpieces of the iconographic tradition were burned. The prime argument fell between the East's assertion that the divinity of Christ was not compromised by his physical and human depiction in the holy icons. Antiorthodox factions in Rome insisted that material portrayals of Christ circumscribed his eternal and spiritual divinity. Interestingly, this objection evaporated conveniently when the Vatican began commissioning images of Christ that numbered into the thousands during the Medieval, Renaissance, and Baroque periods. The Protestant Reformers were spurred, in part, by the ridiculously lavish art of sixteenth-century Roman Catholicism, causing an equal reaction in the opposite direction that still leaves most Protestant sanctuaries unadorned and unconcerned by art.

But there is also an area of utter confusion reigning in the terminology of what is meant, in these days, by "religious" or "spiritual" or "sacred" art. Another barometer that highlights this shifting terminology is illustrated by the four-hundred-page catalog for a 1986 exhibit at the prestigious Los Angeles County Museum of Art, titled *The Spiritual in Abstract Art: 1890–1985.*[16] Although the book and exhibit are hinged on the word *spiritual,* there is not a single publicly professing Christian included among its artists.[17] The catalog's ambitious glossary of spiritual categories includes alchemy, anthroposophy, cabala, gnosticism, hermeticism, Native American and primitive folklore, occult science, and theosophy, but there is not even a tip of a hat to medieval and contemporary Christian mysticism or intellectual traditions. Is it possible that no Christian cultivated an abstract or symbological style of art? This would be a surprise to CIVA, which is currently mounting a traveling exhibit that will include dozens of abstract artists between the ages of twenty and seventy.[18]

In 1988, painter Edward Knippers of Washington, D.C., was the only Christian invited to a panel discussion on spirituality and the arts at the prestigious Hirschorn Museum. He used the opportunity to make a statement about distinction:

> Our topic was "The New Spirituality in Art." The distinctively Christian was my personal concern at the time. I said that one would assume that anything calling itself a religion would have a spiritual dimension in the same way that anything we call water will be wet. But the major issue when it comes to water is not its wetness, but its drinkability. One can die of thirst in the presence of most of the world's water. As with water, so it is with religion. It is not how the religions of the world are alike that is important—that they are all spiritual—but how they are different. Which one can give life, and give it more abundantly?[19]

In the years since this time, more Christians are in the limelight at prestigious modern art arenas, asking the questions. If we can ask them first, in the classroom, as this litany of problems I've presented attempts to demonstrate, our students will be that much further along in their intellectual development, especially with regard to artistic endeavor.

Applications with an Agenda

The security of the Christian classroom, provided it is not "shut away" from contemporary culture, offers one of the premiere sites for wrestling the complicated issues of current art practices to clarity. During 1999, I experimented with students at Union University with a seminar called "Contemporary Issues in Art," devoted to giving an in-depth review of the particular problems associated with contemporary art. Any Christian department preparing artists for a career in the real world ought to require art majors to take such a course.

This particular course was driven by the students' initial questions about art after a few preliminary readings and a review of the main challenges to traditional art posed by modernism and the avant garde. Based on questions that sorted themselves into three main categories, a compendious reader of essays and articles was compiled from secular sources, texts about spiritual art from the non-Christian arena, and some of the typical Christian critiques and assessments on the arts.[20]

As it turned out, these students were more preoccupied with issues of validity and propriety as Christians making art rather than the recent historical lineage of the arts world—the closest significant collections of modern art are five to ten hours away by car. While the students did wish to know how to justify the approaches of conceptualism, abstraction, or minimalism as communicative approaches to art, their main line of inquiry was motivated by questions such as these:

- How far can Christians go in the arts without being unrighteous?
- Should every artwork by a Christian be obviously "spiritual" in content?
- Does there always have to be an explanation for the purpose or meaning of the artwork, especially if it can cause stumbling?
- What are the inappropriate and appropriate uses of the human body or form in art?
- Is going for shock value instead of craft or excellence a weakness in art?

In most cases, the students never actually received pat answers to their questions, and this annoyed them considerably. Nevertheless, if they as individuals continue in the arts as professionals, they will have to resolve these issues on their own terms as practicing artists. No rote set of rules or pat replies can truly stand up against controversy, when controversy arises about art, because in the end the artists' intention and ethic, if not their very personality, are put on trial.

In the Christian arena, artists of faith who experience censorship often receive it from their church community on the one hand or are passive-aggressively drummed out of the professional arts scene by simply being ignored and passed over in regional competitions. The methodology of this particular session was meant to draw out the students' ability to ask questions and to leave them with a body of literature that could be pondered over the coming years (if it is not used for compost or insulation). Our discussions were designed to highlight all the possible answers to the problems posed, but ultimately, students were evaluated on the level of engagement they undertook in the discussion—not whether they had the "right" or "wrong" answers for the questions. That methodology serves for philosophy, ethics, and theology but not at all for contemporary art discussions.

Partial answers to the questions were presented when we viewed contemporary works by artists who do not identify with the Christian community but work with pronounced religious themes, such as mixed media artist Bill Viola, as well as Christians and current members of CIVA. Students also evaluated commercially viable regional galleries in Memphis and Nashville, interviewed art collectors, surveyed attitudes on the campus, considered creating works that would demonstrate the differences between various styles of art, and heard from visiting guest artists while they labored through the reader material.

Because it was unfolding during the progress of "Contemporary Issues in Art," we seized the opportunity to analyze the unholy flap caused by Chris Ofili's collage *The Blessed Virgin Mary* at the Brooklyn Museum show, "Sensations: Young British Artists from the Saatchi Collection." The issues at hand regarding "Sensations" were extremely distorted, yet few Christians of note actually went to the museum and gave any balance to the discussion on the printed page or confronted the exhibit's curators with their

questions. In March 2000, one self-professed Christian pro-
tester hoodwinked the security guards and then triumphantly
smeared a tube of white paint over the work. This reaction-
based, extremely nonconstructive approach to making ourselves heard in the public forum—which parallels the
dynamiting of abortion clinics, in some ways—only polarizes
more negative press for the conservative viewpoint, thus stopping the opportunity for dialogue once again.

Conservative critiques generally reported that Ofili dese-
crated the image of Mary by "smearing" elephant dung over
the image (when it was actually presented in dried clumps) and
encircling the African Madonna with crude magazine cutouts
of genitalia. Some chided Ofili for portraying Mary as a black
African.

In response, Christian art historian Elizabeth Douglas of
Geneva College, Pennsylvania, sent out an E-mail epistle in support of Ofili's choices. She explained that the artist's upbringing
as a devout Nigerian Roman Catholic influenced his use of
dung because, in the harsh outback of Nigeria, elephant dung
is life-sustaining fuel. She also wished to clarify the fact that his
use of magazine imagery was not pornographic but meant to
emphasize Mary's humanity in her role as the mother of God's
son—Mary's womb bore the Lord, and Mary's breasts suckled
him, after all. Douglas, who is African-American, also commented about the racial slurs connected to the work:

> Is it also bad taste that German Renaissance painter
> Dürer painted the Virgin as a plump German blonde? Is
> it bad taste that Michelangelo carved his Pieta with
> Mary, who would have been nearly fifty at the time of
> the crucifixion, bearing the face of an 18 year old, and
> having a body the size of an NFL linebacker? They are
> not described as bad taste, but accepted as reflecting
> the cultural norms of their time and place. . . . Let's
> avoid condemning things before we have examined the
> evidence.[21]

Nevertheless, mere explanations of a controversial work do
not satisfy our reservations about a particularly troubling piece,

nor can they justify it as a truly "good" work of art. Many of the "Sensations" works are distinguished more by their shock value than by the attainment of art that truly has a presence, or provokes a thoughtful response in the viewer, or leaves a sense of aesthetic satisfaction in the onlooker.

During the "Sensations" outcry, it is my view that the political and economic undertones were far more controversial than the actual works. It is far more disturbing that the Brooklyn Museum allowed itself to be used as a showroom for Charles Saatchi, the owner of the collection, who is looking for a "Sensations" buyer to augment his sinking fortunes. It is equally troubling that New York mayor Rudolph Giuliani called attention to the show by threatening to remove city funding from the museum—an ethical consideration that borders on the museum's rights of freedom of expression. Was this a senate election campaign ploy? Should the mayor of New York have the right to limit any American's right to freedom of expression?

In this harshly secular climate, Christians in particular need to be extremely concerned about freedom of expression; our faith is transmitted at public gatherings called worship services, where we are free to speak from the pulpit; we are free to pray in public; we are free to hold marches, conduct events in public arenas, and so on. If the right to freedom of expression is not protected for one group, what prevents the freedom of religious expression, which we take for granted in this country, from being compromised?

Similar dynamics occurred in 1989 when the National Endowment for the Arts (NEA) fielded damaging criticism for funding Robert Mapplethorpe's homoerotic photography, Richard Serrano's *Piss Christ*, and Karen Finley's off-color performance art.

Based on the questions I fielded from audiences I addressed in the 1990s, many Christians seemed obsessed about their right to censor artwork because their hard-earned taxes funded the NEA. As *Time* magazine critic Robert Hughes pointed out to me during a conversation at a CIVA conference in 1993, (a) less than one dollar of each individual tax return funded the

NEA at the time; (b) these three artists represented a miniscule percentage of something like eighty-three hundred grants to individuals and companies funded by the NEA over its history, and (c) if the NEA were suspended, hundreds of small art enterprises, individuals, and performing companies would lose annual funding that constituted the bulk of their budgets—even in amounts as small as $10,000 per annum. Dismantling the NEA also, ironically, removes the possibility of funding for Christians who apply for such opportunities; and if Christians do not get into the arena of the NEA, then our voice within an elite arts organization is dissipated.

Senator Jesse Helms, like Giuliani, promoted a great deal of negative rhetoric about the arts and the NEA, eventually causing NEA director John Frohnmayer to resign. In the end this was actually a great loss, as Frohnmayer was one of the few commentators in the high art world who attended church and understood Christian mores. Whatever possible equilibrium he might have brought to the arts discussion was squandered when he was harried out of the arena. Once more, conservative Christian voices became negative detractors in the public arena who added invective, but nothing constructive, to the art scene.[22]

The solution for Christians who wish to regain a voice that is heard in the arts is much more difficult than being a self-appointed censor. Contemporary art cannot be eradicated. Artists will make "bad" or controversial art, and sell it, and even be rewarded for it with huge press attention and monetary gain, regardless of Christian morals and tenets. The system of contemporary gallery exhibits and museum shows is one that some Christians can enter without losing integrity, but it is not for everyone. Other Christians will continue to create art that is trivial, cliché, and banal, and they will be financially rewarded for it by fellow Christians who collect mass-produced *kitsch*—a German word indicating "inconsequential trash." But this work will not impact the culture to the slightest degree, and nor, some might say, does it glorify the Lord.

To remind myself of the urgency of crossing cultural boundaries, I often revisit a quote I found a few years ago in a front-page article, "And Now, a Word from Our Creator," from the

New York Times Book Review. The author somewhat flippantly described the reappearance of God as a "viable" character in contemporary novels, mentioning works by Flannery O'Connor, Walker Percy, Frederick Buechner, John Updike, Thomas Keneally, and Timothy Winton, among others. O'Connor, a shrewd interpreter of the waywardness of humanity, wrote this in the 1950s:

> When you can assume that your audience holds the same beliefs you do, you can relax a little and use more normal means of talking to it. When you have to assume that it does not, then you have to make your vision apparent by shock. To the hard of hearing, you shout. And for the almost blind, you draw large and startling figures.[23]

Flannery O'Connor, a devout Roman Catholic, was not envisioning Christians talking among themselves within the comfortable ghettoes of a Christian subculture. O'Connor was encouraging a shock-shout-and-startle strategy to engage those who *will* not hear, *will* not see, *will* not touch.

Within our places of worship, it is entirely appropriate to foster art that glorifies God. But if we wish to speak to the public and regain a voice among what culture critic Tom Wolfe calls "art worldlings," we must keep this alternative, sightless, deaf, and hostile audience in mind. "Christian art" ceases to exist as a chapter heading in any textbook on art after the medieval architecture of the tenth through fourteenth centuries. Even art that is not obviously "Christian," but exhibits a sincere and specifically Christian theme, has been summarily dismissed by the world of high art for over a century.

The grandest irony of the present situation is that postmodernism, denigrated by many Christians for valid theoretical reasons, has reopened the door to Christian content. One of the surprising virtues of postmodernism is a propensity to embrace a variety of contents, forms of expression, and artistic approaches. All historical and traditional forms of art have been welcomed back into the fold of contemporary art-making. Christians in the arts are now, more than ever, positioned to make an impact in contemporary culture by reintroducing Christian content to the arts in a variety of styles. Significant bridges are being rebuilt to the culture, thanks to the persistence of our Christian campus art departments, the understated (mostly voluntary) efforts of Christians who administrate arts fellowships, the increasing availability of grants given to Christian endeavors, and the thirty-something-year lead that artists of the faith have used as practice, so that they might "speak" effectively into the culture.

Problem-Breaking Principles

Alongside the litany of problems isolated by this chapter, the educator's responsibility must include positive suggestions and proactive solutions. In teaching, I always mention several foundational principles in ceaseless operation that gird any believer who is attempting to dedicate any work to the ultimate glory of God, whether they accept this operation or not. These have to do with the infinite creativity and ultimate selfhood of God; the intelligence and pattern-breaking example of Jesus Christ; and the communicative yet often wordless bent of the Holy Spirit.

If God is the Creator of the entire universe and is an infinite being, and if we are made in God's image, then it stands to reason that Christians and particularly artists of faith are connected to an infinite source of creative solutions in life. We don't always act as if we have access to an infinite and free source of endless creativity, because the obvious, the trite, and the cliché are safer than mystery and open-ended assertions. But Christians ought to exhibit an innate creativity if they are truly expressing the creative image of the Creator.

On another tangent relating to the *imago dei* versus our image, the dominant mode of making art since the early 1900s has been that of self-expression. Self-expressive modes of art delve deeply into the psyche of the artist, or use art as a cathartic release of emotional energy. Robert Hughes asked in *The Shock of the New*: "Is the Self automatically interesting in art?"

> Few cultures have been so obsessively preoccupied
> with the merely personal as ours . . . . The last [40]

years are littered with the debris of attempts to claim
for the exposure of the self that conceptual dignity
which is the property of art. Every kind of petty documentation, psychic laundry list, and autistic gesture has
been performed, taped, pinned up, filed, and pho-
tographed.[24]

We assume that because we are operating in a seemingly endless era of self-generated art, we as so-called selfless servants of
God cannot participate. Even in a self-obsessed era, Christians
have an option to participate within the mainstream—moreover, Christendom includes an element of self-expression that is
undeniable and goes right to the "top." How does God explain
the being of the Almighty to Moses in Exodus? Roughly translated, God's name is the "I AM," or the "I AM THAT I AM."
This Creator God is therefore the ultimate self in an era of self-
hinged art. Artists of faith who are wittingly gaining perfected
knowledge in the nature of God, in whose image they are made,
will express part of this knowledge as their "self" gained
expression through art. In an age that is saturated with the
visual, it must be said, such awesome and mysterious concepts
may be better served by the nonverbal ideations we call art,
rather than an exclusive menu of verbal treatises. Mystery and
the exploration of deeper existential truths of life have always
been the natural province of art—the question is, whose truths
are being conveyed?

Another operative principle relates to a question that
philosopher Dallas Willard from the University of Southern
California has used to challenge many audiences. If you were
asked, "Who is the most intelligent person that ever walked
the earth?" who naturally comes to mind first? Einstein?
Wittgenstein? [Ben Stein?] [Is that your final answer?] Willard
finds it rather amazing that Christians rarely answer with the
one reply that corresponds to scriptural truth. Scripture tells
us that Jesus Christ was in the beginning, with God, during
the creation. Christ also walked the earth and became intimately familiar with God's creation on human terms. So we
also have to say, our image in God's image is tied up with

God's intelligence, manifested in Jesus Christ. Artists of faith seeking to attain Christlikeness ought to be reflecting a cosmic appreciation for intelligence through their intimate rapport with the Lord, regardless of their IQ levels.

In addition to his numerous job titles—Messiah, Emmanuel, Counselor, Way, Truth, Life, and so on—Jesus Christ was a pattern-breaker. He overcame the apparent triumph of death by the resurrection. The Lord's example is one of bold innovations, response instead of visceral reaction, and nonconformity that fly in the face of superficial word games or pharisaical traps. So we should expect, at least on occasion, to be surprised in the best way by the art of those attempting to follow in the Lord's steps. If art is truly emulating Christ, it ought to have elements of the creatively nonconventional, the healthily subversive, and the surprising.

Made in the image of God, we are also inseparably connected to the Holy Spirit, the communicator who intercedes for us to God with ceaseless groans deeper than words (Rom. 8). A vitally communicative spirit is inseparable from our image in the image of God and may express the most sublime praise and anguish. The Spirit is essential to us because God did not always use obvious means of communication. Can you understand all the parables? Can you grasp the gist of all the prophets' acts (which showcase Jehovah's penchant, incidentally, for wildly creative and provocative performance art)? Is the Book of Job perfectly clear in your perception? Did God ever say, "Go ye out and make obvious art?" There are many examples of open-ended communiques between the people of God and the Creator—otherwise, why would the development of discernment be such a necessity to Christian maturity?

The character of Bezalel as tabernacle designer leads us to a wonderful conclusion in the New Testament, which makes no specific entreaties to artists at all. Bezalel the highly skilled, Bezalel the versatile, Bezalel the willing, the Spirit-attuned, the teacher, and the team member worked on a physical tabernacle that has long ceased to exist. The people were so enthusiastic about the tabernacle that God art-directed through Moses that Moses had to tell them to stop bringing their gold and fine stones. If you've ever been involved in church-building campaigns, you know that people never have to be stopped from bringing in financial contributions; in fact, the extraction of money is often a drawn-out process with no surfeit of "cheerful givers."

So it is with the New Testament temple. In 1 Peter 2:4–10, Peter infers to God's elect that although the third temple in Jerusalem was destroyed and ransacked by the Romans in A.D. 71, the new Christians—as the living stones—have rebuilt the new temple. You, Christian, are a living stone of the new temple, fashioned by an artist of great renown.

Christ is the eternal cornerstone of this spiritual tabernacle—the permanent feature that supports all the other structures; Isaiah foresees this lineage for Christ in chapter 43. Use the imagination God has given you to ponder which architectural element you are: are you a decorative element? A sturdy stone, just doing its job in the middle of a wall of other stones? Perhaps, today, you're feeling more like a rain gutter or a door frame. Perhaps, on other days, you feel like a window—a beautifully carved aperture that lets the light of day pierce the temple's shadows. And who among us serves as a golden but nonfunctional, decorative ornament of great beauty? For art is so often denigrated because it is so nonfunctional in a utilitarian world, and yet God saw fit to include beauty and decoration in the first temple.

During a CIVA conference in 1993, an Orthodox priest and academician, Anthony Ugolnik, charged several hundred CIVA artists with a call many of us cannot forget: "The wasteland of twentieth-century secularism—the desert to which Christ or the monk goes—is alive with possibilities . . . . Refuse to be marginalized. Render holy the process of image-making."[25]

CHAPTER 10

CHRISTIAN WORLDVIEW
AND MUSIC

PAUL MUNSON

WHETHER ONE CONSIDERS the testimony and commands of
Scripture or the historical experience of the church, there is no
overlooking the prominence of music in the Christian life.
About a hundred times in Scripture, God's people are urged to
make music; much of Scripture is in fact song; and just about
everybody seems to have something to sing, from the morning
stars as God laid the cornerstone of the world (Job 38:7), to
those who rebuilt Jerusalem after returning from exile (Neh.
12), from the songs recorded early in Luke's Gospel, to the song
of Moses and of the lamb sung by those who have conquered
the beast and his image and the number of his name (Rev. 15).
In his *Confessions* Augustine testifies: "How deeply was I
moved by the voices of your sweet singing Church! Those
voices flowed into my ears and the truth was distilled into my
heart, which overflowed with my passionate devotion. Tears
ran from my eyes and happy I was in those tears."[1] Pretty heady
stuff! Here is an art through which "truth was distilled" into
the heart of one of the church's greatest theologians. And then
there is Luther's famous dictum assigning to music the highest
place and greatest honor among disciplines, next to theology.[2]

We do not need to rehearse further how rich a gift music has
been in the lives of the saints. We already know. Christians care
so deeply for the gift that they quarrel over it. Today, more than
ever, many, who are merely trying to be good stewards of something so obviously precious, have divided the church over what
Michael Hamilton in *Christianity Today* has called dogmas of

music. "Since the 1950s, denominational divisions have steadily become less important in American church life. We have the baby boom generation (of which I am a part) to thank for much of this. But at bottom we are all still sectarians; we still prefer to congregate with the likeminded. Our new sectarianism is a sectarianism of worship style. The new sectarian creeds are dogmas of music."[3] American church life is marked by dissension over worship, and the accompanying debate has dominated published Christian thought on music. This essay, too, as it surveys the field, will have to focus disproportionately on the role of music in congregational worship.

But let us be clear from the outset: good stewardship of the gift of music involves many things besides just responsibility for what we sing on Sunday mornings. Each of us must decide what music will be ours during the rest of the week as well. We must decide how we will use it and how we will share it. If we are dogmatic, this implies that we are principled. But how do we know where our principles will lead us? Or, more to the point, do we know that our principles are biblical? And—dare I ask—are we even aware of what our principles are?

The truism "Ideas have consequences" has been a loaded expression since Richard Weaver's editors chose it for the title of his 1948 book. What makes the truism so memorable is that, while it seems self-evident, upon reflection we realize that we naively live much of our lives as if it were not true—as if our worldview were only remotely relevant to our daily lives. When we assume that we can act in a "value-free" way we deceive ourselves, for we bring to our every endeavor, including music, the ideas that have shaped us. If the ideas are not our own, they will be someone else's. The ideas that people have about beauty (whether found in an iris, an old ghost story, first love, or a hard linedrive straight down the first-base line) are what philosophers call *aesthetic* ideas. As a worldview aims to make sense of the world as a whole, so aesthetic principles aim to make sense of beauty. If we want our decisions about music to be biblically sound, we ought first to make sure that our aesthetic presuppositions are, too.

The thesis of this essay is that the way we relate to music follows from the way we answer five questions: *Why do we make (or listen to) music? How do we decide which songs to sing (or play or hear)? Does it matter? What does music mean anyway? And what is its moral significance?* While it is beyond the scope of this essay systematically to provide answers for each of these questions, it will be argued that good stewardship of the gift begins with the conscientious application of biblical principles to these issues. And where the church is in an aesthetic muddle, more often than not it is because we have been careless in our first principles.

In recent years, the finest and most comprehensive consideration of music from a distinctively evangelical perspective has been Harold Best's *Music through the Eyes of Faith* (a contribution to the Christian College Coalition's series Through the Eyes of Faith). Best exhorts musicians to reject as their vocational model the romantic conception of the haughty, isolated artist-hero in favor of a biblical model of the humble servant. He exhorts all Christians to think critically about our stylistic prejudices, that we might more richly glorify God in "a Pentecost of musics." This makes for some convicting and inspiring reading. But, as helpful as Best's counsel is in such matters, the case he makes for cultural pluralism rests on aesthetic principles that ultimately make it difficult for him to explain why Christians should be discriminating at all in their musical choices.

> From here on out, I take the position that, with certain exceptions, art and especially music are morally relative and inherently incapable of articulating, for want of a better term, truth speech. They are essentially neutral in their ability to express belief, creed, moral and ethical exactitudes, or even worldview. I also assume that, no matter how passionately artists may believe what they believe or try to show these beliefs in what they imagine and craft, their art remains purposefully "dumb."[4]

It is important to consider these assertions in their context. Best is at pains to correct the simplistic belief, at one time common in the church, that the structures of musical style can be inherently good or evil. Unless combined with words, the abstract vocabulary and syntax of music are incapable of bearing precise propositional truth. Arguing in this way, he is able to drive home a much-needed lesson, that "Christians are biblically justified in fully celebrating artistic activity of the most diverse sort, including that which may have been created in downright unbelief."

But the matter is not as easily resolved as Best would have it, for serious musical thinkers have always recognized a link between style and idea, in part because music almost always *is* combined with words. Musicians make the stylistic decisions they do because they are trying to communicate particular ideas as effectively as possible. Therefore it is not happenstance that medieval music sounds the way it does and that Renaissance music sounds the way it does. One did not merely evolve from the other. The changes in style reflected changes in worldview, and the ideas that animated the Renaissance would become strangely inarticulate if one tried to express them in a medieval idiom (and vice versa).

So what do I say when a student asks me about the beauty he hears in Richard Strauss's *Also sprach Zarathustra* or Dave Matthews's "Crash" or Zimbabwean mbira music intended to induce trance? A biblical perspective leads us to receive with gratitude beauty wherever it may be found, but Best's confidence that art and music are incapable, by their presence and use, of shaping behaviors is dangerously overstated.[5] Not only Plato, but Hitler and Stalin (and Macy's and Penney's) would disagree. So, apparently, would the writer of 1 Samuel (16:23). The meaning of music is not exhausted once we have analyzed its lyrics and its cultural context, nor is music uniquely impotent among *things*—among the drugs and bullets and sugar and fresh air of this fallen, finite world—to shape our character. Like the sower's crops in the parable, we are contingent, yet morally responsible, beings; the Bible sees no contradiction in this.

In clarifying his theory of the moral ambiguity of art, Best turns to Romans 1 and Psalm 19 to draw an analogy between the twofold speech of God (in his Word and in creation) and the (supposedly twofold) speech of artists. His intent is to provide a paradigm that separates truth from beauty by associating truth with direct speech and beauty with creation. As you read his explanation of the paradigm, note how he opposes revelation to creation. He sees so wide a gulf between the theological categories of special revelation and general revelation that he will not use the same word for both and denies to creation its traditional status as a kind of revelation.[6]

> In the separation of revelation and creation, God has provided a clear opportunity for, and a clear distinction between, absolutes (revealed truth) and relativities (the wordless/deedless creation and its counterpart in human handiwork). Each is a separate domain; each is entirely right; and the one should not be confused with the other. Revealed truth is fixed. It is eternal. Handiwork has no fixed reference point within itself. It will pass away.[7]

Just as God speaks in two ways, in morally precise Scriptures and in a morally ambiguous creation, so, too, "if we want to know who the musician really is and what he or she believes, we should go to him or her to observe and listen. The music cannot tell us, even if the music maker wants it to; it is limited to declaring itself and pointing to its maker." Thus, in his eagerness to combat aestheticism (i.e., a view that *equates* beauty with truth) and simplistic interpretations of the moral content of art (i.e., a view that values *only* truth), one of the most articulate Protestant musicians of our day adopts a central doctrine of postmodern criticism. He divorces art from truth by denying that artists speak through their work. No matter how passionately the creators of *Paradise Lost,* the Vietnam War Memorial, or the *Eroica Symphony* may have wanted to tell us something, these works "remain purposefully 'dumb.'" They are "limited to declaring themselves and pointing to their makers" in the same "mute" way that nature points to God.

Even without considering problems in Best's interpretation of Scripture, his analogy can be shown to fail in two respects. First, the difference in purpose that accounts for the difference in function between creation and special revelation has no parallel in the relationship between artistic human speech and more direct kinds of human speech. Sure, a sunrise does not tell us how God saves, but, then again, this was presumably not what it was intended to do. This *was* the intent of J. S. Bach when he wrote his *St. Matthew Passion*. The difference between God's creation and special revelation is that, whereas in creation God intends to glorify himself by all sorts of means (illuminating the heavens, filling the earth with life, etc.), in special revelation he intends to glorify himself specifically through saving sinners. The truth of this salvation can be the subject of any form of human communication, including art.

A second failure of the analogy is that it treats the categories of absolute and relative in a confusing way. In the divine half of the analogy, Best only contrasts the absolute nature of God's truth with the relative nature of creation's beauty. (This allows him by analogy to call the truth embodied in the Christian's life "absolute" and everything else "relative.") But why does he not contrast the *beauty of the Creator* with the beauty of creation? Or the truth of the Creator with that truth which can be expressed or lived by the creature when he has learned it from revelation? Because then he would have to concede that there is an absolute measure of beauty. "The beauty of God," according to Best, "is not aesthetic beauty but moral and ethical beauty. The beauty of the creation is not moral beauty; it is aesthetic beauty, artifactual beauty."[8] But surely this is nonsensical. What does the term "moral beauty" mean, except that goodness is aesthetically beautiful? (And can we even speak of "aesthetic beauty" without being redundant?) Whence comes this confusion? Best's desire to establish biblical grounds for aesthetic relativism puts him in the awkward position of having to assert that God is not beautiful.

Now granted, created beauty *is* relative in the sense that it is finite: its "point of reference" is not within itself but in God's absolute beauty. In this same sense, the truth (or goodness) found in the creature is also relative. That is, the creature is true (or good) to the extent that it conforms to God's absolute truth (or goodness). Hence the distinction Best would make between revelation and creation should help us to distinguish not between absolute truth and relative beauty but between the absolute (in God) and the relative (in the finite), pure and simple. But this is not what Best means when he speaks of artistic beauty as being relative. It appears that he is an aesthetic relativist in the same way that postmoderns are: he believes that *the very essence* of beauty will vary from individual to individual and from group to group (not because the individual's perception is limited and fallen, but) because there is no objective standard. Apparently beauty really does lie in the eye of the beholder.

Or does it? What is beauty anyway? And how does the way we answer this question affect the way we answer the five basic questions about music posed at the beginning of this essay? Well, beauty obviously has to do with form. Everybody agrees on this, but this is also about as far as any agreement gets. According to the dominant view in our culture, something is beautiful if it is pretty, if it appeals to the senses; and, because everybody has a different idea of what is pretty, beauty is said to be a matter of taste, which cannot be accounted for. Or it is whatever we are culturally conditioned to think is beautiful.

We have not always thought this way. Both Augustine and Thomas Aquinas, for example, held that beauty is objective. Beauty, they said, was the form of things that enables us to recognize goodness and truth. We make a big deal of the fact that God called what he created "good." But we forget that he said this in response to *seeing* it. Six times in Genesis 1 "God saw that it was good," and then, in the thirty-first verse, "God saw all that He had made, and behold, it was very good" (NASB). Genesis 2:9 tells us that "out of the ground the LORD God caused to grow every tree that is pleasing to the sight" (NASB). (See also Eccles. 3:11.) God made everything perfectly beautiful in its own way, to imitate his own divine beauty.[9] It is our sin that introduced ugliness into the world and that blinds us to the beauty all around us. And if God made everything perfectly beautiful, then there is an objective measure for beauty and we can think critically about it. But it requires discernment and discipline.

The reason individuals and cultures differ in their notions of beauty is not that its essence is up for grabs but that no finite, fallen mind can comprehend it in its fullness. The historical Christian understanding of beauty acknowledges beauty's transcendental objectivity. If I do not recognize something as beautiful when it *is* beautiful, this is merely because I have not learned to read the artist's language, the semantics of his mode of utterance. If I pay the artist the courtesy of listening in a culturally informed way, I will recognize the beauty. Do not be fooled. In this fallen world, beauty requires something of us, just as truth and goodness do. Consider a sunset. When my daughter was two or three years old, she saw oranges and reds just fine; but she was oblivious to sunsets. Are we to doubt, then, whether a sunset is inherently beautiful? Are our ideas about the beauty of sunsets perhaps a matter of cultural conditioning? Of course not. My daughter lacked the experience and *discipline* needed to *discern* the beauty of sunsets.

Of all the explanations of beauty that I have come across, the one that most concisely gets at what people seem to mean when they say something is beautiful—whether it be a clear, blue sky or a Grünewald crucifixion—is Thomas Aquinas's. He said that beauty must include three qualities: *integrity* (the sense we have that something is whole), *right proportion* (when the parts that comprise something relate to one another in appropriate ways), and *brilliance* (Latin *claritas,* that which illuminates).[10] If this is true, it resolves many nagging questions.

Consider, for example, the old opposition between so-called utilitarian and purist approaches to art, which pits the usefulness of art against its autonomy. Do we value art for its own sake? Or as a means to some other end? If beauty is a formal integrity, proportionality, and brilliance that communicates goodness and truth, then it is by nature functional. It illuminates. Even the most abstract art and absolute (instrumental) music are beautiful to the extent that they communicate something, however intangible. The serious music lover typically feels disdain for advertisers and evangelists who prove indifferent to the aesthetic claims of music, who care only if it boosts sales or moves souls—if it "works." The problem here is not that they *use* (bad) music to communicate their message, but that they are content with a message so impoverished that it can be communicated in ugly forms.

Here is another aesthetic problem solved by the historical Christian theory of beauty. Many people (including the ancient Greeks) associate beauty with balance, sweetness, and consonance. But if this were the case, how could we account for the beauty in music as violent as Verdi's *Otello* or as sad as Górecki's *Third Symphony?* These works are beautiful because they cohere in appropriate ways, their parts fit together in ways appropriate to their subject matter, and they shed light on that subject matter (they help the listener to see—or hear—it in new ways). Hence it is no paradox for something unbalanced, bitter, or dissonant also to be beautiful, if these qualities are fitting.

A list of aesthetic problems clarified by the historical Christian theory of beauty could go on for many pages, and a modest essay on music is not the place for such a list. It is, however, the place to assert the following: that musical pluralism can best (and perhaps only) be championed on the basis of such a theory. The way to broaden someone's musical horizons is to demonstrate *objectively* the beauties of unfamiliar music, to equip him with the listening skills to hear the beauty that exists where previously, in ignorance, he heard only noise—the beauty that exists whether or not he heeds it. Only this kind of experience motivates people, in humility, to appreciate the inexhaustible riches of this world's musics. Harold Best describes the joys of this kind of appreciation vividly: "In these later years of my profession, I find myself laughing and whole again, musically happier than ever, celebrating this vast expanse of sonic creativity, longing with all my heart to be a world musician as a living part of being a world Christian, and delighting in teaching all of this renewed good news. I find myself wanting to dance through a Pentecost of musics."[11]

But, if the very essence of beauty is subjectively defined, why bother? Why should I not be complacent in whatever my current prejudices are? When a genuine aesthetic-relativist considers the forms of multiple traditions, past and present, he may acknowledge the truth of the messages communicated by the forms, but it becomes increasingly difficult for him to see how inseparable the forms are from the message. It becomes increasingly difficult for him to see the forms themselves as anything other than cultural expressions, valid for a particular time and place, and basically interchangeable with other forms in other times and places.

Evangelicals in particular have long suffered a dichotomy between form and content. Although we may fight over forms, in the final analysis we wonder if they might not be "all relative." Perhaps it is only the content that matters, and the Spirit will bless whatever form we use. Perhaps baptisms can be administered in a hot tub[12] or in an animated fire truck with sirens and confetti,[13] without losing in significance. We proclaim the gospel as if it does not matter *how* we proclaim it, as long as we get the *substance* right. A third of a century ago, Marshall McLuhan tried to teach us that the medium is the message; but who listened?

Well, for one thing, the slogan is not entirely accurate. The medium is not the message but an integral part of the message. The historical Christian understanding of beauty is not aestheticist.[14] It does not confuse beauty with truth. Nor does it confuse tackiness with sin. It is not a sin to make bad aesthetic choices (although it might be, if ugly worship and stammering proclamation are the products of laziness or poor stewardship). To say that truth and goodness and beauty are inseparably linked is not to equate them. But pause and consider for a moment what kind of a Christianity would subscribe to the true and the good but not the beautiful. I cannot get the warning of Hans Urs von Balthasar out of my head: "Our situation today shows that beauty demands for itself at least as much courage and decision as do truth and goodness, and she will not allow herself to be separated and banned from her two sisters without taking them along with herself in an act of mysterious vengeance."[15] For, in a world that has bid farewell to beauty, the good loses its attractiveness, and the proofs of truth lose their cogency. Postmoderns inhabit such a world. Forms are never more fragile than in a culture that views cynically the attempts of human beings to reach out to one another (not to mention God's ability to reach us).

How then do we choose our forms? Or, as asked earlier, how do we decide which songs to sing (or play or hear)? To make decisions based on aesthetic principle is to strive to live out the good and the true in the best *way* possible. It is to imagine (as good stewards of our imagination) forms competent to bear the weight of glory. And, since the riches of the goodness and truth and glory of God's creation and salvation are so full, these forms will be diverse. The many different ways that music can function in this world—to encourage soldiers, to pace work and lighten its drudgery, to compound the expressive power of theater, to protest injustice, to pacify babies—has led musicians to develop a vast array of styles. Each is fitted to its function. Each can be a blessing.

Thus three principles emerge. First, aesthetic excellence is the pursuit of forms worthy of our ends. Second, this pursuit will lead us to embrace a wide range of musical ends and styles. Third, this pursuit will lead us to recognize and respect the interdependence of ends and style. Many people, overwhelmed in delight at a particular kind of music, make the mistake of treating it as a kind of all-purpose accompaniment to all of life. Their lives are poorer for it. Obviously Gregorian chants make lousy dance music. Raucous polkas cannot hallow. Commercial jingles generally do not reward aesthetic contemplation. And Wagner's operas are a terrible choice for background music at a party. Beauty is always apt.

Charlie Peacock describes the second principle as a kind of kingdom bias. "A kingdom bias is an ideological bias which favors a comprehensive and diverse picture of musical faithfulness. It is music created by musicians [and appreciated by listeners] called by God, to God, and for God, everywhere and in everything musical. This is what is meant by a comprehensive view of the role of music in the church and in culture. It is a calling that is huge."[16] When we attend only to music that is easily identifiable as "Christian," for example, when we privilege the music of evangelism and corporate worship and neglect the music of courtship, the concert hall, and the playground, not only are we arbitrarily refusing the good gifts of God; we are shirking the cultural mandate he placed on humans at creation (Gen. 1:28; 2:15; 2:19) to use their skills and imagination to order it. All of it. Furthermore, by not taking the lead in transforming culture, we shirk the command of our Lord that his disciples be the "salt of the earth," a light that "shines before men."

Perhaps the most troubling aspect of American evangelical culture is its almost exclusive identification with popular culture. Popular culture, too, is a precious gift of God, to be scorned at our own loss. Popular music can be a source of genuine entertainment, it can be a means to meet people where they are, and—frankly—some of it is profoundly beautiful. But it is not sufficient. And the problem has as much to do with form as it does with content. This is the message of Kenneth Myers's brilliant, readable, and influential book *All God's Children and Blue Suede Shoes: Christians and Popular Culture.*

> It might seem an extreme assertion at first, but I believe *that the challenge of living with popular culture* may well be as serious for modern Christians as persecution and plagues were for the saints of earlier centuries. Being thrown to the lions or living in the shadow of gruesome death are fairly straightforward if unattractive threats. Enemies that come loudly and visibly are usually much easier to fight than those that are undetectable. Physical affliction (even to the point of death) for the sake of Christ is a heavy cross, but at least it can be readily recognized at the time as a trial of faith. But the erosion of character, the spoiling of innocent pleasures, and the cheapening of life itself that often accompany modern popular culture can occur so subtly that we believe nothing has happened. Christian concern about popular culture should be as much about the sensibilities it encourages as about its content.[17]

Make no mistake about what Myers asserts. The form of culture (not just the content) can shape character, affect one's ability to enjoy innocent pleasures, and affect the quality of one's life or the respect one has for it. How?

Two songs sharing the same basic subject matter can be written with different kinds of listeners in mind. One kind of listener looks for forms that will powerfully confirm what he already knows. He is delighted by the familiar, by what stimulates without asking anything of him, by what offers the pleasures of an active emotional life without all the difficulty that normally goes along with one. The other kind of listener looks for forms that reveal to him new ways of thinking, perspectives not his own. He is delighted by adventures that lead him far afield from what he already knows, so that he might transcend his previously limited viewpoint and be enlarged. As a generalization, it can be said that the forms of popular culture tend to speak to the first kind of listening, while the forms of high culture tend to speak to the second kind of listening. Myers quotes at length an analogy from C. S. Lewis's *An Experiment in Criticism*.

> A work of (whatever) art can be either "received" or "used." When we "receive" it we exert our senses and imagination and various other powers according to a pattern invented by the artist. When we "use" it we treat it as assistance for our own activities. The one, to use an old-fashioned image, is like being taken for a bicycle ride by a man who may know roads we have never yet explored. The other is like adding one of those little motor attachments to our own bicycle and then going for one of our familiar rides. These rides may in themselves be good, bad, or indifferent. The "uses" which the many make of the arts may or may not be intrinsically vulgar, depraved, or morbid. That's as may be. "Using" is inferior to "reception" because art, if used rather than received, merely facilitates, brightens, relieves or palliates our life, and does not add to it.[18]

Reception of the arts is, in a sense, like love or justice or the pursuit of knowledge, because it involves stepping outside the safe familiarity of our own experience and putting ourselves in another's place. Myers asks, "Are there natural virtues of sympathy, of love, of justice, of mercy, of wisdom that can be encouraged by aesthetic experience? According to Lewis, learning to 'receive' a work of art does encourage habits of the heart that have effects in other areas of life."[19]

The point is not to deprecate popular music, which is a blessing in its proper place. The point is that a diet consisting *solely* of popular forms is not the healthiest for the soul. At the least, the forms of high culture should comprise the humanities core of our children's education. If the end of liberal learning, the health of the mind, is to be gained through encounter with what Matthew Arnold called "the best which has been thought and said," then classical repertoires should be the focus of music curricula. "In a democratic culture, people believe themselves to be entitled to their tastes," concedes the philosopher Roger Scruton. "But it does not follow that good and bad taste are indistinguishable, or that the education of taste ceases to be a duty."[20]

And finally, as suggested at the beginning of this essay, being a good steward of the gift of music means weighing the arguments in the great debate over church music. Much of this debate has focused on the relation of corporate worship to evangelism. In the final analysis almost everybody seems to agree that worship will be evangelistic, even if that is not its main purpose. The question becomes: *in what way* will it be evangelistic? Just about everybody will at least pay lip service to the idea that worship is the response of believers to the presence of God—a response and presence that the Holy Spirit may use to lay bare the secrets of unbelievers' hearts, that they might exclaim, "God is certainly among you" (1 Cor. 14:25 NASB). There is considerable disagreement, however, about what *forms* are most appropriate to realize this ideal. The problem is therefore (at least in part) an aesthetic one.

Whether rightly or wrongly, many sense a tension between the forms in which (mature) believers respond to the presence of God and the ability of unbelievers or new believers to understand these forms. Consider how Mark Altrogge (author of the chorus "I Stand in Awe of You") describes one of the aesthetic priorities at his church: "When we talk together in our leadership team, we say, 'Everything we do at Lord of Life [Church] on Sunday morning—even Christian things—*should be as sensitive and understandable to unbelievers as possible*'"[21] (emphasis mine). There are degrees of understandability, then, and there can be a tension between our effort to behold the often unpalatable splendor of God and our effort to be sensitive to the seeker. The basic disagreements in the dialogue are over which *forms* strike the right balance between these two efforts.

The consensus of those, like Sally Morgenthaler and Barry Liesch, who advocate the primary use of contemporary popular styles is that, while "the purpose of worship is to glorify God, not to win lost souls," evangelism should be an integral part of worship and that this can only be when churches adopt the vernacular forms already familiar to the unchurched.

> These days, traditional American Christian culture is an anachronism in its own backyard. Some of us are just having a hard time admitting it. . . . If language apart from experience has no meaning, then only that which somehow connects with the secular person's experience and knowledge base is going to be intelligible to the Brads and Brendas of our society. If we truly want to reach them, we must, as John Smith says, "enculturate the truth into the vernacular of a broken world." We must speak in terms a broken world can understand.[22]

But what if those terms prove inadequate to realize what is acknowledged to be the primary purpose of worship? Critics worry that the forms of "praise and worship" choruses alone (for example) cannot possibly give adequate expression to a mature believer's awe-filled response to God.

The consensus of those, like Marva Dawn and David Wells, who advocate the primary use of traditional styles is that believers and churches will reach out to evangelize because their character has been properly formed, in part through the spiritual discipline of corporate worship. This is less likely to happen in worship shaped by popular culture, with its tendencies toward safe familiarity, aimless energy, and emotions had at little cost. Instead, Dawn calls for a worship in which we are "immersed in splendor."

> Taking God seriously is, however, decidedly countercultural. We live in an age and a culture that want instead to turn the worship of God into a matter of personal taste and time, convenience and comfort. Consequently, we need the biggest dose of God we can get when we gather for worship on Sunday morning—to shake us out of this societal sloth and somnambulism and summon us to behold God's splendor and respond with adoration and service and sacrifice. . . . My primary concern in various churches' and denominations' struggles over worship is that so many decisions are being based on criteria other than the most essential—namely, that God be the Subject and Object, the Infinite Center, of our worship.[23]

Very conscious of the aesthetic nature of the problem, she "calls for a process, a *discernment* by the community, a sorting of the best of new and old. However, because tradition is so often thrown out without much thought or consideration, I have *tried to demonstrate its beauty* and validity and importance for our times in order to counterbalance the overaccentuation on the 'contemporary' in current discussions"[24] (emphasis mine). Critics charge that, by slighting the contemporary, writers like Dawn show a certain callousness to the plight of unbelievers and new believers.

Where does the answer lie? We are corporately to *ascribe to the Lord* the glory due his name, to bring an offering, to worship the Lord in holy splendor (1 Chron. 16:29; see also Heb. 13:15), and it all must be done for the edification of the church, as one who prophesies so as to *speak to men* for their upbuilding and encouragement and consolation (1 Cor. 14:3, 26; see also Col. 3:16 NASB).

Of the two repertoires used most widely in American Protestant churches today, it can be argued that traditional English-language hymnody, broadly considered, is the better suited for corporately "ascribing to the Lord the glory due his name."

1. The melodic style of these hymns was conceived congregationally. That is, the melodic contour, range, tessitura, and rhythm were designed for people of no particular vocal accomplishment to sing *together*. On the other hand, the vocal style out of which praise-and-worship music has evolved is conditioned by the expectation that it will be *performed* and *recorded* and then processed passively by its audience. The most sophisticated component of the melody is its rhythm, which is conceived soloistically and heard against the backdrop of an all-pervasive beat. (That is why, when the instruments of the rhythm section are removed, pop/rock melodies will often sound shapeless.[25]) Hence the importance of using a band, if a church wants to be truly innovative in intersecting with mainstream culture. The challenge is in making such an experience truly congregational, so that it is not just a performance with which people are invited to sing along. In the rare congregation (of any stylistic persuasion) where the saints have been taught personally to take responsibility for the songs, there is a sense in which the congregation (or, better yet, the Holy Spirit) leads. The organist or band may accompany, the pastor may still stand up front, perhaps there is even a specially designated music "leader," but the impulse for the music clearly comes from within the congregants, almost all of whom sing with guts and abandon.

2. Traditional hymnody is the product of centuries of selection. Those who sing it are discipled by those who have gone before (Heb. 13:7). The layer upon layer of editorial filtering has resulted in a high incidence of theological, devotional, poetic, and musical quality. Thinkers on both sides of the debate acknowledge the difficulty we face in leading inhabitants of a materialist-humanist world to worship that focuses—not on things or humans—but on God. God, in both his terrible transcendence and astonishing immanence. How is

the poor worship-planner, who is only human—with limited time, experience, and gifts—faithfully to proceed? In part by availing himself or herself of the wisdom of preceding generations. Hymnbooks represent the distillation of that wisdom into a manageable form. If the publishers and committees have done their job, the texts and tunes will be not only rich (in a way that the perspective of a single generation cannot be) but also singable and intelligible (although perhaps not immediately so).

3. Carefully edited hymnbooks[26] nurture the kinds of literacy and sophisticated oral tradition that can sustain biblical thought. When David Wells attempted an empirical comparison of the theological content of a standard Protestant hymnbook with two widely used collections of contemporary choruses, he found that almost all the classical hymns but only 41.1 percent of contemporary choruses developed some aspect of doctrine. The hymnody of postmodern spirituality (as Wells calls the chorus repertoire) "lives off the truth of classical spirituality but frequently leaves that truth unstated as something to be assumed, whereas in the hymnody of classical spirituality the truth itself is celebrated. The one rejoices in what the other hides."[27]

On the other hand, of the two repertoires used most widely in American Protestant churches today, it can be argued that praise-and-worship music, broadly considered, is the better suited for "speaking to men" whose habits have been largely shaped by popular culture. Remember that beauty always communicates. It is unclear how anyone can ascribe to the Lord the glory due his name if they do not understand the language of the ascription. The genius of Protestant worship has always been that it is participatory and in the vernacular. Thanks be to God that he has raised up so many who faithfully write and perform in the vernacular-based genres of Christian contemporary music and praise-and-worship music!

So, then, *the best church-music practice for our day will be passionately engaged with tradition and at the same time passionately committed to renewal and intelligibility.*

The Bible affirms the importance of tradition. It describes God as having used tradition to transmit his Word and its proper interpretation (Deut. 31:19, 21; 1 Cor. 11:2). What higher commendation is there? But, as with all good things, tradition can be abused. We are warned against trusting traditions more than Scripture (Matt. 15:6). What we do not need is the lackadaisical approach to hymn-singing found in most "traditional" churches today.

The Bible enjoins us to sing to the Lord a new song (Pss. 96; 149). Listen again to Marva Dawn: "What are spiritual songs [in Col. 3:16]? Were they new expressions of praise composed at the moment—or ecstatic utterances? We cannot be certain, but what we do know is that God cannot be contained in what we already know. There is always a need for new compositions. . . . Our choices and creations will be guided by the exhortation in Colossians 3:16 [see especially NASB] that we use these spiritual songs to teach and admonish each other. All our music will help believers learn the language of faith and what worship is."[28]

The Bible says that our worship should be intelligible. All things (the hymn, the lesson, the revelation, the tongue, the interpretation) should be done for edification (1 Cor. 14:26). Edification comes from what is intelligible, but we must take care in defining these concepts. In a society where souls are saturated with a commercial-popular aesthetic, we are inclined to conclude that "intelligible" means "easy." If the people we are trying to lead in worship are not accustomed to means of communication that demand something of them (such as sustained reflection, openness to the unfamiliar, and engagement with form and symbol), then we tend to want to avoid these means.

But with what do we replace them? Can something difficult be communicated in an easy way? Dawn again: "I am told by critics that such performances are necessary for people in our television and cyberspace culture, but the very problems of that culture are thus transferred to the churches— for faith is not merely intellectual assent to doctrinal positions or an expression of emotions. . . . Faith is a lived language, and it cannot be learned unless one participates in it and practices it. If one's introduction to Christ comes from a polished performance, how will that person have the courage to live his or her own awkward, stumbling version of the Christ-life?"[29]

John Frame, on the other hand, understands his use of contemporary worship music at New Life Presbyterian Church in Escondido, California, as "becoming all things to all people that we might by all means save some. It is not a compromise of the Gospel, but it is rather a way of removing unnecessary offense so that the offense of the cross itself may be heard all the more vividly, all the more offensively."[30] The message of God's Word will most clearly be proclaimed in the service that makes allowance both for the intelligibility of the message and the fullness of the message.

Practically speaking, this can be achieved through the thoughtful and *idiomatic* use of both accessible, contemporary hymnody *and* classical hymnody. Every believer should expect to find some aspects of congregational worship readily accessible, even as other aspects remain mysterious. As regards evangelism, it should be self-evident that a seeker (by definition) knows that what he or she already has is inadequate. The seeker wants to be stretched.

There remain a few miscellaneous observations about church music that ought to be made. First, the acoustics of a worship space can be a real encouragement or discouragement to congregational singing (of all styles). It is critical that everybody be able simultaneously to hear himself or herself, hear the congregation as a whole, and hear the accompaniment. Where one or more of these layers of the sonic fabric are inaudible, singers will be disheartened (although perhaps not consciously). Where, for example, the space is dead or the song leaders are overmiked so that individual congregants cannot hear their own (or anybody else's) voice, this will communicate the message that theirs does not matter. If the singing in your church seems lifeless, do not assume that the problem is entirely spiritual; you may want to have a professional acoustician check out your sanctuary.

Second, the wise music leader is sensitive to the stylistic integrity of every repertoire he or she employs. The healthiest traditional hymn-singing will be found in congregations which pay close attention to the poetry they sing and are blessed with an organist who accompanies with rhythmic clarity and energy. An approach to accompanying hymns or choruses that crosses over from one style to another will occasionally infuse worship with new life and fresh perspective, but it is unlikely to sustain long-term engagement. For example, the reason Lutheran chorales of the sixteenth and seventeenth centuries seem so moribund today is that they were rhythmically disfigured by fashions of the eighteenth century.[31] The originals were often quite jaunty. Morgenthaler claims that, "If boomers and busters are looking for tradition today, most want it with a little *t* and definitely their way. What exactly is *their* way? Tradition that speaks to the under-fifty crowd in the 1990s is *repackaged* tradition. Why else would a recording company feature Madonna singing 'Silent Night' (no pun intended)? Repackaging means taking the basic content and delivering it in a different way."[32]

The trick here, as always, is in wedding "the basic content" with an appropriate form. Dressing an old hymn in hip attire may win a hearing from otherwise hostile worshipers, but a hymn treated as a praise-and-worship chorus is in fact a praise-and-worship chorus (and probably an awkward one at that) and is unlikely to lead, in the long run, to more substantive hymnody. Crossing over in the opposite direction is often even less successful. When musicians inexperienced in pop-based idioms try to accompany contemporary choruses (perhaps on organ or piano), younger congregants tend to pick up on—and be distracted by—the stylistic dissonance, although they may be impressed by the musicians' sincerity. A helpful handbook for church musicians trying to organize worship in multiple styles is *Leading the Church's Song* (Augsburg Fortress, 1999).

My favorite argument for mixed worship I have saved for the end of my essay. When Christians worship their Lord in songs they feel are not their own, they learn charity and humility. C. S. Lewis, who personally was not fond of hymnody, understood this well.

There are two musical situations on which I think we can be confident that a blessing rests. One is where a priest or an organist, himself a man of trained and delicate taste, humbly and charitably sacrifices his own (aesthetically right) desires and gives the people humbler and coarser fare than he would wish, in a belief (even, as it may be, the erroneous belief) that he can thus bring them to God. The other is where the stupid and unmusical layman humbly and patiently, and above all silently, listens to music which he cannot, or cannot fully, appreciate, in the belief that it somehow glorifies God, and that if it does not edify him this must be his own defect. Neither such a High Brow nor such a Low Brow can be far out of the way. To both, church music will have been a means of grace; not the music they have liked, but the music they have disliked.[33]

CHAPTER 11

CHRISTIAN WORLDVIEW AND THE SOCIAL SCIENCES

Antonio A. Chiareli

IN MY FIRST WEEK as a student in the Ph.D. program in sociology at Northwestern University, I recall sitting in a seminar room with my cohort and listening to a few faculty introduce themselves and talk about their research. I vividly recollect how one of our stellar professors began his talk. As he opened Smelser's huge *Handbook of Sociology* to the table of contents, he proceeded to read out loud each chapter title, in what is perhaps sociology's equivalent of a fully referenced Bible. I remember seeing our "jaws drop" as we heard, in total amazement, this professor comment as he read along, "I've published in this area . . . and in this one. I've also written extensively in this one, and I've published some articles on this subject, and on this other one," and he continued on down the list. Upon reaching chapter 15, however, he paused. He then uttered, "The sociology of religion. . . . Well, I've never written anything on this. I just don't know why serious sociologists bother with such things." Laughter filled the air. Then he continued, uncontested and in the same original manner, on to the final chapter.

I recount this experience for a couple of reasons. First, because I want to illustrate the kind of antireligious environment that exists in the sociology departments—and, I would argue, in the social sciences as a whole—especially in our most distinguished institutions of higher learning and research. Admittedly, that particular professor, being openly atheist, was especially hostile to the idea of religion in the scholarly discipline of sociology. But the fact that not once during my graduate years did

I encounter a Christian sociologist teaching in the discipline's mainstream, is some evidence of its overwhelmingly secular orientation. If they were there, the expression of their views was most likely restricted to a sort of "underground" context that never evident to me. This does not come as a surprise, given that the discipline itself commonly exudes deeply antireligious sentiments in its overall teaching and scholarship. Indeed, those who are looking for the Christian worldview in these non-Christian educational contexts will find their efforts greatly frustrated by its striking absence therein, as in the general academic culture of the social sciences.

A second reason for sharing the above anecdote is that, as a young graduate student, that experience truly had an impact on me—I would not otherwise be able to recall it so vividly after a decade. For many years, though I did not consider myself an atheist, I functioned in academia as a secular sociologist, in large measure because of how I was trained. That was, after all, exactly what my teaching role models taught me to do. I was their disciple.

My conversion to evangelical Christianity has forced me to change that. It has also instilled in me a great concern for the key role that I play, as an academic, in the training of my students. Furthermore, I have come to believe firmly that Christian higher education in general must go the distance in establishing the value of the Christian worldview in the liberal arts. As someone once reminded me, "Everyone is someone's disciple." The question we must ask, then, is this: Whose disciples are we preparing our students to be? I hope the answer to this important question in institutions of Christian higher education is *Jesus Christ.*

When I was invited to write this chapter on the social sciences and the Christian worldview, my urgency to discuss these and other concerns began to weigh heavily on my mind. I wondered what I could say that would not only be fair to sociology but to all other social sciences as well. Above all, however, I wondered how I could best elevate the discussion of the Christian worldview in the social sciences to an edifying level— one that could clearly communicate this worldview's rightful place within these disciplines, to the glory of our Lord, Jesus Christ. In this chapter, I attempt to do just that.

Since the late nineteenth century, but principally since the late 1960s, many important works have addressed the relationship between the social sciences—especially sociology—and Christianity.[1] At the dawn of the new millennium, the idea of scholarship and faith is being studied with renewed interest, particularly in Christian interdisciplinary circles.[2] My aim in this chapter, however, is not to review these works, though such an effort would certainly reveal the increasing vitality of the subject. Instead, I offer a candid discussion not only of the challenges but also the real promise, of integrating the Christian worldview and the social sciences. Let us begin, however, by first examining the merits of this integration from a truth-committed perspective and what is ultimately at stake for Christian higher education in today's society.

AFFIRMING A TRUTH-COMMITTED DIALOGUE AND ITS MEDIATION

This chapter is born out of two of my deepest convictions as a former secular sociologist who now embraces and defends a Christian worldview. One concerns the need for affirming a truth-committed conversation between the social sciences and the Christian worldview. The other concerns the vital role that Christian institutions of higher education must play as the carriers of this dialectical process.

First, I believe that the social sciences provide a magnificent theoretical and empirical opportunity for integrating a biblically grounded approach with the study of our social world. This approach, based on the idea of "reading the world by reading the Word,"[3] is rooted in the understanding that, outside of divine truth, the social sciences will continue to have only partial explanatory power for developing clarifications for our social reality and for devising solutions to its problems. In other words, our comprehension of the social world via existing naturalistic or humanistic theory and praxis remains incomplete.[4]

This is evident, for instance, in the way that the social sciences are much better at describing social phenomena than they are at predicting their outcomes; or defining social conditions rather than solving social ills. I contend, therefore, that only a continuous dialogue between Scripture—and the principles therein—and the observable world can generate more comprehensive and accurate formulations within the social sciences for understanding our human social condition. As Fraser and Campolo have rightly put it, the ultimate goal in this conversation "is to express truth about social reality."[5] If all truth is God's truth, then the challenge of integrating it into the academic arenas of sociology, anthropology, psychology, history, political science, and economics must be met.

Let me elaborate with a familiar example. Consider the basic notion that, as humans, we tend to organize ourselves into collectivities. This is an established and undebatable fact within the social sciences. The secular—and especially anthropological—worldview, for example, argues that this most basic of human tendencies is a result of cultural adaptation. Other branches of it claim that it represents an evolutionary vestige from what is theorized or assumed to be our primal history.[6] The specialized areas of secular physiological and cognitive psychology also investigate how humans are "similar to animals in neuroanatomy, neurophysiology, sensation, learning, and biological drives."[7] According to this reasoning, our tendency to live in groups probably just reflects the basic instincts present in most species in the animal kingdom.

In their attempt, however, to establish theoretical connections between humans and animals through Darwinian cultural and biological evolutionary paradigms, these disciplines have failed to emphasize and explain a basic reality—how Godlike humans really are. How can we fully understand, constrained by such secular paradigms, the reasons why humans are singularly creative and that we have an unmatched ability to think and develop a common language? How do we explain our complete self-awareness or our capacity for self-sacrifice? Why do we possess a spiritual component to our being, which is a belief widely held across virtually all cultures on earth? These and other questions continue to puzzle the scientific community in their persistently self-reliant and secular *modus operandi.*

In the mainstream of the social sciences, however, it is a rarity to find a clear and genuine statement that God's order and workings are recognizable in the social world. The implications of looking at the world through this secular prism are clear. Both the evidence of God's revelation and the witness of creation, not to mention the shared experience of billions of persons of faith, are excluded from the "scientific" process. Yet even a secular anthropologist or psychologist would agree that the practice of systematically ignoring—or at best downplaying—the significance of such overwhelming amounts of data calls into question the validity of any "scientific" approach to the study of humans and their social contexts.

By contrast, the Christian worldview enables us to consider the evidence and principles found in Holy Scripture, in order to arrive at a fuller and arguably less hypothetical understanding of the ways in which we function as social beings. Continuing with this theme of human collectivity, Scripture clearly tells us that, from the beginning, God saw community as a basic and necessary unit of human existence (see Gen. 1:27–28; 2:18, 22–24). Whether in the form of a dyadic union between a man and a woman, or as a nuclear or extended kinship unit, or even as a village or nation, he created us as social interactors, after his own divine image and character as a relational (trinitarian) being.[8] Thus, while some of our behavior and physiology may resemble that of animals, humans are uniquely like God because he designed us that way, with intellect, emotion, and will. Humans are his greatest creation, having dominion over all other living things (Gen. 1:28).

I contend that considering God's perspective in the human equation improves our ability to understand our social behavior, for we are no longer bound only to the search for explanations from the illusive rules of natural law. Nor are we subject to the inadequacies of the postulates about humanity, which are derived from cross-species comparative studies. Instead, a new paradigm emerges that generates a conception of human behavior that is much more coherent with observable reality, and to biblical truth.

Based on this premise, it is still quite possible to accept much of the extensive witness, found in these various disciplines, to this gregarious quality in humans. Granted, the debate over the origins of humanity is bound to endure indefinitely between competing worldviews. But outside of Darwinian frameworks, there is no disagreement from the Christian perspective with the fact that the social sciences offer us some important insights and analytical tools for studying the successes and problems of our intricate social experience, as well as our complex human organizational apparatus. My point here is that the purpose of bridging the Christian worldview and the social sciences is not simply to throw out the scientific method and its body of work. Rather, it is to help inform, challenge, and ultimately contribute to the refinement of many of our current theories and assumptions about the social world.

To be sure, a novel is best explained by its author. Similarly, a painting can best be interpreted by its artist. In the same way, I believe that our human essence is best defined and illumined to us by our Creator. Therefore, I repeat with conviction that a worldview born out of the mind of God, by his revelation, cannot only corroborate but also greatly refine the existing explanatory frameworks within the social sciences. This Christian worldview, however, is of little social scientific value if it retreats in the face of the likely disputes from other worldviews. Rather, it must stand immovable in the truth of Jesus Christ. Only in this way will truth-committed social scientists be able to confidently forge and advance new paradigms that can compete with the reigning and at times erroneous assumptions about the world we live in. In this process, social scientists in Christian higher education must strive to maintain an ongoing dialogue with the world, but one that is firmly grounded in our reading of the Word.

This brings me to a second and related conviction that guides this chapter. It centers on the question of the future of institutional support for the Christian worldview within academia, including the social sciences. I speak here of the role

Christian institutions of higher education must play in the propagation of God's truth through this dialectic "Word-world" process. It is presently evident, however, that with growing urgency, even colleges and universities that genuinely seek to embody the rock of God's truth are faced with the reality of constantly having to assess and ultimately choose between two fundamentally divergent routes in today's educational landscape. For the sake of contrast, I will call them the godly and the worldly path.

Following the godly path means to accept and boldly carry out the challenge of integrating faith and learning by participating in the shaping and teaching of a biblical worldview. Yet the structure and purpose of this worldview must be not only eternally true but also temporally viable. Its robustness and longevity depend on its ability to impart truth in a way that can impact the practical demands of daily life in any social context. Here the social sciences have a significant role to play, since they speak authoritatively about our social experience. The student body must feel convinced—and convicted—that God's principles apply to the college experience as well as to the world at large. This is extremely important for the continued vitality of the overall mission of Christian educational institutions to promote a truth-based biblical worldview.

In an increasingly ideologically diverse educational setting, however, the pressures, especially for students, to negotiate between absolute truth and relativism, between the religious and the secular, become tremendous. This is especially true in an era when technology is capable of transmitting an uncensored parade of postmodernity—to say nothing of immoral and amoral views and graphic contents—at the click of a mouse. Hence the utter importance of continued institutional support for an academic environment that decisively affirms the Christian worldview in relation to the influences from the *kosmos*, or the world/universal order, as New Testament writers called it in the Greek language.

Yet consistently living out the Christian worldview is admittedly a challenge even for the leading Christian institutions of higher education, which must also exist in and interact with the world. It should also be briefly acknowledged here that even among people who consider themselves to be Christians, there is great variance with regard to certain dimensions of faith, denominational doctrine, and adherence thereto. This can represent a difficult challenge to unity in mission. Moreover, it is not easy, from an organizational standpoint, to orchestrate all academic and managerial aspects of the institution, and to ensure a unified mind-set toward a Christian worldview from a plethora of administrators, faculty, staff, and students alike.

Can we say, however, that there is an alternative to affirming a Christian worldview in Christian higher education? This answer is yes and no. That is, an alternative exists. Yet, if we are to commit ourselves to God's truth, we must avoid the path of conformity with secular philosophies. In the postmodern age, choosing this path means to submit increasingly to a dominant secular framework, built on the myth of "cultural relevance," in which truth is diluted or replaced according to the sensitivities of the times. Such an agenda prioritizes pluralism and extreme forms of political correctness, and fails to acknowledge the universal applicability of God's truth, regardless of subcultural variations.

In this way, the Christ-centered educational calling of the Christian institution risks quickly eroding under the persistent pounding of the waves of cultural relativism, produced in what seems to be an ever-expanding sea of secular assimilative tendencies in American and other societies.[9] For the student who is at the mercy of the social sciences and other secular academic disciplines for developing an understanding of the world, following this road only contributes—and tragically so—to the extinguishing of his or her faith flame, because the *kosmos* does not know Christ.

Unfortunately, as history shows, this secular path has been trampled on and beaten down by the passage of countless institutions, originally founded on Christian principles, that have embraced the many liberal rationalist interpretations of the world, openly leaving aside the infinite benefits of God's perspective. As Charles Malik makes clear, the world's leading and most prestigious institutions, such as Harvard, Oxford,

Sorbonne, and many others, "were all founded on and dedicated to Jesus Christ, [but] in the course of time they swerved from that foundation and dedication."[10] Malik further explains that, in raising the banner of Western-style "progress," such institutions gradually but steadily moved away from Christ and the church because these came to be seen as relics of the past.

But while the worldly path is taken up by this most secular academic procession, the godly path lies relatively uncharted, still awaiting Christian pioneers whose conviction and spirit rejects the forced separation of truth and experience, revelation and science, faith and reason. If we, in Christian higher education, are to remain true to our task and "be imitators of God" (Eph. 5:1), we must not forsake Scripture's caution to "not conform any longer to the pattern of this world" (Rom. 12:2). We must therefore daily seek the godly path, in light of all wisdom abiding in God's Word, made known to us by his Spirit, as we labor under the lordship of the living Christ.

In my view, there is no better realm than the social sciences to develop the truth-committed approaches that will solidify the foundation of Christian higher education into the future. Achieving a symbiotic relationship between, in this case, the Christian worldview in the social sciences and Christian institutions of higher education will ensure that both sides will thrive in the new millennium as they resist the secular pull of the world.

With these convictions in mind, I proceed to develop the rest of this chapter. In the next section, I discuss the rationale for the common perception in the secular social sciences that its integration with the Christian worldview is highly problematic. I then reiterate the promise of this integration. Finally, I close the chapter with a word of caution against adopting a "value-stretch" approach in the mediation by Christian higher education between the Word and the world.

THE PROBLEMS AND PROMISE OF INTEGRATION

Although I strongly defend the merging of Christian faith and scientific learning, affirming a Christian worldview in the realm of the social sciences can be very problematic. In part, this is because here we are talking about disciplines that emerged and developed—and quite intentionally so—virtually outside the bounds of any biblical framework. Simply put, disciplines such as sociology, psychology, and economics were created by the world and are largely characterized by being of the world and developed for the world. Their foundational and operational ideologies therefore pose significant obstacles to asserting the value of a Christian worldview within these fields.

This is not to say, of course, that the social sciences are not interested in the study of religious systems, expressions, and their phenomenology. Indeed, as I show below, the social sciences have much to say about religion. Yet their approach to doing it—with very few exceptions—is blatantly and self-consciously nonreligious. In sociological textbooks on the subject, for instance, this treatment of religion is allegedly done for the sake of what is regarded as scientific "objectivity" in analysis.[11] While I agree that a certain distance from one's research data is well advised for the sake of analytical clarity, this does not imply that only a "value-free" approach should be used when examining cultures and their religions. Any amount of objectivity, after all, requires some standard of truth.

Obstacles to Integration

In their intense modern quest for knowledge, the great majority of social scientists have become participants in what I call the "tyranny of scientific rationality."[12] Significant barriers based on principles thereof have therefore been created, which seemingly impede a successful "marriage" between the social sciences and the Christian worldview. Below, I provide three assumptions that in my estimation are most salient in the arguments against this integration. They can be stated as follows:

1. All worldviews or ideological frames are subjective constructions developed to sustain a particular claim about reality. Their study requires the use of relativistic approaches. Consequently, religious worldviews that make claims about absolute truth contribute no more to the development of

scientific knowledge than do other socially constructed worldviews.

2. Religious systems are viewed critically in the social sciences, usually as ideological instruments of social control. As such, religious claims are commonly distrusted as a basis for objective scientific knowledge.

3. Knowledge based on experimentation and other rational processes is built on empirical evidence. The nonempirical nature of belief systems dictates that religious values must be distinguished from science and set apart from the scientific method in the social disciplines.

Although I grant that these assumptions do not encompass the universe of possible rationales on the issue, they do strongly suggest that much of the problem with the acceptance of the Christian worldview is epistemologically based. That is, it centers on a persistent preoccupation with the nature of scientific knowledge, reflected in questions such as these: What is acceptable knowledge? What is not? Should science consider nonempirical knowledge? Are there transcendent truths or only truth-*claims*?

First, as secular sociological and anthropological theories contend, all worldviews are ideologically based and culturally subjective in nature.[13] Different worldviews are seen as being subjectively "packaged," according to the core beliefs of different cultural subgroups. Each ideological "package" is sustained by the norms and values of a specific subculture and, in turn, determines the ways in which that subculture sees and comprehends all reality. Religious worldviews present an especially difficult analytical challenge to the scientific method because many of their beliefs are deemed not only culturally specific but also founded on claims about "absolute truth" from supernatural authority. The Christian worldview is considered a textbook example of this.

Because social scientists acknowledge that there are thousands of different and subjectively constructed worldviews out there (e.g., the Christian, the Marxist, the liberal feminist, the radical homosexual, the pacifist, the technoscientific, the atheist, and so on), the only way to make analytical sense of this complex diversity is to adopt a relativistic stance in the study of the social world. In this way, and in various degrees depending on the methodological approach, the social scientific method tends to treat all worldviews as subjectively true—but only within and given their own cultural context. The alternative to this would be to strip the analysis of all subjective elements, opting instead to deal only with the empirical condition at hand. With the possible exceptions of political science and history, which are interested in factual accuracy, this alternative is less common in the social sciences, since it tends to impoverish the analysis. Whatever the method, the result of this process is the negation of the Christian belief in absolute truth because it is presumed—ironically by faith—not to exist on its own, but only through the expression of this particular "social construction of reality."[14]

Grounded in the relativist paradigm, then, secular social scientists—if they consider it at all—only accept the Christian worldview's notion of absolute truth as a subjective interpretive frame. In essence, God's absolute truth is undermined and supplanted by the much more accommodating notion that it constitutes only one of many truth claims. Consequently, it cannot be taken as an objective reference point to guide social scientific analyses.

There is a second concern about the nature of knowledge, which seems to constitute an obstacle to the integration between the social sciences and the Christian worldview. That is, critics believe that if religious knowledge is ideological, then it must possess a hidden political agenda. Consequently, we must be suspicious of it. Some scholars, then, critique ideology as something to be highly cautious about. For instance, in his influential work, John B. Thompson defines ideology as "meaning in the service of power."[15] By this, he means that ideologies are constructed out of meanings that serve to sustain unequal relations of power, to the benefit of the powerful. Any worldview, in this sense, must be questioned for its true intent.

Along these lines, other scholars study certain forms of collective action, such as social movement organizations, and their attempts to promote a particular worldview or ideological "frame." Christian and other organizations, critics would claim, are always involved in the "politics of signification,"[16] as they attempt to push their views onto target populations. Promoting a frame or "schemata of interpretation"[17] that reflects Christian values and goals, for instance, can be seen as a means toward political gain. This argument, too, tends to undermine the Christian notion of absolute truth because it is reduced to an insidious mechanism for political motives.

By all secular accounts, therefore, the notion of a worldview being superior to all others—and a religious one at that—runs counter to basic axioms of the social sciences, at least in the sense that it precludes all other interpretive frames from also contributing to our understanding of reality. To the mainstream secular sociologist, this sounds biased and tending toward hegemonic oppression, and to the anthropologist, ethnocentrically imposing. The psychologist may consider it dangerously dogmatic and conducive to delusions and abuse. The historian might find it naïvely presumptuous. The political scientist likely sees it as ideologically coercive and exploitative. Finally, for the secular economist, it is all too restrictive, reactionary, and thus irrationally unproductive. In sum, comprehending all reality through the prism of an all-encompassing biblical worldview seems an absurdity to the proponents of the social scientific method.

Much of this rationale, however, is most likely influenced by the ways in which historians, sociologists, anthropologists, and political scientists have studied religion and its past.[18] Historians, for instance, have vividly recounted the violent legacy of humanity's religious conquests. Clark reminds us of the devastating results of combative religious zeal, as he writes:

> Historical examples include crusades, holy wars, inquisitions, and witch hunts; bloody battles between Muslims and Christians; and violent persecution of Anabaptists, Quakers, Catholics, and Mormons. As Pascal noted in *Lettres Provinciales*, "Men never do

evil so completely and cheerfully as when they do it from religious conviction."[19]

From the sociology of religion, we see formulations of religion as an agent—for good and for evil—of social control. Those who embrace a functionalist view focus on how religion is instrumental in generating cohesion and order in society. Others, however, illustrate their arguments with the above examples, as they maintain that religion generates conflict. They contend that religion is used as a tool for domination by the power elite in each society and, in the Marxist tradition, as an opiate or pacifier of the oppressed masses.[20]

Microsociological approaches, on the other hand, look at how religious meanings and symbols are created through social interaction, paralleling much of the anthropological orientation toward the study of systems of religious beliefs and rituals across cultures and the values they embody.[21] Lastly, political scientists have paid close attention to the phenomenon of "civil religion."[22] The main idea behind this concept is that the relationship between religion and state politics can generate a sense of righteous citizenship in society. Rulers and citizens act in history to bring about what they see as God's vision for, say, an orderly, lawful, and just society.

In America, for example, the belief in democracy constitutes the civil religion, and many religious texts are invoked by presidents and other politicians in order to defend it. Although the concept of civil religion is in some ways compatible with the Christian worldview, it certainly does not derive from the gospel of Jesus Christ. Rather, it refers to a belief in a broader definition of God—not necessarily that of the Judeo-Christian tradition—as something of a "higher power" that is deeply interested in a particular unfolding of a society's history.

My main point here is that the treatment of religion in the secular social sciences has either represented it as a social control ideology, or as experientially subjective, or as a secularized idea that is only functionally transcendental, for the purpose of running a society. These views of religion have greatly influenced the skepticism with which it is seen by the social scientific community, when it comes to subscribing to the idea of an integration between the Christian worldview and their disciplines. All of these representations, however, are quite distinct from the idea of absolute truth that is at the core of the Christian worldview. This must not be confused with "religion," as I argue in the next section.

A final and brief observation on the obstacles to integration is the following. The ultimate basis for this differentiation between the faith and science brings us back to the realm of the "tyranny of scientific rationality." That is, in the search for scientific knowledge, the demand in the social sciences for empirical support for absolutes creates an impasse for such an integration, since absolutes in the Christian worldview's sense rest squarely in the realm of belief and supernatural authority. As such, its scientific validation via experimentation, empirical observation, and the like becomes highly problematic, if not impossible. To secular social scientists, this means that the two—the social sciences and the Christian worldview—must be kept distinguished from one another, meaning that integration is largely implausible.

These are some of the claims against integration seen through the prism of the secular social sciences. Because they are indeed substantial, they must be acknowledged and seriously considered if we are to truly entertain the idea of a truth-committed dialogue between faith and science, or the Word and the world, in these social disciplines.

The Promise of Integration: In the Disciplines, in the Classroom, in the World

Recently, in a conversation with a Christian brother of mine, I was reminded of Jesus' own words to the Pharisees, who were trying—to no avail—to incriminate him. He said to a lawyer among them, "Love the Lord your God with all your heart and with all your soul *and with all your mind*. This is the first and greatest commandment" (Matt. 22:37–38, emphasis added).

It seems to me that Christians, in general, want to compartmentalize our thought life. For instance, we seek God with our minds at church but may exclude him from our vacation planning. Or we may ask for his guidance during a prayer meeting but refuse to bring him into a professional debate at a secular academic conference. Thus, Christians are often guilty of contributing to the very cognitive segregation we must seek to avoid, between the realm of faith and that of rational thinking. For myself, if I am to obey this greatest of commandments and love him also with all of my mind, I must be characterized, in belief and in action, by the conviction that the sociologist need not reject the Christian faith perspective any more than the Christian needs to deny the usefulness of serious sociological analysis. Granted, in light of the challenges presented above, this is not an easy task. Yet I maintain that the Christian worldview is workable and indeed valuable within the social sciences.

My goal here is to provide some arguments toward this claim, not as a premise for conversion, but as a testament to the truth of Jesus' words and to the idea of a truth-committed dialogue between the Christian worldview and the social sciences. In this next section, I will do so largely by providing a brief critique of the above assumptions and arguments against integration, sponsored throughout the social scientific community.

"Word-World" Integration in the Disciplines

It is important to address the claim in the secular social sciences about the subjective nature of ideology, in particular with regard to worldviews that are founded on absolute truth beliefs. I disagree with the secular argument, based on the relativistic approach, that the diversity of worldviews determines their undifferentiated contribution to scientific knowledge. It is a logical fallacy to argue that, because many views of reality exist and because they are therefore considered subjectively true only within their own cultural contexts, that absolute truth does not exist.

Consider, for instance, the various existing religious worldviews. Among them, Confucianism and some strains of Buddhism claim there is no deity. Other Buddhists argue only the existence of lesser gods. Meanwhile, Islam and Judaism believe in a unitarian God. Christianity, on the other hand, defends the doctrine of the Trinity.[23] "Who is right?" one might ask. The relativist approach claims, "All are right!" Yet in the relativist's overzealous attempt to consider all cultural and religious variance as contextually true, logic and truth gets thrown out. If these religious worldviews make such varied—and in fact oppositional—claims about reality, it is illogical to conclude that they are all correct, is it not?

Let us be reasonable! From the standpoint of rational logic, our only options in this conundrum are either that all religious views on God are wrong, or that only one claim is right and true.[24] There are no other logical options, certainly not one that considers them all to be true. Moreover, what does all of this diversity in belief have to do with the actual existence and true essence of God? His Word tells us that—in three persons—he is! And that reality lies outside of the contrasting *human* opinions about him.

The analysis in Robert Clark's work, based on a classic article by Moberg, makes this point on cultural relativity most succinctly. Clark writes:

> This relativistic conclusion is based on a logical error. As Moberg (1962) has pointed out, one cannot legitimately infer from the fact of cultural diversity that there are not any absolute and ultimate values and standards. A difference of opinion among different peoples as to what is true "in no way proves that the object toward which the opinion refers does not exist." (Moberg, 1962: 39). Cultural variety only demonstrates a difference in judgement regarding what is true, good, and beautiful. These judgements, which are culturally relative, can coexist with absolute and ultimate standards that transcend relativism and social construction.[25]

At minimum, one can say, based on this argument, that the opinions at work in the secular social sciences that negate absolute truth are founded on dubious epistemological constructions, which are often based on *a priori* assumptions about the subjective nature of all that is seen as religious. These opinions must therefore be viewed and evaluated with caution. To say that all worldviews contribute subjectively and equally to scientific knowledge is inconsistent with any notion of rationality in the social sciences, which claim to seek objectivity in analysis even when faced with subjective ideas.

In my estimation, what makes the Christian worldview so robust and time-tested is that, quite to the contrary of other worldviews, it is not interested in convincing by argumentation, but rather in convicting by proclaiming truth. It is objective because it is truth based. And most satisfying to the analytical and truth-seeking human mind, the Christian worldview does not require blind devotion. Rather, it commands a serious and intelligent study of the nature of humans, the condition of the world, and the character and attributes of the true and triune God. Rooted in this commitment to truth, the social sciences only stand to benefit from the Christian perspective, as the "Word-world" dialogue guides the integrative process.

But what should be the Christian worldview's response to secular social science, as the latter points to the ideological use of religion as a mechanism for social control? And how can Christian social scientists deal with the obstacles to integration, which stem from the nonempirical nature of faith? Again, we come back to an epistemological and methodological debate.

First, it is not difficult to point out that religion, as a system or social institution, is man-made. This is the case even in Christianity, for we acknowledge that although one body of Holy Scriptures is used, at least within Protestantism, the various denominations were all founded and organized by men. The history of misuse of religion over the centuries arguably only reflects the fallen nature of humans and has absolutely nothing to do with the character and will of God. Thus, the claim that religion can be controlling or oppressive is fundamentally a critique of human institutions, not of God and his truth. From the viewpoint of epistemology, this makes all the difference. Proponents of the Christian worldview in the social sciences must be clear in the affirmation of this reality.

As sociologist Peter Berger argues, the phenomenon "religion" does rightly belong in the realm of social scientific analysis, in the sense that it is a human product. In his view, it is a human projection. However, well hidden in his argumentation is his belief that some element of Christian faith might transcend the religious infrastructure and the very human vessels that experience it.[26] At any rate, what is crucial to establish is that the gripes we find in the social sciences against the subject of religion lie outside of God's transcendent truth, found in his Word. It is a commitment to his truth, and not to religious systems and traditions, that must undergird the integration that we seek.

Lastly, we come to a methodological challenge. How can disciplines based on experimentation and empirical observation, for instance, merge with a worldview that is founded largely on nonempirical elements, such as faith and supernatural belief? Are these not quite distinct orientations that must be kept mutually separate? To this, we must respond in the words of John Stott, who wrote, "There was a time when [God] chose to speak, and to clothe himself with a body which could be seen and touched."[27]

Even today, no reasonable argument can be made against the historicity of Jesus Christ. For the Christian, the evidence is compelling. For everyone else, it probably is not. Still, the argument against nonempiricism falls apart elsewhere as well. Can we measure the love of a parent toward a child? Is female intuition empirically proven? Is there anything tangibly concrete about guilt or innocence? The answer is no. Yet scientists cannot dispute their existence and thus cling to circumstantial evidence about such abstract concepts in order to justify their existence. But God's circumstantial evidence is his Word and his creation. It seems only consistent with this rationale that we treat his evidence in like manner.

In sum, nonempirical evidence, because it is not based on sensory inputs, restricts the scientific method's ability to regard it as conducive to objective knowledge. I would argue, however, that the notion of "hard" evidence is somewhat overrated in the social sciences and that there is room in certain discussions for considering the metaphysical. As we strive to integrate the Christian worldview and the social sciences, we must be open to a paradigm shift regarding the nature of knowledge and our methodological practice if we are to commit ourselves to discovering truth via the social disciplines.

"Word-World" Integration in the Classroom and in the World

Unlike what is perhaps the case with the physical sciences, I believe it is not enough in the social sciences to restrict the Christian witness simply to "acting Christianly" in the classroom. True, we are called to reflect God's redemptive nature and to show love and compassion toward our students, as we engage them in our disciplines. However, the social sciences provide us educators with an excellent opportunity to embark on a truth-committed exploration of our fields. Here, I will make my point by drawing mainly from the discipline of sociology.

Think, for instance, of the subjects that a sociologist typically teaches—hopefully not all in one semester: social problems, social and economic justice, community studies, the family, world religions, deviance and criminology, intergroup relations, social stratification, social change, social policy, research methods, and so on. The possibilities for applying the "Word-world" dialogue are endless. Such an approach is particularly applicable to dealing with pragmatic questions related to why things go wrong in society.

One excellent example is the recent proliferation of violence and shootings in American schools. The "Word-world" approach can also help us to think truthfully about pressing issues, such as the problem of racial prejudice and persecution in the world, or social injustice and the worsening contrast between the rich and the poor in America, etc. By infusing our classroom discussions with God's principles of justice, compassion, righteousness, etc., and by developing their applicability to social issues, we bring home to students the "living" character of his Word, as it is shown to be extremely relevant even in our contemporary world.

This is a challenging process, and perfecting it proves to be an ongoing task. Yet it is also liberating, in the sense that seeking truth is rewarding. One of my most popular lectures, for instance, compares what I call the "Jesus movement" of the first century and two other social movements (the civil rights movement in America and the landless movement in Brazil) by looking at four criteria developed in political sociology for social movement success. By considering these criteria, students see how and why the other movements enjoyed much success. By the same *human* criteria, however, we conclude that the "Jesus movement" should have failed miserably. So why did it become the most influential movement—religious or otherwise—in all of history? The lively discussion that ensues about the human-divine nature of Christ and the idea of fulfillment of Scriptures, among other things, always proves to be eye-opening. This is only one of many examples of this integrative approach.

The history of the social sciences also affords us an opportunity to establish links with the Christian worldview. For instance, sociology first developed as a discipline that was fundamentally interested in the nature of urban social problems, which emerged most significantly in the wake of the French and Industrial revolutions. The doctrine of man's sin-nature, for instance, provides a context for the study of such social problems, at the same time that it sheds the light of God's Word on the reasons for why they persist. Numerous other applications would be possible here. For now, however, the above examples are sufficient to illustrate how a dialectical "Word-world" approach validates not only the rich sociological literature but also engages the teacher-scholar and the student in a truth-committed exercise that is both competent, stimulating, and glorifying to God.

Finally, in the sense of social action, we can conceptualize a sort of "gospel-embedded" sociology that goes beyond the experience of a classroom-confined Christian sociology. Rather, it calls Christian scholars and their students to bridge the divide between theory and practice through their engagement with society for the cause of Christ. It is active and reflective, and thus valuably praxis based. This must be the principal outcome of the integration between the Christian worldview and the social sciences, since such an educational approach proves paramount to the formation of individuals who will impact their communities in truth and love, both as professionals and as followers of Christ. Therein lies the intrinsic value of "reading the world by reading the Word" for the social sciences in particular and for the liberal arts as a whole.

THE DANGER OF "VALUE-STRETCH"

A fundamental reason for reviewing the problems and the promise of the integration I speak of is to demonstrate that if this "Word-world" dialogue is to take place in any promising way, it will most likely not happen—at least not imminently—in the secular university setting. That is precisely why it is most important that this integration be dynamically carried out in our Christian institutions of higher education.

In a literary masterpiece that could rightly be considered a "Christian Worldview Manifesto," Charles Colson and Nancy Pearcey in part challenge Christian educational institutions and their members with the following statement:

> Christian education is not simply a matter of starting class with Bible reading and prayer, then teaching subjects out of secular textbooks. It consists of teaching everything, from science and mathematics to literature and the arts, within the framework of an integrated biblical worldview. It means teaching students to relate every academic discipline to God's truth and his self-revelation in Scripture, while detecting and critiquing nonbiblical worldview assumptions.[28]

As we have seen from the many reasons given earlier, to embrace such a task proves challenging for the Christian academic and his or her audience. This is especially true if we consider its concrete sociocultural ramifications. In many ways, it means declaring war on the various ideologies and structures that undergird the contemporary and mainstream American educational *status quo*. In the world of academia, this means to take to the intellectual battlefield and confront the very disciplines that in the past three centuries have either emerged out of, or gradually but steadily declined into, strongholds of materialism, humanism, moral and cultural relativism, and secularism. These ideological arenas have sustained dominant worldviews in an academic environment whose scholarship has produced arguments that, in effect, have been used—sometimes convincingly—to undercut and degrade the very foundations and precepts of our Christian faith, heritage, and thought.

Ultimately, to undertake the task of Christian education constitutes a countercultural challenge that in today's postmodernity corresponds to a revolutionary struggle. Yet, in this case the final aim is decidedly nothing but noble: to marshal our every material and spiritual resource, in order to train future Christian leaders, who will then go out and fulfill not only the Great Commission, but also, as Colson and Pearcey put it, God's "cultural mandate" to effect social and cultural change for the cause of Christ, toward the "culmination of His work in creation."[29]

It is important to assert the impracticality of conducting this "Word-world" integrative experiment anywhere other than in Christian educational institutions. For obvious reasons, support for this undertaking is largely absent in secular venues. It is equally important, however, to be cognizant of the danger of complacency in Christian institutions of higher education, which inevitably leads to "value-stretch."

In sociological theory, the concept of "value-stretch" refers to a condition in which the gap between "ideal value preference and achievement expectations becomes too great."[30] Therefore, while not renouncing such values, we tend to become satisfied with less, in order to meet our lower expectations of ourselves, given the context in which we operate. Here, the context is the secular superstructure, which incessantly works to supplant the Christian worldview with its own. In practice, this can happen in a number of ways in Christian institutions of higher education. Issues surrounding enrollment growth, national and world visibility, professional acclaim, external or public funding, program accreditation, recruitment appeal, and so forth can cause our best Christian institutions to become vulnerable to secular philosophies. In all these areas, integrity and commitment to truth must prevail over ambitions that stem from worldly ideas of success.

If there be anything I would wish for readers to understand from this essay, it is the realization that *there is no such thing as a neutral educational process,* especially not in the social sciences. It either functions to teach conformity to or freedom from the world. As we seek to integrate the social sciences and the Christian worldview, to better grasp the sum and substance of the human social experience, we must remind ourselves of the need to recommit daily to God's truth. The choice between disseminating the Christian worldview in an uncompromising fashion or blending with the world and abandoning the idea of absolute truth will always be before us. One path brings glory to God and to the holy name of Jesus. The other suppresses truth, at great peril to the role of Christian higher education in the cause of Christ.

May we, Christian educators and visionaries, be ever conscious of this awesome choice and opt to be witnesses and agents in the process of pointing men and women to freedom in him.

Quaecumque Sunt Vera

CHAPTER 12

CHRISTIAN WORLDVIEW AND MEDIA

KINA MALLARD

WHEN WILLIAM J. BENNETT accepted the post of chairman of the National Endowment for the Humanities during President Reagan's administration, he intended to review the NEH grants and set a new course for the endowment. His first project was the film *From the Ashes . . . Nicaragua.* After reviewing the piece, he denounced it in *The New York Times* as "unabashed socialist-realism propaganda . . . . It is political propaganda, not the humanities." As one might imagine, his assessment did not earn points with most of the media elite and placed a cloud of skepticism over his new role.

Bennett describes this experience as his baptism into politics, the first of many conflicts that can best be understood as a fight for the culture, the social and the moral environment in which we raise our children. He writes:

> The battle for culture refers to the struggle over the principles, sentiments, ideas, and political attitudes that define the permissible and the impermissible, the acceptable and the unacceptable, the preferred and the disdained, in speech, expression, attitude, conduct, and politics. This battle is about music, art, poetry, literature, television programming, and movies; the modes of expression and conversation, official and unofficial that express who and what we are, what we believe and how we act.[1]

William Bennett's role as chairman of the NEH forced him to fight his battles in the "culture wars" under intense public scrutiny. While most followers of Christ are not called to fight the culture war in public, we do struggle with how to interact with our culture, particularly the media. As PBS film critic Michael Medved writes:

> What matters ultimately in the culture wars is what we do in our daily lives—not the big statements that we broadcast to the world at large, but the small messages we send through our families and our neighborhoods and our communities. . . . The future will depend not so much on the movers and shakers in the centers of power, but on the hopes that we generate in our own communities, our schools, our churches, synagogues, and families.[2]

A FRAMEWORK FOR EXPLORING, CHALLENGING, AND ARTICULATING OUR INNER-CULTURAL CONFLICT

This chapter will explore how Christians respond to the tension produced by this culture conflict. Chuck Colson, coauthor of the best-seller *How Now Shall We Live?* writes, "The real [culture] war is a cosmic struggle between worldviews—between the Christian worldview and the various secular and spiritual worldviews arrayed against it. This is what we must understand if we are going to be effective both in evangelizing our world today and in transforming it to reflect the wisdom of the Creator."[3] This author suggests that the Thomas-Kilmann Conflict Model provides Christians with a framework to explore, challenge, and articulate the various responses to the inner conflict produced by a culture that will never reflect the face of Christ.

Whether or not the media influence our lives is a topic debated by academicians, philosophers, advocacy groups, and media moguls, but most would acknowledge that the media, like everything we are exposed to, influences us. Artists and writers have acknowledged this truth for centuries. As T. S. Eliot wrote:

> The author of a work of imagination is trying to affect us wholly, as human beings, whether he knows it or not; and we are affected by it . . . whether we intend to be or not . . . . Everything we eat has some other effect upon us than merely the pleasure of taste or mastication; it affects us during the process of assimilation, and I believe that exactly the same is true of anything we read. . . . Though we read literature merely for pleasure [or see a movie, go to a play, hear music, or experience other forms of art] this never affects simply a sort of special sense; it affects us as entire human beings; it affects our moral and religious existence.[4]

For Christians, interaction with the media affects our daily lives greatly and frequently causes inner conflict. The "of the world but not in the world" dichotomy creates cognitive dissonance, and we are left confused, frustrated, and lacking in direction. This dissonance occurs because the media are alluring and pervasive, and for most of us, avoiding all media contact is not a viable option. Apart from choosing a monastic life, one cannot escape cultural influences. Grappling with how to "deal with" the media creates tension for most Christians and is directly related to their biblical worldview.

H. Richard Niebuhr, author of *Christ and Culture*, reminds us that more frequently the debate about Christ and culture is carried on among Christians and in the hidden depths of individual conscience. This issue is not debated as the struggle and accommodation of belief with unbelief but as the wrestling and the reconciliation of faith with faith.[5] The conflict that results from this daily wrestling causes individuals to explore different levels of interaction with the media. Christians deal with this intrapersonal or inner conflict the same way they manage their interpersonal conflicts—employing one of five strategies of conflict management.

The Thomas Kilmann Conflict Model explains five ways that individuals manage their conflict.[6] Two of these, accommodating and avoiding, are less assertive than the last three: compromising, competing, and collaborating. This chapter will explore these five approaches as strategies Christians adapt when struggling with the inner tension of the media and their moral roles and responsibilities.

THE PASSIVE APPROACHES:
AVOIDING AND ACCOMMODATING

Avoiding

One Sunday night in a revival service, an evangelist preached heartily against the evils of popular culture. His message was clear. Television was bad. Popular music was bad. Newsstand magazines were bad. Christians should purge their homes from the evil influences of the modern media. He challenged the congregation to bring their evil the next night and lay it at the altar. The following night as the music softly played and the evangelist persuaded, one by one members of the church walked the aisle with their televisions, GameBoys, *Sports Illustrated,* CD players, and romance novels.

Avoiding the media as a strategy is both unassertive and uncooperative. Individuals are content to live their lives the way they prescribe it without concern for how the media might be influencing those around them. The tension between Christianity and the media is simply not addressed. The avoidance response to the media includes diplomatically sidestepping the issue, ridding homes of media technology, and/or withdrawing completely from media influence.

For some, the approach of "cleaning one's house" of all media is the only solution. Bill Strom, in *More than Talk,* calls this the separatist position—a position that rejects both media technologies and media content. Some Mennonite, Amish, and Hutterite groups fall into this category. Strom argues, "To the Amish, worldliness denotes specific behaviors and lifestyles. High school, cars, cameras, tape recorders, television, films, showy houses, certain farm machinery and bicycles, all tagged *worldly,* are censured."[7]

As mentioned earlier, this approach lacks practicality. Regardless of our limits on media in our homes, most of our children do leave our houses and are immediately exposed to billboards, newspapers, magazines, and other media. C. S. Lewis acknowledges that one is not, in fact, going to read nothing. Lewis writes, "If you don't read good books you will read bad ones. If you don't go on thinking rationally, you will think irrationally. If you reject aesthetic satisfaction, you will fall into sensual satisfactions."[8]

Many Christians believe that "good" literature must be orthodox literature, that anything worth reading must be the product of a Christian worldview. Those who avoid popular culture adhere to this viewpoint. Afraid of exposing their children to anything not published by a Christian publisher or aired on CBN, they withdraw from popular culture.

Sometimes avoiding takes on the appearance of giving up. Chuck Colson writes, "Battle weary, we are tempted to withdraw into the safety of our sanctuaries, to keep busy by plugging into every program offered by our megachurches, hoping to keep ourselves and our children safe from the coming desolation."[9] Further, avoiding can take the form of legalism and violates the principle of Christian freedom. Just as we *chose* to follow Christ, we must discern and choose ways to make Christlike decisions.

Avoiding the media prevents Christian influence in changing and shaping the direction of the media as well as denies the opportunity to experience what God might reveal through the use of technology and media content. "Turning our backs on the culture is a betrayal of our biblical mandate and our own heritage because it denies God's sovereignty over all of life," writes Colson. "Nothing could be deadlier for the church—or more ill-timed. To abandon the battlefield now is to desert the cause just when we are seeing the first signs that historic Christianity may be on the verge of a great breakthrough."[10]

Accommodating

The second passive response is accommodation. Those who accommodate the media refuse to see a relationship between their spiritual life and their work/leisure life. They accommodate the press by "buying into it" and accepting it quietly. A common comment of accommodaters is, "If you don't like what's on TV, just turn it off." They are ambivalent about whether use of the media has any effect on the consumer and would prefer not to acknowledge the tension. With this approach you do not have to think; you just float along, navigating the media to avoid anything unpleasant or challenging. Many Christians accept this conflict strategy and take the easy way out by ignoring the fact that media messages might have an impact. They drift through life in denial that they could ever be affected by what they absorb.

The opinion that ideas cannot hurt people is one often touted by those who promote sex and violence in the media. Unfortunately, many Christians buy into this belief. When the U.S. Surgeon General called for a restriction on beer advertisements, columnist James J. Kilpatrick countered, "There is no evidence—repeat no evidence—that beer commercials inexorably lead children down the primrose path to a drunkard's grave." However, one must acknowledge that the entire advertising industry is based on the idea that the media *do* have influence on its audience. It is absurd to think that media does not have negative effects on the consumer but do have positive effects. Even at the onset of television, Edward R. Murrow acknowledged TV's power, "This instrument can teach, it can illuminate; yes, and it can even inspire. But it can do so only to the extent that humans are determined to use it to those ends." Michael Medved gives the following description of how illogical the "no effects" argument is:

> Imagine a forthcoming feature film with a torrid sex scene between two charismatic stars. On the nightstand beside the bed is a subtle product placement—say a bottle of mouthwash, with its label turned toward the camera. The current logic of the motion picture business suggests that the typical member of the audience turns his eyes away from two naked, gorgeous bodies in transports of passion and instead focuses all attention

on the bottle of mouthwash at the edge of the frame. How else can one explain the assumption that the mouthwash label will influence the viewers' future behavior, but the vivid sex scene will not? In short, the industry's position is both flagrantly dishonest and lavishly illogical.[11]

Yet many Christians believe that the media has little impact—or at least that it has little impact on *them*. Which leads to another aspect of accommodation. Medved calls this aspect a second line of defense and while he uses it as a defense of the film industry, Christians also accommodate all media by adopting it. This argument concedes the obvious fact that some connection exists between disturbing movie themes and our most pressing social problems but insists that the *problems* shape the themes, rather than vice versa. This "art is a reflection of the world" approach diffuses the responsibility of the media and in turn diffuses the responsibility of Christian accommodaters to be concerned or even cognizant of what they are viewing or reading. After all, if television is merely a reflection of the world, then it cannot be any more influential than going to the mall.

But the impact of media in our society has been validated by too many research studies to be ignored. In 1990 at the conference on "The Impact of the Media on Children and the Family," academicians from leading universities presented research and conducted workshops. At the end of the three-day workshop, one of the organizers reported: "Given the diversity of participants, they reached a surprising consensus that values in much of the mass media, especially in violent and sexually explicit materials, are on the collision course with traditional family values and the protection of children. This review found harmful effects in 86 percent of the studies and ends the debate about whether or not there is harm."[12]

For those who believe that their favorite TV show merely imitates real life, a twenty-five-year study by George Gerbner and his associates at the Annenburg School of Communications found that violent acts occurred on television some fifty-five times more frequently than they did in the real world. Many other studies have been conducted that have found the same results. Clearly, the impact of media influence on society cannot be dismissed. The accommodating approach is perhaps the most detrimental for Christians. In the home, it denies the opportunity for discussion with children about the values of the parents toward the media, and in society the silence of the accommodator is a quiet support for media offerings that undermine Christian values. Our world cries for Christian voices that will not hide their heads in the sand but will take an informed and active approach to cultural influences.

THE ACTIVE APPROACHES: COMPROMISING, COMPETING, COLLABORATING

While avoiding and accommodating involve little thought or energy, compromising, competing, and collaborating are active and dynamic approaches to the inner conflict of Christians and the media. Each of these approaches has its strengths and weaknesses, but all require Christians to think through and talk about how they will manage this pervasive cultural part of their lives.

Compromising

For many Christians who take a lukewarm approach to the conflict of media versus biblical worldview, the solution to the "of the world but not in the world" tension is to compromise. The Thomas-Kilmann model shows that this approach is intermediate in both assertiveness and cooperativeness. It is the path of least resistance and the choice that will be easiest to explain to non-Christian friends.

The objective of compromise as a conflict management strategy is to find some expedient, mutually acceptable solution that partially satisfies both parties, or in this case, both tensions. When you compromise, you are willing to win some and lose some but unwilling to give in totally as in accommodating. Likewise, it addresses an issue more directly than avoiding but does not explore it in as much depth as collaborating, which affords greater opportunity for understanding another's viewpoint. Compromising for the purposes of this discussion is a "sift through and choose" method that could involve compartmentalizing your life or splitting the difference between what is and is not acceptable media fare.

Some Christians employ the dualistic strategy of compartmentalizing their lives. They compromise by seeing a split between what is sacred and what is secular. This was the approach of Martin Luther, who saw a clear distinction between activities of the Christian. Niebuhr writes the following of Luther: "He seems to have a double attitude toward reason and philosophy, toward business and trade, toward religious organizations and rites, as well as toward state and politics. These antinomies and paradoxes have often led to the suggestion that Luther divided his life into compartments, or taught that the Christian right hand should not know what a man's worldly left hand was doing."[13] Niebuhr discusses how Luther's moral and religious development eventually led him to the avoidance position—to reject life in culture as incompatible with the gospel.

Compromising also can mean splitting the difference. For many Christians, the compromise takes almost a formula approach. Families decide together what their limits will be. They may choose to go to only movies that are PG or PG-13 but avoid the R-rated movies. Or they may limit their television viewing and computer time to a specific number of hours per week. Parents might talk to their children about the effects of what they watch on television but provide little monitoring of what they actually watch.

Competing

Competing is both assertive and uncooperative. The Christian who chooses to compete with secular media pursues his or her own concerns and interests with little regard to the other person or group. Thomas and Kilmann describe competing as a power-oriented mode in which one uses whatever power seems appropriate to win one's own position. Competing might mean "standing up for your rights," dogmatically defending a position that you believe is correct, or simply trying to win.

One chooses to compete with the media because he or she feels compelled to *do something*—to join the debate—to make a public statement. However, before engaging in this approach, one must first examine if one is truly called and equipped for the caustic comments and strong challenges to be faced. Justice Oliver Wendell Holmes Jr. said, "The place for a man who is complete in all powers is in the fight." The key to this quote is "*complete* in all powers." Those choosing to compete must ask if they are complete. Or as Frederica Mathewes-Green challenges, ask yourself, "Am I really that holy?"[14]

Those concerned with morality and the media choose to compete in several ways. They advocate censorship, organize boycotts, and create advocacy and watchdog groups. Michael Medved asserts that official censorship is not the answer and moves in a counterproductive direction. He cites the 1990 Florida obscenity arrest of 2 Live Crew as an example of how censorship can backfire. Before the arrest, 2 Live Crew was a little-known band with a small following. Their arrest catapulted them into overnight heroes and spokespersons for freedom of speech.

Some acts of meeting the media head-on have been successful, however. "The ability to employ the power of embarrassment and to pressure the entertainment industry toward a more wholesome posture presupposes the establishment of institutions devoted to that purpose. Fortunately, many such organizations already exist and play a vital part in the continuing combat over the values of the popular culture."[15] For example, Chuck Colson tells about an advertisement for the car company Saab that sold the philosophy of autonomy and rebellion against authority. He publicly criticized this ad on his *BreakPoint* program and received a call from Saab's U.S. president, a Christian, who had made the decision to withdraw the ads. Watchdog organizations have their critics and do not always exhibit Christian practice, and this is unfortunate. However, they can be highly effective in gaining the ear of the media and pressuring them to change if prayer and good sense fuel their strategy.

Joel Carpenter cautions the well-intended Christian from entering the "culture wars." An approach that is too aggressive and poorly thought out can cause an internal backlash. Not only will the overly zealous spokesperson push away those he or she is opposing; they can also confuse committed Christians. People can become so "ashamed of their combative compatriots that they start sympathizing with ideas and perspectives of which they should be more critical. Evangelical scholars' embarrassed and loathing reactions to Randall Terry and Pat Robertson have led many to sympathize with contemporary secular ideas more than they should."[16] As Philip Yancey warns in *What's So Amazing about Grace,* legalistic approaches of moral superiority demonstrate a spirit of ungrace.[17] For the competitive strategy to work, the approach must be holy, not holier-than-thou.

Competing can also involve Christians producing quality entertainment from a biblical worldview. The popular *Veggie Tales* series is an example of how Christians can compete head-to-head with the secular media. *Veggie Tales* has successfully crossed over in marketing, sales, and audience appeal to the secular market without compromising the Christian message.

Collaborating

Collaborating over cultural concerns for Christians usually takes place in the home and church; however, some Christians are called to enter the public realm and to advocate change in the media industry. Collaboration is both assertive and cooperative—the opposite of avoiding—and involves an attempt to work with the other person or group to find some solution that fully satisfies the issues of both parties. It means digging into an issue to identify the underlying concerns of those holding opposing views and finding an alternative solution that meets both sets of concerns. Collaborating between two persons takes four forms:

1. Exploring a disagreement to learn from each other's insights;
2. Concluding to resolve some condition that would otherwise harm them;
3. Competing for resources or confronting; and
4. Finding a creative solution to a problem.

To collaborate with anyone about anything, one first has to have some knowledge of the topic. This is the step many Christians overlook. Quick to react to emotionalism and guilt feelings, they begin the debate without having first studied to show themselves approved. Derek Kidner writes that the books of wisdom in the Bible summon us to "think hard as well as humbly; to keep our eyes open, to use our conscience and our common sense, and not to shirk the most disturbing questions."[18]

Paul writes in Philippians 4:8, "Whatever is true, whatever is noble, whatever is right, whatever is pure, whatever is lovely, whatever is admirable—if anything is excellent or praise-worthy—think about such things." Kenneth Myers notes that "Paul is commanding the Philippians (and, by extension, all believers) to discipline their minds and hearts to reflect on excellence. He does not qualify his statement to say they should only think about excellent 'spiritual' matters—matters pertaining to God directly. So it seems legitimate to believe that anything in the creative realm that qualifies as being excellent or praiseworthy is good to reflect upon."[19]

Collaboration recognizes that it is not the task of the church to *impose* its convictions on the world, but it is the obligation of the church to *declare* its convictions to the world. Christians are responsible to live in a non-Christian world according to the teachings of their Lord and the Scriptures that testify of him. John Akers challenges us in *Christianity Today,* "Where are the creative men and women—the writers, the artists, the filmmakers—who will capture the imagination of our confused world in the name of Christ? Where are those who will expose by their work the vanities and contradictions of our age, and affirm with all the skill they can muster that only in Christ 'are hidden all the treasures and wisdom and knowledge?'"[20]

To collaborate effectively Christians must realize that the tension is not over depictions of violence or sex on TV or the mockery of family values—the tension is over competing worldviews. Collaborating allows us to fulfill the Christian's responsibility to redeem our surrounding culture.

THE CHRISTIAN'S RESPONSE

Conflict in any situation is unavoidable and ultimately can be positive. Those struggling with the tension in values between the Bible and modern culture should find themselves thinking more deeply about their faith and how they should live it daily. Conflict opens up dialogue, and dialogue is the first step to agreement.

Experts agree that those skilled in managing conflict in interpersonal relationships know when to discern which of the five strategies should be employed for a given situation. There are times when emotions are running high and temporarily avoiding an issue may be the best route, and there are times when competition can be the only way to bring about change.

Even though there are times when it is appropriate to choose one method over another, some approaches are generally more effective than others. Those choosing the softer methods (avoiding and accommodating) must acknowledge that these passive methods are not very practical. Further, one's personality and calling can help determine what conflict method is chosen. Medved warns:

> The point is there is no refuge today from the ubiquitous presence of the popular culture. Even those who make a personal decision not to partake of its products will find its influence inescapable. You can put your TV in the closet, avoid movies altogether, and use earplugs to spare your ears from the sounds of rap or heavy metal, but these forms of entertainment will still change your life through their influence on everyone else in this society. Though you may struggle to protect your own

kids from material that encourages violence or irresponsible sex, you can't possibly protect them from all the other kids in your community who have received full exposure.[21]

As Christians we should discern not only what approaches are best but also how God is calling us to respond. David P. Gushee, Graves professor of moral philosophy at Union University, gives the following principles for participation for Christians to consider:[22]

1. "Does your decision reflect the responsible test of freedom in Christ?" First Corinthians 10:23 reminds us there are things that are lawful, but not profitable and do not edify. The key to this first principle is the word *responsible*. What may be a responsible choice for me as an adult may not be a responsible choice for my child.

If we believe that the Jesus Christ through the Bible reveals truth for all levels of our lives, then we must believe that He can guide in our decisions about how to use the media. Colson encourages us to stand firm on the principles of Christianity. "Only Christianity offers a way to understand the physical and the moral order. Only Christianity offers a comprehensive worldview that covers all areas of life and thought, every aspect of creation. Only Christianity offers a way to live in line with the real world."[23]

2. "Does this form of entertainment hit any of my areas of weakness?" The Lord's Prayer asks that we not be led into temptation. At different periods of our lives, we have different weaknesses. Satan is looking for those areas where we show a proclivity to sin. Since Satan cannot read our minds, he learns our weaknesses from what he observes us watching, reading, and hearing.

3. "Should I spend money and time on this activity?" This is perhaps the most difficult question to answer. I have friends who choose not to own a television or computer, not because they are opposed on moral grounds, but because they see these media as time wasters. Myers writes: "Many of the decisions we make about our involvement in popular culture are not

questions about good and evil. When I decide not to read a certain book, I am not necessarily saying that to read it would be a sin. It is much more likely that I believe it to be imprudent to take the time to read that book at this time in my life."[24]

Paul reminds us in 1 Corinthians that although something may be permissible, it may not be beneficial or constructive. The ability to make the tough calls when it comes to time and money stewardship is a sign of Christian maturity and responsibility.

These guidelines will help individuals and families decide their level of involvement in culture, but if Christians are to shape a biblical worldview, they have a responsibility to support those on all fronts. While I may choose a more passive means of dealing with my inner conflict, I can still support those who are equipped and called to fight the battle in a public forum. Through financial resources and prayer, I can encourage art and media projects that reflect Christian views. Praying, giving of time and money, and helping to equip others are not just worthy endeavors; they are necessary pursuits if we are to reclaim our future. William J. Bennett writes:

> The good news is that this cultural virus has created its own antibodies. Americans are regaining the confidence to express publicly the common sense sentiments they hold privately. They are learning again that the things a society collectively chooses to affirm and condemn, encourage and discourage, make all the difference. . . . This renewed understanding on a whole range of social issues is the first critical step in the "revaluing" of America. Values that were once in exile are being welcomed home. The American people are renewing their commitment to our common principles. And so the task of cultural reconstruction has begun.[25]

The postmodern view of communication posits that all communication is subjective. The importance of the sender's decoding of a message is emphasized and the sender's true meaning is minimized as contemporary researchers argue that meaning is in the eyes and ears of the beholder. Believing in the subjectivity of all communication and the absence of "truth," Christians can fall prey to becoming trapped into society's definition of cultural reality.

What Christians must realize is that the reason for communication and cultural confusion goes back to the Fall—to the original sin of Adam and Eve. It is only when we understand conflict through a biblical set of assumptions that we can choose how to respond. For example, if you believe that all communication is fundamentally flawed as a result of sin, then you will recognize as Augustine recognized that our ability to communicate always depends on God's grace.

As we look at our culture and our world, we will realize there will always be a gap between what is and what we, as Christians, would like things to be. Our culture will always be imperfect, and we will always be imperfect in our response to it. As Quentin Schultze writes, "We are restricted by the ambiguity of symbols, by postmodern subjectivity, and by our failure to recognize and use our gifts."[26]

This final point—the failure to recognize our gifts—is critical for understanding how individuals should reconcile their inner conflict with their culture. Some Christians have the ethos to participate in the public arena. They can compete with the media giants because they are gifted writers, speakers, and change agents. Others have been given the gift of facilitation. They can come to the table to collaborate and weigh in the biblical perspective on controversial issues. Still others may avoid direct interaction with the media but may assert their opinions in polls, discussion groups, and letters to those who are called to be cultural change agents. Christians must realize that while the battle is not ours, we do have the ability to be cocreators of culture. We can and must be the change agents that will reclaim our culture for Christ.

CHAPTER 13

CHRISTIAN WORLDVIEW AND TEACHING

Thomas R. Rosebrough

Perhaps the most important question we can ask ourselves is, What do I believe? The question is even more critical for those who teach. In the classroom, whether it is a public high school, a Christian college, or a state university, the teacher's belief system—what we shall term *worldview*—does make a difference in a student's life. We all believe in something or someone. This belief lends a distinct perspective that attentive students will perceive. All students need a perspective, a certain context created by their teachers. This context of belief can be temporal or timeless, hopeless or hopeful, egocentric or transcendent, judgmental or redemptive.

Generation X and the Net Generation care about their spirituality, even though they might think about it differently from other generations.[1] As we shall see below, a sense of purpose in life is a very strong question among youth and most Americans in the twenty-first century. Our students are asking, What about today? What about tomorrow? But they often do not ask about yesterday as they consider their context of belief, their worldview. To this postmodern generation the past seems irrelevant as the culture teaches that the values of our religious heritage are extraneous to their lives. Our students need assurance that there is a God to believe in, One who is good and the same yesterday, today, and tomorrow.

WHAT ARE THE PREVAILING WORLDVIEWS IN AMERICAN EDUCATION?

In order to understand the worldviews in contemporary American education, we must perceive the conflicting visions of public education in the United States. Debates over the mission, content, and methods of public education usually have involved conflicting visions of American identity, of how to deal with the differences in gender, race, class, ethnicity, and sexual orientation. There are those who have always opposed spending classroom time on teaching students how to think critically about their belief system, contending instead that schools should focus on promoting intellectual skills and mastery of certain subjects. The result is that these critics regard any effort to sensitize students to the differences in belief as divisive or even a potential threat to the social glue that binds our democratic society together.

The critics inhabit both sides of the political fence. The conservative right side often argues for an unchanging, truly "American" classroom culture. The liberal left espouses values such as tolerance for difference and respect for diversity as "American" to their core. These differences are purely political so that neither side can fairly appeal to a universally agreed-upon vision of America, its history, or its future.

A Christian worldview cuts through the political morass. It recognizes that the political world does indeed exist—we are to give our due to Caesar. It also recognizes that this "real" world of public schools can exist independently of beliefs—it can and does function every day without the benefit of consciously held worldviews. Many, if not most, people, including teachers, have never reflected on what they believe. Consider the many decisions that teachers must make daily. Teachers must judge between right and wrong as they guide their students. If truth is not seen as transcendent—apart and above the consequences of the teachers' decisions—it becomes relative and constantly changing in nature. The Christian worldview includes the assertion that Christ himself is the *truth*, thus positing a non-relativistic and unchanging approach to morality. This aspect of worldview as well as other theistic assumptions have been challenged recently, especially during the last forty years.

Many believe that public education in America is in a state of moral confusion. They no longer see Christianity and its teachings being utilized as the basis of morality and ethics in American schooling. Allan Bloom[2] even suggests that ethnic minority groups' insistence on preserving their culture may weaken a belief in God and country that has helped unify the American people.

Many American educators, in contrast, applaud the demise of Christianity as the primary religious and educational force in our country's schools. Pai and Adler[3] argue, for example, that insisting on a Christian worldview for our schools would return us to the Puritan era, in which cultural diversity was seen as harmful to the national unity. The authors do not fault Bloom for being apprehensive about the possible effects of becoming preoccupied with cultural diversity. Where Pai and Adler blame Bloom is for his failure to recognize "that the specific contents of the fundamental beliefs . . . . are determined by the cultures in which they are found . . . . He does not recognize that these deeper beliefs are reflections of each culture's unique worldview." Pai and Adler rail against the ethnocentric attitude ("allegedly superior Anglo norms of the dominant group") because they believe it intensifies the sense of alienation and discrimination experienced by the ethnic and racial minority groups.

Multicultural education, as articulated by Pai and Adler, actually seems quite compatible with our democratic society. A person's ability to function effectively in a socioculturally diverse society "depends on the individual's specific knowledge about other subcultures and the skills needed to function appropriately in varying cultural contexts." Most would probably agree with John Dewey that there is an "intrinsic connection between the prospects of democracy and belief in the potentialities of human nature—for its own sake."[4] Many believe cultural pluralism as an ideology holds the stronger argument, that tolerance of diverse cultures and beliefs in our schools is the single most vital virtue. How could one argue that diversity is not enriching? Human life does become more interesting and even exciting when there are many varied ways of thinking, feeling, and viewing the world.

A Christian worldview sees tolerance for cultural diversity as a compelling virtue. Indeed, Galatians 5 implies that it is one of the fruits of the spirit with love, kindness, and patience. Christian educators must travel beyond the traditional notion of tolerance lest they become perceived as patronizing—a superior group willing to tolerate someone "inferior." The question, however, is not whether we should tolerate diverse cultures and beliefs. The question is whether there are times when such toleration compromises transcendent values in the Christian worldview. When, as Stan Gaede[5] has asked, is tolerance not a virtue? It is a question that underlines worldview differences.

WHAT IS WORLDVIEW?

The problem with discussing a person's worldview, as James Sire[6] points out, is that it is almost too obvious to mention. The way people think, the assumptions they make, the approach they take to solving problems or making decisions are all based on a framework or structure shaped by several basic questions and answers: questions everyone has asked ourselves and answers everyone has given either consciously or unconsciously. Sire says we all assume that something is there rather than that nothing is there. What varies is that everyone does not agree on *what* that something is.

Worldview is different from faith. Faith is a belief in something or someone unseen or unheard or even unrecognized. For Christians, it is a trust in revealed truth that transcends one's senses, an expectation that something good can happen because of one's faith in God's goodness and power. Worldview, on the other hand, is a bit more analytic. It is a set of questions and answers about the way one perceives life. For most people the set of assumptions called worldview is largely unconscious and definitely unexamined.

For example, the worldview of the screenwriter and director of the May 2000, CBS television movie version of *Jesus* is obvious to the viewer. Their Jesus is something of a fun-loving surfer-dude. Their Jesus dances, smiles a lot, expresses a faint sexual interest in women, is emotional with his mother. In short, their Jesus is quite human. The filmmakers also showed the divine side through his miracles, especially the raising of Lazarus and Jesus' own resurrection. The writing and directing of *Jesus* was guided by a set of assumptions, a worldview, not by faith, though faith may have been a factor.

Anyone's worldview examination can begin with a simple question, What do you believe? or, What do you believe in? Most people in twenty-first-century America will still say they believe in God or a "higher power." Those who do not believe in God are more likely to say that he exists only in the minds of those who believe. One such atheistic group with a contentious worldview to Christians in this century is naturalism.

In a recent book, Colson and Pearcey[7] contend that the major challenge defining people's lives in contemporary America is theism versus naturalism. Naturalism is a mode of thought, a worldview, that excludes the supernatural and spiritual. Naturalism claims that God did not create us, saying that it is theists who have created the idea of God, or that believers through the act of belief create God. God does not exist for naturalists: natural causes alone explain everything that exists.

"Existence" was the subject of a recent survey conducted at Union University with graduate and undergraduate students. The survey, conducted by graduate student Tiffany Stehle and this writer, was modeled after a similar one published in *USA Today* (April 1999) that asked, "If you could ask God one question and knew that you would receive a clearly audible answer, what would that question be?" The answers are absolutely consistent with what the *USA Today* survey found. The highest percentage of responses, overwhelmingly, had to do with *What is my purpose in life?* The second most popular category of responses was *Why is there such pain and suffering in this world?* And the third strongest response was *What happens to us after we die?*

All of the questions in the survey are basic worldview questions. Christians and naturalists have rather different answers to those three questions:

- *Purpose in life.* For Christians, one finds it in God; specifically, our purpose is to live to glorify God. For naturalists, there is no higher purpose, only to live for the material world.
- *Pain and suffering.* For Christians, Satan brought it with him into this world when Adam and Eve fell from grace. God can give believers the grace to cope. For naturalists, suffering in this world is a part of the natural order. The fittest will survive.
- *After death.* For Christians, our souls live for eternity and we enter it through Christ, the "way, the truth, and the life." Christians believe in the unseen God and the unknown life after death. For naturalists, this natural world, this cosmos we perceive with our senses, is all there is.

Other questions, utilizing a Christian-naturalist dichotomy, comprise the set of assumptions constituting our worldview:

1. What is real in this world? Christians say it is God. Naturalists would say the material cosmos.
2. What is a human being? For Christians, humankind is created in God's image. For naturalists, humans are finite, evolved mammals or even complex machines. This question has rather obvious implications for the issue of fetal tissue research.
3. What is the meaning of human history? Christians say it is a linear playing out of God's plan: after the Fall, Christ came, died, rose from the dead, sent his Spirit, and will come again to establish his heavenly kingdom. Naturalists contend that history is linear but meaningless.
4. Finally, but not exhaustedly, What is the basis for morality? Christians assert that morality is objective—based on the transcendent principles of God as found in the Ten Commandments and the Sermon on the Mount. Naturalists and other atheists say there is no ultimate objective basis for morality—humans create their own subjective standards. It is this last basic

worldview question relating to morality that is so vital to teaching, as we shall see later in this chapter.

HOW IS THE CHRISTIAN WORLDVIEW UNIQUE?

Is the Christian worldview unlike any other? Are the answers to the questions stated above enough to make a case for Christianity as the compelling worldview that Christians think it is? Understanding Christianity is to learn that while it has a corporate dimension, it is also simple and individual. Saving society for Christians begins with saving individuals from their bent toward sin, the original sin of Adam and Eve. And the most powerful evidence of one who is saved is one who extends grace to others. The worldview questions stated earlier and their "Christian answers" form a simple framework, a starting point for a most profound theology. But it is grace, what Martin Luther termed as God's middle name, that makes the Christian worldview unique.

As stated simply by C. S. Lewis, "To be a Christian means to forgive the inexcusable, because God has forgiven the inexcusable in you."[8] Philip Yancey tells a story about a British conference on comparative religions. The conferees were debating what belief, if any, was unique to the Christian faith. The debate ensued for a length of time until Lewis wandered into the room and asked, "What's the rumpus about?" Informed of the subject for debate, Lewis responded, "Oh, that's easy. It's grace." The conferees, after some thought, had to agree. The Buddhists have their eightfold path, the Hindus the doctrine of karma, the Jews their covenant, and the Muslims a code of law—each offering a way to earn approval. Only Christianity dares to assert that God's love is unconditional.[9]

Grace is the defining component of Christianity. It is undeserved favor and unearned love. For believers in Christ, grace is free because Jesus paid the price on Calvary. Christians are called to serve as agents of grace in a hostile world, indeed, in a world that often considers forgiveness and mercy as antithetical to the workings of society. The "natural" human being intuitively rejects grace and embraces justice because he or she does not perceive that a price has been paid. Differences in worldviews have impacted American education historically.

WHAT IS THE HISTORICAL CONTEXT OF WORLDVIEW IN AMERICAN EDUCATION?

The Age of Enlightenment is now three centuries old. Francis Bacon and Charles Darwin have strongly asserted that science, especially biology, has a certain redemptive power. It is through science that our lives here on earth are better—it brings us basic human comforts not enjoyed by our forefathers. But it seems that what was once a subtle message has now become increasingly explicit in the schools. The message is to replace a theistic worldview with a scientific-naturalistic worldview. This view states that the world somehow came into reality without God's creating intervention. In *The Blind Watchmaker,* Oxford zoologist Richard Dawkins has made a case that the universe did not require an intelligent agent to establish evolution. Our schools, backed by Supreme Court decisions, accuse theists of being opposed to science whenever they question evolutionary science and naturalist interpretations of the origin of the universe.

The role of religious faith in America's support of public education can be traced to the worldviews of the founding fathers. The words of the Northwest Ordinance of 1787, passed by those who drafted and signed America's constitution, are revealing: "Religion, morality and knowledge being necessary for good government and the happiness of mankind, schools and the means for education shall forever be encouraged." If one checks the chartering constitutions of the states of Ohio, Kentucky, Nebraska, and others, one finds these same words or a close paraphrasing. Why? They were following the Northwest Ordinance's guidelines for entering statehood. Each new territory, in order to apply for statehood, had to organize schools, hire teachers, and otherwise show that the new state would encourage education. Not just any educational system, but one built on religion, morality, and knowledge. Such schooling would surely supply American democracy with wise citizens who could make discerning decisions in the voting booth.

It is ironic that twenty-first-century America has discovered Christian beliefs to be offensive. It has taken the American court system almost two centuries to make the discovery. The *Engel v. Vitale* decision in 1962 found an innocuous prayer required by the New York regents to be unconstitutional because it was potentially offensive to nonbelievers in the public schools. The prayer was theistic, not specifically Christian, but it was required by the state. The state of New York was subscribing to a long-held belief that education has social as well as academic ends. As Thomas Lickona, foremost authority on character education in the public schools, has argued, "The purpose of education has always been to help people become smart and help people become good."[10]

Brown v. Topeka in 1954 had already documented a new idea to the courts, the idea that children could be harmed psychologically by certain public school embarrassments. It logically followed for the Supreme Court to move from race to religion and not allow children, potentially offended by the prayer, to be simply excused from its recitation.

It was another two decades before many Christians realized the implications of the *Engel* decision. In the 1980 *Stone v. Graham* case, originating in Kentucky, the Supreme Court banned the Ten Commandments from being posted on public school walls. The verdict on American public education seemed clear—the very basis for common law and morality in the Western world was unwelcome in public schools because it violated religious neutrality.

Other more recent cases underline the separation of state from America's religious heritage: *Lee v. Weisman* (1992) banned clergy-led graduation prayers, leaving the door open for student-led prayer in the public school setting. However, *Sante Fe Independent School District v. Doe* (2000) has raised the wall of separation between church and state. The majority opinion banned pregame prayers led by high school students because, as Justice Stevens wrote, "An objective high school student would perceive the . . . prayer as stamped with her school's seal of approval." Chief Justice Rehnquist said in dissent that the majority opinion "bristles with hostility to all things religious in public life."

Another case handed down at the same time as the *Sante Fe* decision, *Mitchell v. Helms,* adds more confusion as it seemingly lowers the proverbial wall of separation. *Helms* upheld the provision of computers and library books to religious schools under federal Title VI. Such aid, dating back to the "child benefit theory" set by the Supreme Court in 1947, is apparently viewed as "neutral" support by the court.

A deeply disturbing "nonneutral" case, at least from the viewpoint of many Christians, occurred in 1996 in Medford, New Jersey. Zachary Hood, a first-grade student in a Medford public school, brought a favorite story to school as part of an assignment. Zachary chose the story "A Big Family" from *The Beginner's Bible.* It centered on Jacob and Esau's reconciliation—no mention of God or his miracles. The teacher refused to read it to the class for fear that reading the Bible "might influence" other students. The school principal supported the teacher, saying the reading was the "equivalent of praying." Zachary's mother took it to court. The lower court upheld the school, saying that it wanted to prevent the misperception by children that the school was endorsing religion. A twelve-judge circuit court in Philadelphia in 2000 split evenly on the issue, in effect upholding the lower court's decision. The Supreme Court refused to hear the case in 2001. The courts sided with the school's right to restrict speech (including individual religious expression) for educational reasons.

WHAT IS WORLDVIEW AS RELATED TO THE FUNCTION OF THE CLASSROOM TEACHER?

The role of the classroom teacher is a distinctive one in the professions. Unlike medicine and law, teaching is primarily a social act. Medical doctors and attorneys can practice their professions largely devoid of the need for social influence. The best family doctors and attorneys are attuned to the social needs of their clients, but their essential tasks can be performed without great attention to social and emotional needs. This is not the case with teachers. To be effective, teachers must attend to their client's social and emotional needs. It is true that many teachers do not, but the act of teaching by its nature focuses on the axiological issues of right and wrong, good and bad.

Education is as multifaceted as its students. One could argue that education has two major goals, academic (the three Rs) and social (the three Cs—character, cooperation, courage). If we had to choose one or the other for children, which goal would it be? Most would probably choose socialization because we fear the adverse societal consequences. Both goals are desirable and represent the traditional ends of schooling. Both goals are also compatible, even complementary.

At least three worldview questions especially address these traditional goals: *prime reality, human being,* and *morality.*

What Is Prime Reality?

In other words, what is real in this world? Who is in charge? Is there a God who wants to order human lives? Did God create reality? All these represent the foundation of a worldview. In a sense, creation is the basis of human dignity, for one's origin defines who one is, why one exists, and how people should treat one another.

What Is a Human Being?

Christianity and other theistic worldviews teach that humankind is created in God's image, that humans are spiritual beings in their essence. Atheistic worldviews such as naturalism or nihilism claim humans are nothing more than complex machines. How people view themselves makes a difference in the classroom. Christianity asserts that human beings were created as free, moral agents with opportunity to make choices, good and evil. The human tendency toward sin leads people to make bad choices. The human sense of the divine can lead one toward the good, toward Christ who endues purpose in each life. The role of Christ was and is to defeat humanity's sinful tendencies. An understanding of who we are can help us discern the nature of suffering in this world. Human nature became morally distorted with Adam, leading to a morally and often physically distorted world.

What Is the Basis for Morality?

For those with nontheistic worldviews, morality is relational to human beings. It is subjective in the sense that right and wrong can change, based on the circumstances people find themselves in. Morality is consequential for the atheist in that moral decisions are dependent on one's perception of the consequences of the decision. For Christians morality is objective and transcendent. One's ethics is based on objective standards such as the Ten Commandments and/or the Sermon on the Mount. Morality is based on the character of God as good, loving, and holy—it is transcendent or apart from humans as they make their moral decisions.

HOW IS A TEACHER'S WORLDVIEW INFLUENTIAL IN A CLASSROOM?

Does a teacher's worldview make a difference in the classroom? How does a teacher respond to the three worldview areas cited above: prime reality, nature of human beings, and basis of morality? Let's take each in turn to examine the teacher's impact.

Prime Reality

We live in a time when teachers in the public sector, and I would assert we are affected in the private sector as well, are reluctant even to mention God in the classroom. The courts have made it unconstitutional for the God of previous generations to be prime reality in American life. *Religion* is a politically incorrect word. *Spiritual* is socially acceptable because it is more individual in its tone. Many fear that losing the heritage that religion has played in American history will adversely our affect democracy. Why? Jefferson saw clearly in his vision for democracy that the workings of government depend on the values of lawmakers and of the governed. If citizens are dishonest, deceitful, proud, boastful, unkind, and immoral, then government will be the same. The founding fathers knew this truth when they wrote the words of the Northwest Ordinance of 1787: democracy is dependent upon people who are educated in "religion, morality and knowledge."

Thomas Lickona suggests ways we can incorporate religion's contribution in our schools:

1. Teach role religion played in our moral beginnings as a nation. "Endowed by our Creator with certain inalienable rights"—we must teach that these rights are God-given and government cannot take them away.

2. Our country's major social reform movements have been inspired by religious vision, from the abolition of slavery to the civil rights movement. Those who have violated it do not diminish the power of this vision.

3. Understand the role of religious motivation in the lives of individuals. An examination of some textbooks in our public schools shows that Mother Teresa was simply a social reformer with a heart for the poor. We must insist that the truth of her faith and sense of personal call from Christ be revealed and included in educational history.

4. Include religion in curricula. For example, where sex education is taught in the public sector, let's assert religion's role. To exclude the idea of "it violates my religious beliefs to have sex before marriage" is to violate religious neutrality.

5. Include religion in social issues. What do the major world religions (Christianity, Judaism, Islam) have to say about the plight of the poor? Jesus teaches that our very salvation depends on how we treat the poor.

6. Engage students in discussions about moral truth. The claims of Christianity are that moral truth is objective, that is, independent of the knower. We can teach that adultery is wrong, slavery is wrong, racism is wrong, cheating is wrong, child abuse is wrong. And that they are wrong because of objective moral truth, even if people do not seem to know it.

7. Challenge students to develop a vision of life that addresses the purpose of life. The media culture says happiness is maximizing one's pleasure. Christianity says that our sense of fulfillment comes from serving God. We can ask students the question, "What will you be most proud of at the end of your life?"[11]

A Human Being

A teacher's worldview makes a difference in students' perception and conception of the nature of a human being. "In Adam's fall we sinned all" (based on Romans 5) is a famous catechism from *The New England Primer* of Colonial America. In twenty-first-century America teachers need graceful ways to teach students that we all have sinned and fallen short. "All" includes teachers. Immanuel Kant spoke clearly to the nature of a human being in his formulation of the principle of human dignity: "Act so that you treat humanity, whether in your own person or in that of another, always as an end and never as a means only."[12] Teachers who are not humble, sensitive, and fair to their students may model a worldview of human beings that is arrogant, conveying that only students are sinners; and that perhaps the reason they are sinners is not because they lack Jesus but because they lack the infinite knowledge of their professor.

Basis of Morality

A teacher's worldview affects students' sense of right and wrong. Just as a court system will surely fail if it becomes arbitrary and capricious, so will a teacher's classroom system collapse as well. To be arbitrary is to decide without evidence. To be capricious is to decide without consistency. Teachers must set up a classroom that includes a structure for assessment that objectively evaluates student work and does so consistently and fairly. Morality in a Christian worldview transcends the individual, including individual teachers. The greatest challenge for teachers is to assess students fairly, consistently, and even gracefully.

HOW DO WE LIVE A LIFE OF FAITH IN TEACHING?

We began by making a distinction between faith and worldview. Now we must put them together again. Worldview to Christians is meaningless without faith. Faith is the holy glue that inspires and cements our worldview. So, how can we live our faith as teachers? How can we promote "alternative teaching," a distinctively Christian worldview choice for teaching? Here are a few suggestions.

1. We must first recognize what a life of faith is. I believe it involves advancing the kingdom of God in small ways every day. His ways are usually small, subtle, and simple: a smile, a gesture of kindness, a simple presence in a room in a time of trouble, a humble act of servanthood, a word of encouragement, a show of sensitivity like knowing when to remain silent, a patient attitude in a time of stress. Elton Trueblood reminds us that a life of faith is often a false dichotomy between word and deed.[13] A kind word goes even further than a cup of water to the thirsty. Our words as teachers can be a part of Jesus' living water, the kind of refreshment that can eternally satisfy.

2. We must recognize what an educated person is. Edward Tingley says the majority of modern universities assume everyone has this recognition because education is just what the university does.[14] I think there are three issues here: (1) An educated person must be more than a vessel filled with information. There must be holism in education. Learning must touch the soul as well as the mind. (2) A person educated in a discipline must be broadly as well as narrowly educated. Classic liberal learning was valuable in itself and was intended to assist one in living well because it required something of a personal dialogue between knowledge issues and the learner. This dialogue assists the learner in knowing who he or she is as a person interacting with society. (3) Classic liberal learning is not enough, however. Students entering this new millennium must be prepared to earn a living as well. Jesus was a carpenter. Paul was a tent maker. An educated person at a Christian liberal arts university addresses learning holistically, employing what Elton Trueblood called the "*divine and*": in mind *and* soul as well as in liberal arts *and* the professions. Twenty-first-century higher education must address the holistic issue at both these levels. We do not have to settle for the demands of the conjunction *or* in education.

3. How we teach is vital as well. Trueblood reminds us that we teach too much. He says, "In the modern college there is too much teaching and not enough learning." Our tendency is to do

the work for students when they ought to do it themselves. A part of our faith can be our trust in our students' ability to learn. The *constructivist* approach to learning popularized by the great Swiss epistemologist, Jean Piaget, views learning as constructed by learner. Recent neuroscience discoveries confirm that the human brain is a pattern-seeking device that craves variety, challenge, and structure. Let's teach less and allow our students to learn more.

4. A sharp distinction exists between how Christian teachers live their faith in the public versus the private sectors; indeed, the public schools of twenty-first-century America are not legally receptive to a life of faith, especially the Christian faith. No one in either sector, however, can stop teachers from having private prayer. One of my favorite books on education is Postman and Weingartner's *Teaching as a Subversive Activity.*[15] It is about teachers who might dare to teach less and expect more from students. While the thesis of this book is not religious, a Christian teacher can "subvert" a classroom full of students by committing in prayer before each school day, perhaps arriving early for class to pray for each student in the as-yet-empty desks or chairs.

5. While it is counter-court even to say God's name in a devotional way in public schools, we can respond privately but not in a proselytizing way to student inquiries about faith. For example, a student may ask how God can allow senseless tragedies like school shootings. An adolescent does not want a philosophical debate in such circumstances. The student wants reassurance. I think the characteristic of God we should focus on in such situations, whether in a public school or in a higher education classroom, is his goodness. Yes, our God is omnipotent, omniscient, transcendent, redeeming, and holy, but above all he is good and loving.

6. Living our faith in the classroom has at least two integrative aspects in: (1) the teacher-student dynamic, and (2) the discipline itself. *Discipline integration* generally receives the most attention as teachers seek to find fundamental assumptions that guide their discipline. For example, in the field of education, one can ask integrative questions which can lead us to discover

the assumptions, like: "What are the implications of teaching all children as gifted?" or, "How can the practice of ability grouping be reconciled with cognitive learning?" Another way to uncover foundational assumptions in the discipline of education is to look at the history of ideas. For example, the idea of the kindergarten was born in the mind of the German mathematician, Friedrich Froebel, from his love of the logic of God's natural order and creation.

It is, however, the former integrative aspect, the *teacher-student dynamic,* that fuels my passion for living our faith in the classroom. I believe that the process—the *how* of learning—is at least as important as the disciplinary assumptions—the *what* of learning. All teachers, regardless of their *a priori* understandings of their discipline, can apply Galatians 5:22–23: "But the fruit of the Spirit is love, joy, peace, patience, kindness, goodness, faithfulness, gentleness and self-control." All of these attributes speak of process, of how teachers can guide learning. Long after students have forgotten ideas they should have learned in their discipline, the influence of a godly teacher remains.

7. Students need perspective from their adult teachers. They need reassurance that certain values are timeless, that morality is based on a transcendent standard and that their teacher is committed to holding to that standard. Michael Novak[16] writes eloquently about the Christian gift of conscience. He defines *conscience* as the practical habit of discerning the right thing to do in immediate circumstances and by which we blame ourselves for failing to utilize the light of discernment. As teachers we must live the moral life in front of students. As Novak points out, in earlier Christian ages the moral life was thought of as a way of life to be lived, a set of paths to follow with Christ as model and the lives of the saints as pathbreakers. Dare we as teachers be pathbreakers?

It has been my belief as expressed in this writing that teachers must examine their *worldview* belief system because students have to learn and keep learning how to live. This examination can lead to an alternative teaching, a way of living our faith as teachers in a culturally pluralistic world. What we believe as teachers does make a difference in the lives of those with whom we interact. Knowing the questions is at least as important as knowing the answers. It is through seeking to answer the critical questions of faith that we can live an examined life. For teachers and students it is critical: the examined life is better.

CHAPTER 14

CHRISTIAN WORLDVIEW AND HEALTH CARE

SUSAN R. JACOB

EVOLUTION OF HEALTH CARE

"AT ONE TIME medicine and religion were so thoroughly united that a medicine man was a priest."[1] Many cultures still regard healers this way. In the West, religion and medicine remained closely linked until the end of the medieval period. The first hospitals were established in monasteries, and physicians were often monks, and nurses were often nuns. The church was a predominant force in health care, which was based on the Christian concepts of charity and sanctity of life.[2] The link between religion and medicine was also evidenced in diagnoses because many devastating illnesses like the plague were often attributed to spiritual causes and were thought to be God's retribution for sin.[3]

The scientific revolution, having its roots in the work of Descartes, Hume, and Locke, brought a separation of medicine and religion by promoting a new method for seeking knowledge. Truth could only be discerned through the examination of empirical data and a rational scientific method. Experimental science disputed the authority of the church, and its former command over truth began to crumble. Since the experimental method could not readily be applied to God or personal experiences with God, religion was rooted out of all science, including medicine.[4] As the scientific worldview gained momentum in the West, physicians were forced to use only the techniques that stood up under the scrutiny of the experimental method of modern science.

Today in the twenty-first century, health care professionals bear the brunt of this unfortunate split between religion and medicine. History reveals lengthy periods of antagonism between science and medicine. In the health field clergy and physicians have not always collaborated in providing holistic health care to patients. Medical education is focused heavily on the sciences with little time left for future physicians to study the humanities while theological students concentrate on languages, history, literature, sociology, philosophy, and psychology. The paths of these two professionals often cross at the bedside of the sick. Physicians and clergy rarely communicate, however, with each other regarding the physical or spiritual health of their patients but rather engage in small talk when encountering one another at the patient's bedside.

The health care professionals who have long been attuned to the spiritual needs of patients are nurses. They have realized that people need more than excellent scientific medical care. On the other hand, physicians guided by Cartesian philosophy have been trained to practice only the techniques that have been proven in a laboratory. Fortunately, nurses have historically acted to bridge the gulf between physicians and clergy by suggesting that pastors and physicians talk with each other about the holistic needs of the patients whom they have in common.[5]

CLINICAL STUDIES LINKING FAITH AND HEALTH

Even though Christian health care professionals have intuitively known that faith and health are interrelated, there was little clinical evidence until recently that documented the link between faith and health. Pioneering work by medical researchers such as Benson, Dossey, and Koenig coupled with increased media coverage of the topic along with alternative healing methods have changed this fact. Scientific evidence has shown that religious involvement prevents illness and helps people recover from illness and live longer.[6]

The Western world often views health as optimal physical status; and the mind, influenced by Western thought, envisions a robust physical stature when reflecting on health. The concept of health commonly implies an absence of physical symptoms as well as normal laboratory and test results. The medical establishment has reluctantly given some recognition to mental health as a valid entity. However, to be included in the medical model, psychiatry has had to bend to the view of the mind as brain and of suffering as a statistically validated disease classification. Health insurance companies, insisting on physical evidence regarding diagnosis and treatment, lag behind in validating many mental conditions as reimbursable, and therefore, many go untreated.[7]

The current health care system has a tendency to have a one-dimensional materialistic view of health. Nevertheless, numerous medical research studies have documented a clear mind-body relationship. The medical literature reveals an increasing number of studies showing that spirituality shares a mutual relationship with both mind and body.[8] Interrelationships between the socioeconomic aspects of the person and other dimensions of functional independence have also been demonstrated. This is reflected in Engel's call for a biopsychosocial approach to health care.[9]

There is compelling scientific evidence that spiritual practices, including prayer and regular church attendance, significantly affect health. The impact of prayer on health has basically been studied in two ways. The effects of intercessory prayer on healing have been documented. In addition, the effects of prayer on physical and mental well-being as well as on the coping ability of individuals have been studied extensively.[10]

Oxman in 1995 studied 232 patients who underwent open-heart surgery. The overall death rate was 9 percent in the first six months after surgery, but for those who were regular church attendees the rate was only 6 percent. A number of other studies also point to the value of church attendance or religious involvement for positive health outcomes.[11] Church involvement for both Caucasians and African-Americans has been consistently related to personal adjustment, happiness and life satisfaction, psychological well-being, lower suicide rates, and less depression.[12]

Medical researchers at Duke University's Center for the Study of Religion/Spirituality and Health track the influence of religious beliefs and lifestyle on physical and mental health. Studies have shown how strong belief may affect immune system responses, lower blood pressure, and extend survival. Churchgoing elderly have nearly half the stroke rate of their less religiously active peers. A random health survey of 3,963 people in 1986 revealed that both systolic and diastolic blood pressure were lower among frequent church attenders than among people who attended church less often.[13]

ASSUMPTIONS OF THE CHRISTIAN WORLDVIEW

Documented empirical evidence of the correlation between faith and health make it imperative for Christian health care professionals to base personal and patient decisions on values emanating from the Christian worldview. This worldview must be foundational for the Christian transdisciplinary health care team. Basic beliefs must undergird ethical decision making on a daily basis. There is such a wide gap today between societal beliefs and values and Christian beliefs and values that Christian health care professionals have an obligation to guide patient decision making and alternative health care choices. Decisions should be based on the following assumptions inherent in the Christian worldview.

God is our omnipotent, omniscient, loving Creator who is sovereign. He is the one leading our life's journey. We have been given deliverance by the blood of the Lamb and are now being directed by God on a journey through life, which will end in the kingdom. God's leading is always loving and wise for believers. God works everything for our good—to conform us to Christlikeness (Rom. 8:28–29; 5:1–5). We must acknowledge that we are not totally in control of everything in our lives and express our confidence in a God who can care for us when we ourselves cannot. Spiritual maturity involves trusting that God will answer our prayers according to our real needs as he sees them and not as we with our limited vision see them.[14]

Christians are guided by the Holy Bible, which is the inerrant, inspired, written Word of God. The Christian worldview affirms the truthfulness and the authority of the Scriptures, which serve as a standard by which beliefs and opinions can be tested. Building on this foundation, we can relate to one another in love and humility, bringing about truth, fellowship, and community.[15]

Petitionary prayer should not be to control God but to relinquish control and acknowledge God's presence and guidance in our lives. The ultimate goal of prayer should not be to get our needs met but to draw near to God. We must not forget the five purposes of prayer: praise and adoration; thanksgiving; confession; petition; and intercession.

People are faced with many challenges and enemies, including disease and suffering. We must remember that God is sovereign. Nothing touches us that God does not allow. God is allowing every situation we face in life, including illness. Illness is designed to shape us in the image of Christ. God often provides both miraculous and natural means for our deliverance. God saved Hezekiah's life through medical and miraculous treatment (Isa. 38). God provides healing though confession and prayer (James 5:13–16).

However, suffering is an essential aspect of God's sanctifying of his people, and sometimes God deems his personal presence in our lives a sufficient substitute for physical healing (2 Cor. 12:7–10).[16] Sickness, suffering, and death are evils that plague man, but they are not the greatest evil. The greatest evil would be to lose God and to have reason to doubt his faithfulness. God defeats and destroys the negative powers of sickness and death, but he does it by claiming the realm as his own and bringing it to its own logical end. The perfection and power of God are displayed in the acceptance of suffering.[17] It has been said that God whispers to us in our pleasures, speaks to us in our work, and shouts to us in our pain.

HOLISTIC HEALTH CARE

God is the healer of the whole person, and he motivates and directs the work of Christian health care professionals who are called to a life of service. The Christian perspective of health includes our whole lives. Health of body, mind, and spirit is viewed as a gift from God to be nurtured and used in his service.

In the Christian tradition, health is seen as holistic and dynamic. Good health is not an end in itself but rather an enabler, giving us the energy and vitality to serve and love others.[18]

APPLYING THE CHRISTIAN WORLDVIEW TO HEALTH CARE

Standards from the Joint Commission for Accreditation of Health Care Organizations are explicit about the patient's right to care that considers his personal dignity and respects spiritual values.[19] Practitioners who are confident and secure in their own faith can extrapolate from their beliefs to interventions with patients. Health care professionals must be challenged to remember their Christian values and to better understand and apply their beliefs. Only then can they adopt a true "discipleship strategy" where they are integrating their faith into their professional practice.[20] Several guides are available to assist with this task. For example, Reed's Spiritual Perspective Scale is a ten-item questionnaire that uses a six-point scale to measure spiritual perspective. It measures the extent that the spiritual perspective permeates one's life and spiritually related interaction.[21]

Illness often triggers emotional, mental, physical, and spiritual pain. The health care provider must be aware of spiritual concerns in order to address those concerns and detect spiritual distress or despair. Christian health care professionals must encourage faith, give hope, and surround patients with love. In addition, there are practical methods that can be employed in ministering to the health of others.

Spiritual ill health involves an alienation from God.[22] Therefore, patients should be assessed for signs of discouragement, anxiety, disrupted trust in God, anger toward God, and loss of hope. Spiritual crises can occur when there is failure to attain a life's goal, an inability to come to terms with aging, or a need for total control over one's life.

Spiritual assessment is one of the elements necessary for providing holistic care. Special religious needs such as inability to acquire foods required by beliefs, inability to participate in usual religious activities, and lack of ability to read Scripture should be addressed. Enhanced inclusive spiritual support can be provided to patients by facilitating the process of finding meaning and purpose in life; supporting the faith needs of patients by providing time for ritual and devotional practices; referring patients to other members of the health care team for counseling if spiritual distress occurs; and collaborating with the patient's pastor.[23]

BIOETHICAL ISSUES IN HEALTH CARE

Bioethical dilemmas entail medical situations that arise in human relationships where a clear right or wrong answer is not immediately apparent. Christians are faced daily with making difficult choices related to life-and-death issues; caring, not killing; organ transplantation; informed consent; alternative treatment issues; resource allocation; and quality of life versus quantity of life.

Problems arise because we feel an obligation to do the right thing before God and our fellow man, but because of our sinful nature we often do the wrong thing, as the apostle Paul found in his experience in Romans 7:15–20. Christians have a responsibility to respond to situations from a Christian perspective, and they should seek Christian counsel when making difficult decisions. Christian health care professionals have a responsibility to provide guidance to patients based on their Christian worldview.

Advances in medical science and technology have given rise to two sets of major problems related to optimal health care. The first set of problems deals with the adequate distribution and availability of heath care, and the second set revolves around recognizing the problems associated with technological advances.[24] Health care sciences demand that moral consideration be given to what is right or what ought to be done in a health care situation. Such situations may range from individual clinical situations for an individual patient and family to health policy decisions related to distribution of resources. As the business and economic aspects of health care tend to become an overriding issue in health care and patients become customers rather than persons in need of care, Christian health care providers experience frustration. Values-based health care is imperative in a time when concern is raised over health care mergers, acquisitions, changing health plans, and deteriorating relationships between patients and health care providers.

It is imperative that health care professionals operating under the Christian worldview carry out their obligation to patients by helping them solve ethical dilemmas from a Christian perspective. Additionally, Christian health care providers must have a raised consciousness and take a pro-active role in developing and supporting health policy decisions that are morally sound. Christians must take a stand and make or guide choices based on a Christian perspective in at least four interrelated areas: (1) clinical, (2) allocation, (3) human experimentation, and (4) health policy.[25]

Clinical Issues

Health care providers face ethical and bioethical dilemmas every day. Situations where medicine can prolong the life of an eight-year-old child, but the parents refuse medical treatment are difficult. Cases involving the elderly often evoke questions of whether or not consent to treatment was "informed." Other clinical issues surround the question of quality versus quantity of life.[26] Care of the acutely or chronically ill creates difficult questions for which there are no easy answers.

Allocation Issues

A topic that has recently received a lot of attention is that of rationing or allocating scarce medical resources. Numerous ethical questions surround this issue, including what criteria should be used to determine which patient receives needed medical care and which patient does not. Should the criteria be age, contribution to society, or benefit to the patient when determining resource allocation? Financial ability to secure medical care is also a determinant for health, which presents another ethical dilemma in a nation where many people do not have health care insurance. The preamble to the World Health Organization (WHO) constitution states that the highest attainable standard of health is one of the fundamental rights of every human being, regardless of race, religion, political belief, or economic or social conditions.[27]

However, the United States seems more like a nation that views health care as a commodity or big business. Managed care has become the new delivery system, which is focused on the "bottom line," and many patients are discharged from the hospital "quicker and sicker." Therefore, the United States could be viewed as the only industrialized country that has not defined health care as a right for everyone, but rather as a commodity.[28]

Human Experimentation Issues

At a time when the abortion debate has focused on gruesome late-stage pregnancies, clinics have been quietly adopting and refining drug and surgical techniques that end pregnancies earlier than ever.[29] Earlier, easier abortions by pill, injection, or vacuum are now available and present a choice that has been made by far too many women in today's society. Christian health care professionals need to be reminding women that the fetus is a baby—a human being.

Consider the theological significance of advances in "reproductive technology." Artificial reproduction includes many different techniques such as artificial insemination from a donor sperm or from the husband's sperm, in vitro fertilization.[30] Surrogate parenting may mean that the surrogate mother may conceive a child from the sperm of the husband of the woman who will rear the child, or she may only gestate and carry to term an embryo fertilized in vitro from gametes of the rearing parents. Human freedom intervenes to make such choices possible. However, Christian choices must be carefully considered.

It cannot be right to rule out all human intervention in the procreative process because the use of reason and will to free ourselves from some of the constraints of nature is itself part of our God-given nature. Some exercises of freedom—even when they transcend the constraints of nature—are good and should be affirmed. Other exercises of freedom, even when they bring desirable results, may override limits that ought not to be transcended. Only with difficulty can we draw needed lines here, and it is not surprising that even Christians disagree on the many questions surrounding contraception.[31]

Health Policy Issues

Health policy issues involve ethical value dimensions that usually focus on economic, legal, and political factors. Therefore, not all values are ethical or moral values.[32] Health policy development and implementation must take into account ethical issues. The President's Commission for the Study of Ethical Problems in Medicine and Biomedical and Behavioral Research (1983) concluded that society has an ethical obligation to ensure equitable access to health care for all.[33] This obligation rests on the special importance of health care to relief of suffering, prevention of premature death, restoration of functioning, increasing opportunity, provision of information about individual health status, and showing evidence of mutual empathy and compassion.[34]

When faced with ethical dilemmas, the Christian worldview guides decision making by requiring answers to the following four questions: (1) What does the Bible teach us? (2) What does our conscience tell us? (3) What have other Christians done? (4) What does the Holy Spirit tell us to do?[35]

SPIRITUAL DIMENSIONS OF HEALTH

Christian health care professionals have often been part of church hospital visitation teams where they visited patients, witnessed to them, and prayed for them and with them on Sunday. However, on Monday the same healing professionals returned to their jobs and visited many of the same patients but refrained from thinking about or mentioning anything spiritual for fear of missing an important symptom or offending the hospital staff or the patient. Today, however, the health professions and the church are both becoming more aware of each other and terms such as *biopsychosocial, wellness, wholeness,* and *transformation* are being used.[36]

Health has more recently been viewed in the holistic model as a multidimensional concept. Five dimensions are used to discuss health: physical, emotional, intellectual or mental, social, and spiritual. These dimensions overlap and interact.[37] A change in one often affects the others, whereas a balance among the five dimensions results in optimal health. Perhaps the least understood by the health care system today is the spiritual dimension. Older definitions of health do not include the spiritual dimension. Recognition of spirituality as a component of health has been slow, perhaps because there is no commonly agreed-upon definition of spiritual health. Perspectives that are identified in the literature include: sense of fulfillment, values and beliefs of community and self, wholeness in life, and well-being.[38]

The church has many advantages as a healing institution. Common health problems that affect the health of Americans include grief and loss events, unemployment, family conflict, emotional problems, loneliness, and isolation. These problems have been identified as significant contributors to illness.[39] The Christian perspective on health care recognizes the church as a healing institution. Care for all people is part of the church's mission in carrying out the gospel. Care for the whole person includes the interrelationship of body, mind, and spirit.

The Bible addresses the interrelationship between body and soul numerous times. The New Testament tells us in Luke 9:2 that when Jesus sent out the disciples, he told them not only to preach the kingdom of God but also to heal the sick. Churches have traditionally functioned well in ministering to the needs of the sick or those who are in crisis. Members rally around those who are ill to provide support such as meal preparation, housecleaning, and transportation to the doctor and hospital visitation.

Education is another area in which vibrant churches usually function well. Classes on health-related topics such as stress management, cardiopulmonary resuscitation, and financial planning are often offered.[40] The potential for health ministry to church congregations extends beyond crisis care and education. Most of the work should be in the areas of health promotion and disease prevention. Through seminars, workshops, and discussion groups church members begin to understand that a healthy lifestyle is part of being a responsible steward of one's life.

Distinguishing between the medical model and the spiritual model requires a look at cure and healing. Cure may occur without healing, and healing may occur without cure. Cure separates the body from the soul, whereas healing embraces the whole. Cure ignores grief while healing assumes grief, and finally, cure rejects death and views it as a defeat when healing includes death among the blessed outcomes of holistic care.[41]

Much of what happens in churches throughout the country has been documented in research to have a positive effect on health and well-being: social support, prayer, music and worship, opportunities to be cared for and to care for others.[42] All of these factors along with faith foster an attitude of hope that has also been widely reported in the literature as having a positive effect on health. The relationship between hope and health-promoting lifestyles in adults with Parkinson's Disease, children with cancer, and the bereaved and the grief process has been well researched.[43]

Our belief and faith—concepts commonly thought to be related to the spirit or the mind—actually pervade all aspects of humankind. The person who lives with hope actually interprets life differently than someone who does not live with hope, and therefore, he or she thinks and acts differently.[44] People who live with a hopeful faith actually have more physical energy, more mental clarity, and more freedom in relationships with others.[45] Faith encourages an essential optimism.[46] The best physicians know that their art must cooperate with powers beyond their own.[47] Patients should give physicians respect and gratitude but not devotion. People must place their ultimate hope for health and wholeness in God, who himself has been broken by death. Hope can be defined as longing for something with the expectation of obtaining it, and Christian hope entails having joy despite our circumstances because of our eternal hope that is in Christ Jesus.

The popularity of physician-assisted suicide points to the failure of the health care system to address the spiritual opportunity presented by illness, particularly terminal illness. It means that many patients do not trust the health care system to alleviate lingering pain and control devastating symptoms in the last weeks of life. Spiritual pain and distress that often accompany chronic and terminal illness also goes unrecognized by many health care professionals. The cries of those patients who long for an easy way out in order to avoid intense suffering point to the need for a more compassionate, caring health care system that recognizes and deals effectively with the needs of the whole person.[48]

NEW MODELS FOR HOLISTIC HEALTH CARE

Several new models for holistic health care augment and support the role of the church in health care. Parish nursing and faith communities are programs that are centered in church congregations; these programs are often referred to as congregational health programs or health ministries. There is growing interest on the part of pastors and churches in the United States in promoting the physical and emotional as well as spiritual health of the church members. Body Soul and Spirit, on the other hand, is a program available in comprehensive cancer centers in the United States. This program incorporates the patient's faith and faith community into the holistic treatment plan for the patient and family.

Parish Nursing

The role of the church in health care can be very important and should not be overlooked. Structured programs that have taken the lead in providing health care for congregations include the parish nurse program, health ministry programs, and congregational health programs.[49] Parish nursing is a unique, specialized practice of professional nursing that focuses on the promotion of health within the context of the values, beliefs, and practices of a faith community, such as a church or synagogue. Parish nursing takes into account the mission and ministry of the faith community to its members and the community it serves. Health is viewed not only as the absence of disease but as a sense of physical, social, psychological and spiritual well-being, and of being in harmony with oneself, the environment, others, and God. The concept of parish nursing considers healing as the process of integrating the body, mind, and spirit to create wholeness, health, and a sense of well-being, even when cure may not occur. In today's society most illnesses and premature deaths are a result of lifestyle choices such as diet, exercise, substance abuse, violence, and risk-taking behaviors. With this in mind, parish nursing integrates current medical and behavioral knowledge with the beliefs and practices of a faith community to promote holistic health and to prevent or minimize illness.

Faith Community Programs

In Australia there are programs that have been documented by well-designed research studies as significantly cost-efficient, with fiscal savings reported as high as 70 to 90 percent.[50] Such programs have also been demonstrated to have a positive effect on the health of congregations as they fill a gap in the current health care system. These programs are called faith community nursing programs. Results of implementing such programs include improved case management; decreased use of other health services including emergency admissions and readmissions; fewer relapses requiring hospital admission; improved individual and family functioning; improved confidence and coping ability; less suicide; patients' increased knowledge and skills related to their condition; enhanced ability for self-care, and, therefore, independent living and less loneliness and isolation. Health care professionals functioning in this program assist individuals in their spiritual development, enabling them to resist or remove the stressors that cause disease and distress.[51]

Body Soul and Spirit

Body Soul and Spirit is a program being offered to patients as part of their comprehensive therapy at Cancer Treatment Centers of America which operates at hospitals nationwide. This program offers spiritual counseling in addition to surgery, chemotherapy, radiation, and other therapeutic treatment. Counselors work with patients and their families and loved ones to offer a variety of spiritual services. These services include individual and group prayer, meeting with clergy of the patient's choice, weekly religious and communion services, and support groups that focus on faith, healing, and the positive aspects of life.[52]

IMPLICATIONS FOR EDUCATION, PRACTICE, AND RESEARCH

Education

Universities stand at the forefront of the culture. Therefore, the Christian university is in a great place to critique the culture. Educators must equip students for lives of engagement as transformation agents.[53] Educators must integrate faith and learning in the classroom. Faith, spirituality, and ethics and moral reasoning must be woven into the curricula of physicians, professional nurses, social workers, and other health care professionals. Spirituality must be threaded through courses much like therapeutic communication. Elective courses on spirituality in health care, bioethical issues, and the faith factor in health are only one means of assuring that students are equipped with the foundation needed to provide ethical, individualized health care to patients and families.

The academic and clinical training of professional and lay workers in the physical health, mental health, social work, and spiritual health disciplines must have a broad interdisciplinary base. This will require continuous dialogue and collaboration among the disciplines to develop a transdisciplinary whole-person curriculum.[54]

Medical mission trips are another valuable way to introduce students in the health professions to sacrificing self in an effort to meet the needs of those less fortunate. The exposure to different cultures and religious, political, and socioeconomic conditions in the educational process is invaluable in establishing a lifelong commitment to serving others.

Service learning helps develop student character. Having experienced more than volunteer work and more than a traditional classroom environment, students enter the classroom for life and follow a path toward public and community engagement and scholarship. Service learning is also an ideal way for Christian universities and colleges to build partnerships and respond to the needs of their communities. Service learning is a particularly useful mechanism for meeting the needs of vulnerable, underserved populations.

Practice

Christian health care professionals need to lead the way in applying the holistic approach. Holistic care honors the spiritual dimension of people's lives and offers an approach to healing that combines medicine and spirituality. "Partnerships between religious groups and health providers are a channel for health promotion efforts to vulnerable populations and must be approached from the culture of the community."[55] Perhaps the establishment of a lay health advisor program would be best in small rural communities, whereas the parish nurse mode would be a better model for larger congregations who have a larger budget that could potentially support health promotion and disease prevention programs.[56]

Sponsoring whole-person services in relation to problems such as alcoholism, substance abuse, and domestic violence should be a priority of the church as a healing community. Every local church has the potential to provide such health promotion programs through the use of lay volunteers. The Christian health care provider, therefore, has an obligation to be a trainer and a trainer of trainers.

Study findings provide support that nursing interventions can be directed toward inspiring hope, encouraging supportive relationships and participation in spiritual activities, recommending a well-balanced diet, and facilitating physical activity. Health care providers can promote health through hope and its impact on health-promoting behaviors.[57]

In their individual encounters with patients, Christian health care professionals must recognize the value of prayer, Bible reading, and church attendance or fellowship with believers. As research has shown, significant healing and support for most people comes from being part of a vital, healthy fellowship that focuses on worship, service, and outreach rather than becoming individually focused on the particular dysfunction.[58] Spiritual assessments should be done on each patient so that individual needs can be addressed. The inclusion of prayer and congregational support should be the norm in primary health care in the home and hospital facilities. Christian practitioners must act as advocates in their health care organizations for inclusion of the spiritual dimension in patient care.

Research

In order to reverse the imbalance between spirituality and health care, we must expand our vision of science and reestablish the importance of religion and spirituality to health and well-being. Studies must be conducted that examine the relationship of individuals' experiences and beliefs on their health status and overall well-being. More well-designed longitudinal studies are needed to evaluate the impact of faith on health. Although longitudinal studies are more difficult and expensive to conduct, it is imperative that they be carried out to answer such questions as "Do people who attend church weekly develop fewer cases of cancer than people who attend once a year or never?"[59] Frequency of church attendance has been a variable used as an indicator assessing religiosity. The recognition of the complex, multidimensional nature of religious beliefs and practice demands more well-designed research studies in the future. For example, studies that use measures of intrinsic and extrinsic religiosity and patients' perceptions of the importance and effects of their beliefs are needed to evaluate the faith factor's impact more carefully.[60]

Further research is needed to clarify the concepts of hope and hopefulness and to determine the relationship between hope and a health-promoting lifestyle. People are living longer, and therefore people will be living longer with chronic diseases.[61] The goal of Healthy People 2010, our national health care plan, is to increase the life span of healthy individuals. Therefore, treatment goals must include the reduction of symptoms, increasing functional capacity, limiting disease progression, and mitigating psychological consequences.[62] Christian scholars need to investigate the effect of hope and faith on these factors.

Research needs to be carried out that explores the effectiveness of historical and existing models of integrated or whole-person primary health care in various cultures. This would facilitate awareness of successful models of care as well as encourage others to refine and adapt them to local conditions.[63]

Christian health care professionals must be supportive of the research process and facilitate the efforts of researchers in their clinical settings. They must read widely and critically to inform themselves of research results that could have an impact on the health of their patients. Christian practitioners have an obligation to apply the results of reputable studies to their clinical practice in order to facilitate more positive health outcomes for patients.

CONCLUSION

Although there are acknowledged deficits in Western health care when it comes to appreciating faith and the human spirit, we must not dismiss our conventional health care system completely. Instead, we should suggest practical ways for patients and health care professionals to make faith an integral part of health care.

No longer can wholeness be an afterthought if health care is to lead to health for all as has been mandated by our national goals for health care. A totally new model of health care must emerge that truly looks at the whole person. The experience of the doctor and patient sharing prayer and Scripture reading should be more common than not.

Physicians and other transdisciplinary health care team members have an obligation to share research results with patients. Just as the physician warns the patient that cigarette smoking increases the chance of cancer and cardiovascular disease, he or she should also be justified in telling a patient that a change in religious practices such as attending church less frequently may have negative health consequences to the patient's health.

The physician, professional nurse, social worker, and other members of the health care team must be attuned to spiritual distress in patients and refer the patient appropriately to his or her pastor or hospital chaplain. We may see an increased capacity for healing when health care professionals as well as patients become more open to God's healing power. As society continues to recognize the need for spirituality in all dimensions of life, perhaps we will see a more holistic health care system emerge in which there will be greater opportunities for healing of the mind, body, and spirit.[64]

CHAPTER 15

CHRISTIAN WORLDVIEW
AND SOCIAL WORK

MARY ANNE POE

A CAMPUS MINISTER responsible for discipleship and community ministries at a Christian university asked me recently, "What is there in the Bible to help me understand the importance of social ministries?" This bright young man, with a strong Christian church and family background, a Christian college degree, and a seminary degree, understood thoroughly the assignment he had been given to disciple college students toward a deeper spiritual life—prayer, Bible study, worship, and evangelism. But he had no grounding in the Christian imperatives to care for the disadvantaged. He was humbly and sincerely asking a social work professor to help him understand the relevance and importance of leading students to be involved in ministries with the poor, the disabled, and otherwise disenfranchised populations. His evangelical preparation had not included biblical teaching toward that end. This man's question and lack of knowledge and preparation for his job assignment are representative of a major gap in much of evangelical Christianity of the twenty-first century.

The social work profession has played a role in creating this chasm. While attending a professional meeting for social work educators recently, I participated in a roundtable discussion about the role and relationship of Christian faith with the profession of social work. Social work educators, who were also Christians, were trying to assess their place in the profession and determine the best strategies for attaining credibility and gaining a voice in how the profession continues to develop. It was clear that these Christians felt like an unwelcome minority in the profession, suspected of compromising the profession by their Christian beliefs. During the twentieth century the social work profession emerged from its infancy and defined itself. It clarified a knowledge base, values, and skills, and it organized into professional associations. In the process of professionalizing, though, it abandoned the connection to its spiritual and religious heritage. For much of the century, the religious and spiritual impetus for social work practice was dismissed.

At the dawning of a new millennium, both evangelical Christianity and the social work profession seem to be searching for a way back to an earlier congruence. Though evangelical Christianity and the social work profession cannot and should not attempt to be defined by each other or to be united in any deliberate fashion, they do share significant points of congruence. Both would benefit from a respect and appreciation for the other. This chapter is an effort to trace historical developments in the worldviews of evangelical Christianity and the social work profession. It offers a rationale for recovering some of the shared heritage.

Historical Background—Judeo-Christian Traditions

One function of all societies is to tend to its citizens who cannot or will not care for themselves. The practice in some societies has been to protect the community from the burden of care. Old or disabled Eskimos would go off or be sent away to die. Lepers have been corralled into colonies, and children with or without disabilities were abandoned when they became an extra burden. Modern China limits families to having only one child to raise, resulting in countless abortions. In the United States, abortion laws conveniently allow people to eliminate the burden of care for an infant in the event of an unwanted pregnancy.

Most, if not all, societies rely on some degree of mutual aid. The early Egyptian, Mesopotamian, and Assyrian cultures tended to emphasize the importance of not doing harm. Early Chinese records indicate similar behavioral rules in relation to social welfare. The Egyptian holy book, *The Book of the Dead*, contained a list of seven acts of mercy and an early version of what is commonly called the Golden Rule: "Do to the doer in order to cause him to do [for thee]."[1] There is gain to be realized by merciful behavior. Care of others comes in varying degrees and with varying motivations. It is usually accompanied by the notion of reciprocity. Mutual aid is especially evident when communities experience danger, crisis, or a pervasive lack of material resources.[2]

A culture's view about life itself informs the manner in which those with disadvantages are treated. The early Hebrew culture had quite distinctive guidelines, inspired by their covenant obligations to God. Their treatment of the poor, strangers, widows and orphans, and the disabled was guided by the Hebrew view of God as Creator of all life. One honored God by honoring life regardless of the circumstances of that life. The care for people in need was a responsibility of each individual and also a communal obligation. Laws were in place to systematize and guarantee at least minimal care. Jewish individuals and communities used this theological system to evaluate their relationships with the disadvantaged. The biblical narrative of Hebrew history repeatedly bears witness to God's concern for the disadvantaged, and the prophets of God warn of judgment on communities that fail to value life and give aid to the poor and needy.[3]

The Jewish concept of charity, *tsedakah*, is just as easily translated as "justice."[4] This suggests a reciprocal benefit between those who have need of charity and those who have need to do justice. The prophet Micah sums up this rule of life. "He has showed you, O man, what is good. And what does the LORD require of you? To act justly and to love mercy and to walk humbly with your God" (Mic. 6:8). The exchange of resources among members of the community was believed to be the will of God designed to provide social welfare. Specific practices developed to reflect this worldview. These practices included hospitality to strangers, care of widows and orphans, redemption of lawbreakers, adjustments to material resources through Sabbath years and the year of Jubilee, and kindness to slaves and debtors with avenues toward freedom.[5]

A Christian worldview subscribes to this Hebrew view with the additional idea that Jesus' life serves as a model for redeemed human life and work. Jesus' life and practices in relation to the community of believers and to unbelievers offers a blueprint to which all Christians throughout history have been beckoned. The invitation Jesus extended in the Gospels was "follow me." It remains the invitation extended to those who would call themselves Christians today.

Following Jesus, or doing what Jesus did, has provided the impetus through Christian history to care for the poor, the sick, the widowed, the orphaned, the disabled, the stranger, and any other in a disadvantaged condition. Jesus commanded his followers to love as he loved. It is a person's love and commitment to God that should compel compassionate acts toward others, not the idea of reciprocal benefit or simple obedience to a law of justice. Jesus noted the common practice of mutual aid in the Sermon on the Mount (Matt. 5:43–48) and taught that his followers were to be different. One cares for another because that other person is made in the image of God, not because the other person can bring benefit to you. Jesus taught his disciples that their behaviors toward those who were hungry, thirsty, naked, sick, imprisoned, or strangers was behavior directed toward God: "Whatever you did for one of the least of these brothers of mine, you did for me"(Matt. 25:40).

The four Gospels in the New Testament describe Jesus' life as one attentive to the concerns of the oppressed and one that challenges the indifference of those who are privileged. Jesus did not just teach about compassion. He demonstrated it by the way he lived his life. He healed the sick, touched the lepers, fed the hungry, socialized with the outcasts, and confronted the privileged and hypocritical. Early church members followed the example of Jesus. They sold their possessions to share with the poor. Believers made provision for widows and orphans. They gave hospitality to strangers and shelter to the homeless. In subsequent Christian history, not all "followers" of Jesus have behaved as he intended. The fact that some do not adhere to the model yet claim to do so does not mean the model is invalid.

Another biblical principle that has guided Christian practice is the value of work and the responsibility to provide for one's family: "If a man will not work, he shall not eat" (2 Thess. 3:10). Historic Christianity has emphasized that work is not punishment but an expression of personhood and the image of God. The biblical record indicates that Adam and Eve had work to do prior to the Fall. Jesus labored as a carpenter until he began his public ministry. Meaningful work helps to establish a person's dignity, and failure to work diminishes a person's sense of being.

The two biblical principles of compassion and the value of work have had profound implications for social welfare history. As Christianity became more institutionalized, both in the East and the West, so did its good works. Social services of all kinds were delivered through the church structure. These services had varying degrees of balance between the principles of compassion and the value of work.

The church was the delivery system for social services until urbanization and industrialization began to change the fabric of society during the fifteenth and sixteenth centuries.[6] It was during this period that the government role in social welfare ascended. The Elizabethan Poor Law of 1601 was a turning point in this regard. The poor law assumed that government had a responsibility to help the needy. One way the state could help was by organizing a social welfare structure with guidelines for all to follow.[7] The impetus to provide for those who could not provide for themselves arose from a church tradition and Judeo-Christian worldview. Even as government's role increased, the church continued to give leadership to social welfare policies and programs. Clergy were often the local administrators for the implementation of the poor law. The balance had tipped regarding which biblical principle prevailed.

The value of work and one's responsibility to provide for one's family dominated the formulation of laws to organize for the poor. The more difficult law of compassion and mercy was often relegated to a remote secondary consideration in these matters. The "principle of least eligibility" ensured that no one receiving assistance would have more than someone who was working.[8] Stringent safeguards were established to prevent undeserving people from receiving help. This principle still guides social welfare policies in the United States.

Social Welfare History in the United States

Social welfare history in the United States is firmly embedded in the Judeo-Christian tradition from its European heritage.[9] The church organized social services sometimes informally but often in more formal ways such as hospices, orphanages, traveler's aid stations, and homes for the aged. The great awakenings of the eighteenth and nineteenth centuries in Europe and America resulted in a proliferation of services to the needy. George Whitefield and George Muller established orphanages, and Jonathan Edwards worked to protect Indians from exploitative settlers. Others established schools. The fruit of revival included leaders in the abolitionist movement, such as William Wilberforce in Great Britain, Harriet Beecher Stowe, John Woolman, Charles Finney, and many others.

Church colleges provided stations on the underground railroad and advocated for abolition. Evangelicals also fought for labor reform on behalf of white workers and children. They devoted resources to humane care for the mentally ill. They worked to reform the justice system and prisons.[10] In these revivals there was no dichotomy between the spiritual and physical realities. Both soul salvation and social reform were sought.[11]

On the secular front, increasing industrialization and urbanization altered the nature of communities, the role of government, and families. The manner in which social services were delivered reflected the changes. By the late nineteenth century, generally the period of time identified as giving birth to the profession of social work, the church and its constituents were struggling with how to deliver social services in an environment increasingly dependent on government to resolve social ills. Until the twentieth century social services occurred as a result of individuals, communities, churches, and government cooperating rather informally because of a shared belief in providing help to those in need. Social work, as a profession, has been secular in nature from its beginning. The values that drove the formation of the profession and the kinds of services provided were religious. The roots of social work are generally identified in three distinct movements: the Charity Organization Society, the social settlement movement, and a movement to establish large institutions to address various problems. All three of these movements experienced rapid growth in the nineteenth century, and all grew out of the church.[12] The contribution of the practice of Christian faith to these three movements, however, has been generally neglected in histories of the profession of social work.[13] Also neglected in social work history has been the record of continued development and delivery of services to populations-at-risk by church and denominational groups. Churches or church-related organizations continue to provide many services to the poor, orphans, homeless, sick, imprisoned, and elderly.

The remainder of this chapter will address questions that arise from an examination of the factors that influenced the development of the profession of social work and evangelical Christianity in the twentieth century. What were the cultural forces that propelled social work as a profession to adopt in the twentieth century an often adversarial relationship with the church, though it had been birthed from Judeo-Christian parents? What theological forces pushed the delivery of social services away from a central focus of evangelical Christian life and practice?

Social Work's Divorce from the Church

The social work profession is a multifaceted one. The three movements identified earlier represent different ideological bases for practice and different targets for solving social problems. Generally, large institutions to house the poor, the aged or the mentally ill, and orphans began to replace local arrangements for the care of dependent populations in the eighteenth and nineteenth centuries. The earliest institutions were sponsored by

Catholic and Protestant religious groups. Later, state-controlled boards of charity regulated the proliferating institutions, and "professionals" emerged who became the experts on the needs, care, and regulation of the occupants of the institutions.[14] The institutions represented a progressive and comprehensive system of care for that time that mirrored the ideological shift of responsibility for dependent groups from the family and community to the state.

By the late nineteenth century the experiment with large state institutions began to show its weaknesses. Though they lasted well into the twentieth century, it became clear much earlier that the costs, the numbers of dependent people, and the lack of real humane treatment for these groups in large state institutions was not an effective means to solve society's need to provide care. The institutions did, though, create a class of individuals who were forerunners to social work professionals.[15]

The Charity Organization Society (COS), originally established in England in the mid-nineteenth century, advocated for a systematic, scientific approach to eradicating the ill effects of poverty. In the early history of the COS, the poor were helped by volunteers, mostly wealthy women called "friendly visitors," whose aim was to reform the poor, teach them skills for successful living, and move them from dependency to independency.[16] This charity work evolved into a set of specific skills that could be taught to workers, especially skills that equipped them to "diagnose" the reasons for an individual's poverty.

Mary Richmond, administrator of the COS in Baltimore and Philadelphia, was the prime mover in developing and articulating this movement's goals. She helped to found training schools and authored in 1917 the first textbook, *Social Diagnosis*. Her interest in social casework had germinated by involvement in church activities and by a faith-based concern for the weak and oppressed.[17] The first school of social work in the United States, the New York School of Philanthropy (now Columbia University School of Social Work), founded in 1904, was a result of the work of the COS movement.[18]

Current clinical social work practice can be traced to these early roots. The focus for solving problems was to bring healing and reform to individuals and families. Though the COS originated from a religious impetus to provide charity, it took a turn away from faith-based practice in favor of scientific materialism. Emphasis was put on individual problems, skills, techniques for casework practice, and development of professional identity and status for the caseworker. The "science" of helping was the foundation for practice. People could be cured of their problems if a correct diagnosis and treatment plan were followed. The agenda of the COS movement was rehabilitation, reform, and development of those individuals who required charity, not social reform.

The third movement reflects a different dimension of social work history. The Social Settlement movement viewed poverty and other social problems not simply as individual defects to be corrected by caseworkers but focused attention on environmental factors. Social settlements sought to empower the poor and change social structures through organized social change. Labor unions, political activism and governmental reform, and community development organizations characterized the efforts of the Social Settlement Movement. Jane Addams established Hull House, the best-known settlement house, in Chicago in 1889. Young, well-to-do women with Protestant backgrounds were the primary supporters of the Social Settlement Movement, as had been true for the COS. Settlement houses have generally been identified as secular in nature, but many had religious roots.[19]

The Social Settlement movement, like the COS, turned to scientific research and ideology for an understanding of unjust conditions. They turned to government or social institutions to address the social ills they studied. They eventually joined hands with the COS movement. The two movements shared a concern for the same social problems and eventually recognized that problems generally had both individual and environmental causes. The union of workers from the COS movement, Social Settlement movement, and state institutions converged during the mid-twentieth century to give shape, form, and structure to the nascent profession of social work.

Nearly all social services were conducted through religious channels until the latter part of the nineteenth century.[20] In the early twentieth century the profession began to take shape beside the American culture that was increasingly enamored with scientific materialism and humanism. The profession in its early days was predominantly white, female, and Protestant. In many ways it abandoned in the twentieth century its very early connections with a traditional Judeo-Christian worldview and substituted the naturalistic ideology of the progressive era. It adopted this secular perspective as it worked to achieve parity with other professions in society and with other disciplines in the academy. It retained the Judeo-Christian tradition of values that emphasized kindness and justice.[21] Its methods and knowledge base reflected the views of the prevailing culture. The shift in the predominant worldview during this time in American history can perhaps best be tracked by examining the dynamics of theological discourse of the same period.

Evangelical Christian Thought and Social Welfare

During the nineteenth century the church expressed itself in relation to the prevailing culture by either reacting against it or incorporating it as its own. Two religious movements within Protestantism are especially significant for the development of social welfare practices—one standing as an alternative or answer to culture and one adopting the emerging naturalistic philosophy of the day. These two theological movements or perspectives had a significant impact on the manner in which society addressed social problems and eventually influenced the emerging social work profession.

The first theological movement to impact social welfare practices in the nineteenth century was revivalism. Timothy Smith, Norris Magnuson, and Earle E. Cairns have written extensively about the role of the great awakenings and personal holiness in addressing social problems.[22] Revivalism prioritized an emphasis on regenerate souls, transformed by the power of Christ and called to service in the world. Progressive theology and agitation for social reform generally accompanied nine-teenth-century revivals.[23] The ultimate goal for the revivalists was that Christian faith would be a dynamic force for broad social change as well as for individual salvation. Regenerate people worked to "save" or convert others. Out of evangelistic zeal, numerous social ministries came into existence.

Lucretia Mott helped to establish the Philadelphia Female Anti-Slavery Society in 1833. Fanny Crosby started an urban mission center in New York.[24] Perhaps the best known is the Salvation Army, started in 1877 by William and Catherine Booth. The Salvation Army continues into the twenty-first century as a primary source of social services in the United States. The Young Men's Christian Association, the Volunteers of America, the Women's Christian Temperance Union, and numerous mission and education societies were created as a result of revivals in Europe and America.[25]

Evangelism and social services were partners. These partners provided a holistic view of the mission of the church—concern for a future life, i.e., salvation of the soul, and concern for the present work of the kingdom to aid society by eliminating or preventing injustice in all its forms. Many revivalists of the eighteenth and nineteenth centuries believed that Christianity should influence society through political and social reform. Historians have believed that England was spared much civil disorder because of the influence of revivals.[26] Other results of revivalist fervor were evident in the abolitionist movement, temperance, child welfare and advocacy, women's rights, and labor laws. Religious leaders also fought politically for religious toleration and nondiscrimination. Social and political action was the means of attaining a just and caring society. The various ministries or social services had their impetus from religious faith put into action.

The second theological movement to affect social welfare during this time was nineteenth-century liberalism and, of particular relevance for social work, the social gospel movement. The theological liberalism of this period was an attempt to conform theological thought and biblical interpretation to the increasingly influential scientific naturalism of the day.

Particularly after the Civil War, American religion experienced a rapid growth in concern for a wide range of social issues. Sometimes this fervor for social reform overshadowed the earlier prominence of soul salvation. Theologians like Walter Rauschenbush and Washington Gladden articulated the new theology for the academy. Charles Sheldon popularized it through writings in the journal *The Christian Herald* and the novel *In His Steps*.[27] Ironically, Sheldon's provocative phrase "What would Jesus do?" has emerged as a mantra for conservative Christianity in recent years.

The new liberalism was concerned with understanding the causes of suffering and injustice and working toward reconstructing society to reflect Christian principles. It focused on the present kingdom of God, rather than a future heavenly kingdom. Many seminaries reorganized to emphasize sociology—a newly developing social science influenced by Marxism and social Darwinism.[28] This "Christian sociology" tended to be more concerned with science than theology. Personal salvation and evangelism were viewed as obsolete. Sin and hell were doctrines no longer addressed by liberal preachers of the late nineteenth century. Instead, social Darwinism, Marxism, naturalism, and humanism filtered into liberal Christian theology to lead religious reformers to hope for a more just society based on social change activism, expressed through these secular philosophies.

The rift between conservative Christians as represented in revivalism and the holiness tradition and liberal Christians as represented by the social gospel has a deep theological/worldview chasm to bridge. Basic doctrines of the Christian faith as historically understood by the church were undergoing rigorous challenge by the new liberalism of the nineteenth century. Particularly challenged were ideas about the nature of Scripture, Christology, the nature of humankind, and the doctrine of creation. Concerns for the evangelical Christian centered around guarding the "fundamentals" of the faith from these liberal new ideas. Addressing social issues of the day took a secondary seat. The result for the twentieth-century evangelical church has been a conflicted relationship between evangelism and social action.

The revivalists viewed Scripture as divinely inspired, God-breathed, the actual work of God, which should be accepted as truth without mixture of error. For nineteenth-century liberals, Scripture was to be studied like any other naturalistic phenomenon. Higher criticism of the Scripture that had developed in Europe during the nineteenth century reduced the Bible to a literary text to be studied in a manner similar to that used for any other ancient text. Scientific reasoning questioned the veracity of long-accepted biblical stories as recorded in Scripture.

Understanding the historical Jesus and questioning the Christ of faith was another dilemma that proved problematic between revivalist or conservative Christians and liberal theologians. Was Jesus simply a great teacher to be emulated as Sheldon had intimated in his novel? Or was Jesus the Son of God, redeemer of humankind, who entered human history as a man to establish a way of salvation as orthodox Christianity had taught? Liberal theologians dismissed beliefs in supernatural events, such as the virgin birth, miracles, and the resurrection. Conservative Christians refuted liberal theology and held steadfastly to traditional orthodox Christology.

Understandings of the nature of human life and creation took divergent paths at this juncture in Unites States history. Social Darwinism coaxed liberals toward humanism and efforts to perfect society through social and political activism. God may have created life, but people were in charge of it now. The profession of social work became a partner with this ideology early in its development in the twentieth century. In the academy, social work depended on theoretical constructions borrowed from the social sciences, also heavily influenced by scientific materialism that had exercised such an impact on liberal theology. Evangelical Christianity, appalled by the abandonment of orthodox theology, fled from any affiliation with the humanism of the social gospel. With this theological impasse, the practice of caring for society's disadvantaged groups continued its shift away from the oversight of the church to the prerogatives of the state, and specifically the growing profession of social work.

Evangelical Christianity in the United States expanded by growing churches, denominations, mission societies, and schools. Until the fundamentalist-modernist controversy of the early twentieth century, evangelical Christianity also led in the establishment of social ministries.[29] Though many of these entities continued to do some social ministries, the goal of the ministries was always first and foremost the salvation of souls. Social ministries for conservatives simply became a means to an end; the disadvantaged were targets for evangelism. The thrust of the ministries was not so much an outgrowth of radical discipleship to follow Jesus and do what Jesus did as it had been in the revivalist periods of the nineteenth century. Rather, the present life and future life of individuals were separate and largely unrelated ideas. The focus was on readiness for a future life. Any emphasis on social ministry was suspect because of the social gospel. Evangelical Christianity dismissed liberal theology as heresy and dismissed social work in the process.

Social work developed in the context of these theological battles. The delivery of social services was historically church-based, but the profession was developing in the academy as a consequence of the theological struggles. Theological liberalism partnered with the new philosophies of the day, such as naturalism or Marxism to give social work, as a profession, an acceptable academic foundation. After Mary Richmond's first school of philanthropy, other schools followed quickly. The profession had to prove itself in the academy and in society by developing a distinctive knowledge base and skills that distinguished it from other disciplines, such as psychology and sociology. It also had to build credibility and validity to its existence. Though the values to care for the disadvantaged that gave rise to the practices of social work emerged from orthodox Judeo-Christian traditions, and especially revivalism in the nineteenth century, the profession was growing out of a more secularized academy and naturalistic worldview. The result for social work has been an uneasy relationship with faith communities and the theology of the church while its practice still reflects the historic commitments of the church to aid the disadvantaged.

Recovering a Shared Heritage

Worldviews make a difference in the way problems are addressed. They shape the values that guide life and human behavior. When early Christians sold their possessions and shared with the poor among them, they were motivated by their understanding of God, relationships among people, and the value of life. When the profession of social work was developing through government institutions, the Charity Organization Society, and social settlements, the architects of the profession interpreted their world through a particular perspective on the value of life and relationships among people—a worldview that was most influenced by Judeo-Christian thought.[30] Their value systems propelled them toward action to alleviate pain and injustice and to establish a more perfect society. Both Christian faith and social work practice share a belief that social welfare is important. How narrowly or broadly social welfare is defined and how it should be attained lead to divergent practices for achieving it. Different worldviews place emphasis on different values.

The social work profession, guided by the code of ethics established by the National Association of Social Workers (NASW), summarizes the social workers' responsibilities to society by stating, "The social worker should promote the general welfare of society." The worker's primary obligation is one of service to clients. Clients have value and should be treated respectfully regardless of their life circumstances. Social workers should "make every effort to foster maximum self-determination on the part of clients."[31] The rudiments of this ethical system are not lodged in a profession created in the twentieth century. Rather, the basis is in a religious system thousands of years old. The value of personhood, personal responsibility, and self-determination is at its core a value system fostered by belief in a Creator God who loves the ones created. People are autonomous and fallible but also capable of great good. People cannot judge others because all share a common fallible nature. Relationships among people and with God give rise to the greatest good that is possible. People have free choice, but often need help from others. Love is the ultimate value.[32]

The values of the profession of social work, as expressed in the NASW code of ethics, are not sustainable apart from the Judeo-Christian worldview from which they emerged. David Sherwood asserts that it is only fair to ask the question, "Where did these values come from and what gives them moral authority?"[33] Naturalism, socialism, humanism, and capitalism—dominant philosophies of the twentieth century that have helped to shape programs and policies for social welfare—do not support the values espoused by social work to respect the worth and dignity of each person regardless of their circumstances. If the material world is the extent of reality, if there is no God who created life and gave it meaning, then there is no basis for valuing life apart from the contribution that life can make to the material world. Thus, the disabled, elderly, and mentally ill are inconvenient to the advancement of society. There is no reason to value these people, since they make no contribution to a naturalistic or capitalistic system. Economically these groups are a drain on resources and become dependent on social welfare. They have no intrinsic value as Christian orthodoxy asserts.

I began my social work education in the context of a theological seminary in 1979. The tension between social work and Christian faith was evident. Social work education included the idea that social workers should not impose their personal values on clients, especially proselytizing for religious beliefs. Social workers should be value neutral in relationship to the client. I had no difficulty respecting people by not pushing my values on them, but I did not think it possible for anyone to be value neutral. I believed that people were made by God and in God's image. I knew they were responsible to God for their own life decisions and therefore could easily support their right to self-determination. I could not judge them because I knew I could not withstand judgment myself. I also knew that the church had historically provided social services of all kinds and that my Christian faith compelled me toward doing what Jesus had done. My Christian faith and the new social work values I was learning seemed congruent to me. My professors at seminary assisted in exploring this relationship between Christian faith and social work practice. The tension was a bit puzzling. I attended graduate school in social work at a publicly funded university a few years later while also working as a pastor in a local church doing social ministries. In the graduate school context, my Christian faith was suspect. Social work practitioners and educators seemed to regard Christian faith and practice as antithetical to the values of the profession.[34] Christians were thought to be judgmental and disrespectful to people who did not believe as they did. They were thought to value people only as objects for evangelism. Social workers wondered how Christians could work with people who behaved in ways that Christians thought sinful.

The Christian evangelical world of which I was a part during my graduate education viewed social work with equal suspicion. As a profession it was linked with the social gospel and liberal political and theological thought.[35] Other pastors had cautioned me of the theological liberalism that drove social ministry projects. Ministries to feed the hungry or provide shelter to the homeless were always secondary to evangelism and often nonexistent in the minds of conservative church leaders.

Since completing my education, I have worked in a variety of settings, both church related and nonsectarian. In this span of time the culture of this country has changed and so has the culture of the profession of social work. Appreciation for religious faith and practice has grown among social work professionals, although conservative, evangelical Christianity is still under suspicion by many. Like the larger culture, the profession has shifted from strict adherence to scientific materialism or naturalism to what is called postmodernity. The basic mission of social work and the values that guide the profession endure.

Evangelical Christians who are professional social work practitioners and educators have succeeded in recent years in gaining a voice and respectability within the profession, largely because of the efforts of the North American Association of

Christians in Social Work (NACSW). Charitable choice legislation passed in the Welfare Reform Act of 1996 has opened possibilities for faith-based organizations to partner with the government in delivery of services to disadvantaged populations. Church-based institutions do not have to give up their faith teachings in order to participate in charitable choice projects. The profession is struggling with how to collaborate with faith-based agencies in new ways.[36]

The social work profession, evangelical Christians, and the government each have different roles to play and resources to provide for social welfare. They can help one another. The church can acknowledge the wealth of knowledge and skill that social work can provide in helping oppressed populations. It can support publicly sponsored welfare efforts simply because the beneficiaries are part of God's creation and because Jesus helped people, whether or not they deserved it or behaved as he would have wanted. The church can utilize the model of Jesus for helping rather than cooperating with or raging against the popular philosophies or worldviews of the day, such as naturalism, humanism, capitalism, and postmodernity.

Social work's mission is to maximize human well-being by caring for those who are least able to care for themselves. The profession of social work would profit by respecting the faith that has guided churches to organize throughout the centuries to care for the poor, sick, disabled, orphans, strangers, incarcerated, and elderly. Professionals can seek to work collaboratively with faith-based agencies under the new charitable choice provisions. Christians in social work can assist the profession in regaining a shared commitment to oppressed groups in a way that is appropriate for the twenty-first century.[37] Respectful and cooperative initiatives among government entities, social work professionals, and faith-based groups could result in a world that is more compassionate and more helpful to those who have need of society's care. Perhaps the social work profession and evangelical Christians should reclaim some of their common heritage of service.

CHAPTER 16

CHRISTIAN WORLDVIEW
AND THE WORLD OF BUSINESS

DONALD L. LESTER WITH WALTON PADELFORD

AS ADULTS COME TOGETHER in organizations to pursue careers, their worldviews come with them. Over time organizations develop worldviews that are institutionalized through their cultures. Organizational cultures reflect ways of thinking, values, and acceptable behavior of individuals in the organizational setting. Most organizations are concerned with some kind of business, either for-profit or not-for-profit.

Cultures are outward, overt manifestations of organizational worldviews. Cultures are shaped by founders to facilitate the most important reason for organizations to exist, which is the mission. An organization's mission states what business they are in and why. Or, put another way, what is the business of each business.

In the most traditional sense, economists view the business of business to be the maximization of profits. According to this view, sometimes referred to as libertarianism, as a firm pursues a profit-driven strategy, society tends to reap benefits far beyond the obvious continued existence of the business. Maximized profits lead to continued business growth and development, which translates into more jobs, better wages, and an overall economic benefit to society. What is best for society in terms of its relationship to the world of business has become known as the social good concept. What is good for society has been much discussed in the business literature over the last several decades.

A second school of thought gives overt, conscious attention to societal needs and ills that can be ameliorated by the world of business. This outlook has come to be known as social responsibility. There are many levels of commitment to social responsibility, but the primary focus involves businesses acting in the interest of society in a deliberate manner. If businesses view segments of society as stakeholders—people or groups who have a strong interest in the success of the organization—then they should be willing to give back to society a measure of their success. Examples include voluntarily reducing pollutants in the atmosphere, financially supporting educational institutions, or sponsoring community fund-raising activities for local charities.

A third school of thought emphasizes virtue. In this view, the character of the person is being formed through the experiences of life. Through the various tests and trials of the business world, a person's character as well as the character of the business organization is being honed.

This chapter describes libertarianism, social responsibility, and the moral-virtue approach to business ethics as a progression. It concludes with a discussion of an ethical foundation as a basis for the existence of the firm that goes beyond libertarianism, social responsibility, or serving mankind. This foundation is the firm's purpose, embodied in the notion of a Christian worldview—a worldview founded on holiness, justice, and love.

The Ethical Responsibility of the Firm

The study of individual behavior in organizations is based on ethics. The concept of ethics has become a widely debated topic in the field of business and the study of organizations. The term itself is constantly being defined and redefined by business theorists, practitioners, and philosophers. Since firms are composed of people, and since people are actors who constantly exhibit behavior, a relevant definition of ethics for business is as follows:

"Ethics is a branch of philosophy dealing with values related to human conduct, with respect to the rightness and wrongness of certain actions, and to the goodness and badness of the motives and ends of such actions."[1]

Much of the debate found in the business ethics literature centers on the aforementioned concept of social responsibility. Social responsibility is a multidisciplinary term that spans the fields of sociology, philosophy, economics, management, ethics, psychology, and religion.[2] For the business scholar, social responsibility refers to management's obligation to make choices and take actions that will contribute to the welfare and interest of both society and organizations.[3] The conundrum in this definition concerns the contribution to the interests of society. One person's idea of a valid contribution does not necessarily agree with that of another.[4] Although there are many opinions concerning the appropriate level of social responsibility required by a firm, an alternative or opposite concept also exists.

The chief proponent of this alternative school is Milton Friedman, and the theme espoused is that the primary social responsibility of a firm is to maximize profits.[5] This libertarian economic perspective is rooted in the theory of the firm; being economically responsible to all stakeholders is the fiduciary duty of management. This economic responsibility is accomplished solely through the maximization of profits.[6]

For those who believe the firm's social responsibility goes beyond that of a purely economic support of stakeholders (including stockholders, suppliers, customers, employees, managers, and so forth), finding a common ground for this agreement has been difficult. Proposed models of total social responsibility for the corporation do not overlook economic maximization. Rather, they combine this emphasis with legal, ethical, and discretionary responsibility. The basis for this line of thinking is that moral agents exist in business, and each individual should do what is right in any sector of society.

An Ethical Framework of the Business of Business

Business ethicists have, at times, relied on the philosopher Immanuel Kant for guidance in determining the ethical responsibility of the firm. Kant argued for the existence of a "categorical imperative," which reflects the belief that be-havior should not be performed unless the actor is willing to accept such behavior as guidelines by which to establish law. Kant also espoused the concept of duty, which suggests that the pursuit of rewards when performing a task is unethical; only the performance of duty for duty's sake receives moral approbation.

In an effort to develop a conceptualization of the ethical behavior of business, it is necessary to identify two distinct areas of ethical philosophy. The first is deontology, which focuses on universal statements of right and wrong, or a list of rules, concerning the duties and rights of individuals. This is an ethical approach without regard to the consequences of the individual's actions. Only action from pure ethical prin-ciple is in view here. Kant said: "There is a categorical imper-ative which states that one ought never to act unless one is willing to have the maxim on which one acts become uni-versal law."[7] If not, it is unethical. Deontology focuses on methods or intentions of an individual with regard to a specific behavior.[8]

The second area of philosophy that pertains to ethical con-siderations in business is utilitarianism. This concept can be neatly summarized as "the greatest good for the greatest num-ber." For every action, perform a social cost/benefit analysis and act on the results. The total of all utilities resulting from an act should be greater than the total of all utilities resulting from any other act in question to be regarded as ethical.[9]

Contrasting these two popular notions of ethical philo-sophy, deontology appears more appropriate for the study of the business of business than does utilitarianism. Deontology provides a more expedient approach to daily decision making and individual action, which is critical in a competitive business environment. Utilitarianism implies a cost/benefit analysis for every action. The challenging and fast-paced arena of business responds more favorably to a rules approach. However, since these are philosophies devised by men, an argument could be made for either.

A third ethical philosophy concerns the practice and promotion of moral virtues as a basis for the business of business. Many organizations publish mission statements that utilize moral virtues to describe the actions of their organizational members. Examples include honesty, service, courage, integrity, and so forth. Organization members see vices, as opposed to virtues, as extreme examples of behavior—behavior that involves going too far or not far enough. If moral virtues are habits that provide a reasonable framework for behavior, then vices, such as dishonesty, greed, or avarice, should be clearly identifiable as outside the scope of appropriate organizational behavior.

Whether individuals or other organizations are treated fairly tends to be a central theme for virtuous organizations. If a firm operates within the boundaries of the law and treats its stakeholders fairly, it is considered morally virtuous. The problem with moral virtues as an ethical philosophy is that they describe the kind of people an organization desires to employ without specifically addressing their behavior. Rather, virtues tend to clarify and edify deontology and utilitarianism.[10]

An example of the virtue of service as a primary business ethical consideration will be illustrated by an unlikely source coming from the nineteenth century, that of popular literature. Service as a virtue will be used to demonstrate that an adherence to Christian virtues, while admirable in the competitive world of business, stops short of actually presenting a Christian worldview.

Beyond Social Responsibility

Charles Dickens was a nineteenth-century English writer who had a particular gift for creating very distinct fictional characters. The members of the poor working class in England, generally portrayed as overworked, underpaid, and relegated to a lifetime of hardship, were dearly loved by Dickens's readers. The source of the misery of the working class was the English industrialist.

Dickens characterized the English industrialist as greedy, manipulative, and uncaring. This depiction grew out of

Dickens's own experience as a child laborer. He witnessed abuses of children and the poor working class firsthand as a child, and the experience tended to be reflected in much of his work.

Nowhere is this more embodied than in the fable *A Christmas Carol*, published in 1843. This book excels in the clear and concise presentation of greed and selfishness personified in the character Ebeneezer Scrooge. His pursuit of profit maximization was portrayed as being at the expense of his employees and his firm's community stakeholders. When visited at his business by fellow businessmen collecting funds for the poor to be distributed at Christmas, Scrooge refused to donate, referring instead to opportunities provided by the workhouses and prisons.

The passage of the book that is the most relevant to the current discourse is a speech made by the ghost of Jacob Marley, Scrooge's late business partner, warning Scrooge of his fate if he did not change his ways: "It is required of every man . . . that the spirit within him should walk abroad among his fellowmen, and travel far and wide; and if that spirit goes not forth in life, it is condemned to do so after death. It is doomed to wander through the world . . . and witness what it cannot share, but might have shared on earth, and turned to happiness."[11]

The ghost of Marley subsequently explains to Scrooge that the real business of mankind is the common good established through virtues such as charity, mercy, and kindness. The hours toiled in a business are only a drop of water in an ocean of serving mankind.

Dickens presented a plan for business behavior that is rooted in Christian ethics but stops short of completely espousing a Christian worldview. Dickens would characterize the business of business as serving mankind.

The conceptualization of ethics taken from *A Christmas Carol* rejects the libertarian view completely, while seeing the social responsibility position as inadequate. The concept of serving mankind is not to be viewed as a line item on the budget or a program of public relations.

Dickens was proposing that a business go beyond ethical foundations such as deontology or utilitarianism, and use as a standard for its actions the ideal of serving mankind. This concept is certainly rooted in Christian ethics. The real Christian worldview, however, is rooted in the love of God.

The Christian Worldview and Business

For a business to distinguish itself as truly Christian, it has to move beyond ideals and virtues. Deontology, utilitarianism, and moral virtues all seek to emulate the ideal man. A Christian organization, however, seeks to emulate God. To be sure, these ethical philosophies are not mutually exclusive. There are many examples where one overlaps the other. However, what separates them is an organization's primary reason for existence.

If an organization is seeking to emulate God, it is necessary to try to understand the essence of God. According to the authority of the Bible (without which there is no foundation for a Christian worldview), God is holy, just, and loving.[12] A Christian organization is built on and managed by a foundation of holiness, justice, and love—three virtues that sound much different from the typical virtuous mission statements of most modern organizations.

There are many references to the holiness of God in Scripture. One such example is in Psalm 30:4: "Sing unto the Lord, O ye saints of his, and give thanks at the remembrance of his holiness" (KJV). The fact that God is just is reiterated throughout the Bible, including the following passage in Proverbs 3:33: "The curse of the LORD is in the house of the wicked, but he blesseth the habitation of the just." Understanding love is impossible without understanding God, as noted in 1 John 4:8: "He that loveth not knoweth not God; for God is love" (KJV).

God is many things, so a natural question would be, "Why holiness, justice, and love?" Micah 6:8 provides this insight: "He hath showed thee, O man, what is good; and what doth the LORD require of thee, but to do justly, and to love mercy, and to walk humbly with thy God?" (KJV). This verse is a prescription for the ethical behavior of organizations that choose to honor God. If organizational members are bound by a strong Christian ethic, they will attempt to honor God in their work and the management of their work. The guidelines provided in this verse are simple: do justly, love mercy, and walk humbly with God.

Alexander Hill singles out holiness, justice, and love because of their importance to ethical decision making and the business of business. Hill describes holiness, justice, and love as being necessary and sufficient. Each must balance the other much like the three-legged stool requires the balance of each leg to maintain stability. No one leg can stand on its own. Each is incomplete without the other two. All three conditions must be met before an action can be considered moral.[13]

Embracing holiness without the temperance of justice and love can become too legalistic. Justice without holiness and love may prove too stringent. And love without the guidance of holiness and justice can turn into maudlin sentimentality.

In the dog-eat-dog world of business, how does an organization maintain its Christian worldview? The answer lies in the strength and commitment of organizational members to its culture and mission. As previously mentioned, organizational culture is, for the most part, shaped by the beliefs, values, and attitudes of the founder. As the organization grows and develops and more and more people become a part of it, the founder's set of beliefs, or his worldview, is adopted by each new member. For an organization's worldview to be truly Christian usually requires that the founder act out his Christian faith on a daily basis and surround himself with other Christians. The leadership of any organization is crucially important to the founding and maintaining of a given organizational culture. Organizations are composed of people, and leadership sets the ethical tone for the organization.

It is important to remember that no matter how well new employees are screened as to their compatibility with the Christian worldview, some sinful behavior is going to occur. Such is the nature of man. However, a strong Christian culture, supported by a guiding mission statement and nurtured by the founder and current leaders, is possible.

Organizations such as ServiceMaster, Chik-fil-A, Polaroid, and others are in business and prospering with very strong Christian cultures. These companies separate themselves from others by being openly Christian. At ServiceMaster, for example, God is openly recognized. William Pollard, former CEO of ServiceMaster, described his nineteen thousand employees as being made in the image of God.[14] When that is the basis upon which employees are viewed by management, each worker gets treated as a person of value and worth. The old business adage that "past behavior predicts future performance" is exchanged at companies like ServiceMaster for a belief that God changes people into new "creatures" and their actions become new, not a mirror of their past.

Christian organizations go beyond posting an impressive mission statement and a list of values on the wall at corporate headquarters. They strive to honor God in everything they do by concentrating on achieving the delicate balance between holiness, justice, and love.

The Individual Christian in a Bad Business Organization

It is good to think about organizations with well-functioning, Christian ethical roots. But how can the individual Christian glorify God in a bad business organization? How can the Christian glorify God in a mainstream organization, or one that functions with a secular worldview?

Part of Christian spirituality is seeing reality as it really exists. "Vanity of vanities saith the Preacher, vanity of vanities, all is vanity" (Eccl. 1:2 KJV). Life in this world takes on a certain "under the sun" perspective. The business world provides us with an opportunity to earn a living, to eat, and to take care of our families. This is good even if the business organization itself is not consciously operating for God's glory.

There are actually three main benefits that we may enjoy in this life "under the sun": the ability to enjoy our food, the gift of a good marriage, and the ability to enjoy our work (Eccl. 2:10, 24–26; 9:9). The writer of Ecclesiastes makes clear that these things are a gift from God, what the Puritans might have called "common grace." God gives these good gifts to the redeemed and the unredeemed alike. So it is possible that we may or may not be enjoying these benefits.

If our work is bitter, it is nonetheless necessary for the sustenance of our families. We may have to stay in a bad organization for a long time. Therefore, we can thank God for our daily bread under a bad work situation. God's glory might shine more clearly through a worker in a bad situation who exhibits an industrious and loving attitude than through similar workers in ethically upright organizations.

The remedy for a Christian in a bad work situation is really the maintenance of a biblical perspective. The world is passing away along with its works. The glory of God is at stake wherever the worker is stationed. So through God's sustaining grace it is possible to work in bad situations for his glory.

CONCLUSION: A LOOK AT ETHICS AND VALUES

Ethics as a concept fits into the framework of the business world for a simple reason: The actions of businesses affect individuals, the common good, and society as a whole. A business cannot benefit society or the common good if it is not run in accord with moral principles. From one society to another there is strong consensus on many issues. Examples include: Do good and avoid evil, respect lives and truth, and cooperate and be helpful to one's fellowman.[15] A business that is not run in accord with moral principles is one that is based only upon self-interest.

At some point a company must look to its values, its corporate mission, and its driving force and evaluate them critically. Companies that have been through this process and have outstanding results to show for it include Johnson & Johnson, Control Data, McDonald's, and Motorola. One of the best examples is Dayton-Hudson, the noted retailer of dry goods, whose corporate constitution states: "The business of business is serving society, not just making money. Profit is our reward for serving society well. Indeed, profit is the means and measure of our service—but not an end in itself."[16]

Companies like Johnson & Johnson and Motorola boast of strong ethical value systems. Yet they are not Christian. One reason for this is that the business world has become so competitive and so diverse. Companies must focus on talent and expertise at the expense of homogeneity. Another is the predilection toward lawsuits in American society based on any form of discrimination. These reasons, as well as the constant oversight of government regulatory agencies, discourage homogeneous Christian organizations.

Walking the walk and talking the talk are just as difficult, probably even more difficult, for an organization as they are for an individual. It takes a strong faith and a dedication to the three tenets of holiness, justice, and love. And it takes a true giving over of one's self and one's organization to the Lord.

In light of the enormous success achieved by some of the firms mentioned above, ethics has become very topical in today's business literature. There are some whose goal is to take advantage of its popularity. Ethics is being sold to the business community as a means of adding to the bottom line. The distinction for the Christian business, however, is to serve Christ. To be successful in the long term, profits must be earned. But for the Christian organization, profits are a reward for a job well done, not just a reason for existence.

CHAPTER 17

CHRISTIAN WORLDVIEW AND STUDENT LIFE

KIMBERLY THORNBURY

THINK BACK to your unique college experience. What springs to mind? While some may remember a eureka moment in chemistry lab or analyzing a particular novel, most will pinpoint a weekend road trip with college roommates, memories at sporting events, or involvement in a specific club or organization.

I remember routine visits to Messiah College's Philadelphia campus where specific majors could spend semesters studying at Temple University while housed with fellow Messiah students and staff. My friends and I would spend evenings sitting on the outside concrete stoop in front of the college's townhouse, sandwiched between two large Temple University fraternity houses on Broad Street. This time spent "stoopin," as it was commonly called, offered hours of laughter and heartfelt discussions about life, God, and the future, and an occasional evangelistic conversation with fraternity men stumbling home. This informal period with friends provided time to discuss the implications of our Christian worldview and our desire to enter the entertainment industry. Upon reflection, these memories clarified what it meant to be a Christian studying at a liberal arts college.

Since 92 percent of a college student's time is spent outside the classroom on average, most memories emerge as co-curricular. Specifically, "Only about forty-eight hours of a typical college student's week are devoted to attending class and studying (Boyer, 1987). About two-thirds of the time in a given week is spent on other activities. If as many as fifty hours are devoted to sleeping, at least seventy hours in a student's week remain."[1] These critical seventy hours are most often spent with peers, the single biggest influencer of the traditional college-age student. Therefore, how colleges help structure these peer interactions is critical, since learning is most effective when it is a social activity where reflection and discussion are involved. The responsibility of a student development professional is to dedicate his or her work to creating and shaping co-curricular environments where such reflection and discussion are nurtured.

Numerous studies bear out the importance of the out-of-classroom experience. One researcher recently commented, "In fact, when asked about what they learned in college, graduates frequently mention that participation in activities outside class increased their confidence, competence, and self-assurance."[2] Other studies confirm the value of out-of-classroom learning experiences. Notably, "Wilson (1996) estimated that more than 70 percent of what a student learns during college results from out-of-class experiences."[3] In other words, these studies confirm that the lion's share of learning occurs beyond the classroom context.

The Rise of the Student Development Profession

Student development as a professional discipline emerged from understanding the importance of the enormous time spent outside the classroom. From the beginning, the student services profession avoided the compartmentalization of higher education and concentrated on the whole person. The most recent edition of the *Handbook for Student Personnel Administrators* explains, "Historical analysis indicates an institutional commitment to caring, respect, and a concern for a student's growth and development. Souls were at stake. Here is found the roots of the idea of the 'wholeness' of the individual, the philosophical underpinnings of modern student personnel work."[4]

Further, a historical analysis of the American college and university reveals the precedent of a class in moral philosophy designed for the purposes of student development. Moral philosophy served as the precursor of the student development professional. Historian Frederick Randolph noted that "the senior course in moral philosophy, often taught by the president of the old-time college, was its most effective, and its most transparent repository of values . . . . Once that died, as in time it did, there would really be no way to prevent the formation of the National Association of Student Personnel Administrators."[5] When moral philosophy faded, student development professionals took its place.

Since the development of a Christian worldview occurs within a context of meaningful community, student development professionals must first find ways to engage students in significant co-curricular activities. Further, those in student development must identify what opportunities, resources, and programs might profitably fill a portion of those seventy hours during the week, thereby encouraging and reinforcing a Christian world and life view during the college years. Student development professionals must ask how student and residence life staff members complement the fine work that conscientious and faithful faculty members do in the classroom.

By force of definition, Christian student development personnel lead students to engage the integration of faith and living. This chapter emphasizes the tremendous influence that time spent outside the classroom contributes toward the development of a Christian worldview. In addition, specific ways student development professionals create structures, systems, and opportunities for students to develop a holistic Christian worldview are reviewed.

A Strategy for Integration

If students spend 92 percent of their time outside the classroom, then student development offices must consciously provide structures and programming that contribute to the student's worldview development and character formation. Francis Wayland, former president of Brown University, believed that "the most important end to be secured in the education of the young is moral character."[6] While most colleges would affirm this goal in campus catalogs, the reality is often quite different. In his book *Campus Rules and Moral*

Community: In Place of In Loco Parentis, David A. Hoekema argues that the modern college's "actions carry another message entirely. The message of its actual conduct—the reality behind the superficial layer of borrowed rhetoric—might be summarized thus: 'We hire excellent scholars for our faculty, maintain a good library, and fill the flower beds for parents' weekend, and we sincerely hope that the students will turn out all right.'"[7]

Creating a moral community and developing students who live by a Christian worldview must be *intentional*. Everyone at the university, from the president to the faculty to the residence hall directors, must be working in tandem to shape their students, and not simply remain spectators or enforcers of behavior.

The Christian college heralds character development of students as a top priority. Colleges understand that "we are what we repeatedly do," as Aristotle observed. This fact places a particular burden and responsibility upon student development professionals at the Christian college, since the programming must not only be worthwhile and values oriented, but it must also contribute to the student's ability to be a better follower of Jesus Christ. Such a vision for student life entails a twofold strategy. The first goal is to get the student involved in the co-curricular, and the second goal, which is decidedly more difficult, seeks to provide the student with opportunities to think critically and Christianly about the world.

Student development professionals assume the challenge of involving students in learning activities that transcend grades, papers, and transcripts. Co-curricular activities do not merely fill a vacuum. Rather, they play a vital role in developing a student's ability to engage meaningfully with the world with respect to their calling. Educational research repeatedly bears witness to this observation. As one recent study showed, "The research is unequivocal: students who are actively involved in both academic and out-of-class activities gain more from the college experience than those who are not so involved." According to another study, "The only factor predictive of adult success—however defined, and including post-college income . . . is participation in out-of-class activities."[8]

Note the force of this contention: the *only* factor predictive of adult success in college is corresponding involvement in co-curricular activities. The truth of such a realization underscores the centrality of student life programming in higher education. If co-curricular programming resides at the heart of the effectiveness of the university, how much more should this principle be true of the unapologetically Christian college or university.

If we are serious about our commitment to develop Christian leaders for the coming generation, then excellence in co-curricular activity needs to be coupled with Christian commitments to right living. Here again, the data supports the notion that student life programming proves to be the decisive factor in moral as well as vocational development. Research conducted in this area pinpoints a direct link between out-of-class involvement and the development of values. A respected team of educated researchers avers that the single most important variable associated with gains during college in social concern or altruistic values is participation in leadership activities.[9]

Christians working in the field of student development are not content with the mere development of "altruistic values" or "social concern" alone. Rather, they strive to inculcate distinctly Christian virtues revealed in Scripture in their leadership training programs. The command of love for God and neighbor directs a student's development in leadership ability in ways unfulfilled by secular institutions.

Institutions of Christian higher education need increasingly to recognize the centrality of co-curricular student development in advancing their mission of making a permanent impact on both the intellect and behavior of their charges. Even the American College Personnel Association, one of the largest secular organizations for student development professionals, argues in their student learning imperative that "the key to enhancing learning and personal development is not simply for faculty to teach more and better, but also to create conditions that motivate and inspire students to devote time and energy to educationally-purposeful activities, both in and outside the classroom."[10] If this sentiment characterizes the ACPA, Christian institutions should pay even greater heed to this vision. As a result, this requires institutions of Christian conviction to think of the office of the dean of students as *facilitating student development* as opposed to simply coordinating student *activities*.

The results are in. Students point to co-curricular involvement when assessing the most rewarding aspects of their college career. The truth is, when most students are surveyed about their college experience, events that took place outside the classroom rule the list. Simply keeping students busy with programs does not work, but creating activities that foster discussion and deepen relationships and convictions will have an impact. Time spent outside the classroom provides students with distinct choices concerning behavior and possible connections to specific truths exposed in the classroom or church. To be sure, we must concern ourselves with knowing truth for truth's sake, but we must also constantly keep before us the applications for day-to-day living. *Phronesis* (practical understanding), Aristotle reminds us in the *Nicomachean Ethics,* is the necessary complement of *sophia* (theoretical wisdom).

How Are Christian Colleges Doing at Developing a Christian Worldview in Student Life?

Research recently done at the Council for Christian Colleges and Universities (CCCU) bears out the conclusion that development of a student's understanding of living in a perplexing world stands at the core of Christian higher education, particularly from the perspective of alumni. Recently conducted research on the topic of "Taking Values Seriously: Assessing the Mission of Church-Related Higher Education" revealed that "alumni at all of the CCCU institutions (except two) rated the impact of 'God in their day to day lives' more strongly than their senior counterparts at the same institution."[11] That same report noted, "Alumni at all of the CCCU institutions (except three) rated the importance of developing a meaningful philosophy of life more strongly than their senior counterparts at the same institutions." Stated differently, graduates grow in their appreciation of Christian worldview, thinking, and behavior the further they are removed from the Christian "bubble."[12]

The Fund for the Improvement of Postsecondary Education (FIPSE) research also uncovered both positive developments and potential warnings. "On average, . . . we should note that alumni at most of the CCCU Institutions considered the biggest influence of college to be in the development of a Christian worldview, and the smallest influence to be in helping them interpret Christian beliefs and values to others."[13] These findings caution Christian institutions of higher education against self-congratulation. Yes, our students are developing a Christian worldview, but they are having a difficult time removing the proverbial bushel from their lamp. To help correct this deficit, student services can develop environments and communities where reflection and discussion about the Christian worldview flourish.

Further, student development professionals can provide springboards for discussions where the Christian worldview is used as a filter for ideas, thoughts, and behavior. Unless students talk about the impact of their faith in the residence hall, cafeteria, and commons, they won't talk about such issues in the workplace.

A developed worldview necessarily impacts daily living. For example, how a student uses power while serving in a leadership position, the values that become exposed when the student works a part-time job on or off campus, or the Internet sites he or she chooses to visit in the privacy of the dorm room should be consistent with publicly shared beliefs. Worldviews are holistic and therefore should not merely be taught or espoused in philosophy or New Testament classes, during chapel, or on spring break mission trips. The student development profession deals with how students learn to think Christianly about the whole of life. As Steve Garber urges, we must discover ways "to make connections between belief and behavior in the college years."[14]

Student development professionals actively engage students in thinking Christianly about belief and behavior, and they are most often present during those teachable moments to help make such connections. One recent teachable moment included a student development staff member who had the sobering task of talking with a student, who—after finishing his 11:00 A.M. ethics class—proceeded straight to the cafeteria and stole food. That student development professional is the one subsequently dialoging with the student and helping him make the connection between his 11:00 A.M. lecture and 12:01 P.M. "values violation." I want to encourage student development professionals who must address these students and initiate dialogue about behaviors that have hurt the students and/or the community.

In an age of tolerance, it is sometimes difficult to be the one to say, "this was wrong" and begin to talk to specific students about the effects of their behavior. But Hebrews 12:11 reminds us, "No discipline seems pleasant at the time, but painful. Later on, however, it produces a harvest of righteousness and peace for those who have been trained by it."

Many student development professionals can pinpoint examples of students who underwent a discipline process and subsequently developed a deeper relationship with the staff member due to the situation. The student development professional sees the discipline process not simply as an open-and-shut case in which fines, community service, and standard reprimands are doled out, but springboards for discussion about worldview, values, and behavior. Students involved in the discipline process are often teachable and more open to making practical life applications.

The Issue of Rules and a Christian Worldview

Often discussions about connections between belief and behavior are fueled by a particular student action that is contrary to community standards. While the number of students who violate community standards is comparatively small, student development officers spend a significant portion of their time in conversations with such students. Thus, the topic of judicial affairs and the development of a Christian worldview and a moral community deserves attention. The judicial aspect of college life provides unique one-on-one opportunities to help students understand the importance of behavior, morality, and community. Hours are spent in discussions that move beyond simply what is "right and wrong" to what is "Christian."

First, student development professionals must distinguish between legalistic rules and community-oriented rules. James Tunstead Burtchaell, author of *The Dying of the Light*, recounts many hard-core rules at historically Christian colleges and universities. One such rule stated, "We will not rearrange the furniture in our room."[15] In a chapter entitled "The Content of Student Codes: Thou Shalt Have No Large Refrigerators," David Hoekema cites numerous recent student handbook rules that include extensive diatribes against extension cords, irons, and cooking equipment defined explicitly at one college as "toasters, toaster ovens, hotplates, frying pans, broilers, microwave ovens, hamburger makers, Crock-Pots, woks, immersion heaters, quick-heat pots, fondue pots, and percolators."[16] Hoekema adds, "A future historian might justifiably draw the conclusion that the most persistent threats to good order on campuses in the 1990s came from small appliances."[17] He also adds that often student handbooks contain lengthy sections on appliances yet fail to articulate a clear standard and moral basis for policies against sex and drinking. Good practices in student affairs include orientation programs focused not simply on curfew hours and the horrors of blue fun tack but a comprehensive program on higher-level values and a greater emphasis on what builds community.

Making the distinction between legalistic rules and community-oriented rules is a subject that can only be worked out within Scripture and the community's theological tradition. Ultimately however, relationships, not rules, create contexts of Christian community. Subsequently, this Christian community will warm toward a system that upholds and affirms values that protect the community. A student development professional's time is better spent helping student leaders to understand the importance of community than devising more and more rules to control behavior.

One recent study suggests that research on group effects on young people has overwhelmingly shown that peer mentors are the best way to foster desirable norms. Further, author David Hoekema explains the importance of the influence of smaller communities and peers. "To form a genuine community, by fostering and encouraging the numerous smaller communities in which students and faculty find their place and form their identity, is the ultimate goal of the entire system of student conduct regulation and discipline."[18] Hoekema concludes:

> One of the persistent themes of recent work in moral philosophy is the indispensable role of community shaping our moral universe . . . . We learn to be moral by modeling ourselves on others whose judgement and integrity we respect . . . to rely on ever more strenuous enforcement of disciplinary rules and codes is an inherently ill-suited tactic, if one's goal is to assist students to become mature and responsible moral agents. Institutions ought rather to devote their efforts to systematic encouragement of the smaller communities contained on campus in which moral reflection and thoughtful choice flourish.[19]

Practical Ways to Encourage Christian Community

A chief student development officer can help create meaningful community by advocating specific ideas in the president's cabinet, allowing the student development staff time to reflect on the value of their programming and initiating thought-provoking discussions with students about their worldview. The following are a few practical suggestions:

1. The chief student development officer can advocate the creation of gathering places around campus. Intentionally creating such spaces, like coffee shops and sitting areas, invites conversation and reflection. New buildings and dormitories can also include comfortable places that draw students out of their individual living quarters.

2. Student development professionals should continue to work intensely with student leaders and serve as positive adult role models. By articulating "communicable ideas," mentors encourage the promotion of biblical ideas about life and behavior that students can take with them into the workplace or secular graduate schools. Short-term or ongoing leadership classes sponsored by student development officers provide another

way of inculcating the Christian worldview to emerging leaders. Many organizations such as residence life, student activities council, and student government conduct biannual retreats. Such retreats can engage these campus leaders with discussions on their role not simply as organizational leaders but as moral leaders for the entire campus.

3. Staff meetings should discuss how the student development office can offer a host of activities for a diverse population yet simultaneously help students make wise choices about how they spend their time. Yet at the same time we help students prioritize quiet time with God in the midst of such activity.

4. Moving student development beyond legalism by encouraging discussion with students about the value of specific activities and programming. For example, do all movies PG and under automatically fall into a Christian worldview? Similarly, are all R-rated movies necessarily harmful or "off limits"? Do the residence life staff and student activities staff take time to guide discussions about what movies should be shown not simply by ratings but by holding up the subject matter in light of a Christian worldview?

5. The student development office can also focus on specific ways to get students involved in the community. One incentive for involvement at Union University includes a student involvement card. This program encourages students to attend eight events during the semester—from lecture series to cultural arts, to athletic events, to special educational activities. Students get their card punched upon attending these activities. When the card is complete, they are able to enter a drawing for desirable prizes, such as scholarships, housing, and meal plan discounts. Again, it is not a matter of keeping the student busy but encouraging him or her to engage in activities that are meaningful and encourage the experience of academia. This idea provides students an extra incentive to hear guest lecture speakers or to attend a theatre production (without faculty having to give them ten extra credit points on their next test!). Such an idea encourages the student to hear a lecture on intelligent design or see *Waiting for Godot* when they might have otherwise avoided these events. This incentive helps them experience a wide variety

of subcommunities within the broader campus community (e.g., the academic community, the arts community, the religious community, the local community, and the athletic community).

6. Four years ago, the campus ministry office at Union University created LIFEgroups, a small-group ministry offered to incoming freshman and transfer students. Two upperclassmen lead each small group and provide an immediate sense of community for these new students. In addition, LIFEgroups offer accountability and encouragement. Trained upperclassmen leaders are also able to help students articulate the value of Christian community. This program and other similar programs are highlighted in the recent Templeton guide to *Colleges That Encourage Character Development*.[20]

7. Student development professionals should also encourage students to take advantage of CCCU "semester away" programs. Promoting these opportunities on a bulletin board, including them in the student handbook, and personal encouragement are some ways to increase involvement in these programs. Journalists on the student newspaper staff can interview students who participated in these semester away programs. These programs offer students real-world experience in such fields as film and politics combined with a residential setting that allows for reflection and dialogue about these experiences.

All of these ideas provide forums or encouragement to stimulate discussion and reflection on college campuses. The work of student development fails if our students remain busy yet never encounter a program that allows them to reflect on how their faith impacts choices. Our students should be talking about what it means to be a *Christian* leader, not simply a leader.

CONCLUSION

Educational research acknowledges the impact that time spent outside the classroom has on students. This time contributes heavily to the shaping of a worldview. At Christian colleges and universities, the goal is to shape that worldview in a Christlike fashion. Programs can be designed that help students think Christianly about their behavior, and spaces can be developed that encourage student reflection and dialogue. Christian colleges for the most part are doing an effective job of developing their students' Christian worldview. In fact, alumni consider this worldview development one of the biggest influences of their college experience. However, student development must work alongside the academic curriculum to help students develop and interpret these Christian beliefs to others. Time spent both inside and outside the classroom offers adult mentors opportunity to ask students why they believe, and how this belief affects behavioral choices. Hanging with friends in a Christian context, as I did "stoopin'" on Broad Street, allows students time to process everything heard in the classroom.

Student development professionals inherited the mantle of moral philosophy once practiced in the early American college. For those to whom this charge has been given, take heart. Yours is an opportunity to solidify the link between belief and behavior through providing educational activities and programming, creating spaces for reflection and dialogue, engaging in decisive moments in the lives of students, and yes, even through the judicial process. The task makes certain that the Christian worldview does not simply stay in the realm of the intellect alone. It is about life in Christian community and further, about learning to make decisions about all of life that bring glory to God.

CHAPTER 18

CHRISTIAN WORLDVIEW
AND CAMPUS MINISTRY

TODD E. BRADY

"I BELIEVE IN CHRISTIANITY as I believe that the Sun has risen, not only because I see it, but because by it I see everything else."[1] With this concise analogy, C. S. Lewis articulated the comprehensive scope that Christianity should play in the believer's life. Merely acknowledging Christianity as one acknowledges the sun, without seeing and understanding everything else in its light, is incomplete and prevents one from experiencing the true and full abundant life that Jesus spoke of in John 10:10. Christianity is not just a truth that we see but a truth by which we see all things.

Chuck Colson says, "The way we see the world can change the world."[2] The Christian college graduate is prepared for life and will make a difference in tomorrow's world not because of the position he will one day hold but because of the perspective he will have on all of life—his worldview. The Christian worldview affects everything. The way one views the world determines the way one thinks about the world. The way one thinks about the world affects how one acts in the world. For that reason, *how* one thinks is more foundational and more important than merely *what* one thinks. The Christian university works to educate students by helping them think in the right way about all things, guiding them to develop a Christian worldview as the foundational framework that allows them to see everything according to truth and leading them to integrate that view into all aspects of life. When one considers the possibilities of

Christian thinking and all of its results and consequences, the ministry of Christian education is exciting indeed!

Ministry on the Christian campus is the intentional and ongoing development of a Christian worldview that is fully integrated into the lives of students. This ministry, or as many would say the "purpose" of Christian institutions, is to "educate students so they will be prepared for the vocation to which God has called them, enabled and equipped with the competencies necessary to think Christianly and to perform skillfully in the world, equipped to be servant leaders who impact the world as change agents based on a full-orbed Christian worldview and lifeview."[3] The ministry belongs to the entire Christian college. It is not an auxiliary aspect of campus life that is facilitated, encouraged, or even coordinated by the faithful and religious few within a particular department or organization.

Ministry is not a *part* of what the Christian college does. It *is* what the Christian college does. The academic courses of the liberal arts curriculum combined with the co-curricular components of a student's experience at a Christian college serve as the ministry of Christian higher education. From an introductory accounting class or an upper level anatomy and physiology class to an intramural sporting event or a weekly chapel service, each activity serves ultimately to help students see life from the Christian vantage point and to integrate what they believe about God with the way they learn and live in the world. To this end we all minister.

The campus ministry of a Christian college serves the college's mission as an essential partner, working in an integrated fashion with other areas, both academic and nonacademic, to promote and develop a Christian worldview in students' lives. It labors with others in the university, encouraging and involving as many students as possible in an active lifestyle of biblical discipleship and service and leading them to become servant leaders in the world.

WHO ARE WE?

Perhaps the most misunderstood area of the Christian college is campus ministry. Often viewed by others as nonacademic and peripheral, campus ministry sometimes is seen as a nonplayer in the true work and purpose of the college. This perception is fostered when those serving in campus ministry fail to see their role as contributors to the comprehensive task of Christian higher education. When this is the case, campus ministry functions merely as a kind of extended youth group providing fun Christian activities and keeping students busy during those times when they are not required to be involved in academic schoolwork. Among those who lead campus ministry, a lack of understanding and unity concerning the ultimate purpose of Christian education breeds in the lives of students a disconnect between their academic and nonacademic life.

Campus ministry must serve as a vital partner within the university, leading students to relate everything they learn and do to their faith. The Christian activities sponsored through a campus ministry office should never be exalted as more important or more spiritual than the other happenings at the college. Rather, campus ministry should seek to encourage students by providing various avenues through which they might further investigate and grow in the Christian life. These avenues cannot be viewed as the only ones that lead to maturity but as some of many that are available to them while they are in college. Too often when campus ministry thinks of its activities and programs as more significant than other things on campus, a subgroup of students who are regular participants in such programs is developed. In student life, this group is often referred to as the "campus ministry clique."

Campus ministry cannot be as effective when it caters only to a select population of students who enjoy participating in a certain type of activity. Campus ministry must function as a facilitator of ministry that belongs to the students and not as an organization to which students belong. To this end, campus ministry must work hard to lead *all* students to reflect on and engage in a lifestyle that follows Christ.

The Christian worldview is developed more effectively when campus ministry works together with the faculty, seeing its role as serving and supporting the work of the faculty. Frequently on Christian campuses, it is easy for some students to become so involved in campus ministry activities that they begin to neglect their academic responsibilities. Although never actually verbalizing it as such, some students expect faculty and others to excuse their lack of responsibility in the classroom since they were, after all, "doing ministry." Campus ministers and faculty must work together to make sure that such dichotomy between supposed "ministry" and "school" does not exist. Together we model and program in such a way that students are led to see all of life, both academic and nonacademic, as ministry. As students are encouraged to take this perspective concerning all of their college pursuits, such a unity of philosophy and practice among campus ministry and faculty fosters a broader and deeper sense of stewardship in the lives of students.

In addition to classroom work, all activities on the college campus should be opportunities designed to serve as catalysts, propelling students to reflect on and integrate the truths of Christianity into their learning and life. When this is done, campus ministry-sponsored Bible studies are more than just isolated spiritual exercises that have no connection to other aspects of life. Mission trips and service projects are not ventures that only serve to help others through willing and energetic college students. Neither is chapel simply an hour set aside to think on religious themes while we wait for the next class. Rather, each of these serves the purpose of helping students connect what they believe about God with the way they learn and live in the world. *All campus ministry is education*—an education that assists students to unite their love for learning with their love for God in the world in which they live.

When this is the driving focus of a campus ministry, not only will students have a greater appreciation for campus ministry, faculty will also. As those teaching in the classroom see that campus ministry's greatest desire is the integration of faith and learning and living, not only will they see our work as valuable, they will want to be a part of it. Faculty will view occasions to be involved in campus ministry initiatives as opportunities for them to use their gifts and contribute to our collective mission—the development of a Christian worldview.

As campus ministry works with the faculty to develop a Christian worldview among students, no other factor is more valuable than the articulate vision and ongoing support of the college's president. He must see that campus ministry is an essential player and partner in the college's mission. If he does not have a unified vision for the role of campus ministry in the overall mission of the college, no amount or quality of programming will ever bring campus ministry to the table of Christian higher education. Unless the president communicates the importance of a campus ministry on the campus, the faculty and others will never see its importance or appreciate it. For this reason, the relationship between the one leading campus ministry and the president is vital.

Continuous assessment and strategizing with the president about how the university as a whole can progress in the task of Christian worldview development is essential. The motivation for true and comprehensive ministry comes not from just one department within the administration. It trickles down from the top, permeating every part of the institution.

WHY ARE WE HERE?

While early universities like Harvard, Yale, Princeton, and Dartmouth were founded by churches to train ministers, the onset of the Enlightenment caused knowledge or "true" education to be seen as something very distinct from faith. With the Enlightenment of the eighteenth century and the increasing secularization of the university in the nineteenth century, many American universities lost the distinctively Christian mission and vision that had at first driven them. For that reason, "religious education" was considered something that should be promoted by organizations apart from or adjacent to the university.

Modern campus ministry began in the early 1900s as an attempt by both denominational and nondenominational groups to reach students on university campuses with the message of Christianity. Through extensive extracurricular programming, such campus ministries sought to evangelize students and provide them with avenues for collective worship, discipleship, and ministry during their university years. In confronting students with Christian truth, this approach to campus ministry has proven effective. However, some think that campus ministry has often been limited because it is not recognized, appreciated, or valued as a contributor to Christian higher education. In fact, it is often seen as contradictory to the mission and purpose of the institution.

Christian schools work from the basis that all truth is God's truth and that true education occurs only when it is approached from the Christian perspective. Life on the Christian campus is not divided into sacred and secular, since all knowledge and reality are within the realm of God's creation. For this reason, campus ministry at the Christian institution has a different role than it does at public institutions. Understanding that ministry (the development of the Christian worldview) is the responsibility of the entire institution, some would question what purpose a campus ministry serves on a Christian college campus. Does a Christian college even need a campus ministry?

The Christian college benefits from a campus ministry because of the distinctive educational role it plays in the lives of students. *Campus ministry is in the education business.* Who we are and what we do as campus ministers is not separate from or auxiliary to the overall work of the Christian higher educational institutions to which we belong. As campus ministers, we must not see ourselves as ministers at educational institutions but as fellow educators in the ministry of education. Our ministry *is* education—the ministry of Christian higher education.

Each aspect of a student's college life, both academic and nonacademic, serves a vital role in his educational pursuits. While the faculty is the most valuable resource of the university, it is not the only player in a student's education. Outside the classroom, student activities are legion. Too often, such activities are seen only as outlets in which students may participate while they are not involved in the classroom. In the midst of collegiate life, campus ministry educates students by helping them acclimate to university life, encouraging them to reflect on all they are learning, and challenging them to integrate their faith intentionally into every area of their lives.

First, campus ministry seeks to influence the student's education at the Christian college by encouraging and fostering an atmosphere where the Christian worldview can be developed most effectively. For this reason, the mission of the college must remain prominent in the minds of those who serve in campus ministry. Such a mind-set concerning the college's mission helps one understand campus ministry's distinctive role. At Union University, campus ministry exists to create and cultivate a climate that serves as a catalyst for the implementation of the university's mission. In such an environment, students are able to carefully investigate and begin understanding how their faith relates to all of life. They are able to do this as everything that occurs through the work of the university leads them to explore in depth the meaning of their faith and to consider its implications in their lives.

Understanding that students are at different places in their personal spiritual pilgrimages, through campus ministry the Christian college recognizes such places and strives to be an environment that fosters holistic education while at the same time encouraging faith development. According to John Westerhoff, a person's faith expands or develops through four distinctive styles. These styles or stages through which one progresses and matures, considering proper experiences are provided, are experienced faith, affiliative faith, searching faith, and owned faith.[4]

Experienced faith is held and expressed as a response to one's interaction and experiences with other believers. It is mostly a mimicking of the words and actions of other Christians. It is most commonly seen in one's childhood. Affiliative faith is based on and centered primarily in the participation of activities within a community of other believers. It is during late adolescence that most people begin to move out of this stage. Those with affiliative faith look for and find great fulfillment in belonging to and participating in an "identity-conscious community of faith."[5]

Teenagers entering the Christian college do so with a faith construct that is inseparably connected to the associations and identification that they have with certain Christian organizations. For some the issue of faith and devotion to God is not a truth or philosophy that shapes their thought and life. To many students who enter college while they are in the affiliative faith stage, Christianity is not something they *believe* but something to which they *belong*.

Since students on college campuses are entering that phase of life where in every generation "people have asked the cosmic questions and wrestled—for better or for worse—with answers," campus ministry must recognize faith development stages in students' lives and see these times as grand opportunities to help them struggle and grow toward a more mature and integrated faith. As students begin to move from an affiliative faith to a searching faith—one that scrutinizes the commonly held beliefs of their faith community and seeks to settle for oneself what is true—the Christian college atmosphere should encourage and motivate them in their searching. Campus ministry works with others in the college community to initiate activities and cultivate an environment that will further propel students in their search for truth. The ultimate goal is to produce a student with an owned faith, one who in an integrated fashion believes and lives according to the truth of Christianity. Owned faith stands for itself.

Everything on the Christian campus should point students to their God, helping them to unite their belief and behavior and preparing them as persons of faith to enter a hostile world that does not accept the claims of Christianity. During their brief time on the campus, a student's involvement in the classroom and his participation in student life should be enveloped in an atmosphere that promotes learning and faith integration. Campus ministry leads the way in cultivating this climate by continuously holding up the banner of God's reality and purpose, helping students see all of life within the context of his creation.

In the educational process, campus ministry continuously encourages students to recognize the supremacy of God in all things. As we carry out the college's mission related to worldview, we must help students see that God is no less present or active in the college algebra class than he is in the midnight dorm Bible study. Our role is to encourage and facilitate the ministry that is occurring in all sectors of the college and to help students see how everything they experience is a part of the comprehensive realm of God. As students study various disciplines, they understand that "the earth is the Lord's, and everything in it, the world, and all who live in it" (Ps. 24:1). A magnificent song, a complex chemical experiment, an incredibly detailed genome—each of these is a part of God's creation and cannot be appreciated fully apart from an acknowledgement of the reality and supremacy of God.

Campus ministry, together with others, helps students see the unity of truth, and in response challenges them to love God for who he is—the source of truth. Campus ministry strives to lead students to combine their love of God and their love for learning—for it is this combination that characterizes us all at the university. As we grow in knowledge and love for God, we do so understanding that he is over all and that "in every thing he might have the supremacy" (Col. 1:18).

Most students at some time will question their involvement in the liberal arts curriculum, often wondering how a particular subject relates to their future. They will often ask, "Why do I need to learn this?" or "What good is it going to be for me to know this stuff?" Those of us serving in campus ministry often encounter students on this level and can help them see the validity of all knowledge. When one begins to grasp God's supremacy, it is quickly obvious that all knowledge and life are sacred. All of creation belongs to God. All truth is sacred, because it is God's. The specific area to which they refer may not help them earn more money or be more successful. But that is not the purpose of Christian higher education. Such knowledge is ultimately about God and has implications for how one believes and behaves in the world. All knowledge is a part of his creation. Through this knowledge we gain a better understanding of him. It is in the environment of the Christian college that a campus ministry reminds students to see all of life in an integrated fashion.

Busy for God

There is a ravenous hunger on the part of college students for spiritual things. Across the country, traditional college students are showing an increased interest in corporate experiences of worship, co-curricular Bible studies, personal and public prayer, and mission and service involvement. Recently, thirty thousand students from throughout the United States assembled in a field near Memphis, Tennessee, to pray for spiritual awakening on their campuses. Bible clubs and prayer times are being formed on both high school and college campuses. Last year at Union University, a group of students requested, initiated, and led four additional praise and worship services in the chapel. Although chapel credit was graciously granted, many of the hundreds of students in attendance seemed motivated solely by a desire to participate in yet another corporate service of worship.

Not only are students zealous to seek God through worship and Bible study, they are also passionate about going into all the world and serving others through missions. The International Mission Board and the North American Mission Board of the Southern Baptist Convention reported in a recent year that over twenty-six hundred college students spent weeks and months serving in local and international ministries.[7] Many students are staying busy and active seeking various ways to express their faith.

Is such activity the ultimate goal of campus ministry? Is our role merely to provide opportunities for students to "get involved in ministry," as if their lack of participation means that they are not involved in ministry? Programs and activities are a major part of what the campus ministry provides. These should be carefully constructed avenues that provide intentional opportunities for students to grow and develop in their faith and to respond with a lifestyle of Christian service. Although we should be eager for students to participate in worship, Bible study, and ministries, we must not be satisfied merely with *what* students do. While it is wonderful to see students actively involved in Christian ministries, campus ministry should work hard to make sure that students are being educated and molded into the likeness of Christ *through* such activities. We must work and teach and minister to make sure that when students are participating in our programs, they have a proper understanding of *why* they are doing what they are doing. Related to campus ministry programs, does a student participate in a mission trip or ministry project for the right reason? Does she attend her small group Bible study with the understanding that the truths of such study have implications not only for her personal piety but for every area of her life?

Holistic education through campus ministry means that we do not encourage a privatized, marginalized, or compartmentalized discipleship that is distant from other areas of knowledge or life. We must not be content that our students are merely active for God or merely gaining knowledge about God. We must consider ourselves successful only when we have led them to reflect on the truth of Scripture as it relates to every area of life and to integrate that truth into every facet of their lives. When a student seriously considers the truth of Christianity and then uses that truth as the framework by which he approaches history, mathematics, literature, sport, leisure, and ultimately all of life, then we may take confidence that our mission is being accomplished.

"Whatever"

When glowing reports of students' involvement in ministries and service are being reported, one might suggest that campus ministry and the Christian college should smile with gratitude to God. To a degree this is true. Ministry involvement and activity reports cannot, however, be a campus ministry's primary focus or measuring rod for effectiveness. In spite of the many things students seem to be doing to express their faith and commitment to God, there also exists at the same time a deep cavern of discord and angst in the hearts and minds of today's students. Today's generation of students is fragmented. From fragmented families and communities, many come to college with experiences that have caused them to have a pessimistic view of the future. Throughout their lives these students have been constant witnesses to crumbling families, devastating tragedies, and crushing disappointments, all of which have shaped them into a generation struggling for happiness and fulfillment. Yet they look ahead desiring truth, hope, stability, and confidence about their own futures.

According to a recent study by two sociologists, the current generation is one where "hope and fear are colliding."[8] This perspective on life often causes students to have an apathetic outlook on much of the reality around them. This generation makes up what Council for Christian Colleges and Universities' Scholar-in-Residence Steve Garber refers to as the "Culture of Whatever." "Whatever" is the one word that characterizes their apathetic attitude toward life. He states that today's youth are numb to the world around them, unaffected by the sights and sounds that relentlessly bombard them. As a result, their response to most things, good or bad, is mostly "whatever." He says many youth are stepping into adulthood and could not care less about anything.[9]

In *Fabric of Faithfulness*, Garber goes on to claim that those students who develop and articulate a clear worldview are the ones who are able to accept and address the challenges of living in today's pluralistic society. A student is prepared for life in the world when he sees the coherence of truth and lives according to that truth. Unless students make the connection between what they know and how they live on a day-to-day basis, their learning will be an ever-increasing collection of facts that remain fragmented, compartmentalized, and isolated from where they live and prevents them from having an influence in the world. Their supposed "knowledge" will be cold, dry facts lying dormant on the back shelf of their minds. When knowledge becomes disconnected from the way we live our lives, learning is reduced to an exercise that merely prepares us to answer questions of trivia—information that has no purpose and is not productive.

As Garber reminds us, "Knowledge of—leads to responsibility to—which results in concern for."[10] This is true education— knowledge that results in responsibility and concern. Knowledge connected to the reality of the world produces a person who cares about and responds appropriately to the world around him. Like faith, knowledge without works is dead. It always results in action. Knowledge of truth always leads to hope, not apathy.

Campus ministry functions best in Christian education when it serves as a bridge that allows real and tangible connections to be made between the reality and implications of truth and the manner in which students look at and live their lives. This is done by meeting all students wherever they may be in their relationship with God and challenging them to reflect on their lives as they relate to God and his purposes. Students who are preparing for vocational Christian ministry should receive the necessary tools and experiences needed to think and live Christianly in the world. So also should those who are preparing to be teachers, nurses, architects, lawyers, and accountants. Campus ministers cannot see as their only target those students who are preparing for vocations such as pastor or minister or missionary. These students are part of what the Christian university is doing, but its mission is much broader and more extensive. Regardless of chosen careers, all students should be encouraged to develop a sense of *vocatio* or "calling" about their future work.

The nurse, the teacher, the architect, the musician—all should do what they do as an expression of their love for God and in the name of Christ. Each person should approach his discipline, whatever it may be, understanding that it leads not just to a job, but to a life through which God is glorified and humanity is benefited. Campus ministry works to accomplish this among all students by helping them see that all of life is sacred before God and that every believer is a steward, called by God to live for him. Our desire is to see all students seeking to live Colossians 3:17: "And whatever you do, whether in word or deed, do it all in the name of the Lord Jesus, giving thanks to God the Father through him."

The Things We Do

A proper understanding of campus ministry's unique role and purpose on the Christian college campus should serve as the motivation for all programming and activities. One of the most visible aspects of campus ministry programming is the chapel ministry. While the Christian university labors to help students see the Christian faith as the unifying principle by which one relates learning to life, it is only natural that such a community desire to participate in corporate experiences of worship. Not only do we work hard to be a community of scholars; we are a community of faith who seeks to love God with all our hearts, minds, souls, and strength. The chapel ministry should lead students to worship God and to integrate their faith with every aspect of their lives. It is a place where God is exalted and worshiped, and it is a place where we again and again are reminded of the blessing and responsibility that are ours as redeemed humanity before God.

The chapel service is not merely a separate exercise of compartmentalized worship required of students so that the university will appear or remain Christian. Rather, it is the time when the entire university assembles to worship and celebrate the living God. While some students question the necessity of an ongoing chapel program, and while an increasing number of colleges offer "chapel credit" for activities such as cultural events, music recitals, and community service projects, campus ministry and the Christian college communicate and model the primacy of participating in corporate worship and the irreplaceable value of sitting under the discipline of the preaching and teaching of God's Word.[11] There are many other avenues for instruction and faith development on the college campus, but none can replace the corporate gathering for worship and biblical teaching.

The Christian college is not a church. However, we are a faith community and should desire to be obedient to the command to assemble together for such a purpose. Nowhere is the Christian college's unity and focus more evident than that time when a diverse faculty, staff, and student body come together, united by the one who is "the image of the invisible God, the firstborn over creation." We do so understanding that "by him all things were created: things in heaven and on earth, visible and invisible, whether thrones or powers or rulers or authorities; all things were created by him and for him. He is before all things, and in him all things hold together" (Col. 1:16–17). The chapel service is that place where the entire university community reflects anew that all truth is God's truth and that the only proper response as human beings created in God's image are worship and stewardship.

There is great potential for the chapel service to serve as a significant component in the formation and development of a student's Christian worldview. While not all will agree with everything that each speaker says or with how every service is conducted, there should be no doubt in anyone's mind that the worship of God and the desire for truth in the Christian faith are what motivates everything that occurs in the chapel. Also, during a student's college career, the chapel should afford him the opportunity to observe how different people from diverse backgrounds relate their faith to their work, their families, and ultimately their lives. While the campus minister regularly speaks and leads, it should be realized that every faculty and staff member is a "campus minister" and is living out his faith and calling through his particular discipline. For this reason, faculty should often have the opportunity to participate in and lead the weekly chapel services. Of course, students will expect to hear the campus minister relating his faith to his life in the chapel, but how much more effective for students to hear the professor of business administration or the associate professor of chemistry speaking about the reality of faith in his or her life? The chapel is where we *all* worship God and learn more about how we can integrate our faith with every part of our learning and living.

Along with the chapel, campus ministry cultivates a community in which students are encouraged to explore the Christian faith and the implications of that faith through avenues of discipleship and service. Understanding that new students are more open to searching and questions, campus ministry provides opportunities outside the classroom for students to build relationships, explore faith, and study Scripture within the context of comfortable and nonthreatening environments.

Arliss Dickerson, veteran campus minister at Arkansas State University, says, "A specialized Freshmen Ministry is the single most effective strategy for developing a larger college ministry."[12] While this seems to be true, perhaps no other program immediately impacts the life of a student more than a ministry to new students. Freshmen and transfer students approach university life hesitantly and are more open and willing to investigate and participate in such programs. From the moment a student steps on the college grounds, campus ministry works to communicate the essence of who the university is, to assimilate him into university life, and to model for him what the integrated Christian life is. At Union, this is done through LIFEgroups, a student-led small group ministry that ministers to new students by providing the following:

- an immediate place of belonging,
- aid in the transition being made to a new environment,
- an upperclassman leader/mentor who models/exemplifies Christian leadership,
- a place that fosters genuineness and sincerity,
- peer assistance, guidance, and encouragement in personal spiritual formation, and
- a community in which to discuss and grow in the Christian faith.

Recognizing that many students enter college in the affiliative faith stage, a specialized small group ministry to new students provides the needed encouragement and support as one matures socially, academically, and spiritually. A student's relationships with university personnel are key to a satisfying and positive college career. However, a structure that allows students to build immediate and authentic relationships with fellow students is perhaps more important. Unless students feel that they are accepted and cared for by other students, and unless they have a genuine sense of belonging within the college community, they will be less likely to continue their education there. It is in such a student-oriented environment that new students adapt to life on the Christian college campus and are prepared to begin their journey in Christian higher education. The opportunity to develop student leaders who have a Christian worldview and who impact the lives of younger students in a positive way is the most important thing a campus ministry provides.

Once students assimilate to life at the Christian university and continue growing in their knowledge of truth, campus ministry provides ongoing extracurricular opportunities for discipleship and growth. While the life stages and concerns of college students should be considered as opportunities are designed, the ultimate goal of all discipleship ministry is the integrated life. From retreats and Bible studies to lectures and accountability groups, each discipleship program should lead students to see the truth of God's creation and revelation more clearly and to respond appropriately.

Campus ministry helps to develop the Christian worldview in the life of a student not only through discipleship programming (ministry to students) but also through opportunities for service and ministry (ministry through students) outside the classroom. These opportunities must not be driven by a desire for involvement but by a desire for understanding. Arthur Holmes attests that "Christian service activities often reinforce sixth-grade theological half-concepts and bad high school habits of speech."[13] This is true if those coordinating such activities through the office of campus ministry are not driven by a solid theology that conscientiously and responsibly guides students to relate what they are doing to the proper and Christian motivation behind such activities. Through ministry projects, students are able to impact those areas where they serve. This impact in various communities is one of campus ministry's definite goals.

However, the more far-reaching impact occurs in the life of a student through his involvement in and reflection on what he is doing. For many, an international mission project that is theologically driven and intentionally designed will open up a new horizon of thinking that will forever change the way a student thinks and looks at the world. As some have said, "No other thing impacted me more than a campus-ministry-sponsored global outreach trip." Working in a different country among different cultures with people who live and think differently often causes students to consider worldview issues like never before. Once a student begins being assimilated to the college campus, one of campus ministry's greatest goals should be to engage as many students as possible in other cultures. For it is there where Christian thinking that leads to the glory of God is often encouraged most.

A thoroughly God-centered and God-focused philosophy must drive a campus ministry's strategy for student missions and service. Allowing students to explore and exercise their gifts through active hands-on ministry in different cultural contexts promotes reflection and prompts students to consider the stewardship of their lives as Christians in God's world. When students participate in service and ministry, when they are taught the proper motivation for ministry—the glory of God— they begin to understand God's eternal purpose and to see their privilege and responsibility in participating as stewards in his kingdom. A vision of redeemed humanity's final place before God creates a mind-set and lifestyle that are theocentric in motivation and practice.

Campus ministry has the incredible opportunity of shaping a Christian worldview in the lives of students at Christian colleges. To be engaged actively in this challenge means that we must be theologically driven and culturally relevant in all of our initiatives, leading students to integrate their beliefs about God and the world with their behavior. This cannot occur if campus ministry is an island on the periphery of the institution's educational vision. Understanding that it is not our programs alone that lead students toward a more fully developed Christian worldview, we serve as an essential partner in the entire process of Christian higher education. We labor as coeducators toward the common goal of an educated student who has a clearly developed and articulated Christian worldview and who impacts culture as a servant leader. It is the responsibility of campus ministries to submit to and serve the mission of our universities, working with all whom God has assembled for the development of a Christian worldview in the lives of students.

SHAPING THE ACADEMIC ENTERPRISE: AN INTERVIEW WITH CARLA SANDERSON, PROVOST, UNION UNIVERSITY

What is the goal of Christian higher education?

A QUARTER CENTURY AGO Arthur F. Holmes wrote *The Idea of a Christian College* to shape thoughts about and objectives of Christian higher education. This book has provided a conceptual framework for shaping the academic enterprise at Christian colleges and universities all these many years. The goal of such a framework is to remain faithful to the heritage of academic excellence and distinctive Christian commitment. Certainly this is a high calling for the present team of academic administrators and faculty in Christian higher education today. Now is the time to take the next step forward and extend excellence and commitment into a new century filled with greater challenges and even greater opportunities. As we enter this new century, or at least the first quarter of it, we are called to wrestle with new issues and new questions as we think through the idea of a Christian college.

What is the role of faculty in achieving this goal?

Driven by a clear vision and understanding of what the mission of the Christian university should be, the primary vehicle for ensuring the successful future of a Christian college or university is the faculty. Following Peter Drucker, who has led many of the world's leading corporations toward a clear and concise understanding of what business they are in, the faculty in Christian higher education must commit themselves to a commonly held vision and worldview.

In *Scholarship Reconsidered*, Ernest Boyer describes our current system of higher education as a system where confusion over goals diminishes the sense of shared community. In this community, there should be no confusion over goals, administrative goals versus faculty goals, our goals versus their goals. Coming to this understanding is a must for every Christian college faculty of the future.

In a recently published book entitled *Failing the Future*, Annette Kolodny urges faculty to assume a new responsibility for finding such understanding. Dr. Kolodny calls for a coming together of faculty teams for shared decision making and planning, faculty of "divergent and convergent minds" working as teams, teams carefully considered and selected so that the talents and perspectives of faculty team members blend together in complementary ways. In this deliberate, faculty-driven way, team members are placed in a position to work toward establishing an understanding of identity and purpose, and finding the cohesion that is so obviously missing. Faculty come to own the process and commit themselves to the pursuit of turning confusion to enlightenment and understanding. Faculty become a part of the solution and, as Kolodny states, faculty "must own the solutions, or there will be no real solutions" to the problems we face in higher education today.

Yet many faculty are not well acquainted with the larger questions of campus-wide identity and purpose. Many are unaccustomed to the level of involvement in decision making that is characteristic of a faculty-driven process. Many have not seen themselves in the "real solutions" business. Further, the nature of a typical academic department structure is a disincentive for larger understanding to emerge. Most faculties organize themselves in committees, but even then the scope and purpose of committees may be limiting and the composition of members arbitrary. Careful consideration of incentives and disincentives, faculty strengths and talents, and long-held academy views on structure and governance must be challenged if the faculty-driven future of which Kolodny writes is to be passed and not failed.

As Christian colleges consider this approach for the future, it is imperative that we realize our potential in all of this. We must rise to the occasion that presents itself to us and take our place as leaders in community-building on higher education campuses. No other faculty in higher education is in a better position to achieve a cohesive identity and unity of purpose than the Christian college faculty. In Christ, we find our identity and our purpose. In Christ, we know the source of all truth. In Christ, we have a strong sense of community. In him, we have a clear grasp of what it is we are called to do and what it is we are trying to achieve every time we walk into a classroom or laboratory or meet up with a student in a coffee shop. And in Christ, we find our place at the higher education table, helping to shape the academic enterprise for the good of the public and the building of the kingdom.

What challenges do we face as we look toward the future?

The challenge for Christian faculty to rise up and respond to higher education's need for cohesion and campus community comes at a time when threats of secularization abound. James Tunstead Burtchaell's recent book *The Dying of the Light* chronicles examples of Christian colleges losing their grip on their identities. The threat of becoming more and more secular is real and is growing as pluralistic, postmodern world and life views permeate our society. It will take a strong faculty identity with a distinctive purpose that includes a deliberate attempt to combat secularization to seize the opportunity for the distinctiveness that society yearns for and the kingdom impact to which our calling leads us.

Another challenge I believe both the church and we face is that we are moving into a time of greater public demand for more educational accountability and financial efficiency, a time that demands more specialized training and more job-related focus. While recognizing that factors such as graduate placement rates, job markets, and cost effectiveness will become increasingly important to external constituents and accrediting bodies, we must remember that the opportunity to shape Christian higher education is about far more than jobs and markets; the opportunity is about more than shaping educational experiences that are economically sound or cost productive. It is of profound importance that we must never allow anything to take precedence over our ultimate goal to shape young people, their lives, their service, and their relationship to humanity and to God.

We must always fight the threat that excessive regulation and external entities will challenge us to shape education from a purely economical or materialistic view. We must do so by articulating who we are and defining the intrinsic value we offer. This strong sense of identity must be described to mesh well with the small but growing importance that society places on virtue. In doing so we will find ways to maintain autonomy and distinctiveness on our Christian college campuses.

What role should faculty assume in addressing these challenges?

Faculty are crucial in all of this. It is at their hands, through the offering of their minds, that education happens. Faculty need strong leaders to support them and create for them an environment where student learning and growth can take place. They need opportunities to address threats, dialogue about society's needs, and address the challenges they face by ever-changing mores that come with each new generation of students. Faculty need to come together to determine the meaning of Christian higher education within the context of the particular mission of their college or university (for example, what does a Christian, liberal-arts-based education really mean?). They need leaders for this, leaders who celebrate faculty thinking together, leaders who will bring them to the discussion table to search for and wrestle with understanding that comes from God's truth. More than technology, more than the latest pedagogical trend, more than anything, faculty need a strong sense of who they are as a collective body and what it is they have been brought together to do.

Of obvious importance are the individuals who make up the Christian college faculty. There is no more important role for the administration and trustee body than finding faculty equipped for the high calling that is ours in Christian education. Meticulous care and attention to detail are musts with every prospective candidate under consideration. The employment process should be externally far-reaching and internally inclusive. Department members, chairs, deans and/or the provost, and the president must come together as a team first to define the need and then search for individuals not just right for higher education but right for Christian higher education at a particular college at a particular point in its history.

The need-identification process on a Christian college campus is far more than just determining what credentials are needed to meet workload demands. The process may be impacted by the need for someone who can model the teacher-scholar role, who has experience in alternate delivery systems, or who can provide needed ethnic or international diversity. Always the process should be impacted by the need for men and women of faith, called to live out their faith commitment as teachers. Attempts should be made to get to know as much about the applicant as possible before the campus visit. While each team member has a particular area of focus in the interview process, such as academic preparation, experience, scholarship, university fit, faith commitment, and so on, the importance of unity and consensus cannot be overemphasized. All focus areas are equally important and must be equally valued by each member of the search team.

Can you address the imperative of faculty development?

Faculty development is the next vital step. Each Christian college that is serious about its future will take steps to ensure opportunities for the ongoing development of its faculty. Creating a well-supported structure for faculty development is vital. Many effective models exist, including the Center for Faculty Development model where faculty goals can be advanced through a regular and ongoing delivery of development opportunities. The center is about think tanks, panels, discussion assemblies, bibliographies, reading groups, colloquia, Web sites, and newsletters. Faculty development centers serve new faculty with orientation and mentor programs, chairs and deans with leadership development initiatives, but most of all individuals as members of a team. The center is a place to champion the vision and purposes of the institution, a very direct extension of the work of the president and his or her administrative team.

The best faculty development center is a faculty-led center where the agenda of initiatives and offerings is set by faculty who understand and embrace the vision for the college. The center will champion such things as teaching, scholarship, community, and service. The major thread running through all center initiatives is the Christian world and life view. Thus, there is no work on campus more important than faculty development.

Would you agree that Christian colleges are primarily teaching institutions?

The successful future of Christian higher education will depend on faculty who prize and develop classroom teaching in a way never before required. Faculty must accept the challenge to reconsider former paradigms and pedagogical theory. The twenty-first century has ushered in a time when both the substance and method of delivery of education are being challenged. Regarding substance, Ernest Boyer reminds us that teaching is more than just transmitting knowledge; it is "transforming and extending it as well." Traditional disciplinary thinking is being replaced by newly accepted wisdom that looks at issues and knowledge across traditional discipline boundaries. New ways of knowing and relating have emerged. Models such as cooperative learning, service learning, problem-based learning, and team-centered learning and teaching are calling for consideration of a very fluid concept of learning. The substance of the classroom has never been more dynamic, whether the classroom is within the walls of the college or in an underprivileged neighborhood across town.

Regarding method, distance learning and use of the Internet as a delivery system remind us that teaching where we are physically, face-to-face with our students, using chalk, over-heads, or even PowerPoint, is not the only way students of the future will complete their degree requirements. Methods will become available to us that we never dreamed possible. Face-to-face interaction will come to mean something altogether new as technological advances allow the distance between our computer-linked faces to span the globe. No delivery system must ever take the place of the human, real-time encounter between student and teacher for the vast majority of our purposes in Christian higher education.

Yet new delivery systems must be developed to complement and expand our current capabilities where such an encounter is not possible. Interfaces that open up new laboratory opportunities, classes that connect two cultures, and degree programs that extend our mission and purposes to otherwise unreached student populations are just a few examples of how new methods can ensure the successful future of the Christian college classroom.

If teaching is so important, what is the role of scholarship?

The important balance between the classroom teacher role and the scholar role must be determined. It must be clearly understood that the primary role is the teaching role. One of the threats we face in Christian higher education is the temptation of trying to become all things. Our distinctiveness is the teacher-student relationship. Yet even while faculty accept the primacy of their teaching role, they must also be allowed the freedom and resources to concentrate as scholars on important issues within their discipline, to become "torchbearers" for their disciplines, modeling for their students the research role, enticing them to pursue graduate study, enabling them to perpetuate the future of their specific discipline.

Finally, select faculty must be strongly encouraged to concentrate as scholars on contributing to, or in some cases pioneering in, the highly significant work of establishing a Christian world and life view within their disciplines. Christian scholarship of this sort can serve to perpetuate the future of Christian higher education in general.

Harold Heie and George Marsden, among others, have shaped our thinking about this idea of Christian scholarship. Heie contends that it is integral to one's calling as a Christian educator that one share with the larger academic community the results of first-order scholarship informed by Christian perspectives. He encourages us to "offer thoroughly Christian wisdom for public application." Christian educators on our campuses need to offer their disciplines, as well as the communities in which we live, the unique Christian worldview perspective. Only then can full understanding and truth emerge. Corwin Smith explains the worldview role of Christian scholars in anthropological terms. Smith says it is like someone trying to describe things within one community to another community so that both communities have greater understanding. The Christian scholar must try to describe his or her Christianly informed view of the disciplines to other scholars in the discipline so that every member of the discipline has greater understanding.

Similarly, Marsden has suggested that there must be room for explicit Christian points of view within the academy. Marsden likewise encourages Christian scholars to offer first-order work. He writes, "My ideal for Christian scholarship is one that not only looks for the bearing of one's Christian convictions on one's academic thought, but also reflects Christian attitudes that shape the tone of one's scholarship. Christian commitments should lead one toward scholarly rigor and integrity. Scholarship with these qualities will ultimately have the greatest impact in the academy and the greatest chance of being accepted."

A broad view of scholarship needs to be adopted on our campuses. Faculty come from graduate schools with a paradigm for acceptable and noteworthy scholarship. Perhaps in some disciplines our campuses cannot foster the development of that form of scholarship. Certainly in some they can. Thus, suitable definitions of scholarship must be explored. Perhaps a grassroots approach to the question of definition is best. Asking each department first to define what suitable scholarship means within its discipline is an important first step.

Sharing definitions and inviting dialogue among members of the entire faculty team can work to enlarge the perspective of scholarship on every Christian college campus.

What role do students play in building and shaping a Christian academic community?

A profound theme for the successful future of our campuses is the establishment of a dynamic learning community. Careful attention must be given to the students we recruit and support through scholarships, the community we build for them, and the learning environment we create for them. The goal is to graduate students who have learned to deal knowledgeably and competently, and with moral sensitivity, to a rapidly changing world. We must ensure their development of the knowledge and skills needed for global interdependence. We must enable our students to see how they and their nations are linked to others in a dynamically changing contemporary global context. And we must do so through a Christian worldview framework where issues of truth, values, compassion, and servanthood are absolute and are meshed with the subject matter of a major or professional program to enlarge our students' sense of humanity and calling in the world.

Our students must be active, engaged learners, taking on serious conversation with faculty and our on-campus guests about important issues and ideas. Such conversation and growth must evolve from our classrooms out into faculty offices and labs, into the dining hall, the art gallery, into our churches and homes, across the entire community.

Why are students interested in Christian colleges?

There seems to be a heightened interest in what Christian colleges have to offer students. Increases in enrollment are documented across all of Christian higher education. The source is likely twofold. Many committed Christian parents and students are more serious about preparing for a life of dedicated Christian service. Coming from Christian primary and secondary schools and from home-school preparation, a growing number of parents and students seek Christian college education as a continuation of their educational choice and philosophy.

Other students come because they or their parents are troubled by the fragmented approach to higher education that they find on secular campuses and are worried about the moral climate they find there. They come because they hope to find a safe (some parents would add "and supervised") environment where they can study with outstanding professors in cohesive programs of study. Christian colleges must seek students who are not just interested in what the college experience will do *for* them but seek students who are interested in what the experience will do *to* them.

What aspects contribute to the idea of a Christian learning community?

The concept of community is an excellent model by which to shape the overall Christian college student experience. Most of our campuses are residential, a feature that we should emphasize and value as we look to the future. Christian education is holistic and can best be provided in community. A giant in the learning community concept is retired Calvin College provost, Gordon Van Harn. In a tribute to Van Harn on his retirement, Anthony Diekma, then president of Calvin, writes about students and faculty in community, "The nature of our conversation—of our daily talking together—must center on our common educational tasks. (Gordon Van Harn) sees learning as a communal task: students and faculty together acquiring knowledge and insight, and mutually supporting one another in the common enterprise of learning."

Students on our campuses consider strong academic advising to be the most important characteristic of academic quality. Students who choose Christian college education expect full-time faculty to do all the teaching and be readily available to mentor them in the discipline and advise them on matters related to their successful pursuit of a degree. According to a recent survey, 80 percent of students believe that colleges like ours can help them "customize" their education to meet special interests and learning needs without the usual hurdles that are expected on larger campuses. They believe that colleges like ours are best equipped to prepare them to become whole individuals.

A partnership between academics and student life is a first step in establishing a learning community culture where this can happen. A structure that brings students and faculty together outside the classroom is another. Physical spaces on campus that are inviting to both can bring people together. Structural entities like centers with commonly shared purposes is a way to facilitate faculty and student exchange (center for Christian leadership, center for scientific study, center for international study, center for service learning, etc., are examples). Well-planned events that stir the interest of many is yet another opportunity to build community. In whatever creative way possible, our campuses need to hone the concept of learning communities, a concept that is likely to be highly characteristic of successful and dynamic campuses in the future.

What is the place of a core curriculum in such a learning community?

Ensuring the right blend of the disciplines within a core curriculum, matched with the right majors and programs, in order to educate a new generation of students is of great importance in shaping the academic enterprise for the twenty-first century. Again, the Christian college faculty is the key. The distinctive core curriculum and programs of study on each campus need to be a direct reflection of the widely held college vision and a direct reflection of the faculty that is assembled there, and their characteristic strengths and talents. Faculty need to establish clear goals for the core, goals they own and use to design complementary programs and majors to complete the big picture of an undergraduate Christian education.

Fragmentation often characterizes secular campuses and may also threaten ours. We are called to revive the responsibility of a faculty as a whole for the curriculum as a whole. We must call ourselves to an ongoing review and potential realignment of all academic initiatives, including and especially our curricula, to fit a bold, comprehensive, future-directed, Christ-centered mission and purposes for our colleges.

Curriculum review and revision affords an opportunity like no other to reshape the tradition of a college and the future for its graduates. Our revisions need to respond boldly to economic trends and expanding student groups, remembering that liberal arts and professional education should become increasingly more combined where the core and the major become much more integrated and intimately connected than ever before. It is a holistically educated person we are seeking to graduate, one who understands how each aspect of his or her education fits together.

Recently Arthur Holmes, retired chair of the department of philosophy at Wheaton College, served as scholar-in-residence on our campus. In a closing conversation before his departure, he was asked what would be the most challenging issue facing Christian higher education in the twenty-first century. His response was pluralism as a way of seeing the world. Holmes urged Christian colleges to arm themselves with strong thinkers who are positioned to advocate for truth. He urges us to grow our philosophy departments so as to graduate more students equipped with a philosophical framework for exploring the difficult questions of tomorrow. This will require a change in the ethos on many of our campuses where faculty and students come to value the role of the Christian philosopher in the same way we value the role of ministers and church leaders. We need philosophy faculty who are first-rate teachers, well received by students, enthusiastic, and inspiring. We need faculty who can lead students to explore and make sense of what they believe in a pluralistic world. We need Christian students who will wrestle with new ways of seeing the world as they ask the question, "What is objectively true?"

Besides postmodernism, for what other future challenges must Christian colleges be prepared?

We also need to consider the challenge to explore "new directions of global understanding." Christian college campuses are well suited to prepare graduates for work in an internationalized society because many of the questions of tomorrow will be about the search for common understanding and common values. A Christian thinker with a liberal arts education will be well positioned for the searching critique and civil discourse about these fundamental issues that will continue to surface as the world's issues become more shared and less diverse.

Karen Longman, former vice president for the Council of Christian Colleges and Universities and current vice president for academic affairs at Greenville College, poses an important question: "What if Christian colleges were known as places that opened up the world for our incoming students?" The concept of globalization is more than just an emerging new concept for Christian colleges; it is a part of Christ's mandate for our lives. The Great Commission compels us to seize the opportunity to enter open doors that were once closed. The world needs Christian businessmen and women, teachers, nurses, physcians, social workers, therapists, counselors, scientists, computer scientists, specialists in media and the arts, journalists, writers, poets, historians, political scientists, theologians, ministers, musicians, specialists in language . . . the list goes on. The world needs Christ and will receive him at the hands of graduates who are prepared to live and work anywhere in the world to which he leads.

AFTERWORD

DAVID S. DOCKERY AND
GREGORY ALAN THORNBURY

IN A DELIGHTFUL RECENT EDITION of *The Hedgehog Review,*
the editors of said journal posed a question of astonishing
poignancy to some of the most able minds in higher education
today: "What is the university for?"[1] What followed was a
wonderful consideration of the scope and purpose of higher
learning in America today. Academics such as Jackson Lear and
Mark Edmunson wondered out loud whether it is possible to
save the liberal arts in an anti-humanities culture. Other writers rightly savored the role of the university as a place for
prophetic voices and serious intellectual argumentation. Still
others assessed and explained the precursors to the present state
of higher education in America.

Perhaps the most compelling piece in the journal came in the
form of an exchange on "The Moral Purposes of the
University," featuring Harvard professor Julie Reuben, Notre
Dame historian George Marsden, and philosopher Richard
Rorty of the University of Virginia. For their part, Reuben and
Marsden lament the decline of the university's role in the arena
of moral guidance for America's young adults. Rorty, to the
contrary, denies any such desire or role for the American university: "If the students aren't reasonably honest and decent
people by the time they hit the university, I don't see that there
is much that we in higher education can do about it."[2]

One might respond that Rorty has, of course, missed the
point. No one suggests that the university *alone* is responsible
for the moral formation of youth, but neither can anyone deny
that the traditional undergraduate years are a seedbed for character development. As he admits in his contribution to *The*

Hedgehog Review, Rorty essentially thinks that religion is worthless at best and harmful at worst, and really would not mind at all if the church simply went away for good. By way of contrast, academics like Reuben and Marsden realize the potential for the university to build upon the solid foundation begun by faithful churches and parents. The university, at least theoretically, can guard such a trust.

This volume has demonstrated that a Christian university is an ideal place for vigorous Christian intellectual engagement and character development to occur. Although Christians should support and pray for those who seek to influence the secular university for the cause of God and truth, they must also recognize that it is the Christian institution that can, by virtue of its worldview commitments, make consistent advances morally, culturally, and theologically in the lives of coming generations. Because the Christian university holds to fundamental presuppositions about the nature of God and reality, it stands poised to be a wonderful context for vigorous and rigorous intellectual discussion. In his response to Richard Rorty in *The Hedgehog Review,* George Marsden replied:

> I've often commented that the difference between teaching at Calvin College and being in a secular university environment is something like this: People will say, "in order to have really fruitful intellectual life, you have to be open to the widest diversity of opinion." My response to that is that the most vital intellectual community I've been in was at Calvin College, and the reason for this was that when we talked about things, we didn't always have to go back to square one to engage an issue. We could work from square three or four and then argue very vigorously about that. Professor Rorty and I are so far apart on the fundamental issues that it's hard to know how we could possibly talk about them, because on such basic issues we simply judge things differently.[3]

Marsden's experience at Calvin College reflects the same spirit of faithful intellectual inquiry found in the pages of this volume. Simply put, Christian colleges like Union University take as their mission the very thing that today only a very few in the secular academy desire: the wedding of robust academic interest with genuine moral courage. Those of us in Christian higher education take heart that the hopes of so many stalwarts past and present are being realized year after year in colleges and universities committed to the Christian worldview.

ENDNOTES

Introduction: Shaping a Christian Worldview

1. See Daniel Yankelovich, *Coming to Public Judgement: Making Democracy Work in a Complex World* (Syracuse, NY: Syracuse University Press, 1991).

2. See Charles Colson and Nancy Pearcey, *How Now Shall We Live?* (Wheaton: Tyndale, 1999).

3. James Orr, *The Christian View of God and the World* (Grand Rapids, Mich.: Kregel, 1989), 16. The term *worldview* probably can be traced to Immanuel Kant's use of *Weltanschauung* in *Kritik der Urteilskraft* (1790).

4. Ibid.

5. Cf. Abraham Kuyper, The Stone Lectures, Princeton University, 1898.

6. See T. S. Eliot, *Christianity and Culture* (New York: Harcourt, 1940), 22.

Chapter 1, The Authority of Scripture

1. Louis Igou Hodges, *"New Dimensions in Scripture,"* in *New Dimensions in Evangelical Thought: Essays in Honor of Millard J. Erickson,* ed. David S. Dockery (Downers Grove, Ill.: IVP, 1998), 209.

2. For various approaches to the question of the Bible's authority, some from within and others from without the evangelical movement, see in addition to the systematic theologies detailed below, D. A. Carson and John Woodbridge, eds., *Hermeneutics, Authority, and Canon* (Grand Rapids, Mich.: Zondervan, 1986); Duane A. Garrett and Richard R. Melick Jr., *Authority and Interpretation: A Baptist Perspective* (Grand Rapids, Mich.: Baker Book House, 1987); James Montgomery Boice, *The Foundation of Biblical Authority* (Grand Rapids, Mich.: Zondervan Publishing House, 1978); Herman Ridderbos, *Studies in Scripture and its Authority* (Grand Rapids, Mich.: Eerdmans, 1978); Robert Gnuse, *The Authority of the Bible: Theories of Inspiration, Revelation and the Canon of Scripture* (New York: Paulist Press, 1985); Jack Rogers, ed., *Biblical Authority* (Waco, Tex.: Word Books, 1977); David L. Bartlett, *The Shape of Scriptural Authority* (Philadelphia: Fortress Press, 1983); L. William

Countryman, *Biblical Authority or Biblical Tyranny?: Scripture and the Christian Pilgrimage* (Valley Forge, Pa.: Trinity Press International, 1994).

3. Quoted in Carolyn J. Mooney, "Devout Professors on the Offensive," *Chronicle of Higher Education,* 4 May 1994, p. A18. See the comments in George M. Marsden, *The Outrageous Idea of Christian Scholarship* (New York: Oxford University Press, 1997), 5; Joel A. Carpenter, "Sustaining Christian Intellectual Commitments: Lessons from the Recent Past," in *The Future of Christian Higher Education,* ed. David S. Dockery and David P. Gushee (Nashville: Broadman & Holman, 1999), 105.

4. Thomas Kuhn, *The Structure of Scientific Revolutions* (Chicago: University of Chicago Press, 1962). See also James Conant and John Haugeland, eds., *The Road Since Structure: Philosophical Essays, 1970–1993, with an Autobiographical Interview* (Chicago: University of Chicago Press, 2000).

5. Mary Stewart Van Leeuwen, "Five Uneasy Questions, or: Will Success Spoil Christian Psychologists," *Journal of Psychology and Christianity* 15 (1996): 151.

6. See especially Marsden, *The Outrageous Idea of Christian Scholarship,* 44–58. Marsden notes, "Traditional religious viewpoints, I am saying, can be just as hospitable to scientifically sound investigation as many other viewpoints, all of which are ultimately grounded in some faith or other. Hence religious perspectives ought to be recognized as legitimate in the mainstream academy so long as their proponents are willing to support the rules necessary for constructive exchange of ideas in a pluralistic setting" (p. 45).

7. See especially Arthur Holmes, *All Truth Is God's Truth* (Grand Rapids, Mich.: Eerdmans, 1977).

8. Marsden asks (*The Outrageous Idea,* 47), "Is there something peculiar, though, about self-consciously Christian scholars that make them particularly likely to violate the essential canons of scientific investigation of the mainstream academy? Regarding most of the technical scholarship that makes up the vast majority of academic inquiry, there is no reason to expect such a difference. In the corridors of the pragmatic academy Christians and non-Christians can readily share basic standards of evidence and argument. These standards work in separating good arguments from bad, and on many topics they can establish a sort of 'public knowledge' that personas from many ideological sub-communities can agree on and which are not simply matters of opinion."

9. George Marsden, *The Soul of the American University: From Protestant Establishment to Established Nonbelief* (New York: Oxford University Press, 1994), 34.

10. Ibid.

11. James Tunstead Burtchaell, *The Dying of the Light: The Disengagement of Colleges & Universities from Their Christian Churches*

(Grand Rapids, Mich.: William B. Eerdmans Publishing Co., 1998); Carpenter, "Sustaining Christian Intellectual Commitments: Lessons from the Recent Past," 105–19.

12. This endeavor is gaining some attention in broader circles. See Alan Wolfe, "The Opening of the Evangelical Mind," *Atlantic Monthly* (October 2000).

13. Mark Noll, *Between Faith and Criticism: Evangelicals, Scholarship and the Bible in America* (San Francisco: Harper and Row, 1986), 6.

14. Contra, for example, the position put forward by Jack Rogers and Donald McKim, *The Authority and Interpretation of the Bible: An Historical Approach* (New York: Harper and Row, 1979) and Stanley Grenz, *Renewing the Center: Evangelical Theology in a Post-theological Era* (Grand Rapids, Mich.: Baker Academic, 2000), 53–84. See especially the extensive, devastating appraisal of Rogers and McKim by historian John D. Woodbridge, "Biblical Authority: Toward an Evaluation of the Rogers and McKim Proposal," in *Biblical Authority and Conservative Perspectives*, ed. Douglas Moo (Grand Rapids, Mich.: Kregel Publications, 1997), 9–64.

15. Wayne Grudem, in his *Systematic Theology* (Grand Rapids, Mich.: Zondervan, 1994), 47–138, departs from the pattern by moving from a general discussion of "The Word of God" in its various forms, to a discussion of the canon of the written Word of God, and then to "The Four Characteristics of Scripture," which are authority, clarity, necessity, and sufficiency. Thus the discussion of authority precedes the discussion of inerrancy and the distinctions between general revelation and special revelation are covered later under the necessity of Scripture.

16. Carl F. H. Henry, *God, Revelation and Authority, Vol. IV: God Who Speaks and Shows, Fifteen Theses, Part Three* (Waco, Tex.: Word, 1979), 68, 162.

17. Millard Erickson, *Christian Theology* (Grand Rapids, Mich.: Baker Book House, 1985), 153–259.

18. Ibid., 199.

19. Ibid., 221–22.

20. David S. Dockery, *Christian Scripture* (Nashville, Tenn.: Broadman & Holman, 1995), 15–75.

21. Ibid., 62.

22. Ibid., 70–71.

23. Some, of course, will charge that this reasoning is circular, but as Erickson points out, any appeal to an ultimate authority is open to the charge: "Either it bases its starting point upon itself, in which case it is guilty of circularity, or it bases itself upon some foundation other than that upon which it bases all its other articles, in which case it is guilty of inconsistency . . . . Note, however, that we are guilty of circularity only if the testimony of Scripture is taken as settling the matter. But surely the

Scripture writer's own claim should be taken into consideration as part of the process of formulating our hypothesis of the nature of Scripture." Erickson, *Christian Theology*, 201.

24. Stanley J. Grenz, *Theology for the Community of God* (Nashville: Broadman & Holman Publishers, 1994), 22.

25. Stanley J. Grenz, *Renewing the Center: Evangelical Theology in a Post-Theological Era*, 81–84.

26. Millard J. Erickson, *The Evangelical Left*, 81.

27. Grenz, *Theology for the Community of God*, 21–26. Donald Carson states, "[Grenz] prefers the direction illumined by Schleiermacher, arguing that the three sources or norms for theology are Scripture, tradition, and culture. This is, to say the least, decidedly unhelpful. Quite apart from the extraordinary complexities of linking Scripture and tradition in this way, the addition of culture is astonishing." See Donald Carson, *The Gagging of God*, 481.

28. Grenz, *Theology for the Community of God*, 22.

29. So Millard J. Erickson, *Postmodernizing the Faith: Evangelical Responses to the Challenge of Postmodernism* (Grand Rapids, Mich.: Baker Books, 1998), 97–98.

30. Erickson, *Postmodernizing the Faith*, 101.

31. Kevin J. Vanhoozer, *Is There a Meaning in This Text?: The Bible, the Reader and the Morality of Literary Knowledge* (Grand Rapids, Mich.: Zondervan, 1998), 86.

32. J. L. Austin, *How to Do Things with Words* (Cambridge, Mass.: Harvard University Press, 1962); John R. Searle, *Speech Acts: An Essay in the Philosophy of Language* (Cambridge: Cambridge University Press, 1969). On the application of speech-act theory to biblical interpretation, see Anthony Thiselton, *New Horizons in Hermeneutics: The Theory and Practice of Transforming Biblical Reading* (Grand Rapids, Mich.: Zondervan, 1992); "Interpreting God and the Postmodern Self: On Meaning, Manipulation and Promise," *Scottish Journal of Theology: Current Issues in Theology* (Edinburgh: T. & T. Clark, 1995).

33. Kevin J. Vanhoozer, "The Voice and the Actor: A Dramatic Proposal about the Ministry and Minstrelsy of Theology," in John G. Stackhouse Jr., ed., *Evangelical Futures: A Conversation on Theological Method* (Grand Rapid, Mich.: Baker Books, 2000), 63.

34. Ibid., 69, 76, 100.

35. We disagree with Jack Rogers and Donald McKim, who suggested that God's accommodation to human language necessitates that we make a distinction between the general message of Scripture and the details of the Scripture, which by virtue of their human origin are riddled with errors.

36. For different approaches to the doctrine of inspiration, see Dockery, *Christian Scripture*, 37–60; Erickson, *Christian Theology*, 206–20.

37. Erickson, *Christian Theology*, 199.

38. See James I. Packer, "The Adequacy of Human Language," in *Inerrancy*, ed. Norman L. Geisler (1980): 219–20. It should be noted here that "faith," as used by Packer, is not the modern conception of faith as "a leap in the dark" or a "choice to believe against all the evidence." A better depiction or analogy of biblical faith is the relational dynamic we often call "trust." In relationships we come to trust another because he or she has been shown to be trustworthy over time. Biblical faith involves trusting the God who has revealed himself to be trustworthy in contexts of human history in his established communities.

39. Vanhoozer, *Is There a Meaning in This Text*, 349.

40. Alistar E. McGrath, *Studies in Doctrine* (Grand Rapids, Mich.: Zondervan, 1997), 14.

Chapter 2, The Lessons of History

1. "Enrollments Surge at Christian Colleges," *The Chronicle of Higher Education*, 5 March 1999.

2. Beth McMurtrie, "Future of Religious Colleges Is Bright, Say Scholars and Administrators," *The Chronicle of Higher Education*, 9 October 2000, 1. [database online], accessed 9 October 2000, http://chronicle.com/daily/2000/20/2000100905n.htm; Internet.

3. Ibid., 1.

4. Alan Wolfe, "The Opening of the Evangelical Mind," *The Atlantic Monthly*, October 2000, 56–75.

5. Ibid.

6. Ibid.

7. James Tunstead Burtchaell, *The Dying of the Light: The Disengagement of Colleges and Universities from Their Christian Churches* (Grand Rapids, Mich.:William B. Eerdmans Publishing Co., 1998). George M. Marsden, *The Soul of the American University: From Protestant Establishment to Established Nonbelief* (New York: Oxford University Press, 1994).

8. Burtchaell, *The Dying of the Light*, 819.

9. Marsden, *The Soul of the American University*, 431.

10. George M. Marsden, *The Outrageous Idea of Christian Scholarship* (New York: Oxford University Press, 1997).

11. Northumberland Baptist Association, *Minutes, 1832* (n. p. n. d.), 2; cited in J. Orin Oliphant, *The Rise of Bucknell University* (New York: Appleton-Century-Crofts, 1965), 22.

12. Lewis Edwin Theiss, *Centennial History of Bucknell University: 1846–1946* (Williamsport, Pa.: Grit Publishing Co., 1946), 129.

13. The term "regular Baptist" refers to churches that were Calvinistic in theology and worship practice. Such "regular" Baptist churches were set over and against churches of Arminian persuasion (Separate or General Baptists) whose revivalistic and emotionalistic doctrine and practice were frowned on by the majority of Baptist churches in the wake of the First Great Awakening. Such Arminian churches were considered "irregular" in both doctrine and practice. For further consideration of this issue, see Robert G. Torbet, *A History of the Baptists* (Valley Forge: Judson Press, 1963).

14. Stephen W. Taylor, in the Philadelphia *Christian Chronicle*, 23 September 1846; cited in Oliphant, *The Rise of Bucknell University,* 31.

15. Oliphant, *The Rise of Bucknell University,* 255.

16. Ibid., 361.

17. Ibid., 362.

18. See, for example, Michael Payne, "Delving into the People Who Shaped the Bible," in *The Daily Item,* 10 December 2000.

19. Charlotte Allen, "The Postmodern Mission," *Lingua Franca,* December/January 2000, 50.

20. Roy Atwood and Douglas Wilson, *The Quest for Authentic Higher Learning* (Moscow, Idaho: Canon Press, 1996), 21.

21. John Calvin, *Institutes of the Christian Religion,* ed. John T. McNeill (Philadelphia: Westminster Press, 1960), 4.1.1, 1012.

22. Barna Research Group, "Confidence in the Church," 1991 Barna Research Group Study [database on-line]; available from http://barna.org.

23. Mark E. Dever, *Nine Marks of a Healthy Church* (Wheaton, Ill.: Crossway Books, 2000), 14.

24. D. A. Carson, "Can There Be a Christian University?" *The Southern Baptist Journal of Theology,* 1 (Fall 1997): 28.

25. John Baird, *More Than Knowledge* (St. David's, Pa.: Eastern College, 1992), 3.

26. Carl F. H. Henry, *God, Revelation, and Authority,* 6 vols. (Wheaton, Ill.: Crossway Books, 1999).

27. Carl F. H. Henry, *Gods of This Age or God of the Ages?* R. Albert Mohler Jr., ed. (Nashville: Broadman & Holman, 1994), 78.

28. Colin Gunton, "The Indispensability of Theological Understanding: Theology in the University," in *Essentials of Christian Community* (Edinburgh: T & T Clark, 1996), 267.

29. Wolfe, "The Opening of the Evangelical Mind," 56.

30. Gerald Bray, *Creeds, Councils, and Christ* (Great Britain: Mentor, 1997), 10.

31. Marsden, *The Soul of the American University,* 101.

32. Søren Kierkegaard, *Attack upon "Christendom,"* trans. Walter Lowrie (Princeton, N.J.: Princeton University Press), 224.

33. Ibid., 223. On a historiographical note, it appears that in this same passage Kierkegaard was the first philosopher or theologian who employed the phrase "to think Christianly."

Chapter 3, Theological and Philosophical Foundations

1. T. S. Eliot, "Modern Education and the Classics," in *Selected Essays*, new ed. (New York: Harcourt, Brace and Company, 1950), 452.

2. I would thus argue that a Christian doctrine of creation requires a realist, rather than an antirealist view of how we relate to the world. Simply put, realism affirms that there is an external (to me) world that truly exists independent of my thoughts and/or experience. Anti-realism affirms that the external world is dependent on my thoughts and/or experience. See Keith Yandell, "Modernism, Post-Modernism, and the Minimalist Canons of Common Grace," *Christian Scholar's Review* 27 (Fall 1997): 15–26.

3. Richard M. Weaver, "Gnostics of Education," in *Visions of Order: The Cultural Crisis of Our Time* (Wilmington, Del.: Intercollegiate Studies Institute, 1964; reprint, 1995), 126.

4. Marion Montgomery, *The Truth of Things: Liberal Arts and the Recovery of Reality* (Dallas: Spence Publishing Company, 1999).

5. Weaver, "Gnostics of Education," 118ff.

6. Ibid., 120.

7. Ibid.

8. Graeme Goldsworthy, *According to Plan: The Unfolding Revelation of God in the Bible* (Leicester, England: InterVarsity Press, 1991), 56. This theme is particularly prominent in the writings of Cornelius Van Til. Cf. Greg Bahnsen, *Van Til's Apologetic: Readings and Analysis* (Philadelphia, Pa.: Presbyterian and Reformed Publishing Company, 1998).

9. When I use the word *autonomous* here, I am speaking of it in the classic liberal sense used by such thinkers as John Stuart Mill. Mill argued that the individual is the primary unit in society, and that the individual really "owns" himself. A Christian might appreciate Mill's emphasis on liberty, but a Christian's whole foundation and understanding of liberty is ultimately quite different. We do not own ourselves at all. We are either slaves to Christ or slaves to sin. The primary unit in society is the family (and thus neither the individual nor the omnipotent state is the primary unit of society). On the Christian view, then, we come into the world *already* in a network of relationships—relationships that render us accountable to others beside ourselves. While I cannot agree with it in all regards, the understanding of modernity and postmodernity advocated by James McClendon and Nancey Murphy is certainly helpful in thinking through these issues. See their article, "Distinguishing Modern and Postmodern Theologies," *Modern Theology* 5 (April 1989): 191–217.

10. On this point we certainly hit an area of contention. As soon as someone speaks of "God's interpretation of reality" (which I am doing), one often hears the following responses: "This is impossible"; "There is no bird's-eye view of reality"; "The Enlightenment quest for absolute certainty has failed"; etc. This position is understandable coming from the non-Christian, but when Christians begin to speak this way, it is worthy to stop and take note. I am not claiming to have *exhaustive* knowledge of what God thinks on this or that issue. I am claiming that we can, and indeed do, have *true* knowledge of what God thinks on this or that issue. The contemporary claim (heard, if even in a softer form, from some Christian thinkers) that we cannot possess any sort of metanarrative that explains and gives purpose to all of human life is at its heart a rejection of the notion that God has the ability to speak, and that humans have the capacity to hear and understand such speech. Richard Lints is certainly correct, that at this point Christians must reject the claim of certain "postmodern" thinkers (whatever that means) that we are so tradition-bound, so embedded in our historical particularity, that we cannot have access to either transcendent truths or a metanarrative. Cf. Richard Lints, *The Fabric of Theology: A Prolegomenon to Evangelical Theology* (Grand Rapids, Mich.: William B. Eerdmans Publishing Company, 1993). Lints writes (p. 252), "Postmodern theology has to be 'from below' because the gospel is 'from below.' The postmoderns will brook no compromise on this point—which is why there will always remain a theological chasm between the evangelical and the postmodern theological visions. The fundamental methodological movement of the evangelical theological framework is not from the ground of human experience to the superstructure of ideology but rather from the interpretive superstructure of biblical ideology to an understanding of human experience." On the importance of a full-orbed doctrine of revelation, I was immensely helped early in my studies by C. S. Lewis's essay, "Modern Theology and Biblical Criticism," in *Christian Reflections* (Grand Rapids, Mich.: William B. Eerdmans Publishing Company, 1967), 152–66.

11. Exactly how Adam represents us broaches an important issue in Christian theology. For an excellent treatment of the doctrine of original sin, see the recent work by Henri Blocher, *Original Sin: Illuminating the Riddle* (Grand Rapids, Mich.: William B. Eerdmans Publishing Company, 1997). Blocher is essentially Augustinian-Reformed and traces the history of the doctrine and then offers his own position in the final chapter.

12. For a helpful discussion of sanctification in the New Testament, see David Peterson, *Possessed by God: A New Testament Theology of Sanctification and Holiness* (Grand Rapids, Mich.: William B. Eerdmans Publishing Company, 1995).

13. See John Calvin, *Institutes of the Christian Religion*, vol. 20, The Library of Christian Classics, ed. John T. McNeill, trans. Ford Lewis

Battles (Philadelphia: The Westminster Press, 1960), I.V.12 (pp. 64–65). Calvin writes, "For as rashness and superficiality are joined to ignorance and darkness, scarcely a single person has ever been found who did not fashion for himself an idol or specter in place of God. Surely, just as waters boil up from a vast, full spring, so does an immense crowd of gods flow forth from the human mind, while each one, in wandering about with too much license, wrongly invents this or that about God himself."

14. Cf. John Murray, *Redemption Accomplished and Applied* (Grand Rapids, Mich.: William B. Eerdmans Publishing Company, 1955).

15. By speaking of a *telos* under the rubric of redemption, I am not denying that there is a *telos* in creation, and I am not trying to drive a wedge between creation and redemption (as if a *telos* only suddenly sprang into existence with redemption). Creation and redemption are both part of God's sovereign plan, and there is both continuity and discontinuity between them. Colin Gunton has expressed concern that Western theological thought, due largely to the influence of Augustine, has tended to divorce creation from redemption. Among his many writings, see Colin Gunton, "The Doctrine of Creation," in *The Cambridge Companion to Christian Doctrine*, ed. Colin E. Gunton (Cambridge: Cambridge University Press, 1997), 141–57; idem, *The One, the Three and the Many: God, Creation and the Culture of Modernity* (Cambridge: Cambridge University Press, 1994); idem, *The Triune Creator: A Historical and Systematic Study* (Grand Rapids, Mich.: William B. Eerdmans Publishing Company, 1998). I offer a critique of Gunton in my unpublished dissertation, "Colin Gunton and Failure of Augustine: An Exposition and Analysis of the Theology of Colin Gunton in Light of Augustine's *De Trinitate*" (Ph.D. diss., Baylor University, 2000).

16. Augustine, *The City of God*, trans. Marcus Dods (New York: The Modern Library, 1950), X.24, 29.

17. Augustine, *The Trinity* IV.4 The Works of Saint Augustine. A Translation for the 21st Century, trans., Edmund Hill, ed. John E. Rotelle (Brooklyn, N.Y.: New City Press, 1991).

18. Earl C. Muller, "Rhetorical and Theological Issues in the Structuring of Augustine's *De Trinitate*," in *Studia Patristica* XXVII, ed. Elizabeth A. Livingstone (Leuven: Peeters, 1993), 359.

19. Weaver, "Gnostics of Education," 122. Weaver goes on to write, "Intermediate causes are of course the subject matter of science, and hence this attitude has the effect of orienting all education toward science." If Weaver is correct, then a thoroughgoing Christian approach to education would simultaneously (1) give proper place to the reality of ultimate causes (i.e., first and final causes), and (2) remove modern science as the *de facto* queen of the sciences. Modern science would not thereby be rejected or jettisoned. Rather, a truly Christian view of education would have no reason or motivation for seeing modern science as superior or as

more important than other disciplines. And further, the empirical method would be seen as one way of knowing among others, and a truly Christian epistemology and world and life view would recognize that the empirical method is not "neutral" or "value-free" or "presuppositionless" or "faith neutral" but depends on a whole host of presuppositions that are often not stated or recognized (e.g., the object being examined really is there; I am really seeing what is truly there; there is a correspondence between my mind and reality; etc.).

20. Of course, in one sense we simply *cannot* "dethrone" Christ from his proper place of lordship. However, I have texts such as 1 Peter 3:15 in mind, where Peter can write, "but sanctify [i.e., 'set apart'] Christ as Lord in your hearts" (NASB). Christ *is* Lord, but as Christians we are always to be about the task of looking at our hearts to see if we are truly "sanctifying Christ" as Lord in our hearts.

21. Christopher Derrick, *Escape from Scepticism: Liberal Education as If Truth Mattered* (La Salle, Ill.: Sherwood Sugden & Company, 1977), 111.

22. Richard John Neuhaus, "The Christian University: Eleven Theses," *First Things* 59 (January 1996): 22.

23. These definitions come from David S. Dockery, *The Doctrine of the Bible* (Nashville, Tenn.: Convention Press, 1991), 12–19.

24. I have not attempted to deal in detail here with the issue of biblical authority. For such a discussion see the chapter by George H. Guthrie in chapter 1 of this volume.

25. Of course, this whole essay is an attempt to apply the teachings of Scripture to the educational task. However, it is necessary intentionally to affirm the centrality of Scripture to such a task.

26. Neuhaus, "The Christian University," 22.

27. Ronald H. Nash, *The Word of God and the Mind of Man: The Crisis of Revealed Truth in Contemporary Theology* (Phillipsburg, N.J.: Presbyterian and Reformed Publishing, 1992), 81.

28. Ibid.

29. Ibid., 59.

30. This is not a particularly easy passage to translate. There is some debate as to whether "coming into the world" is describing the Logos (Christ) or "every man" (i.e., is it [1] "the true light which, coming into the world", or [2] "every man coming into the world."). However, in either reading the central point remains: it is the Logos which "enlightens" (*photizo*–"shed light on," "shine," "give light to," "illuminate") every man.

31. Augustine, *The Teacher* (*De Magistro*), vol. 9, Ancient Christian Writers, trans. Joseph M. Collerman (New York: Newman Press, 1978), book 1 (p. 131).

32. Ibid., *The Teacher* 11.33, 34 (pp. 173–74).

33. Ibid., 11.34 (p. 174).

34. Ibid., 11.38 (p. 177).

35. Ibid., 12.40 (p. 179).

36. For more on Augustine and illumination, see Ronald H. Nash, *The Light of the Mind: St. Augustine's Theory of Knowledge* (Lexington, Ky.: The University Press of Kentucky, 1969); idem, *The Word of God and the Mind of Man* (esp. ch. 8, "The Christian Rationalism of St. Augustine").

37. Dallas Willard, "The Unhinging of the American Mind: Derrida as Pretext," in *European Philosophy and the American Academy*, ed. Barry Smith (La Salle, Ill.: The Hegeler Institute Monist Library of Philosophy, 1994), 4. Willard's essay is one of the most sane and helpful pieces I have read on the perplexing (but already fading?) issue of deconstructionism.

38. Ibid., 6.

39. Ibid., 9–14. Willard argues that ultimately Jacques Derrida offered nothing genuinely new to the world of philosophy. He simply reflected the three tendencies just mentioned. Willard writes, "Derrida is a brilliant and fascinating individual who has been able to make a personal style look like cognitive substance in a professional context where knowledge in the traditional sense has already been socially displaced" (p. 18).

40. John Henry Newman, *The Idea of a University Defined and Illustrated in Nine Discourses Delivered to the Catholics of Dublin In Occasional Lectures and Essays Addressed to the Members of the Catholic University*, ed. Martin J. Svaglic (Notre Dame, Ind.: University of Notre Dame Press, 1982), 77.

41. Ibid.

42. This is the title of Marion Montgomery's most recent book, and Montgomery gets it from Thomas Aquinas.

43. Derrick, *Escape from Scepticism*, 100.

44. Persons such as Frederick Wilhelmsen are skeptical of most "Great Books programs." See his, "The Great Books: Enemies of Wisdom," *Modern Age* (Summer/Fall 1987): 323–31. Wilhelmsen's article is an important read, particularly for Christians concerned with plotting out a trajectory for true education. The appeal of "Great Books" can be quite strong, but all components of genuinely Christian education must always be seen in light of the greater ends of education: the formation of a wise and virtuous person, and the glory of God. Wilhelmsen writes (p. 327), "The Great Books approach tends inevitably towards producing the skill needed to read intelligently a philosophical work, but it does not, of itself, help turn a man into an incipient philosopher." This is the heart of Wilhelmsen's concern. We should note, however, that a knowledge of the history of thought and ideas *is* essential to a truly liberal education. Indeed, it is hard to imagine any true education that does not consist of a massive and thorough immersion in the central texts and thinkers of one's culture.

45. John Henry Newman, *The Idea of a University*, 75.

46. I use the terms *evangelical* and *Roman Catholic* in their historic and theological sense. That is, I am using both terms to describe respective positions that have histories and that have a body of confessional literature that constitutes the central tenets of each tradition. Thus, I am not using "evangelical" simply to describe a twentieth-century phenomenon featuring such luminaries as Billy Graham, Carl F. H. Henry, etc. I am using *evangelical* essentially in its Reformation sense as that movement which believed it necessary to attempt to correct perceived errors in the Roman Catholic Church. This tradition has a body of confessional literature such as the Westminster Confession of Faith, the Heidelberg Catechism, the Formula of Concord, the Thirty-Nine Articles, and the London Confession. Roman Catholicism also has a confessional heritage that can be easily accessed through its own writings, for example, the most recent *Catechism of the Catholic Church* (Rome: Urbi et Orbi Communications, 1994).

47. Augustine, *Sermons* 43, 7, 9 (*Patrologia Latina* 38, 257–58).

48. See the helpful article by Ted M. Dorman, "*Fides Quaerens Intellectum*: The Soul of a Christian University," *The Southern Baptist Journal of Theology* 1, no. 3 (1997): 58–67.

49. Van Til's understanding has not been accepted by all Christian apologists and scholars. Ronald Nash accuses Van Til of "irrationality," and Van Til and Gordon H. Clark had a rather acrimonious feud over these issues. Ronald Nash's disagreements with Van Til can be found in his *The Word of God and the Mind of Man*. John Frame offers a summary of the Van Til/Clark feud in Frame's *Cornelius Van Til: An Analysis of His Thought* (Phillipsburg, N.J.: Presbyterian and Reformed Publishing, 1995), 97–113. Cf. Frame, *The Doctrine of the Knowledge of God. A Theology of Lordship* (Philipsburg, N.J.: Presbyterian and Reformed Publishing Company, 1987), 21–40. One of Clark's disciples, John W. Robbins, has written a critique of Van Til, *Cornelius Van Til: The Man and the Myth* (Jefferson, Md.: The Trinity Foundation, 1986).

50. Cornelius Van Til, *Toward a Reformed Apologetics* (Philadelphia: privately printed, 1972); quoted in Greg L. Bahnsen, *Van Til's Apologetic: Readings and Analysis* (Philipsburg, N.J.: Presbyterian & Reformed Publishing Company, 1998), 22.

51. Bahnsen, *Van Til's Apologetic*, 4–5.

52. Ibid., 5.

53. Ibid., 6.

54. Cornelius Van Til, "My Credo," in *Jerusalem and Athens: Critical Discussions on the Theology and Apologetics of Cornelius Van Til*, ed. E. R. Geehan (Philadelphia: Presbyterian and Reformed, 1971), 4–5; quoted in Bahnsen, *Van Til's Apologetic*, 20.

55. I have not attempted in this section to tackle all the issues related to faith, rationality, and epistemology. A key work is the important text

by Alvin Plantinga and Nicholas Wolterstorff, *Faith and Rationality: Reason and Belief in God* (South Bend, Ind.: University of Notre Dame Press, 1983). Also see Paul Helm, *Faith and Understanding* (Grand Rapids, Mich.: William B. Eerdmans Publishing Company, 1997); Paul Helm, ed., *Faith and Reason* (Oxford: Oxford University Press, 1999).

56. Augustine, *The Trinity* XV.20 (pp. 409–10).

57. Augustine, *Teaching Christianity* (*De Doctrina Christiania*), trans. Edmund Hill, ed. John E. Rotelle (Brooklyn, N.Y.: New City Press, 1992), I.2 (pp. 106–107). The translator of the New City Press translation has translated *De Doctrina Christiana* as "Teaching Christianity." I have retained the traditional English title "On Christian Doctrine" simply for clarity's sake, since most readers are more familiar with that title.

58. Ibid., I.3.

59. Ibid., I.5.

60. *Logocentrism* can be used in different ways. Derrida rejects the Enlightenment enthronement of reason (a certain type of "logocentrism"—where the *logos* denotes reason). But he rejects also any sort of "logocentrism" where *Christ* is the *Logos* at the center of reality.

61. George Steiner, *Real Presences* (Chicago: The University of Chicago Press, 1989), 119.

62. Because God communicates, and we are made in his image, we have the ability to communicate. Derrida has rejected the reality of such a God, and his denial of meaningful communication is ultimately predicated on his *theological* commitment (or lack thereof). Again Steiner (p. 120): "It is Derrida's strength to have seen so plainly that the issue is neither linguistic-aesthetic nor philosophical in any traditional, debatable sense— where such tradition and debate incorporate, perpetuate the very ghosts which are to be exorcized. The issue is, quite simply, that of the meaning of meaning as it is re-insured by the postulate of the existence of God. 'In the beginning was the Word.' There was no such beginning, says deconstruction; only the play of sounds and markers amid the mutations of time." Derrida's sad and nihilistic paradigm must be rejected by the Christian and by the Christian university. In its place, the Christian affirms that since this is a world created by a communicating God, communication is indeed a possibility. For a helpful critique of Derrida that uses certain Augustinian insights, see R. V. Young, "Derrida or Deity? Deconstruction in the Presence of the Word," and "Deconstruction and the Fear and Loathing of Logos," in *At War with the Word: Literary Theory and Liberal Education* (Wilmington, Del.: Intercollegiate Studies Institute, 1999), 31–58, 59–84. Young's conclusion is as follows: "He [i.e., Derrida] is the manifestation of what happens when philosophic reason is drained of religious faith, and he is right about the alienated, deconstructed, angst-ridden postmodern world." Also see David Lyle Jeffrey, *People of the Book: Christian Identity and Literary Culture* (Grand

Rapids, Mich.: William B. Eerdmans Publishing Company, 1996). See also Daniel E. Ritchie, *Reconstructing Literature in an Ideological Age: A Biblical Poetics and Literary from Milton to Burke* (Grand Rapids, Mich.: William B. Eerdmans Publishing Company), 268–88. Also helpful is J. I. Packer, "The Adequacy of Human Language," in *Honouring the Written Word of God*, vol. 3, The Collected Shorter Writings of J. I. Packer (Carlisle, U.K.: Paternoster Press, 1999), 23–49.

63. This reality could be illustrated by a number of Scripture references. One such example is found in Revelation 12. In the context, John speaks of a war in heaven between Michael and his angels and the dragon (12:7). The great dragon is defeated (12:9), and John states that "they [i.e., Michael and his angels] overcame him [i.e., the dragon] because of the blood of the Lamb and because of the word of their testimony" (12:11 NASB). What is important to note (whether one takes Revelation 12 to be referring to first-century events, the life of the church, or to some future event), is that the dragon is defeated by "the blood of the lamb" (i.e., the cross), and by "the word of their testimony" (i.e., presumably a testimony of what Jesus had done—which would certainly include the cross and resurrection). The cross does not only, in a sense, work backwards (Heb. 9:15; cf. Rom. 3:25), but the power of the cross is also the *means* by which evil (here the dragon) in the *future* is defeated.

64. For insight into the past/future components, see John Piper, *Future Grace* (Sisters, Oreg.: Multnomah Books, 1995). *Future Grace* is more concerned with the future component of the Christian faith, although the past-looking component is not denied. Graeme Goldsworthy's work has been very helpful to me in understanding the centrality of the gospel for all of history. See his *Gospel in Revelation: Gospel and Apocalypse* (Carlisle, U.K.: The Paternoster Press, 1994), and *According to Plan: The Unfolding Revelation of God in the Bible* (Leicester, England: InterVarsity Press, 1991). On the future (or eschatological) orientation of the whole of Scripture, see William J. Dumbrell, *The Search for Order: Biblical Eschatology in Focus* (Grand Rapids, Mich.: Baker Book House, 1994).

65. Weaver, "Gnostics of Education," 132–33.

66. On this general theme, see the excellent essay by the late Mel Bradford, "Against the Barbarians," in *Against the Barbarians and Other Reflections on Familiar Themes* (Columbia and London: University of Missouri Press, 1992): 7–16.

67. T. S. Eliot, "Modern Education and the Classics," in *Selected Essays*, new edition (New York: Harcourt, Brace and Company, 1950), 452.

68. A helpful essay on understanding different types and levels of goals is Jonathan Edwards's work, "The End for Which God Created the World." The essay has been reprinted with a lengthy introductory essay (really a small book itself) by John Piper. See John Piper, *God's Passion for His Glory: Living the Vision of Jonathan Edwards, with the Complete*

Text of "The End for Which God Created the World" (Wheaton, Ill.: Crossway Books, 1998).

69. See John Dewey, *The School and Society,* ed. Jo Ann Boydston (Carbondale and Edwardsville, Ill.: Southern Illinois University Press; London and Amsterdam: Feffer & Simons, Inc., 1980); idem, *Democracy and Education: An Introduction to the Philosophy of Education* (New York: The Macmillan Company, 1917).

70. Dewey, *Democracy and Education,* 117. Dewey writes (p. 127), "Educators have to be on their guard against ends that are alleged to be general and ultimate." Dewey rejects "externally imposed aims," those aims "imposed" on the aims/goals of education from the outside. Dewey writes, "In education, the currency of these externally imposed aims is responsible for the emphasis put upon the notion of preparation for a remote future and for rendering the work of both teacher and pupil mechanical and slavish" (p. 129). That is, according to Dewey, ultimate, transcendent goals are corrupting of genuine education.

71. To the reader who has never seen "equality" or "democracy" spoken of in negative terms, I would highly recommend the winsome essay by C. S. Lewis, "Screwtape Proposes a Toast." The essay appears as an appendix to most editions of Lewis's *The Screwtape Letters.* Lewis's essay is an explicit critique of education in the U.S. Lewis's key point is that one must choose between excellence and equality. You simply cannot have both. By challenging students toward excellence, it is inevitable that there will be different levels of performance, and some will simply perform at a higher level. If true "equality" is the goal, then educators must be constantly seeking to discourage students from academic excellence.

72. Russell Kirk, Foreward to Thomas Molnar, *The Future of Education* (New York: Fleet Publishing Corporation, 1961), 11.

73. Russell Kirk, "The Revitalized College: A Model," in *Education in a Free Society,* ed. Anne Husted Burleigh (Indianapolis: Liberty Press, 1978), 135–36.

74. This exchange is found in William Bentley Ball, *Mere Creatures of the State?: A View from the Courtroom* (Notre Dame, Ind.: Crisis Books, 1994), 69. Chapter 5 of this volume is devoted to the *Wisconsin v. Yoder* case, in which the state of Wisconsin was trying to intimidate an Amish community in Wisconsin because the Amish would not send their children to the government schools. Ball's books is an excellent primer on the sad reality of the civil government's and educational establishment's hostility to those who do not want to send their children to government schools.

75. This memorable phrase is the title of a book by A. J. Conyers, *The Eclipse of Heaven: Rediscovering the Hope of a World Beyond* (Downers Grove: InterVarsity Press, 1992; reprint, St. Augustine Press, 1999). Conyers's basic thesis is that in the modern world there has indeed been an "eclipse of heaven," in that the lives of most modern people are not

informed, as in past ages, by a vision of the future, by a transcendent reality—God and his heaven.

76. James V. Schall, "The Recovery of Permanent Things," in *Another Sort of Learning. Selected Contrary Essays on How Finally to Acquire an Education While Still in College or Anywhere Else: Containing Some Belated Advice about How to Employ Your Leisure Time When Ultimate Questions Remain Perplexing in Spite of Your Highest Earned Academic Degree, Together with Sundry Book Lists Nowhere Else in Captivity to Be Found* (San Francisco: Ignatius Press, 1988), 176.

77. C. S. Lewis, "Learning in War-Time," in *The Weight of Glory and Other Addresses* (Grand Rapids, Mich.: William B. Eerdmans Publishing Company, 1941), 43–54.

78. Ibid., 49.

79. James Boswell, *The Life of Samuel Johnson,* vol. I (London: Oxford, 1931), 418; quoted in James V. Schall, "On Teaching the Important Things," in *Another Sort of Learning,* 46.

80. Among the many studies, see George M. Marsden, *The Soul of the American University: From Protestant Establishment to Established Nonbelief* (New York: Oxford University Press, 1994); James Tunstead Burtchaell, *The Dying of the Light: The Disengagement of Colleges and Universities from Their Christian Churches* (Grand Rapids, Mich.: William B. Eerdmans Publishing Company, 1998).

81. I would like to thank my colleague Paul Munson for comments, criticisms, and conversations during the writing of this paper, which hopefully contributed to a better final product.

Chapter 4, The Influence of C. S. Lewis

1. W. Brown Patterson, "C. S. Lewis: Personal Reflections," in *Sewanee,* Spring 1999, 10–11.

2. C. S. Lewis, *The Abolition of Man* (New York: Macmillan, 1955), 28–29.

3. Patterson, "C. S. Lewis: Personal Reflections," 10.

4. C. S. Lewis, *A Preface to Paradise Lost* (New York: Oxford University Press, 1961), v.

5. George Sayers, *Jack: C. S. Lewis and His Times* (San Francisco: Harper & Row, Publishers, 1988), 179.

6. Lewis, *Preface,* 1.

7. Ibid., 5.

8. Ibid., 9.

9. Ibid., 21.

10. Ibid., 22.

11. Sayers, *Jack,* 182.

12. Lewis, *Abolition,* 14.

13. Michael D. Aeschliman, *The Restitution of Man: C. S. Lewis and the Case Against Scientism* (Grand Rapids, Mich.: William B. Eerdmans, 1983), 67.

14. Lewis, *Abolition,* 15.

15. Ibid., 16–17.

16. Ibid., 23.

17. Sayers, *Jack,* 244.

18. Ibid., 244.

19. Ibid., 244.

20. Lewis, *Abolition,* 34.

21. Ibid.

22. Lewis, *Preface,* 29.

23. Ibid., 29–30.

24. Ibid., 54.

25. Sayers, *Jack,* 168–170.

26. C. S. Lewis, *Mere Christianity* (London: Fontana Books, 1960), 45. The phrase "farther back and higher up" anticipates the great refrain in the final chapter of the final book of *The Chronicles of Narnia.* In *The Last Battle* those who arrive at the "ideal" Narnia exclaim "further up and further in."

27. Ibid., 70.

28. Lewis, *Preface,* 55.

29. Ibid., 56–57.

30. Ibid., 126.

31. Ibid., 127.

32. Ibid., 95. Here we find Lewis using the term "mere Christianity," which he would later adopt as the title for the collection of radio broadcasts he made during the war. Lewis borrowed the term from Richard Baxter, the prominent Puritan pastor and theologian who came to prominence during the Commonwealth and Protectorate, only to suffer under the great persecution during the Restoration. See "Mere Christianity" in *The C. S. Lewis Readers' Encyclopedia,* ed. by Jeffrey D. Schultz and John G. West Jr. (Grand Rapids, Mich.: Zondervan Publishing House, 1998), 270.

33. Sayers, *Jack,* 163–64.

34. Lewis, *Preface,* 101.

35. C. S. Lewis, "Evil and God," in *God in the Dock,* ed. Walter Hooper (Grand Rapids, Mich.: William B. Eerdmans Publishing Co., 1970), 22.

36. Ibid., 22.

37. Ibid., 23.

38. Ibid., 24.

39. Ibid., 104.

40. Ibid., 105.

41. Sayers, *Jack*, 185.

42. Lewis, *Preface*, 116.

43. Sayers, *Jack*, 180.

44. Thomas Talbott, "The Problem of Pain," *The C. S. Lewis Readers' Encyclopedia*, 340.

Chapter 5, Christian Worldview, Ethics, and Culture

1. Thomas Cahill, *The Gifts of the Jews* (New York: Doubleday, 1998), ch. 1.

2. Stanley J. Grenz, *The Moral Quest* (Downers Grove: InterVarsity, 1997), 78.

3. Marx, quoted in Richard Norman, *The Moral Philosophers*, 1st ed. (Oxford: Oxford University Press, 1983), 188.

4. The figure comes from the authoritative recent work on Communism: *The Black Book of Communism*, edited by Stephane Courtois et. al. (Cambridge: Harvard University Press, 1999), 4.

5. Grenz, *Moral Quest*.

6. For a fuller discussion, see David P. Gushee and Robert H. Long, *A Bolder Pulpit* (Valley Forge: Judson Press, 1998), 40–42.

7. For an important recent work structured along precisely these lines, see Charles Colson and Nancy Pearcey, *How Now Shall We Live?* (Wheaton: Tyndale, 1999).

8. For an account of this development, see Barbara Dafoe Whitehead, *The Divorce Culture* (New York: Knopf, 1997).

9. For a similar discussion of the importance of evangelism and church as social change strategies, see Stephen Charles Mott, *Biblical Ethics and Social Change* (New York: Oxford, 1982), chs. 6–7.

10. David P. Gushee, ed., *Christians and Politics Beyond the Culture Wars* (Grand Rapids, Mich.: Baker, 2000), 30.

Chapter 6, Faith and Learning

1. John Naisbitt, *Megatrends: Ten New Directions Transforming Our Lives* (New York: Warner Books, 1982), 24.

2. U.S. Bureau of the Census, *Statistical Abstract of the United States: 1998* (Austin, Tex.: Hoover's Business Press, 1998), 580–81.

3. Win Treese, "The Internet Index, Number 24." [database on-line] available at: <http://new-website.openmarket.com/intindex/99-05-s.htm>.

4. Ibid.

5. Naisbitt, *Megatrends*, 24.

6. U.S. Bureau of the Census, 826.

7. Mark S. Lettman, ed., *A Statistical Portrait of the United States: Social Conditions and Trends* (Lanham, Md.: Bernan Press, 1998), 140–43.

8. Charles William Eliot, "Address on the Opening of the New Building," *American Museum of Natural History 8th and 9th Annual Reports* (1878): 49–52.

9. Ibid.

10. Del Ratzsch, *Philosophy of Science* (Downers Grove, Ill.: InterVarsity Press, 1986), 104.

11. *On Prescription against Heretics,* chap. 7, trans. Peter Holmes, in The Ante-Nicene Fathers, ed. Alexander Roberts and James Donaldson, 10 vols. (New York: Charles Scribner's Sons, 1896–1903), 3:246.

12. Ian G. Barbour, *Religion and Science: Historical and Contemporary Issues* (New York: HarperCollins, 1997), 77–105.

13. John Brooke and Geoffrey Cantor, *Reconstructing Nature: The Engagement of Science and Religion* (Edinburgh: T&T Clark, 1998), chapter 8.

14. Harry L. Poe and Jimmy H. Davis, *Science and Religion: An Evangelical Dialogue* (Nashville: Broadman & Holman, 2000).

15. For a similar experience, see also Harold Heie, "Integration and Conversation," in *The University Through the Eyes of Faith,* ed. S. Moore (Indianapolis, Ind.: Light and Life Communications, 1988), 62.

16. Paul Tillich, "The Relationship Today Between Science and Religion," in *The Student Seeks an Answer,* ed. John A. Clark, Ingraham Lectures in Philosophy and Religion at Colby College, 1951–1959 (Waterville, Maine: Colby College Press, 1960), 302.

17. Stephen Jay Gould, *Rocks of Ages: Science and Religion in the Fullness of Life* (New York: The Ballantine Publishing Group, 1999), 4.

18. John Dewey, *Quest for Certainty: A Study of the Relation of Knowledge and Action* (New York: Capricorn Books Edition, 1960; originally published 1929), 255–56.

19. Arthur Holmes, *All Truth Is God's Truth* (Grand Rapids, Mich.: William B. Eerdmans Publishing Co., 1977).

20. John Paul II, "Message," in *Physics, Philosophy, and Theology: A Common Quest for Understanding,* ed. Robert John Russell, William R. Stoeger, and George V. Coyne (Vatican Observatory: Vatican City State and Notre Dame: University of Notre Dame, 1988), M13.

21. Heie, "Integration and Conversation," 63.

22. Robert T. Pennock, *Tower of Babel: The Evidence against the New Creationism* (Cambridge, Mass.: MIT Press, 1999), 271.

23. For a further discussion of this topic, please see Barbour, *Religion and Science,* pp. 106–136.

24. For a more detailed discussion of this concept, please see Alfred North Whitehead, *Science and the Modern World* (New York: Macmillan, 1925), chap. 1; E. L. Mascall, *Christian Theology and Natural Science* (New York: The Ronald Press Company, 1956), chap. 3; and Nancy

Pearcey and Charles B. Thaxton, *The Soul of Science: Christian Faith and Natural Philosophy* (Wheaton, Ill.: Crossway Books, 1994), chap. 1.

25. Quoted in David C. Lindberg and Ronald L. Numbers, *God and Nature: Historical Essays on the Encounter between Christianity and Science* (Berkeley, Calif.: University of California Press, 1986), 322.

26. Private conversations with Michael Dembski and Paul Nelson.

27. For a more detailed discussion of these first two cases, please see *Teaching Science in a Climate of Controversy: A View from the American Scientific Affiliation* (Ipswich, Mass.: American Scientific Affiliation, 1986), 18–21.

28. Christopher P. Sloan, "Feather for T. Rex? New birdlike fossils are missing links in dinosaur evolution," *National Geographic* 196 (November 1999): 98–107.

29. R. Monastersky, "All Mixed Up over Birds and Dinosaurs," *Science News* 157 (January 15, 2000): 38.

30. Xu Xing, "letter to the editor" *National Geographic* 197 (March 2000): Forum.

Chapter 7, Christian Worldview and Literature

1. Leland Ryken, "Afterword," *Contemporary Literary Theory: A Christian Appraisal*, eds. Clarence Walhout and Leland Ryken (Grand Rapids, Mich.: William B. Eerdmans Publishing Company, 1991), 299.

2. Louise Rosenblatt, *The Reader, the Text, the Poem* (Carbondale, Ill.: Southern Illinois University Press, 1978).

3. Charles. E. May, *The Short Story: The Reality of Artifice* (New York: Twayne Publishers, 1995), 68.

4. Percy Bysshe Shelley, "Ode to the West Wind," in *The Norton Anthology of World Masterpieces*, ed. Maynard Mack et al., ex. ed. in 2 vols. (New York: W.W. Norton, 1995), 2:815.

5. Susan V. Gallagher and Roger Lundin, *Literature Through the Eyes of Faith* (San Francisco: HarperSanFrancisco, 1989), 131.

6. Earl J. Wilcox and Gloria Godfrey Jones, "Guest Editors' Introduction," *CEA Critic* 62 (1999): 1.

7. David Lyle Jeffrey, *A Dictionary of Biblical Tradition in English Literature* (Grand Rapids, Mich.: William B. Eerdmans Publishing Company, 1992).

8. Roland Bartel with James S. Ackerman and Thayer S. Warshaw, *Biblical Images in Literature* (Nashville: Abingdon Press, 1975).

9. Charles E. Bressler, *Literary Criticism: An Introduction to Theory and Practice* (Englewood Cliffs, N.J.: Prentice Hall, 1994), 115.

10. Clarence Walhout, "Marxist Criticism," *Contemporary Literary Theory: A Christian Appraisal*, eds. Clarence Walhout and Leland Ryken (Grand Rapids, Mich.: William B. Eerdmans Publishing Company, 1991), 91.

11. Robert Browning, "My Last Duchess," in *The Norton Anthology of World Masterpieces*, ed. Maynard Mack et al., ex. ed. in 2 vols. (New York: W.W. Norton, 1995), 2:896–97.

12. Susan Van Zanten Gallagher, "Feminist Literary Criticism: A Chorus of Ethical Voices," *Contemporary Literary Theory: A Christian Appraisal,* eds. Clarence Walhout and Leland Ryken (Grand Rapids, Mich.: William B. Eerdmans Publishing Company, 1991), 246.

13. Alan Jacobs, "Psychological Criticism: From the Imagination to Freud and Beyond," *Contemporary Literary Theory: A Christian Appraisal,* 121.

14. Bressler, *Literary Criticism,* 72–73.

15. Alan Jacobs, "Deconstruction," *Contemporary Literary Theory: A Christian Appraisal,* eds. Clarence Walhout and Leland Ryken (Grand Rapids, Mich.: William B. Eerdmans Publishing Company, 1991), 195.

16. Ibid.

Chapter 8, Christian Worldview and Natural Science

1. David R. Williams, 22 June 2000. http://nssdc.gsfc.nasa.gov/planetary/news/mars_water_pr_20000622.html. See also pictures uploaded to the Malin Space Science Systems Web site at http://barsoom.msss.com/newhome.html.

2. NASA plans two missions, but is already lagging behind a little. Hence I've combined the two missions in my scenario. See the Europa Orbiter home page at http://www.jpl.nasa.gov/pluto/euroarbiter.htm.

3. John Polkinghorne, *Faith of a Physicist* (Minneapolis: Fortress Press, 1996), 5. See also R. Netz, "The Origins of Mathematical Physics: New Light on an Old Question," *Physics Today* 53:6, 36.

4. A misunderstanding of Karl Popper's philosophy, the hallmark of which is that "falsifiability" defines science. Although there is truth in Popper's proposition, it is in my opinion too facile even if understood correctly.

5. J. Polkinghorne, *Scientists as Theologians* (London: SPCK, 1996), 16.

6. Polkinghorne's justification for this winsome strategy is explicated in *Faith of a Physicist,* 1–8.

7. Loren Eisley, quoted in Nancy Pearcey and Charles B. Thaxton, *The Soul of Science* (Wheaton, Ill.: Crossway Books), 17.

8. This Enlightenment spirit is exemplified by P. S. Laplace, whose riposte "I have no need of that hypothesis" was delivered in response that God's direct intervention was needed to completely explain the mechanics of the solar system. His statement cannot explain why science is possible. Quoted in Stanley L. Jaki, *Miracles and Physics* (Front Royal, Va: Christendom Press, 1999), 32.

9. J. I. Packer, *A Quest for Godliness* (Wheaton, Ill.: Crossway Books, 1990), 21–34. Packer's book is very accessible to the theological layman yet is an excellent compendium of sources for Puritan writings.

10. Ibid, 21–34.

11. Westminster Confession of Faith, chapter 2 (Inverness: Free Presbyterian Publications, 1983). See also the second chapter of the Baptist 1689 Second London Confession.

12. Jaki, *Miracles and Physics,* viii from the Foreword.

13. See the reprints of Theodore Beza's and Zacharias Ursinus's excellent articles in *The Classical Christian* 1, November/December 1999, "The Law and the Gospel," 2–7.

14. Louis Berkhof, *Systematic Theology* (Grand Rapids, Mich.: William B. Eerdmans, 1941), 57–58.

15. Fang Lizhi, *Bringing Down the Great Wall: Writings on Science, Culture, and Democracy in China* (New York: Alfred A. Knopf, 1991), 30–37.

16. Berkhof, *Systematic Theology,* 57–63.

17. Ibid, 64–81.

18. Ibid., 71.

19. Ibid, 36–37.

20. Benjamin B. Warfield, *The Inspiration and Authority of the Bible* (Phillipsburg, N.J.: Presbyterian and Reformed, 1948), 105–128.

21. Ibid, 131–66.

22. Polkinghorne asserts the same in *Faith of a Physicist,* 7–8.

23. Van Til, *Why I Believe in God,* ed. Jonathan Barlow (Center for Reformed Theology and Apologetics, 1996); Van Til lays out a more sophisticated version of this argument in *The Defense of the Faith* (Philadelphia: Presbyterian and Reformed), 1955.

24. G. C. Berkouwer, *Man, The Image of God* (Grand Rapids, Mich.: William B. Eerdmans, 1962), 67–118.

25. Colin Gunton, *Christ and Creation* (Carlisle, U.K.: Paternoster, 1992), 99–127. The outworking through church history of the doctrine of man being created in the image of God is surveyed in Gunton, Berkouwer, and Berkhof.

26. Ibid., 99–127.

27. Reinhold Niebuhr, *The Irony of American History* (New York: Charles Scribner's Sons, 1954), 46–54.

28. Peter Green, *Ancient Greece: An Illustrated History* (London: Thanes and Hudson, 1973), 30–35. Classical historians are often mystified that the Greeks never developed modern science or a truly technological society.

29. Roland Bainton, *The Reformation of the Sixteenth Century* (Boston: Beacon Press, 1952), 244–61.

30. Extracted from G. E. R. Lloyd's book, *Greek Science After Aristotle* (New York: W. W. Norton, 1973). To these might be added doctors and engineers, who after all are close to our experimental scientists. Most Greek intellectuals eschewed the work of the engineer.

31. To understand a culture's thought, it helps to imagine you are a member of that culture. This can require a radically different mind-set from your own. This "Gestalt Switch" is described by Thomas Kuhn in *The Structure of Scientific Revolutions* (Chicago: University of Chicago Press, 1962), 11–114, as important in understanding new scientific theories, whose underlying "paradigms" may be different from those underlying old theories.

32. G. A. Marsch, "Enlightened Hearts and Cynical Eyes: Why Christian Faith and Doctrine Are Critical Scientific Tools." Published on the Council for Christian Colleges and Universities (CCCU) Web site at http://www.cccu.org/projects/workshops/marsch.htm, 2001; see also Pearcey and Thaxton, *The Soul of Science*, chapter 1.

33. Plutarch, "Life of Marcellus," reprinted in *Makers of Rome* (New York: Viking Penguin, 1965), chapter 17, 3. G. E. R. Lloyd, *Greek Science*, 95, reckons that Plutarch was grinding Platonist axes and was exaggerating Archimedes's distaste for engineering. Yet he clearly admits that "the educated elite whom Plutarch typifies generally combined contempt for the life of the engineer with ignorance concerning his work. This attitude, which had the weighty support of Plato and Aristotle, is, without a doubt, the dominant one in writers of all periods in antiquity."

34. Pearcey and Thaxton, *The Soul of Science*, throughout offer an appraisal of Aristotelianism as a spur (or hindrance) to the scientific program. They rightly consider it an impedance to the progress of physics, but it proved more applicable to biology, where the relation of Aristotelianism forms to function is germane.

35. I am indebted to Professor Arthur Holmes for his superb, stimulating lecture on the life and works of Francis Bacon: "Francis Bacon and the Scientific Revolution," delivered at Union University as part of its Scholar-in-Residence series. See also his *Fact, Value and God* (Grand Rapids, Mich.: William B. Eerdmans Publishing Co., 1997), 84–99.

36. From Francis Bacon's *Novum Organum,* quoted in Schaeffer, 134–35.

37. Robert Frodeman, ed., *Earth Matters: The Earth Sciences, Philosophy, and the Claims of Community* (Upper Saddle River, N.J.: Prentice Hall, 2000), 46.

38. Marsch, Ibid., http://www.cccu.org/projects/workshops/marsch.htm.

39. See 1 Kings 3:3–14, cf. 1 Kings 12:1–16.

40. J. R. R. Tolkien, *The Two Towers* (New York: Ballantine Books, 1965), 202–204. There is a well-thought-out environmental ethic por-

trayed throughout Tolkien's books, showing that excellent fiction can edify in the strongest manner.

41. Gunton, *Christ and Creation*, 99–127.

42. Peter Warshall, "Four Ways to Look at Earth," in *Earth Matters*, 196.

43. Bainton, *The Reformation of the Sixteenth Century*, 244–61; see also Roland Bainton, *Here I Stand: A Life of Martin Luther* (New York: New American Library, Mentor Books, 1950), 223–37. However, lest Protestants get too swelled with pride, I ought to remind the reader that orthodox evangelicals haven't made a huge imprint on twentieth-century science, and I myself have worked with and under superb Roman Catholic scientists over the years. I believe in using my Protestant heritage as a spur for excellence, not a cudgel against the Roman church.

44. The ideal of progress is generally alien to pagan cultures. A more detailed analysis of cultural optimism will have to appear elsewhere.

45. C. S. Lewis, *The Weight of Glory* (New York: Macmillan 1980), 19. I believe parents ought always to keep this excellent point in mind.

46. For example, see a description of the Puritan soldier in action at the Battle of the Dunes, 1658, described in A. Livesey's *Great Commanders and Their Battles* (New York: MacMillan, 1987), 62–67. Also see descriptions of Cromwell's military campaigns throughout Christopher Hill's *God's Englishman: Oliver Cromwell and the English Revolution* (New York: Harper and Row, 1970).

47. See Hugh Ross's Web site "The Creation Date Controversy" [database on-line]; available at: http://www.leaderu.com/real/ri9403/date.html.

48. Since Marcy and Butler's pivotal work in 1995, extrasolar planets are being discovered so rapidly, the best way to keep up with the progress is accomplished by accessing the Web sites of the investigators in the field. Two good on-line extrasolar planet catalogues can be found at http://cfa-www.harvard.edu/planets/catalog.html and at http://exoplanets.org/planet_table.html.

49. See the terrestrial planet finder mission Web site, sponsored by the Jet Propulsion Laboratories and NASA at http://tpf.jpl.nasa.gov.

Chapter 9, Christian Worldview and the Arts

1. Calvin Seerveld delivered "The Halo of the Human Imagination" on July 1, 1991, at Oxford University, during the C. S. Lewis Foundation's interdisciplinary summer institute, "Muses Unbound: Transfiguring the Imagination." Tapes are available through the Foundation, P. O. Box 8008, Redlands, CA 92375, or at 1-888-CSLEWIS.

2. Those surveyed were listed in the Christians in the Visual Arts directory and accessible via E-mail but do not represent the totality of Christian college and university art departments, by any means. Institutions included: Azusa Pacific University, Calif.; Biola University, Calif.; Bethel

College, Minn.; Gordon College, Mass.; Greenville College, Ill.; Houghton College, N.Y.; Indiana Wesleyan University, Ind.; Messiah College, Pa.; Northwest Nazarene University, Id.; Redeemer College, Canada; Roberts Wesleyan College, N.Y.; Taylor University, Ind.; Union University, Tenn.; and Wheaton College, Ill.

3. Like several other key art and Christianity books, *Modern Art and the Death of a Culture* was initially released by InterVarsity Press (Downer's Grove, Ill., 1970) and reissued by Crossway Books (Wheaton, Ill., 1994).

4. Goodwin founded the influential London's Art Centre Group with the financial help of Cliff Richards, Britain's Elvis Presley; in his sixties, he founded the Genesis Arts Trust and still speaks publicly throughout the world. Telephone, 011-44-171-240-6980; genesisarts@btinternet.com.

5. Margaret Miles, *Image as Insight* (Boston: Beacon Press, 1985), 33. Miles taught at Harvard University Divinity School and is now dean of theology at the Graduate Theological Union, Berkeley, Calif.

6. C. S. Lewis, "Meditations in a Toolshed" in *An Experiment in Criticism* (London: Cambridge University Press, 1961), n.p.

7. I know this because I have been involved with Lewis's home, The Kilns, since 1991; after a twelve-year restoration project, it is slated to become a center for Christian scholars. For more information, contact the C. S. Lewis Foundation, 1-888-CSLEWIS.

8. Lewis, "Meditations in a Toolshed," 88.

9. Ibid., n.p.

10. Jaroslav Pelikan, *The Illustrated Jesus Through the Centuries* (New Haven: Yale University, 1996), 6.

11. Dan Cray, "Art of Selling Kitsch," *Time*, 30 August 1999, 62–63.

12. Robert Hughes *The Shock of the New* (New York: Alfred A. Knopf, 1991) is useful to conservative Christians because Hughes is one of the few secular critics who cannot accept many claims of contemporary art as valid. Within this discussion, written initially as a British Broadcasting Corporation television series in 1980, Hughes often credits Joseph Beuys with the formation of conceptual art; "being and doing" enters the text on page 400.

13. It is to my chagrin that I have never located the primary source of the Flaubert quote, which I discovered on an ad for an art paper company, nor have I pinpointed the oft-quoted Picasso paraphrase of Flaubert—yet these are standard phrases in use today.

14. Thomas Mathews, *The Clash of Gods: A Reinterpretation of Early Christian Art* (Princeton: Princeton University Press, 1993), 180.

15. The Iconoclastic Controversy is often hardly given a nod in most art survey texts; several interesting sources that can lead to interesting class discussions, if students are primed to take sides, are: St. John of Damascus's *On the Divine Images*; St. Theodore the Studite's *On the Holy*

Icons; Leonid Ouspensky's *The Meaning of Icons*; and Paul Evdokimov's *The Art of the Icon: A Theology of Beauty.*

16. Edward Weisberger, ed., *The Spiritual in Abstract Art: 1890–1985* (New York: Abbeville Press, 1986).

17. Lewis, *An Experiment in Criticism*, n.p.

18. CIVA's Web site showcases an exhibit of works by members, and the availability of traveling exhibits, at www.civa.org.

19. From Edward Knippers's statement for a panel discussion on "The Narrative in Art," CIVA Conference, Biola University, 1989.

20. Secular sources included readings from *Theories and Documents of Contemporary Art: A Sourcebook of Artists' Writings* (Stiles and Selz, Berkeley: University of California Press, 1996) and Greil Marcus' entertainingly flip assessment of pop culture, *Lipstick Traces: A Secret History of the Twentieth Century* (Cambridge: Harvard University Press, 1989), as well as current articles about new installations and exhibitions. Readings on spiritual though not specifically Christian art are represented here by Mark C. Taylor's book, *Disfiguring: Art, Architecture, and Religion* (Chicago: University of Chicago Press, 1992); *Mapping the Terrain: New Genre Public Art*, edited by Suzanne Lacy (Seattle: Bay Press, 1995), and Susan J. Barnes' work, *The Rothko Chapel: An Act of Faith* (Austin: University of Texas Press, 1987). The Christian discussion was evaluated through excerpts from Gene Edward Veith's *State of the Arts: From Bezalel to Mapplethorpe* (Wheaton, Ill.: Crossway Books, 1991) and Hilary Brand and Adrienne Chaplin, *Art and Soul: Signposts for Christians in the Arts* (Carlisle: Solway/Paternoster Press, 1999), as well as forays into the works of Calvin Seerveld, Douglas Adams, Jeremy Begbie, Jane and John Dillenberger, Hans Rookmaaker, and Francis Schaeffer.

21. Douglas's comments were first sent out by E-mail but appeared in the March 2000 CIVA Newsletter, which was devoted to "Sensations" and other controversies and also offered direct quotes from Ofili and media treatments of the event.

22. Frohymeyer's earnest comments about this were recorded in a *Newsweek* interview, "The Nature of the Beast," 16 March 1992, 69.

23. "And Now, A Word from Our Creator," *New York Times Book Review,* 12 February 1989, n.p.

24. Hughes, *The Shock of the New,* 268.

25. Anthony Ugolnik, author of *The Illuminating Icon*, spoke on the subject at the CIVA Conference in Messiah College, Pennsylvania, 1993.

Chapter 10, Christian Worldview and Music

1. Augustine, *Confessions* 9.6.14.

2. Martin Luther, *Tischreden*, 7034.

3. Michael S. Hamilton, "The Triumph of the Praise Songs," *Christianity Today* 12 July 1999, 21–30.

4. Harold M. Best, *Music through the Eyes of Faith* (San Francisco: HarperSanFrancisco, 1993), 42.

5. Ibid., 48–57.

6. To do so, Best must read his proof texts contrary to their plain meaning. He must argue that God has *not* made his invisible attributes evident "in the things that have been made" and that the heavens do *not* tell the glory of God (they only point to it). For a more orthodox approach, one that acknowledges "a coherence and complementary relationship between 'general' and 'special' revelation," see what Brad Green has to say about "Revelation, Scripture and the Possibility of Knowledge" elsewhere in this volume.

7. Best, *Music through the Eyes of Faith*, 47.

8. Ibid., 43–44.

9. Aquinas, *Expositio super Dionysium De divinis nominibus* (*On the Divine Names*), 4.5. Augustine applies this idea directly to music in a most delightful way in his letter to Jerome of Bethlehem on the origin of the human soul. *Epistulae* (*Letters*), 166.13. For a more recent formulation, see Jonathan Edwards, *A Dissertation Concerning the Nature of True Virtue*, chapter 3.

10. *Summa theologiae* 1.39.8 reply. Species autem sive pulchritudo habet similitudinem cum propriis Filii. Nam ad pulchritudinem tria requiruntur. Primo quidem integritas, sive perfectio, quae enim diminuta sunt, hoc ipso turpia sunt; et debita proportio sive consonantia; et iterum claritas, unde quae habent colorem nitidum pulchra esse dicuntur.

11. Best, *Music through the Eyes of Faith*, 4.

12. Sally Morgenthaler, *Worship Evangelism: Inviting Unbelievers into the Presence of God* (Grand Rapids, Mich.: Zondervan, 1999), 137.

13. As in the children's ministry of First Baptist Church, Springdale, Arkansas.

14. Aestheticism is to beauty what dry intellectualism is to truth and what legalism is to goodness. They are idolatrous.

15. Hans Urs von Balthasar, *The Glory of the Lord: A Theological Aesthetics*, vol. 1, *Seeing the Form*, trans. Erasmo Leiva-Merikakis (San Francisco: Ignatius Press, 1982), 18.

16. Charlie Peacock, *At the Crossroads: An Insider's Look at the Past, Present, and Future of Contemporary Christian Music* (Nashville: Broadman & Holman, 1999), 64.

17. Kenneth A. Myers, *All God's Children and Blue Suede Shoes: Christians and Popular Culture* (Wheaton: Crossway Books, 1989), xii–xiii.

18. C. S. Lewis, *An Essay in Criticism* (Cambridge: Cambridge University Press, 1961), 88. Quoted in Myers, *All God's Children*, 91–92.

19. Myers, *All God's Children*, 97.

20. Roger Scruton, *The Aesthetics of Music* (Oxford: Oxford University Press, 1997), 498.

21. From an interview excerpted in Morgenthaler, *Worship Evangelism*, 89.

22. Morgenthaler, *Worship Evangelism*, 127–28.

23. Marva Dawn, *A Royal "Waste" of Time: The Splendor of Worshiping God and Being Church for the World* (Grand Rapids, Mich.: Eerdmans, 1999), 8.

24. Ibid., 5.

25. Carol Doran illustrates this with a poignant story. "Two of my teenaged daughters and I were on a long road trip when they suggested, half in jest, that we make the time pass faster by singing with one another. Remembering all the times our family used to sing on long trips when I was growing up, I asked enthusiastically, 'What shall we sing?' It turned out that all my daughters were able to remember were a few silly songs from childhood such as 'the ants go marching two by two, hurrah, hurrah!' and some jingles from television commercials. The rock music they listen to was not practical for singing because its effects depend upon an incessant beat and loud accompaniment. Its melody was not strong enough to stand alone." *Trouble at the Table: Gathering the Tribes for Worship* (Nashville: Abingdon Press, 1992), 50.

26. For a discussion of aesthetic problems associated with the exclusive use of projection screens in congregational singing, see Dawn, *Royal "Waste" of Time*, 285–95.

27. The idea of the church was treated in 21.6 percent of the classical hymns and in 1.2 percent of the choruses. The themes of sin, penitence, and the longing for holiness appeared in only 3.6 percent of the choruses, the holiness of God in only 4.3 percent. Cited in *Losing Our Virtue: Why the Church Must Recover Its Moral Vision* (Grand Rapids, Mich.: Eerdmans, 1998), 44–45.

28. Dawn, *Royal "Waste" of Time*, 16.

29. Ibid., 125.

30. John M. Frame, *Contemporary Worship Music: A Biblical Defense* (Phillipsburg, N.J.: Presbyterian and Reformed Publishing Company, 1997), 96.

31. By baroque harmonizations. Of course the poetry, too, has been disfigured by the insistence of translators that the English be made to rhyme at all cost.

32. Morgenthaler, *Worship Evangelism*, 136.

33. C. S. Lewis, "On Church Music" in *Christian Reflections* (Grand Rapids, Mich.: Eerdmans, 1967), 96–97.

Chapter 11, Christian Worldview and the Social Sciences

1. These include, among many others, Charles R. Henderson, "Sociology and Theology," *American Journal of Sociology* 1 (1895): 381–83; Shailer Matthews, "Christian Sociology" [series], *American Journal of Sociology* 1 (1895): 182–94, 359–80, 457–72, 604–617, 771–84; 2 (1896): 108–17, 274–87, 416–32; David Lyon, "The Idea of a Christian Sociology: Some Historical Precedents and Current Concerns," *Sociological Analysis* 44 (3): 227–42; Peter L. Berger, *The Sacred Canopy: Elements of a Sociological Theory of Religion* (Garden City, N.Y.: Doubleday, 1967); Ronald J. Burwell, "Sleeping with an Elephant: The Uneasy Alliance between Christian Faith and Sociology," *Christian Scholar's Review* 5: 195–203; Richard Perkins, *Looking Both Ways: Exploring the Interface between Christianity and Sociology* (Grand Rapids, Mich.: Baker Book House, 1987); William H. Swatos Jr., ed., *Religious Sociology* (Westport, Conn.: Greenwood Press, 1987); Michael R. Leming, Raymond G. DeVries, and Brendan F. J. Furnish, eds., *The Sociological Perspective: A Value-Committed Introduction* (Grand Rapids, Mich.: Zondervan Publishing House, 1989); and David A. Fraser and Tony Campolo, *Sociology through the Eyes of Faith* (San Francisco, Calif.: HarperSanFrancisco Publishers, 1992).

2. See, for instance, George Marsden, *The Outrageous Idea of Christian Scholarship* (New York, N.Y.: Oxford University Press, 1997); and David S. Dockery and David P. Gushee, eds., *The Future of Christian Higher Education* (Nashville, Tenn.: Broadman & Holman Publishers, 1999).

3. This reference to the connection between the written word and the world is borrowed from the works of the late Paulo Freire, a well-known Brazilian theologian and educator. His approach was to teach the poor and oppressed peasants how to read, in order to name and transform their world politically. Much of his pedagogy and imagery, commonly used in Christian Base Communities in Brazil, is arguably applicable to the relationship between reading God's Word and understanding the world through a Christian prism. See, for instance, Paulo Freire, *Pedagogy of the Oppressed* (New York, N.Y.: The Seabury Press, 1970).

4. Naturalists (also known as positivists) believe in and look for natural laws governing all empirical phenomena. They are committed to a "value free" approach that pursues the "objective" study of social facts. Meanwhile, humanists reject the notion of natural law and look instead at how people create and sustain their social situations, usually via interaction and communication based on symbolic meanings and interpretations. In this sense, humanists are "value aware," in that they recognize values as an important subject of study, since they are believed to play an essential role in social interaction. In their majority, however, humanists do strongly

believe that the researcher's values ought not to interfere with but must be segregated from research. In this sense they do agree with naturalists.

5. David A. Fraser and Tony Campolo, *Sociology through the Eyes of Faith,* 300.

6. See Richard A. Barrett, *Culture and Conduct: An Excursion in Anthropology* (Belmont, Calif.: Wadsworth Publishing Company, 1991); and Abraham Rosman and Paula Rubel, *The Tapestry of Culture: An Introduction to Cultural Anthropology,* 7th ed. (Boston, Mass.: McGraw Hill, 2001).

7. See, for instance, Ronald L. Koteskey, *Psychology from a Christian Perspective* (Nashville, Tenn.: Abingdon Press, 1983), 31.

8. On a personal note, it is interesting to me that the Scripture verse that first opened my eyes to the truth of the gospel, leading me in my personal journey with Jesus Christ, was John 1:1–2. "In the beginning was the Word, and the *Word was with God,* and the Word was God. He was *with God in the beginning*" (NIV, italics added). Here, as in numerous other passages of Scripture, the relational essence of God is revealed, in that the Word (the Son) communed perfectly with the Father (and the Holy Spirit) from everlasting.

9. Peter L. Berger discusses the legitimization of either accommodation or resistance as the central crisis in the struggle between theology and pluralism produced by secularization. See Peter L. Berger, *The Sacred Canopy.*

10. Charles Malik, "A Christian Critique of the University," *The Real Issue,* vol. 12 (2) (Feb. 1999): 7.

11. See, among other writers, Ronald L. Johnstone, *Religion in Society: A Sociology of Religion* (Upper Saddle River, N.J.: Prentice Hall, 1997); and Meredith B. McGuire, *Religion: The Social Context* (Belmont, Calif.: Wadsworth Publishing Company, 1997).

12. For excellent treatments of the progressive rationalization of society in capitalist economic systems, see, for instance, Max Weber's numerous essays in Max Weber, *Economy and Society,* vols. 1 and 2, eds., trans., Guenther Roth and Claus Wittich (Berkeley, Calif.: University of California Press, 1978). See also H. H. Gerth and C. Wright Mills, eds., trans., *From Max Weber: Essays in Sociology* (New York, N.Y.: Oxford University Press, 1946); and Jürgen Habermas, "Technology and Science as Ideology," in *Toward a Rational Society* (Boston, Mass.: Beacon Press, 1970).

13. The concept of "worldview" in sociology is most closely associated with the writings of Karl Mannheim. See, for instance, Karl Mannheim, *Essays on the Sociology of Knowledge* (New York, N.Y.: Oxford University Press, 1952; orig. 1923).

14. For formative arguments on the social construction of reality and its relation to religion, see especially Peter L Berger and Thomas

Luckmann, *The Social Construction of Reality* (Garden City, N.Y.: Doubleday, 1967); and Peter L. Berger, *The Sacred Canopy.*

15. John B. Thompson, *Ideology and Modern Culture* (Stanford, Calif.: Stanford University Press, 1990), 7.

16. David A. Snow and Pamela E. Oliver, "Social Movements and Collective Behavior: Social Psychological Dimensions and Considerations," chap. in *Sociological Perspectives on Social Psychology,* ed. 36K. Cook, G. A. Fine, and J. S. House (Boston, Mass.: Allyn and Bacon, 1995), 571–99.

17. David Snow, E. Burke Rochford Jr., Steven K. Worden, and Robert Benford, "Frame Alignment Processes, Micromobilization, and Movement Participation," *American Sociological Review* 51 (1986): 464–81.

18. Here, psychology and economics play a minor role relative to the other disciplines. But it is worth mentioning Freud's view that anxiety and infantile projection are psychological sources of religious belief [See Roger A. Johnson, "David Hume: A Skeptic Examines Religious Beliefs," in *Critical Issues in Modern Religion,* 2nd ed., eds. Roger A. Johnson et. al. (Englewood Cliffs, N.J.: Prentice Hall, 1990), 1–23; Ernest Wallwork, "Sigmund Freud: The Psychoanalytic Diagnosis—Infantile Illusion," in *Critical Issues in Modern Religion,* 2nd ed., eds. Roger A. Johnson et. al. (Englewood Cliffs, N.J.: Prentice Hall, 1990), 118–45]. Meanwhile, the economic interest in religion has largely been related to studying which religious systems have facilitated the emergence of capitalism. Max Weber develops an influential argument about Calvinism in Max Weber, *The Protestant Ethic and the Spirit of Capitalism,* trans., Talcott Parsons (New York, N.Y.: Scribner, 1958; orig. 1904).

19. Robert A. Clark, "Thinking About Culture: Theirs and Ours," in *The Sociological Perspective: A Value-Committed Introduction,* eds. Michael R. Leming, Raymond G. DeVries, and Brendan F. J. Furnish (Grand Rapids, Mich.: Zondervan Publishing House, 1989), 67.

20. For a thorough and concise review of the sociological perspective on religion, see Ronald L. Johnstone, *Religion in Society.*

21. For the anthropological view of religion, see Abraham Rosman and Paula G. Rubel, *The Tapestry of Culture.*

22. For the concept of civil religion, see for instance, Robert N. Bellah, "Civil Religion in America," in *Religion in America,* eds. William G. McLoughlin and Robert N. Bellah (Boston: Houghton Mifflin, 1968); and John A. Coleman, "Civil Religion," *Sociological Analysis* 31, no. 2 (1970).

23. Meredith B. McGuire, *Religion: The Social Context.*

24. I encourage non-Christian readers to examine in theology the important claims about the truth of Christianity and Holy Scripture. Although I am convinced of it, I am not a theologian, and I believe that this area of apologetics lies beyond the scope of this chapter.

25. Robert Clark, "Thinking About Culture: Theirs and Ours," in *The Sociological Perspective: A Value-Committed Introduction,* eds. Michael R. Leming, Raymond G. DeVries, and Brendan F. J. Furnish (Grand Rapids, Mich.: Zondervan Publishing House, 1989), 72. See also David Moberg, "Cultural Relativity and Christian Faith," *Journal of the American Scientific Affiliation* 6: 34–48.

26. Peter L. Berger, *The Sacred Canopy.*

27. John R. W. Stott, *Basic Christianity,* 2nd ed. (Downer Grove, Ill.: Inter-Varsity Press, 1971), 14.

28. Charles Colson and Nancy Pearcey, *How Now Shall We Live* (Wheaton, Ill.: Tyndale House Publishers, 1999), 338.

29. Ibid., 295.

30. See Vincent N. Parrillo, *Strangers to These Shores: Race and Ethnic Relations in the United States,* 5th ed. (Boston, Mass.: Allyn and Bacon, 1997), 49.

Chapter 12, Christian Worldview and Media

1. William Bennett, *The Devaluing of America* (New York: Simon and Schuster, 1992), 10.

2. Michael Medved, speech at the Shavano Insititute, November 1990.

3. Chuck Colson and Nancy Pearcey, *How Now Shall We Live?* (Wheaton, Ill.: Tyndale House Publishers, Inc.), 17.

4. See Frank E. Gaebelein, *The Christian, the Arts and Truth* (Portland: Multnomah Press, 1985), 101.

5. H. Richard Niebuhr, *Christ and Culture* (New York: Harper & Row, Publishers, 1951), 10.

6. Kenneth Thomas and Ralph Kilman, *Thomas-Kilmann Conflict Mode Instrument* (Santa Clara, Calif.: Xicom, Inc. 1974).

7. Bill Strom, *More Than Talk* (Dubuque: Kendall/Hunt Publishing, 1996).

8. C. S. Lewis, *The Weight of Glory* (New York: Simon & Schuster 1996).

9. Colson, *How Now Shall We Live?* x.

10. Ibid.

11. Michael Medved, *Hollywood vs. America* (New York: HarperCollins Publishers), 125.

12. Ibid., 245.

13. Niebuhr, *Christ and Culture,* 171.

14. Frederica Mathewes-Green, Chapel Speech, Union University, 11 October 1999.

15. Medved, *Hollywood vs. America,* 325.

16. Joel Carpenter, "Sustaining Christian Intellectual Commitments: Lessons from the Recent Past," in David S. Dockery and David P. Gushee,

The Future of Christian Higher Education (Nashville: Broadman & Holman Publishers, 1999), 116.

17. Philip Yancey, *What's So Amazing about Grace* (Grand Rapids, Mich.: Zondervan, 1997), 33.

18. Derek Kidner, *The Wisdom of Proverbs, Job and Ecclesiastes* (Downers Grove, Ill.: InterVarsity Press, 1985), 11.

19. Kenneth A. Myers, *All God's Children and Blue Suede Shoes* (Wheaton, Ill.: Crossway Books, 1989), 98.

20. John Akers, *Christianity Today*, June 1989.

21. Medved, *Hollywood vs. America*, 269.

22. David P. Gushee, *The True View: What the Bible Says about Culture*, sermon at NorthBrook Church, Jackson, Tennessee, 11 June 2000.

23. Colson, *How Now Shall We Live?* xi.

24. Myers, *All God's Children and Blue Suede Shoes*, 31.

25. Bennett, *The Devaluing of America*, 256.

26. Quentin J. Schultz, *Communicating for Life* (Grand Rapids, Mich.: Baker-Academic, 2000), 69.

Chapter 13, Christian Worldview and Teaching

1. "A World of Their Own: Searching for a Holy Spirit," *Newsweek* (8 May 2000), 61–63.

2. Allan Bloom, *The Closing of the American Mind* (New York: Simon and Schuster, 1987), 192.

3. Young Pai and Susan A. Adler, *Cultural Foundations of Education* (Columbus, Ohio: Merrill Prentice-Hall, 2001), 114.

4. John Dewey, *Freedom and Culture* (New York: Capricorn Books), 127.

5. Stang D. Gaede, *When Tolerance Is No Virtue* (Downers Grove, Ill.: InterVarsity Press, 1993).

6. James Sire, *The Universe Next Door: A Basic Worldview Catalog, 3d Edition* (Downers Grove, Ill.: InterVarsity Press, 1997), 16.

7. Charles Colson and Nancy Pearcey, *How Now Shall We Live?* (Wheaton, Ill.: Tyndale House Publishers, 1999), 20.

8. C. S. Lewis, "On Forgiveness," in *The Weight of Glory and Other Addresses* (New York: Collier Books/Macmillan, 1980), 125.

9. Philip Yancey, *What's So Amazing About Grace?* (Grand Rapids, Mich.: Zondervan Publishing House, 1997), 41.

10. Thomas Lickona, Eric Schapps, and Catherine Lewis, *Eleven Principles of Effective Character Education* (Washington, D.C.: Character Education Partnership, 1995), 1.

11. Thomas Lickona, *Religion and Character Education* (Educational Leadership: September 1999), 21–27.

12. Immanual Kant, *Critique of Practical Reason* (Indianapolis, Ind.: Bobbs-Merrill, 1956).

13. Elton Trueblood, "The Idea of a College," in *A Philosopher's Way*, ed. by Elizabeth Newby (Nashville, Tenn.: Broadman Press, 1978), 101.

14. Edward Tingley, *Technicians of Learning* (First Things: August/September 2000), 29–35.

15. Neil Postman and C. Weingartner, *Teaching as a Subversive Activity* (New York: Dell Publishing Co., 1969).

16. Michael Novak, "Where Would Civilization Be Without Christianity?" *Christianity Today* (6 December 1999), 50–52.

Chapter 14, Christian Worldview and Health Care

1. Dale Matthews, *The Faith Factor* (New York: Penguin Books, 1998), 17.

2. Elaine Ridgeway and Amelia Broussard, "The Evolution of Nursing" in *Contemporary Nursing: Issues, Trends and Management,* eds. Barbara Cherry and Susan Jacob (St. Louis: Mosby, 1999).

3. Matthews, *The Faith Factor*.

4. Ibid.

5. Granger Westberg and Jill Westberg McNamara, *The Parish Nurse: Providing a Minister of Health for Your Congregation* (Minneapolis: Augsburg Fortress, 1990).

6. Matthews, *The Faith Factor*.

7. E. Anthony Allen, "Wholeness, Salvation and the Christian Health Professional" in *Transforming Health,* ed. Eric Ram (Monrovia: MARC Publications, 1995).

8. Herbert Benson, *Timeless Healing* (New York: Scribner, 1996); Harold Koenig, *The Healing Power of Faith* (New York: Simon and Schuster, 1999); Matthews, *The Faith Factor*.

9. George Engel, "Is Grief a Disease? A Challenge for Medical Research" in *Psychosomatic Medicine* 23 (1961): 18–23.

10. Matthews, *The Faith Factor*.

11. Thomas Oxman, et. al. "Lack of Social Participation or Religious Strength and Comfort as Risk Factors for Death after Cardiac Surgery in the Elderly," *Psychosomatic Medicine* 57 (1995): 5–15.

12. Mary McRae, Patricia Carey, and Roxanna Anderson-Scott, "Black Churches as Therapeutic Systems: A Group Perspective," *Health Education and Behavior* 25 (1998), 778–89.

13. Koenig, 1999.

14. Matthews, *The Faith Factor*.

15. David Dockery, *Basic Christian Beliefs* (Nashville: Broadman & Holman Publishers, 2000).

16. Edward Larson and Darrel Amundsen, *A Different Death* (Downers Grove, Ill.: InterVarsity Press, 1998).

17. Gilbert Meilaender, *Bioethics* (Grand Rapids, Mich.: William B. Eerdmans Publishing Company, 1996).

18. Westberg and McNamara, *The Parish Nurse.*

19. Constance Sumner, "Recognizing and Responding to Spiritual Distress," *American Journal of Nursing* January 1998, 26–31.

20. Arlene Miller and Judith Shelly, *Values in Conflict* (Downers Grove, Ill.: InterVarsity Press, 1991).

21. Sumner, "Recognizing and Responding to Spiritual Distress."

22. E. Anthony Allen, "Wholeness, Salvation and the Christian Health Professional" in *Transforming Health.*

23. Sumner, "Recognizing and Responding to Spiritual Distress," 26–31.

24. Anne Davis, Mila Aroskar, Joan Liaschenko and Theresa Drought, *Ethical Dilemmas in Nursing Practice,* 4th ed. (Stamford, Conn.: Appleton and Lange, 1997).

25. Ibid.

26. Carla Sanderson, "Ethical and Bioethical Issues" in *Nursing and Health Care,* eds. Barbara Cherry and Susan Jacob (St. Louis: Mosby, 2002), 198–218.

27. Preamble to the Constitution of the World Health Organization (Geneva: WHO), 1948.

28. Meilander, *Bioethics.*

29. Painter, *USA Today,* 4 August 1999.

30. Meilander, *Bioethics.*

31. Ibid., 20.

32. Davis et al., *Ethical Dilemmas and Nursing Practice.*

33. President's Commission for the Study of Ethical Problems in Medicine and Biomedical and Behavioral Research: *Securing Access to Health Care. Volume One Report* (Washington, D.C.: U.S. Government Printing Office, 1983), 20.

34. Ibid.

35. Christopher Grundman, "Healing: A Dimension of Ecclesial-Missionary Action" in *Transforming Health,* 77.

36. E. Anthony Allen in "Wholeness, Salvation and the Christian Health Professional," 9.

37. Susan Jacob, "The Grief Process of Older Adult Women Whose Husbands Received Hospice Care," *Journal of Advanced Nursing* 24 (1996): 280–86.

38. John Hjelm and Renee Johnson, "Spiritual Health: An Annotated Bibliography," *Journal of Health Education* 27 (1996): 248–52.

39. Antonio van Loon, "The Development of Faith Community Nursing Programs as a Response to Changing Australian Policy," *Health Education and Behavior,* December 1998, 790–99.

40. Westberg and McNamara, *The Parish Nurse.*

41. Frederick Reklau, *Health Ministries Connection* (Des Moines, Iowa: Health Ministries Association, 1987).

42. Robert Hummer, Richard Rogers, Charles Nam and Christopher Ellison, "Religious Involvement and U.S. Adult Mortality," *Demography* 36 (1999): 273–85; Hana Ayele, Thomas Mulligan, Sylvia Gheorghiu and Carlos Reyes-Ortiz, "Religious Activity Improves Life Satisfaction for Some Physicians and Older Patients," *Journal of the American Geriatric Society* 47 (1999): 453–55; Phillip Waite, Steven Hawks, and Julie Gast, "The Correlation Between Spiritual Well-Being and Health Behaviors," *American Journal of Health Promotion* 13 (1999): 159–62.

43. Susan Fowler, "Hope and a Health Promoting Lifestyle in Persons with Parkinson's Disease," *Journal of Neuroscience Nursing* (1996): 111–16; Kay Herth, "Hope in Older Adults in Community and Institutional Settings," *Issues in Mental Health Nursing*, 14, 139–156; Jacob, "The Grief Process of Older Adult Women, *The Parish Nurse*..

44. Westberg and McNamara, 1990.

45. Ibid.

46. Roberta Rehm, "Religious Faith in Mexican-American Families Dealing with Chronic Childhood Illness," *Image: Journal of Nursing Scholarship* 31 (1999): 33–38.

47. Maelinder, *Bioethics*.

48. Ibid.

49. Westberg and McNamara, *The Parish Nurse*.

50. Van Loon, "The Development of Faith Community Nursing Programs," 790–99, as a response to changing Australian health policy.

51. Ibid.

52. Koenig, *The Healing Power of Faith*.

53. Richard J. Light, *Making the Most of College: Students Speak Their Minds* (Cambridge, Mass.: Harvard University Press, 2001.

54. E. Anthony Allen in "Wholeness, Salvation, and the Christian Health Professional."

55. Mary Simpson and Marilyn King, "God Brought All These Churches Together: Issues in Developing Religion-Health Partnerships in an Appalachian Community," *Public Health Nursing*, February 1999, 41–49.

56. Westberg and McNamara, *The Parish Nurse*.

57. Fowler, "Hope and a Health Promoting Lifestyle."

58. Mary Rado Simpson and Marilyn Gwens King, "God Brought All These Churches Together: Issues in Developing Religion-Health Partnership in an Appalachian Community," *Public Health Policy* 16, no.1: 41–49.

59. Matthews, *The Faith Factor*.

60. Koenig, *The Healing Power of Faith*.

61. Fowler "Hope and a Health Promoting Lifestyle."

62. M. R. Kinney, "Quality of Life Research: Rigor or Rigor Mortis," *Cardiovascular Nursing* 31(1995): 25–28.

63. E. Anthony Allen, "Wholeness, Salvation, and the Christian Health Professional," 9.

64. Matthews, *The Faith Factor.*

Chapter 15, Christian Worldview and Social Work

1. Robert Morris, *Rethinking Social Welfare: Why Care for the Stranger?* (New York: Longman, 1986), 66.

2. Ralph Dolgoff, Donald Feldstein, and Louise Skolnik, *Understanding Social Welfare*, 4th ed. (New York: Longman, 1997), 24.

3. See Ronald J. Sider, *Just Generosity* (Grand Rapids, Mich.: Baker Books, 1999) for a concise discussion of the biblical foundations for treatment of the disadvantaged.

4. Morris, *Rethinking Social Welfare*, 72.

5. Sider, *Just Generosity*, 49–75.

6. Philip R. Popple and Leslie Leighninger, *Social Work, Social Welfare, and American Society*, 2nd ed. (Boston: Allyn and Bacon, 1993), 5.

7. Ibid., 225.

8. Dolgoff, Feldstein, and Skolnik, *Understanding Social Welfare*, 61.

9. Beryl Hugen, ed., *Christianity and Social Work: Readings on the Integration of Christian Faith and Social Work Practice* (Botsford, Conn.: North American Association of Christians in Social Work, 1998), 2.

10. Earle E. Cairns, *An Endless Line of Splendor: Revivals and Their Leaders from the Great Awakening to the Present* (Wheaton, Ill.: Tyndale House, 1986) 44–52.

11. Ibid., 276.

12. Popple and Leighninger, *Social Welfare and American Society*, 98.

13. Peggy Pittman-Munke, "A Different Rootstock: The Lutheran Contribution to the Development of Social Work Prior to 1917," *Social Work and Christianity* 26 (Spring 1999): 40.

14. Popple and Leighninger, *Social Welfare and American Society*, 100.

15. Ibid., 58.

16. Ibid., 59.

17. Ibid., 62.

18. Ibid., 61.

19. Ibid., 100.

20. Space does not allow an analysis of the contributions of Jewish and Catholic groups that were quite significant in the development of social services during the early days of the profession. Also, the contributions of African-Americans are not covered in this analysis of evangelical traditions in providing social services. These groups, along with the evangelical Protestant groups primarily discussed in this paper, relied on a biblical faith and worldview.

21. Alan Keith-Lucas, *So You Want to Be a Social Worker: A Primer for the Christian Student* (St. Davids, Pa.: North American Association of Christians in Social Work, 1985), 1.

22. For a detailed description and analysis of the relationship of revivalism and social reform in the nineteenth and early twentieth centuries, see Timothy L. Smith, *Revivalism and Social Reform: American Protestantism on the Eve of the Civil War* (Gloucester, Mass.: Peter Smith, 1976); Norris Magnuson, *Salvation in the Slums: Evangelical Social Work, 1865–1920* (Metuchen, N.J.: Scarecrow Press, 1977; Grand Rapids, Mich.: Baker Book House, 1990), and Earle E. Cairns, *An Endless Line of Splendor: Revivals and Their Leaders from the Great Awakening to the Present.*

23. Smith, *Revivalism and Social Reform,* 60.

24. Wendy Murray Zoba, "A Woman's Place," *Christianity Today* 44 (August 2000), 42.

25. Cairns, *An Endless Line of Splendor,* 295–96, 304.

26. Ibid., 307.

27. Dallas Willard, *Spirit of the Disciplines* (New York: HarperCollins Publishers, 1988), 8–9.

28. Smith, *Revivalism and Social Reform,* 148.

29. Norris Magnuson's book, *Salvation in the Slums: Evangelical Social Work 1865–1920,* thoroughly examines the record of social ministries in evangelical life until 1920.

30. Keith-Lucas, *So You Want to Be a Social Worker,* 1.

31. National Association of Social Workers, *NASW Code of Ethics,* 1997.

32. Alan Keith-Lucas, *Giving and Taking Help* (Chapel Hill, N.C.: University of North Carolina Press, 1972), 138–42.

33. David Sherwood, "The Relationship Between Beliefs and Values in Social Work Practice: Worldviews Make a Difference," *Social Work and Christianity* 24 (Fall 1997): 122.

34. See the study by Lawrence E. Ressler and David R. Hodge, "Religious Discrimination in Social Work: An International Survey of Christian Social Workers," *Social Work and Christianity* 27 (Spring 2000): 49–70.

35. Dwain A. Pellebon, "Perceptions of Conflict Between Christianity and Social Work: A Preliminary Study," *Social Work and Christianity* 27 (Spring 2000): 36.

36. Sider, *Just Generosity,* 86. Also see David A. Sherwood, "Charitable Choice: Opportunity and Challenge for Christians in Social Work," *Social Work and Christianity* 25 (Spring 1998): 1–23 and David R. Hodge, "Welfare Reform and Religious Providers: An Examination of the New Paradigm," *Social Work and Christianity* 25 (Spring 2000): 24–48.

37. See the article by Edward G. Kuhlmann, "The Idea of Social Work: Back to the Future," *Social Work and Christianity* 26 (Spring 1999): 9–24, for a provocative challenge to the profession and Christians in the profession to explore its roots and regain its moral authority.

Chapter 16, Christian Worldview and the World of Business

1. *Webster's New Collegiate Dictionary* (Springfield, Mass: G&C Merriam, 1973).

2. For a more complete discussion of social responsibility, see M. Cottrill, "Corporate Social Responsibility and the Marketplace," *Journal of Business Ethics*, 9 (1990): 723–29; T. Mulligan, "Justifying Moral Initiative by Business, with Rejoinders to Bill Shaw and Richard Nunan," *Journal of Business Ethics*, 9 (1990): 93–103.

3. K. Davis and W. C. Pilcher, eds., *Ethics, Free Enterprise, and Public Policy* (New York: McGraw-Hill, 1979).

4. D. Sherwin, "The Ethical Roots of the Business System," *Harvard Business Review*, 61 (1983): 183–92.

5. Milton Friedman, "The Social Responsibility of Business Is to Increase Its Profits," *The New York Times Magazine*, 13 September 1970, 32 ff.

6. Richard Nunan, "The Libertarian Conception of Corporate Property: A Critique of Milton Friedman's Views on the Social Responsibility of Business," *Journal of Business Ethics* 7 (1988): 891–906.

7. H. C. Bunke, "Should We Teach Business Ethics?" *Business Horizons* 31 (1988): 2–8.

8. O. C. Ferrell and L. G. Gresham, "A Contingency Framework for Understanding Ethical Decision Making in Marketing," *Journal of Marketing* 49 (1985): 87–97.

9. Ibid.

10. Manuel Velasquez, *Business Ethics, Concepts and Cases*, 4th ed. (Upper Saddle River, N.J.: Prentice-Hall, 1998).

11. Charles Dickens, *A Christmas Carol* (New York: Signet, 1987), 4. *A Christmas Carol* was first published in 1843.

12. Alexander Hill, *Just Business: Christian Ethics for the Marketplace* (Downers Grove, Ill.: InterVarsity Press, 1997).

13. Hill, *Just Business*, 15.

14. Tim W. Ferguson, "Inspired from Above, ServiceMaster Dignifies Those Below," *Wall Street Journal*, 8 May 1990, 25.

15. R. T. DeGeorge and J. A. Pilcher, eds., *Ethics, Free Enterprise, and Public Policy* (New York: Oxford University Press, 1978).

16. "Business Ethics, Nice Guys Finish First," *The Economist* 308 (1988): 58.

Chapter 17, Christian Worldview and Student Life

1. G. H. Kuh, J. H. Schuh, E. J. Whitt, R. E. Andreas, J. W. Lyons, C. C. Strange, L. E. Krehbiel, K. A. MacKay, *Involving Colleges* (San Fransisco: Jossey-Bass, 1991), 12.

2. T. J. Marchese, "A New Conversation About Undergraduate Teaching: An Interview with Prf. Richard J. Light, Convener of the Harvard Assessment Seminars," *AAHE Bulletin* 42 (1990): 3.

3. Kuh, et. al., *Involving Colleges*, 8.

4. M. J. Barr, M. K. Desler, et. al. *The Handbook of Student Affairs Administration*, 2d ed. (San Francisco: Jossey Bass, 2000).

5. Ibid., 33.

6. Derek Bok, *Universities and the Future of America* (Durham, N.C.: Duke University Press, 1990), 63.

7. David Hoekema, *Campus Rules and Moral Community* (Lanhan, Md.: Rowman and Littlefield Publishers, Inc.), 127.

8. Kuh, et. al., *Involving Colleges*, xi.

9. Ernest T. Pascarella, Corrina A. Ethington, John C. Smart, "The Influence of College on Humanitarian/Civic Involvement Values," in *The Journal of Higher Education* 59 (1988): 412–37.

10. "ACPS Student Learning Imperative": [database on-line] available at: http://www.ascdhome.org/imperati.htm.

11. David S. Guthrie and Donald O. Opitz, *FIPSE Through the Eyes of Student Affairs* (Washington, D.C.: Council for Christian Colleges and Universities), 6.

12. Ibid. *the same place as in the preceding endnote //*

13. Ibid.

14. Steven Garber, *The Fabric of Faithfulness* (Downers Grove, Ill.: InterVarsity Press, 1996).

15. William Tunstead Burtchaell, *The Dying of the Light: The Disengagement of Colleges and Universities from Their Christian Churches* (Grand Rapids, Mich.: William B. Eerdmans Publishing Co., 1999), 753.

16. Hoekema, *Campus Rules*, 67.

17. Ibid.

18. Hoekema, *Campus Rules*, 166.

19. Ibid.

20. John Templeton Foundation, *Colleges That Encourage Character Development* (Philadelphia: Templeton Foundation Press, 1999).

Chapter 18, Christian Worldview and Campus Ministry

1. C. S. Lewis, *The Weight of Glory* (New York: Macmillan Publishing Company), 106.

2. Charles W. Colson and Nancy Pearcey, *How Now Shall We Live?* (Wheaton, Ill.: Tyndale House Publishers 1999), 13.

3. David S. Dockery, "The Great Commandment as a Paradigm for Christian Higher Education," in *The Future of Christian Higher Education,* ed. David S. Dockery and David P. Gushee (Nashville: Broadman & Holman Publishers), 9.

4. John H. Westerhoff III, *Will Our Children Have Faith?* 2d. ed. (Toronto: Morehouse Publishing, 2000).

5. Ibid., 93.

6. Steven Garber, *The Fabric of Faithfulness* (Downers Grove, Ill.: InterVarsity Press, 1996), 16.

7. Annual Report of the Southern Baptist Convention (June 2000). Report from the International Mission Board (pp. 195–97). Report from the North American Mission Board (pp. 251–54). Nashville: Convention Press, 2000.

8. A. Levine, and J. S. Cureton, *When Hope and Fear Collide* (San Francisco: Jossey-Bass Publishers), 1998.

9. Steven Garber, "The Culture of 'Whatever.'" Lecture given at Union University, Jackson, Tennessee, 22 March 2000.

10. Ibid.

11. John Yates, "Trading worship for service," *The Tennessean.* February 4, 1997, 1A–2A.

12. Arliss Dickerson, "The 10 Commandments of Collegiate Ministry, Address given in Jonesboro,Ark., 1997.

13. Arthur Holmes, *The Idea of a Christian College* (Grand Rapids, Mich.: William B. Eerdmans Publishing Company, 1987), 84.

Afterword

1. *The Hedgehog Review* 2, no. 3 (Fall 2000). This issue of *The Hedgehog Review* is must reading for Christians interested in the state of and prospects for American higher education.

2. Ibid., 111.

3. Ibid., 118.

CONTRIBUTORS

David S. Dockery has served as President of Union University since 1996. The author or editor of more than twenty books, including *Christian Scripture* and the *Holman Bible Handbook*, Dockery is a recognized leader in Christian Higher Education. He serves on the Board of Directors of the Council for Christian Colleges and Universities. Dockery is a Senior Fellow for the Wilberforce Forum, and a Consulting Editor for *Christianity Today*.

George H. Guthrie serves as the Benjamin W. Perry Professor of Bible and Chair of the Department of Christian Studies at Union University. He is the author of numerous articles and four books, including *The Structure of Hebrews: a Text-Linguistic Analysis* and *The NIV Application Commentary: Hebrews*. He holds the Ph.D. and M.Div. degrees from Southwestern Baptist Theological Seminary and a Th.M. from Trinity Evangelical Divinity School.

Gregory Alan Thornbury is Assistant Professor of Christian Studies and Director of the Carl F. H. Henry Center for Christian Leadership at Union University. He is the co-editor of *Who Will Be Saved?* and author of several articles and book chapters. Thornbury is a Fellow for the Wilberforce Forum, the Research Institute of the Ethics and Religious Liberty Commission (SBC), and the Center for Church Reform. He holds the Ph.D. from The Southern Baptist Theological Seminary.

Brad Green is Assistant Professor of Christian Studies at Union University. His work has focused on the theology of Colin Gunton. He is a contributor to *New Testament*

Interpretation and *Theologians of the Baptist Tradition*. Green holds the Ph.D. from Baylor University.

Harry L. Poe is the Charles Colson Professor of Faith and Culture at Union University. Poe is the author of several books, including *The Gospel and Its Meaning* and *Christian Witness in a Postmodern World*, and *The Designer Universe*. He holds the Ph.D. from The Southern Baptist Theological Seminary and has studied at Oxford University.

David P. Gushee is the Graves Associate Professor of Moral Philosophy at Union University. A prolific author and much sought-after speaker, Gushee serves as a Fellow for the Wilberforce Forum. He is the author or editor of several books, including *The Righteous Gentiles of the Holocaust* and *Toward a Just and Caring Society*. His Ph.D. work was completed at Union Theological Seminary in New York City.

Jimmy H. Davis serves as Associate Provost and Professor of Chemistry at Union University. With Hal Poe, he is the author of *Science and Faith: An Evangelical Dialogue* and *Designer Universe: Intelligent Design and The Existence of God*. Davis holds the Ph.D. from the University of Illinois.

Barbara McMillin is Dean of the College of Arts and Science and Professor of English Literature at Union University. She completed her doctoral work at the University of Mississippi and has done additional study at Harvard University.

Glenn A. Marsch holds the Ph.D. from Florida State University. Currently he serves as Assistant Professor of Physics at Union University. A frequent participant in seminars on Faith and Science, Marsch is an Associate of the Vanderbilt University Center in Molecular Toxicology.

Karen Mulder is the Arts editor for *Christianity Today*. A graduate of Boston University and Yale University, she is currently completing her Ph.D. at the University of Virginia.

Mulder is Assistant Professor of Art at Union University where her focus is in art history.

Paul Munson holds degrees from Wheaton College (B.Mus.) and the University of Michigan (Ph.D.). He is an Assistant Professor of Music at Union University where he teaches music history. He has published the first critical edition of Franz Liszt's oratorio *St. Stanislaus*.

Antonio A. Chiareli holds the Ph.D. from Northwestern University and serves as Associate Professor of Sociology at Union University. His work has focused on the peasant movements and socioeconomic development in Latin America.

Kina Mallard serves as Director of the Center for Faculty Development and Chair of the Communication Arts Department at Union University. Mallard is a frequent contributor to academic leadership forums and the author of several articles and book chapters. She holds the Ph.D. from the University of Tennessee.

Thomas R. Rosebrough holds the Ph.D. from Ohio State University. He serves as Professor of Education and Dean of the School of Education and Human Studies at Union University. Prior to coming to Union Rosebrough served as Dean of the Graduate School at Malone College. His publications have focused on instruction in higher education.

Susan R. Jacob (Ph.D. University of Tennessee, Memphis) serves as Dean and Professor in the School of Nursing at Union University. A recognized scholar in the field of nursing, Jacob is the co-editor of *Contemporary Nursing: Issues, Trends, and Management* and has authored several book chapters and articles in professional journals.

Mary Anne Poe is Associate Professor and Director of the Social Work Program at Union University. A graduate of Vanderbilt University, the University of Louisville, and The

Southern Baptist Theological Seminary, Poe is a leader in the North American Association of Christians in Social Work.

Walton Padelford (Ph.D. Louisiana State University) is Professor of Economics and Acting Dean of the McAfee School of Business Administration. Padelford is recognized for inter-disciplinary emphasis. **Donald L. Lester** is the former dean of the McAfee School of Business Administration and is currently the Director of the Center for Entrepreneurship at Arkansas State University.

Kimberly Thornbury serves as Dean of Students at Union University. She is a graduate of Messiah College and the University of Louisville. An active member of the American College Personnel Association and the Association for Christians in Student Development, she is currently completing her Ph.D. at Regent University (Virginia Beach).

Todd E. Brady is Minister to the University at Union University. A graduate of Southwestern Seminary, Brady is a frequent speaker at conferences across the country on campus ministry.

Carla Sanderson serves as Provost and Professor of Nursing at Union University. Sanderson is a Commissioner for Southern Association of Colleges and Schools and a member of The Board of Directors of the Association for Southern Baptist Colleges and Schools. She holds the Ph.D. from the University of Florida.

NAME INDEX

SCRIPTURE INDEX